INSOLVENCY AND THE
ENTERPRISE ACT 2002

To Nigel

Best wishes

Nick

INSOLVENCY AND THE ENTERPRISE ACT 2002

Stephen Davies QC

Editor

JORDANS

2003

Published by
Jordan Publishing Limited
21 St Thomas Street, Bristol BS1 6JS

© Jordan Publishing Limited 2003

British Library Cataloguing-in-Publication Data
A catalogue record for this book is available from the British Library

ISBN 0 85308 811 X

Typeset by Mendip Communications Ltd, Frome, Somerset
Printed by Henry Ling Limited, The Dorset Press, Dorchester, DT1 1HD

FOREWORD

Just over 20 years agao, the Report of the Review Committee on Insolvency Law and Practice was published. In Chapter Two of the Report, Sir Kenneth Cork's committee described the historical development of insolvency law (corporate and personal), highlighting the landmark statutes which changed the shape of the statutory schemes for administering insolvent estates. Through a series of recommendations, the Cork Committee concluded that wide-ranging reforms were necessary. The Government implemented many (but by no means all) of those recommendations in the Insolvency Act 1986. In particular, a new raft of insolvency procedures was introduced, including voluntary arrangements, administrations and administrative receiverships. Only 16 years later, we now have Part 10 of the Enterprise Act 2002 which has effected equally radical reforms. It abolishes Crown preferences in all insolvencies. In corporate insolvency, the Act abolishes, for the large part, administrative receiverships and fundamentally recasts administration into the rescue procedure of choice. The personal insolvency reforms introduced by the new Act are more far-reaching than any statute since the Bankruptcy Act 1883. It is a sign of the accelerating rate of change in the modern world that these sweeping reforms should come so soon after the reforms of 1986.

The Bar has been subject to the same rate of change. Twenty years ago there were few, if any, members of the Bar practising outside London who specialised in insolvency. It would have appeared inconceivable that a chambers practising in the regions would establish a presence and reputation in this field the equal to any in London, would make their mark as counsel regularly instructed in reported insolvency cases and would master the expertise and practical experience to produce a book such as this. Guildhall Chambers, under the leadership of Stephen Davies QC, within a period of a few years has achieved all this and more. The production of this book reflects their commitment and their contribution to the law and practice of insolvency.

I commend this book to all practitioners of insolvency, lawyers and accountants alike. The new law in its historical context is fully explained and expounded with clarity. Whether advising a corporate lender as to its appropriate remedy or a bankrupt as to the nature and effect of a bankruptcy restriction order, the practitioner will find that this book provides the insight into the law and guidance which he requires.

The Honourable Mr Justice Lightman
February 2003

PREFACE

There are four points which I would like to make in this Preface.

The first is that the appearance of my name on the front sheet signifies that I was the one who roped in our insolvency team to write this book. Theirs has been the hard work and to them is due the lion's share of the credit.

Secondly, as many before us have no doubt found to their cost, busy practices, growing young families and the demands of a modern set of chambers all conspire against book-writing. In our case, the conspiracy was further assisted by the fact that, instead of the safety and comfort of retrospection, we chose to write about the future – unchartered territory and sweeping reforms. Such an exercise is time-consuming for lawyers like us who are trained only to study and assess the impact of existing law on past acts and events. If there is to be a next time, we will take sabbaticals.

This leads to the third point. It is consoling to think that we have not yet had to consider, still less write about, the next chapter in the modernisation of our insolvency laws. There is a sense that it might be no less sweeping: e-filing, mandatory debt counselling, marshalling of enforcement procedures, super-priority funding, external regulation of the insolvency profession, consumer liens and cram-downs (to name but a few areas of prospective reform).

Lastly, we owe thanks: to our spouses, non-spouses, partners and significant others for tolerating further inroads on family and personal life; to Martin West at Jordans whose intelligent guidance, professionalism and unfaltering opti-mism kept us on track; and to Robbie Carnegie at Jordans for his bonhomie and attention to detail. Very special thanks are due both to the Insolvency Service and to PricewaterhouseCoopers. As for the Insolvency Service, Stephen Leinster and Mike Norris have been at the very heart of the corporate and personal insolvency reforms respectively and understand them better than anyone. They have answered our every query and even came to visit us in chambers. There is also the Official Receiver in Cardiff, Paul Cropper, who has unwittingly taught us a great deal over the years about the nuts and bolts of the practice of insolvency – thereby arming us with some of the tools with which to understand the new reforms. As for PwC, they kept us abreast of much of the lobbying in Parliament and Tim Hewson went out of his way to assist us. I could not sign off without mentioning Steve Hill of Moon Beever. A mild-mannered and self-effacing man, Steve's long experience of the law and practice of personal insolvency together with his raw intelligence mark him apart and it has been a privilege to follow the passage of the Bill through Parliament and to discuss the reforms with him.

Stephen Davies QC
Guildhall Chambers
February 2003
www.guildhallchambers.co.uk

CONTRIBUTORS

Guildhall Chambers Insolvency Team
Richard Ascroft
Jeremy Bamford
Nicholas Briggs
Stephen Davies QC
Paul French
Katie Gibb
Martha Maher
Hugh Sims
Matthew Wales

www.guildhallchambers.co.uk/Commercial-Teams/
Insolvency-Company-Members.html

OUTLINE CONTENTS

CONTENTS

TABLE OF CASES

References are to paragraph numbers

TABLE OF STATUTES

References are to paragraph numbers

TABLE OF STATUTORY INSTRUMENTS

References are to paragraph numbers

TABLE OF EUROPEAN MATERIALS

References are to paragraph numbers

TABLE OF OTHER MATERIALS

References are to paragraph numbers

TABLE OF ABBREVIATIONS

BBA	British Bankers Association
BRO	bankruptcy restriction order
BRU	bankruptcy restriction undertaking
CA 1948	Companies Act 1948
CBI	Confederation of British Industry
CCAO	County court administration order
CDDA 1986	Company Directors Disqualification Act 1986
the Cork Report	*Insolvency Law and Practice: Report of the Review Committee* (June 1982) Cmnd 8558
CVA	company voluntary arrangement
CVL	creditors' voluntary liquidation
DIP	debtor-in-possession
DTI	Department of Trade and Industry
EA 2002	Enterprise Act 2002
ECSA	European Coal and Steel Community
ERA 1996	Employment Rights Act 1996
IA 1985	Insolvency Act 1985
IA 1986	Insolvency Act 1986
ICAEW	Institute of Chartered Accountants of England and Wales
ILA	Insolvency Lawyers' Association
IPA	income payment agreement
IPO	income payment order
IR 1986	Insolvency Rules 1986
ISA	Insolvency Services Account
IVA	individual voluntary arrangement
LPA 1925	Law of Property Act 1925
NAEA	National Association of Estate Agents
PPP	public–private partnership
QFCH	qualifying floating charge-holder
R3	Association of Business Recovery Professionals
RSL	registered social landlord
TUPE	Transfer of Undertakings (Protection of Employment) Regulations 1981, SI 1981/1794
the White Paper	DTI White Paper, Productivity and Enterprise, *Insolvency – A Second Chance*, July 2001, Cmmd 5234

Chapter 1

GENERAL INTRODUCTION

'Insolvency is not a very thrilling or amusing subject'
Lord Mishcon[1]

THE 'E' WORD

1.1 We live in an age of political spin. In the old days, an Act of Parliament introducing sweeping reforms of the law of insolvency would be entitled 'Bankruptcy Act' or 'Companies Act' or, latterly, 'Insolvency Act'. Not even George Orwell[2] could have foreseen that such reforms might be introduced in an 'Enterprise Act'. On 2 July 2002, Lord Boardman commented on the 'E' word in the first of the debates in the House of Lords on (what was then) the Enterprise Bill as follows:

> 'This morning I looked up the word "enterprise" in the dictionary. It means boldness, courage and with imagination. I do not find that a good description of the Bill's objectives – insolvency, competition, consumer protection and so on.'

ENTERPRISE ACT 2002

1.2 Nevertheless, the name has stuck and is now on the statute book. The Enterprise Act 2002 (EA 2002) received Royal Assent on 7 November 2002. It is a leviathan of a statute, comprising 281 sections and 26 Schedules. Its preamble outlines the breadth of its scope and the disparate nature of the areas of law for which it legislates:

> 'Establish and provide for the functions of the Office of Fair Trading, the Competition Appeal Tribunal and the Competition Service; to make provision about mergers and market structures and conduct; to amend the constitution and functions of the Competition Commission; to create an offence for those entering into certain anti-competitive agreements; to provide for the disqualification of directors of companies engaging in certain anti-competitive practices; to make other provision about competition law; to amend the law relating to the protection of the collective interests of consumers; to make further provision about the disclosure of information obtained under competition and consumer legislation; *to amend the Insolvency Act 1986 and make*

---

1   *Hansard*, 15 January 1985.
2   *Politics and the English Language* (1946).

other provision about insolvency; and for connected purposes.' (emphasis supplied)

1.3   As its title suggests, this book is concerned only with those parts of the EA 2002 which affect the law and practice of insolvency. These amount to a mere 24 sections in Part 10 and Schedules 16–23.

The approach of the Parliamentary draftsman has been to recognise that the IA 1986 is the primary statute governing corporate and personal insolvency. The result is that Part 10 and the relevant Schedules will not survive over time as provisions in their own right but serve only to introduce amendments to the IA 1986. Nevertheless, for the purposes of this book, it is necessary to refer to the provisions of the EA 2002 rather than the new or amended provisions of the IA 1986.

Explanatory Notes

1.4   As is now customary for such new statutes, there are Explanatory Notes. These have been prepared and produced by the Department of Trade and Industry (DTI) in order to assist the reader in understanding the EA 2002. Whilst they do not form part of the Act and have not been endorsed by Parliament, they are a useful tool of construction.

Corporate insolvency

1.5   By the first five of the following seven sections in Part 10 of the EA 2002, the Government has made fundamental changes to the law and practice of corporate insolvency:

(a)   **Section 248: 'Replacement of Part II of the Insolvency Act 1986'.** This section replaces the existing statutory regime for administrations. The new code is now found in Sch B1 to the Insolvency Act 1986 (IA 1986) (set out in Sch 16 to the EA 2002). Its purpose is to streamline the system of administration, remove the need for a court hearing in most cases whilst retaining its collective nature. The Government hopes that this will make the administration process more accessible, cheaper and less bureaucratic. These sweeping changes will involve many minor amendments to existing legislation, most of which are to be found in Sch 17 to the EA 2002.

(b)   **Section 249: 'Special administration regimes'.** There are specific exceptions from the new code for administration for certain special companies.

(c)   **Section 250: 'Prohibition of appointment of administrative receiver'.** The collective administration procedure will supercede administrative receivership. This is a major reform of corporate insolvency law by restricting the use of administrative receivership in all cases in respect of floating charges created after the coming into force of s 250 save in certain special and specified cases. In this latter respect, new Sch 2A to the IA 1986 is set out in Sch 18 to the EA 2002 dealing with, in particular, certain types of capital market transactions and also 'project companies' – for both of which the power to appoint will remain.

(d) **Section 251: 'Abolition of Crown Preference'.** This section applies to all insolvencies (corporate and personal) and abolishes the Crown's preferential right to recover unpaid taxes ahead of other creditors, thus ending the Crown's statutory right established since 1897 to be paid preferentially out of floating charge assets.

(e) **Section 252: 'Unsecured creditors'.** This section introduces new s 176A into the IA 1986 entitled 'Share of assets for unsecured creditors'. It provides that a percentage or portion (as yet unspecified) of floating charge realisations shall be made available for unsecured creditors. In this book, this will be referred to as 'top-slicing'.

(f) **Section 253: 'Liquidator's powers'.** This rationalises the circumstances in which an office holder requires sanction before issuing certain types of corporate insolvency proceedings. It is not a major reform but a tidying-up provision.

(g) **Section 254: 'Application of insolvency law to foreign company'.** This is a potentially far-reaching provision which is beyond the scope of this book. It enables the Secretary of State by order to apply some or all of the IA 1986 to any company incorporated outside Great Britain.

(h) **Section 255: 'Application of law about company arrangement or administration to non-company'.** This provision was introduced during the passage of the Bill through Parliament and tidies up the law. It enables rules to be made applying the procedures for company voluntary arrangements (CVAs), administrations and schemes of arrangement under s 425 of the Companies Act 1985 to industrial and provident societies, friendly societies and certain other bodies.

Personal insolvency

1.6 By ss 256–269, even greater changes have been introduced to the statutory scheme for personal insolvency:

(a) **Section 256: 'Duration of bankruptcy'.** This new provision has caused much controversy and debate. In future, save in special cases, a bankrupt will obtain his discharge 1 year from the bankruptcy order, at the latest. In the majority of cases, discharge will be obtained between 3 and 6 months by a series of administrative acts. Necessarily, there will be a period of transition in respect of 'old' bankruptcies and these transitional provisions are set out in Sch 19 to EA 2002.

(b) **Section 257: 'Post-discharge restrictions'.** A purpose of the Act is to remove the stigma which has been traditionally associated with the state of bankruptcy save in those cases where a 'bankruptcy restriction order' or BRO is made. This is a new concept which it is thought will apply to no more than 10% of all bankrupts. This section introduces new s 281A of IA 1986 which, in turn, imports the provisions of new Sch 4A. The provisions of new Sch 4A are set out in Sch 20 to EA 2002 and comprise a code under which the Secretary of State or the official receiver can apply for a BRO in a manner and on grounds which are not dissimilar to applications for disqualification orders. Correspondingly, new Sch 4A will provide for undertakings to be given in lieu of a BRO. The effect of a BRO or undertaking is provided for by Sch 21 to EA 2002 which amends various relevant statutory provisions including s 11 of the Company Directors' Disqualification Act 1986 (CDDA 1986).

(c) **Section 258: 'Investigation by Official Receiver'.** Recognising that the vast majority of cases concern consumer debts and otherwise no culpable conduct, the mandatory duty of the official receiver to investigate is to be replaced by a discretion which it is envisaged will be exercised in approximately 10% of cases.

(d) **Section 259: 'Income payments order'.** This provision revises the current regime concerning income payment orders (IPOs).

(e) **Section 260: 'Income payments agreement'.** This is a new concept which, it is expected, will remove the costs and delay of applying for an IPO where the official receiver and the bankrupt can reach a binding agreement to the same effect as an IPO.

(f) **Section 261: 'Bankrupt's home'.** Not part of the original package of reforms, these new provisions were introduced and refined during the passage of the Bill through Parliament. They introduce new ss 283A and 313A of IA 1986. Section 283A provides for a bankrupt's home to cease forming part of the bankruptcy estate if no application for sale for the benefit of creditors is made within 3 years. Section 313A makes special provision for bankrupt's homes which are of low value.

(g) **Section 262: 'Powers of trustee in bankruptcy'.** This section is a tidying-up provision, introducing the requirement that a trustee in bankruptcy now requires sanction before issuing certain types of clawback proceedings.

(h) **Section 263: 'Repeal of certain bankruptcy offences'.** Consistent with the introduction of BROs, this section repeals provisions in the IA 1986 which created criminal offences of failure to keep proper accounting records and gambling and speculation.

(i) **Section 264: 'Individual voluntary arrangement'.** This section imports Sch 22 to EA 2002 – which in turn creates new ss 263A–263G and 389A of IA 1986. These new sections will allow a bankrupt to enter into a fast-track, no-nonsense individual voluntary arrangement (IVA) in which the official receiver will act as nominee or supervisor.

(j) **Section 265: 'Disqualification from office: justice of the peace'.** This and the following two sections make special provisions for those holding particular offices when bankrupt.

(k) **Section 266: 'Disqualification from office: Parliament'.**

(l) **Section 267: 'Disqualification from office: local government'.**

(m) **Section 268: 'Disqualification from office: general'.** This section empowers the Secretary of State to make an order/rules disqualifying certain bankrupts from holding certain offices or positions specified in the order or rules.

(n) **Section 269: 'Minor and consequential amendments'**. This section introduces Sch 23 to EA 2002 which provides for many and varied minor and consequential amendments arising out of this substantial package of reforms.

Money

1.7   Finally, pursuant to ss 270–272, the financial regime under which the Insolvency Service operates will be modernised. One result of this is that the Insolvency Service will be able to separate out the costs that relate to the operation of the Insolvency Services Account (ISA) so as to allocate more fairly those costs amongst the insolvent estates. Another result is the creation of new income for the Insolvency Service from the insolvency profession. These new provisions also rewrite the statutory scheme for managing funds derived from insolvent estates.

Origins and passage of the Bill to Royal Assent

1.8   As appears in the separate introductions to the respective parts of this book devoted to personal and corporate insolvency, it is easier to trace the origins of the reforms affecting corporate insolvency than it is those affecting personal insolvency. For the purposes of this general introduction, the following dates and events should be mentioned.

1999 – By agreement between the Chancellor of the Exchequer and the Secretary of State for Trade and Industry, a Government review of company rescue and business reconstruction mechanisms was set up. Its terms of reference were:

> 'To review aspects of company and insolvency law and practice in the United Kingdom and elsewhere relating to the opportunities for, and the means by which, businesses can resolve short to medium term financial difficulties, so as to preserve maximum economic value, and to make recommendations.'

September 1999	The review group produced consultation document.
November 2000	The review group published a report making a number of recommendations including that:

                (a) a floating charge holder should lose the right to veto the making of an administration order; and
                (b) there should be an improvement in the approach of the Inland Revenue and HM Customs & Excise toward business rescue.

1 April 2001	The revenue authorities responded by operating a joint Inland Revenue/Customs & Excise unit called the Voluntary Arrangements Service.
2 April 2001	Insolvency Act 2000 came into force save provisions reforming CVAs (ss 1–4 and Schs 1–3).
Spring 2001	The Government made a commitment in its 2001 election manifesto to reform the bankruptcy laws to

ensure a second chance for people who go bankrupt through no fault of their own.

20 June 2001   The Queen's Speech:[3]

> 'My Government will introduce legislation to encourage enterprise, strengthen competition laws, and promote safeguards for consumers.'

31 July 2001   White Paper published (Cmnd 5234), 'Productivity and Enterprise – Insolvency: A Second Chance'.[4]

5 October 2001   End of consultation process.

28 November 2001   A summary of responses by consultees was published.

26 March 2002   Enterprise Bill introduced in the House of Commons[5] (Melanie Johnson MP – Parliamentary Under-Secretary of State for Competition, Consumers and Markets was the lead minister responsible for stearing the Bill through Parliament):

> '... a major step towards the Government's objective of making the UK the best place in the world to do business.'

10 April 2002   Second reading debate.[6]

April–May 2002   Standing Commitee B debates during the fourteenth to eighteenth sittings.[7]

13 June 2002   Report stage.[8]

17 June 2002   Third reading debate.[9]

19 June 2002   Updated print of the Bill introduced into the House of Lords.[10] Lord Sainsbury of Turville and Lord McIntosh of Haringey piloted the Bill through the House of Lords.

2 July 2002   Second reading debate in the House of Lords.[11]

---

3   http://www.publications.parliament.uk/pa/ld200102/ldhansrd/
     vo010620/text/10620–01.htm.
4   http://www.insolvency.gov.uk/cwp/5234.htm.
5   *Hansard* reference: Vol 382 Col 703.
6   Hansard reference: Vol 383 Cols 44–120; http://www.parliament.the-stationery-
     office.co.uk/pa/cm200102/cmhansrd/vo020410/debtext/20410–10–head2.
7   *Hansard* reference: Hansard Standing Committee B; http://
     www.publications.parliament.uk/pa/cm200102/cmstand/b/cment.htm.
8   *Hansard* reference: Vol 386 Cols 1033–1109; http://www.parliament.the-stationery-
     office.co.uk/pa/cm200102/cmhansrd/cm020617/debtext/20617–06–head2.
9   *Hansard* reference: Vol 387 Cols 22–125; http://www.parliament.the-stationery-
     office.co.uk/pa/cm200102/cmhansrd/cm020617/debtext/20617–28–spnew3.
10   *Hansard* reference: Vol 636 Col 741.
11   *Hansard* reference: Vol 637 Cols 138–190 http://www.publications.parliament.uk/pa/
     ld199900/ldhansrd/pdvn/lds02/text/20702–04–head0.

16, 18, 22, 29 and 30 July 2002	Committee debates in the House of Lords.[12]
15 and 21 October 2002	Report debate in the House of Lords.[13]
28 October 2002	Third reading debate in the House of Lords.[14]
30 October 2002	House of Commons considerations of Lords' amendments.[15]
7 December 2002	Royal Assent.

INSOLVENCY (AMENDMENT) RULES 2003

1.9 Implementation of the EA 2002 will require secondary legislation, including changes to the Insolvency Rules 1986, SI 1986/1925 (IR 1986). At the time of writing, the Insolvency Service is receiving views of 'key stakeholders'. Prior to being laid in Parliament, the Lord Chancellor must consult the Insolvency Rules Committee on any changes to the Rules.

1.10 At the time of writing, there are two sets of draft rules in circulation for consultation. It is envisaged that, in broad terms, there will be one set of Insolvency (Amendment) Rules to implement all the changes to corporate and personal insolvency. In each case, as the name suggests, they will effect amendments to the IR 1986.

1.11 The Insolvency Rules Committee, chaired by Mr Justice Evans-Lombe, has yet to conclude its deliberations and the ultimate form of the proposed rules remains a matter of speculation. That said, it is clear that they will include the nuts and bolts of the new procedures (including administrations, top-slicing, BROs, IPAs and fast-track IVAs).

1.12 There will be a separate and discrete (ie second) statutory instrument pursuant to IA 1976, s 176A concerning 'the prescribed part' (top-slicing). At the time of writing, these draft provisions are in circulation and are referred to in Chapter 5. It is anticipated that a third statutory instrument will introduce minor and consequential amendments to other primary and secondary legislation (see, eg **5.48**). A fourth statutory instrument is anticipated pursuant to IA 1986, s 72A (see **6.3**).

---

12 *Hansard* reference: Vol 637 Cols 1095–1101, 1119–1166, 1187–1222; Vol 637 Cols 1427–1467, 1488–1544; Vol 638 Cols 132–180; Vol 638 Cols 738–745, 763–806; Vol 638 Cols 821–852 http://www.publications.parliament.uk/pa/ld199900/ldhansrd/pdvn/lds02/text/20730–04–head1.

13 *Hansard* reference: Vol 639 Cols 702–18, 732–3, 782–847; Vol 639 Cols 1070–1086, 1098–1143, 1160–1210; http://www.parliament.the-stationery-office.co.uk/pa/ld199900/ldhansrd/pdvn/lds02/text/21021–09.htm.

14 *Hansard* reference: Vol 640 Cols 12–18, 34–86 http://www.publications.parliament.uk/pa/ld199900/ldhansrd/pdvn/lds02/text/21028–17.htm.

15 http://www.parliament.the-stationery-office.co.uk/pa/cm200102/cmhansrd/cm021030/debtext/21030–25.htm.

SECTION 277 OF EA 2002

1.13   It is necessary to mention s 277 of EA 2002 which is not contained within Part 10 of EA 2002 but in the supplementary provisions of Part 11. Section 277 empowers the Secretary of State to make such:

> 'supplementary, incidental or consequential provision as he thinks appropriate –
>
> (a) for the general purposes, or any particular purpose, of that Act or
> (b) in consequence of any provision made by or under this Act or for giving full effect to it.'

1.14   During the consultation process concerning the new rules following Royal Assent, various small wrinkles have emerged concerning the way in which the EA 2002 is worded or as to its effect in certain circumstances and the indications are that the DTI might well use s 277 to iron these out.

COMMENCEMENT

1.15   The company insolvency provisions, along with the abolition of Crown preference, are expected to come into force early in the 2003 financial year, once the necessary secondary legislation has been put in place. At the time of writing, the predictions are for July 2003. It is important to understand what this means. In any case where there is an existing insolvency process (eg an administrative receivership, administration or company voluntary arrangement), the new provisions will not apply to any subsequent, post-commencement-date insolvency process. So, for instance, the abolition of Crown preference will not apply to a liquidation initiated after the new provisions have come into force if the company was already in administrative receivership, administration or company voluntary arrangement on the commencement date.

1.16   The individual insolvency provisions, along with the changes to the financial regime of the Insolvency Service, are expected to come into force early in the 2004 financial year, once the necessary staff training and infrastructure have been put in place.

1.17   Generally, individuals made bankrupt before commencement, but who have not been discharged, will be discharged either 1 year after implementation or earlier if their discharge is due before then. If an individual has been an undischarged bankrupt in the previous 15 years, he or she will be discharged 5 years after commencement of the provisions, or when a court grants discharge under the current regime, whichever is earlier. Criminal bankrupts can be discharged only by order of the court.

Part 1

CORPORATE INSOLVENCY

Chapter 2

INTRODUCTION TO CORPORATE INSOLVENCY

'It is best not to swap horses while crossing the river'
Abraham Lincoln[1]

WORTHY REFORMS

2.1 The intended reforms were simple and would have been immediately effective. After a long period of gestation, it was proposed that, for all but a handful of special cases, the (selfish) administrative receivership regime would be replaced by a new, revamped (collective) administration procedure. Crown preference moneys and a proportion of floating charge realisations would find their way into the pockets of the unsecured creditors. The most vulnerable creditors would be given a larger stake in the vast majority of corporate insolvencies.

A fatal concession mid-stream

2.2 As the Government was crossing the river from the bank marked *'ancien régime'* to that marked 'streamlined administrations', lobby groups reminded it that a financial institution is a 'person' within the meaning of the human rights legislation. They said that it followed that financial institutions had a right not to be deprived of the 'peaceful enjoyment of [their] possessions' – such possessions included the existing rights to appoint administrative receivers under existing debentures granted to them by their corporate customers. Thus, it would be a breach of the banks' human rights to remove such existing powers. With no opposition, the Government conceded mid-stream that the brave new reforms would only affect debentures created after the coming into force of the new legislation. As is demonstrated in chapters of this book concerned with Crown preference, administrative receiverships and top-slicing, this concession has altered very radically the economic effect of the reforms in a manner which was not alluded to or apparently appreciated in either House during the passage of the Bill through Parliament.

2.3 First, it is necessary to consider whether the Government's concession was correctly made. This, in turn, requires consideration of the public interest which gave rise to the reforms in the first place.

---

1   Address to a delegation from the National Union League, 9 June 1864.

The banks' human rights and the 'control of the use of property in accordance with the public interest'

2.4   The origin of the banks' human rights is Art 1 of the First Protocol to the European Convention for the Protection of Human Rights and Fundamental Freedoms which is in these terms:

> 'Every natural or legal person is entitled to the peaceful enjoyment of his possessions. No one shall be deprived of his possessions except in the public interest and subject to the conditions provided for by law and by the general principles of international law.
>
> The preceding provisions shall not, however, in any way impair the right of a State to enforce such laws as it deems necessary to control the use of property in accordance with the general interest or to secure the payment of taxes or other contributions or penalties.'

2.5   The question is: why did the Government not conclude that the exception in the second paragraph operated in its favour on the grounds that the proposed abolition of the right to appoint administrative receivers under existing debentures was necessary 'in accordance with the general interest' to control the use of the power to appoint by the banks?

The 'general interest' in the abolition of the right to appoint administrative receivers

2.6   What had prompted the Government to propose the abolition of the right to appoint an administrative receiver? The answer is said to be the conduct of the UK clearing banks and that part of the insolvency profession which acts for the clearing banks. A more controversial question (and thankfully one beyond the remit of this book) is whether such charges were/are justified.

2.7   When compared with other major industrialised countries, the UK is probably the most secured creditor-friendly regime in the Western world. At the other end of the spectrum, amongst the least pro-creditor countries are France and the US. In the US, there is an automatic stay on enforcement against assets, an unimpeded right to petition for reorganisation and a statutory regime which allows the company's board to remain in control during reorganisation. Amusingly, this prompted one well known American commentator[2] to observe that:

> '... if an American banker is very, very good, when he dies he will go to the United Kingdom. British banks have far more control than an American secured lender could ever hope to have. Receiverships on the British model are unknown and almost unthinkable in the US. A US Banker could barely imagine a banker's Valhalla in which a bank could veto a reorganisation as a UK bank may effectively veto an administration by appointing an administrative receiver.'

2.8   Over a long period, it was perceived in many quarters that the (still nascent) law relating to corporate rescue had gone off the rails – giving rise to the

---

2   Westbrook 'A Comparison of Bankruptcy Reorganisation in the US with the Administration Procedure in the UK' (1990) 6 *Insolvency Law and Practice* 86 at 87.

introduction of this latest raft of reforms. The origins of this perception are as follows.

The development of the problem – conflicts of interest

2.9   In January 1977, a wide ranging review of insolvency law and practice was set up by the then Secretary of State for Trade and Industry, Mr Edmund Dell, under the chairmanship of Sir Kenneth Cork. Its terms of reference included consideration of 'less formal procedures as alternatives to bankruptcy and company winding-up proceedings in appropriate circumstances'. The Cork Report, published in June 1982, included proposals for two new or revised procedures: administrations and CVAs. Both schemes were implemented by the insolvency legislation of 1985 and 1986. During the passage of the Bill in 1985, the Government was asked by Mr Nicholas Lyell[3] to clarify the matters relating to the conflicts of interest:

> 'Will a chartered accountant who is placed by a bank with a debenture in a position of company doctor to advise the company on its financial affairs be capable thereafter of acting as a receiver if the company is subsequently put into receivership or wound up?'

For the Government, Mr Fletcher dodged the issue, replying:

> 'That is a good question, and it is the sort of point we are currently considering. We must discuss where we should draw the line with regard to the conflict of interest ... I cannot give my hon. Friend the precise answer, because this is the sort of point that the Department wishes to consider further before introducing proposals in the House.'

2.10   Nothing further was said on the topic. Notwithstanding the new collective procedure called 'administration', administrative receivership remained the route of choice for the banks and other debenture holders. It was an easy and quick procedure to initiate for any lender whose security was backed by a floating charge. But it is not a collective procedure and the holder of a floating charge can initiate it at any time, provided the contract with the borrowing company allows. An administrative receiver owes a duty of care to his/her appointor but little in the way of obligations to others. A receiver would appear to have little incentive to maximise returns on assets over and above those required to repay the lender and discharge the expenses of the receivership although in some circumstances he might be liable if he failed to manage the property with due diligence. Receiverships tended to be characterised by poorer returns to creditors than those in CVAs but better than in liquidations. In addition, as debenture holders under UK insolvency law, the banks enjoyed super powers to scoop the pool under their floating charges – powers not available in (or understood by) continental Europe or the US.

2.11   At the end of the boom, presided over by Nigel Lawson as Chancellor of the Exchequer, there was an exceptionally difficult and volatile economic climate in Britain. Within 2 years, receiverships were at record levels. The Treasury (and, latterly, Gordon Brown) became convinced that the banks were

---

3   *Hansard*, 30 April 1985, col 143–144.

partly responsible for the depth of the post-Lawson recession (ie the one which set in at the end of the 1980s). They perceived that many businesses were killed unnecessarily by the precipitate enforcement actions of trigger-happy banks.[4] There was growing public concern about reporting/investigating accountants being appointed administrative receivers. The conflicts created by this process led to litigation.[5]

2.12   In November 1992, a working party was set up by the Insolvency Service to explore why these new company rescue provisions brought into effect by the IA 1986 had been so little used, although with apparent success when they were used. The working party identified various barriers to the greater use of these provisions, including the power of secured creditors (generally banks) to put in an administrative receiver to recover the value of their security.

2.13   In October 1993, it was recommended that secured creditors would be obliged to give 7 days' notice of their intention to appoint a receiver. A number of other issues were consulted on, including the possibility of super-priority to be given to creditors during the moratorium or subsequent CVA.

2.14   In April 1995, the Insolvency Service published revised proposals, together with a summary of the responses to the October 1993 paper. The 7-day notice of the intention to appoint a receiver was reduced to 5 working days. Provisions were proposed to prevent disposal of assets or other abuse by directors during that period of notice, and during a moratorium, in response to the banks' concerns that the assets over which they might hold charges would be dissipated. It also provided that a meeting of creditors could not approve a proposal which would affect the rights of secured creditors without their creditors' concurrence. The idea of statutory super-priority was dropped. The criticisms and concerns led to the formulation of the statement of principles which set out the framework for the relationship between a bank and its corporate customers. Most of the banks signed up to this and it became known as 'the Bankers' Code'. It came into force on 1 July 1997.

2.15   Peter Mandelson, the then Secretary of State for Trade and Industry, visited Silicon Valley during 1997/98 and was impressed with the Americans' attitude to business failure. He liked the Americans' pro-debtor approach and contrasted it with our pro-creditor approach. In December 1998, the *Competitiveness* White Paper restated the new Government's commitment to 'legislate for a stay on creditors' action to allow a business in difficulties up to 3 months to come to an arrangement with its creditors', alongside two reviews into company rescue and the stigma of bankruptcy.

THE FIRST ATTEMPT AT REFORM

2.16   For present purposes, the nub of the problem was summarised in the House of Commons on 3 February 1999 by Mr Richard Page MP when he asked

---

4   'Banks pulling the rug too quickly' a comment by Ross Cranston during the Second Reading of the Bill.

5   See, eg, *Huxford v Stoy Hayward & Co* (1989) 5 BCC 421 and *Sheppard & Cooper Ltd v TSB Bank plc* [1996] BCC 653.

for leave to bring in a Bill to amend the IA 1986 so as to disqualify from appointment as receiver or liquidator of a company any person or company called in to carry out a financial appraisal of that company:

'The Bill aims to remove a long-standing problem in our legislation. Under the present law, firms of accountants that are called in by the banks or other lenders to report on companies in difficulties can be, and often are, appointed as administrative receivers if the findings are sufficiently serious. Those firms of accountants are obliged to safeguard the capital of the lenders: they are not concerned about the continuity and survival of the borrowing company. Indeed, all too often, the accountants have a vested interest in putting the companies on which they report into receivership.

As long ago as 1992, 30 per cent of insolvency practitioners recognised that the issue was a real and not just an apparent conflict of interests. It is like giving a judge and jury £10 for every prisoner whom they set free, but £100 for every prisoner whom they find guilty. No one would think that that was a fair law and no one would say that justice was being done under such rules. The same logic applies to the situation today, in which insolvency practitioners are so often the reporting accountants.

Serious mistakes have been made under the present arrangements. One accounting firm investigating a company to whom a bank had lent money reported that it was in serious difficulties. The accountants recommended that their related firm of insolvency practitioners should be brought in to act as receivers. It took the intervention of the Postern Executive group, a group specialising in business recovery, and a report from a second firm of accountants to persuade the bank that a mistake had been made. In due course, the loan was repaid, the secured and unsecured creditors were paid and hundreds of jobs were saved.

I could cite numerous examples, but I shall give only one more. The owner of a dairy business in Pembrokeshire sought the advice of his bank on the value of his stock. He was visited by a 24-year-old accountant who worked for one of the big five. After a single day on the farm, that expert valued the cheese held in the dairy at half the figure the owner had calculated. The visit cost the owner £3,000. The accountancy firm – surprise, surprise – was appointed to act by the bank as the receiver for the business. As events turned out, the receiver could not milk 200 cows a day or keep them in good health for sale and, when the original owner obtained another valuation for his stock, the bank granted him overdraft facilities of £1 million and he was able to save much of his operation.

All those problems flowed from the visit of a young accountant who was inexperienced in farming, but whose firm could have benefited from the dairy business going into receivership. Legal action was unsuccessful, because receivers have a duty of care only to the party that appoints them: the bank. For individuals and companies who face adverse reports, there is, sadly, usually no effective remedy short of legal action. Directors of companies being investigated are all too often presented with winding-up petitions without any opportunity to make representation or any avenue of appeal. That is neither fair nor right. No wonder accountants are often said to exist to kill the wounded and count the dead.

Reputable bodies working in the industry recognise the need for action. For example, the Royal Bank of Scotland has altered its entire approach to companies in difficulties. For it, receivership is the last resort. The results have been dramatic. In 1992, it had an 11 per cent receivership rate. Four years later, that figure had dropped to only 5 per cent. In 1996, it put only 48 companies into receivership, a fall of 82 per cent over four years. The more positive approach meant that some 79 companies and almost 5,600 jobs were saved. Even with the companies put into liquidation, the new approach meant that it was possible to sell off many parts as viable concerns.

The key element in the strategy is the bank's decision not to appoint investigating accountants as receivers. It has recognised the conflict of interest that investigating accountants may face and acted to remove it. It prefers to diagnose the problems that borrowing companies face and strengthen their management capability to deal with them. If only all banks would adopt such an approach.

There are wider lessons to be learned for the eight bodies engaged in licensing insolvency practitioners. They should have acted long ago to resolve this issue. My major contention about the potential conflicts of interest that arise when investigating accountants act as administrative receivers was conceded by Lord McIntosh of Haringey speaking for the Government in another place last week. However, I do not accept his repetition of the old argument about the advantages in terms of knowledge that a firm of investigative accountants has about a business when appointed as the administrative receiver. That only perpetuates the existing problem over the conflict of interest.

The promise of legislation to provide for a moratorium on creditors' actions while a company is in difficulties and proposals are formulated is all very well but neither that nor the joint Treasury and Department of Trade and Industry review of the law on company rescue mechanisms promised in last December's competitiveness White Paper offers the remedies that are needed right now, especially as the economy may move into recession.

There have been too many delays in tackling the matter. Those professionally involved, such as the banks, lending institutions and, above all, the companies that have experienced scrutiny by investigating accountants, understand the conflict of interest. The case for independent regulation of those who play both roles, perhaps through an insolvency commissioner, is strong. I prefer effective self-regulation to Government action, but if the eight bodies engaged in insolvency licensing cannot take the necessary steps to end this obvious conflict of interest, the duty to act falls upon Parliament and the Government.

I know that the Government are studying changing the Insolvency Act 1986 and that this issue, as we know from the Mansion House speech, is attracting Ministers' attention. That is all to the good and I welcome it, but action is needed now, not in two, three or four years. The Bill reflects important changes of attitude towards that problem outside Whitehall and Westminster. It provides a solution to that long-standing conflict of interest and I commend it to the House.'

2.17   The Bill did not survive but the point had been made. Having earlier identified the 'moral hazard' and the 'inevitable' conflicts of interest which arise in such cases,[6] the DTI's review[7] summarised the problem as follows:

'The thrust of this issue is that companies are placed unnecessarily or precipitately into receivership because of self interest of insolvency practitioners, appointed to investigate those companies' affairs, recommending their own appointment as administrative receivers because they wish to earn further fees for so acting ... In

---

6   In the DTI's consultation document issued in September 1999 (Ch 9).

7   *A Review of Company Rescue and Business Reconstruction Mechanisms by the Insolvency Service*, July 2000, paras 115–121.

1993 the Royal Bank of Scotland (RBS) announced a change of policy so that it would not, other than in exceptional circumstances, appoint insolvency practitioners who had carried out an investigation into a company as administrative receivers of that company. This was as a result of concerns expressed during the recession of the early 1990s (administrative receivership appointments peaked in 1992) that many such appointments following investigations were due more to the desire of insolvency practitioners to earn further fees than to the need to protect and realise banks' security ... The great majority of non-professional respondents to the consultation argued that the practice should be prohibited. A common argument was that, even if it were not in fact a problem, nonetheless the general perception of a conflict of interest was so strong as to mean that public confidence could never be likely to be engendered ... We therefore recommend that the very real issue of the perception of conflict of interest be dealt with both by the banks, through an amendment to the Statements of Principles and by the profession in changes to its ethical guidance. We also believe that this is an area in which the newly formed Insolvency Practices Council could usefully provide a degree of informed public interest input.'

It was inevitable that something would be done about these perceived problems.

'Insolvent Abuse'

2.18   In the meantime, there was a separate but related body of criticism which centered on the conduct of the professionals who were practising corporate insolvency on behalf of the banks. The problems were the subject of several studies,[8] including a paper entitled *Insolvent Abuse: Regulating the Insolvency Industry*,[9] which lamented the absence of any independent regulation of the insolvency industry and declared that numerous businesses had been unnecessarily placed into receivership to boost the income of insolvency practitioners:

> 'Conflicts of interests are rampant in the insolvency industry. At the heart of it are the insolvency practitioners whose main aim, like other businesses, is to maximise their fees and income. To remain in business, they need a constant supply of new clients. In big accountancy firms, managers are set targets for generating fees and income. Their salaries and promotion are linked to their performance. There is always a temptation to meet targets and generate income by putting healthy businesses into receivership and by prolonging the receiverships ... The "reporting accountant" could conclude that the business being reported upon is doing well, and receive a one-off fee. The accountants could recommend receivership and/or liquidation, and then urge the bank to appoint them as receivers and liquidators. In this case, the firm will collect fees for many years. Insolvent abuse is clearly institutionalised in the structures and processes of market economies.'

8   See, eg, Arnold, Cooper and Sikka 'Insolvency, Market Professionalism and the Commodification of Professional Expertise' (1999), to be found at http://aux.zicklin.baruch.cuny.edu/critical/html2/8018arnold.html.

9   Jim Cousins MP, Austin Mitchell MP, Sikka, Cooper and Arnold (2000): see http://www.commerce.adelaide.edu.au/apira/papers/Cousins135.pdf.

THE INFLUENCE OF THE BANKS ON THE PRACTICE OF CORPORATE INSOLVENCY

2.19   In a more general sense, it is well known that the influence of the clearing banks and other financial institutions on insolvency law and practice is phenomenal. Take the *Brumark* decision, which was published in June 2001. In their heart of hearts, lawyers and accountants who practise insolvency law know (or certainly should know) that, in every practical sense, the decision of the Privy Council on an appeal from New Zealand, made up of a formidable panel of Law Lords, represents an unequivocal and binding statement of English law to the effect that almost all purported fixed charges on book debts in standard form bank debentures created only floating charges. And yet, since June 2001, the banks have taken the line that their purported fixed charges are enforceable as such.[10] The majority of the larger firms of solicitors and accountants could not be seen to disagree. In turn, banks make it clear that they will not take kindly to opposition on this or any other related subject. The entirety of the profession knows that this is going on but there is a conspiracy of silence. The result is an unhealthy stockpiling of book debt realisations in many corporate insolvencies due to the refusal by the banks to accept that *Brumark* affects their purported fixed charges. To date, only the smaller practitioners have made applications to court for directions pursuant to their professional guidelines.[11] At that stage, having marked its disapproval of the opposition, the bank will concede the point so as to avoid the creation of a precedent (as if one were needed). This brings us back to the banks' human rights and the question of whether proposed reforms ought to have been regarded as coming within the 'general interest' exception referred to above.

Did the human rights legislation really prevent a removal of the banks' existing rights to appoint an administrative receiver?

2.20   It was the perceived abuses of administrative receiverships referred to in this introduction which caused the Government to introduce reforms. It was, at least, clearly arguable that the proposed abolition of the right to appoint administrative receivers under existing debentures was necessary 'in accordance with the general interest' to control the use of the power to appoint by the banks and therefore not a breach of the First Protocol (see **2.4**). One can only speculate why the Government simply conceded such an important point. Perhaps it was no more than political expediency – to avoid having to fight the banks, thereby jeopardising the swift passage of all the reforms onto the statute book. Whatever the reason, as appears elsewhere in this book, the result of the concession is that hundreds of millions of pounds which would otherwise have gone to unsecured creditors will enure for the benefit of the banks' shareholders.

---

10   An attitude characterised by Sir Gavin Lightman in his address to the R3 2002 annual
       conference in Portugal as not in accordance with the banks' 'social duty'.
11   See R3 *Technical Bulletins* Nos 47 (March 2002) and 50 (May 2002).

CROWN PREFERENCE AND TOP-SLICING

2.21 Whilst Mr Brown and the Treasury wanted to abolish administrative receiverships, for its part, the DTI had long wanted to follow the trend in other countries (most recently, Germany and Australia) by abolishing the super-rights of the Crown which have become known as 'Crown preference'. There were the makings of an economic trade-off. As one MP was later to comment during the debate on 17 June 2002: 'The Chancellor's fingerprints are all over this Bill'.

2.22 It is worth mentioning briefly the abolition of Crown preference in the general context of the corporate insolvency reforms. The scope of the Crown's preferential status was reduced as part of the 1986 reforms to cover income tax deducted by employers under PAYE, deductions made by contractors in the construction industry from payments to sub-contractors and National Insurance contributions, all for amounts due in the year prior to the insolvency. Value added tax accruing during the 6 months prior to the insolvency and a range of other withholding taxes and duties were also preferential. Some £60 million to £90 million of preferential debt has been recovered in insolvencies every year.

2.23 There have, historically, been two principal arguments in favour of the Crown's status as a preferential creditor. First, the Crown is an involuntary creditor. It neither chooses its debtors nor has the ability to tailor the terms on which it becomes a creditor. Secondly, Crown debts are debts due to the public purse and the benefits to society as a whole of the collection of taxes due to the Crown (and the expenditure of such revenues on public 'goods') outweigh the benefits to or claims of individual creditors except, to a limited extent, employees. But the Crown was not unique in being an involuntary creditor in that any creditor whose claim against a company or individual arises as a result of a wrongful (tortious) act is also an involuntary one. Further, those who are creditors for consumer deposits do not see themselves as contracting with the company in a way that means they are advancing credit to it. Small, unsecured creditors might argue that the Crown had both other remedies available to it which they did not enjoy (eg the power to levy distress and impose penalties) as well as the resources to devote to the efficient collection of tax.

2.24 However, it was thought that the position of unsecured creditors would not necessarily be improved if the Crown's preferential status was removed. In cases where a company had assets which were subject to a floating charge, such removal would in the first place benefit the floating charge-holder. Only if there were sufficient funds to repay the charge-holder in full would unsecured creditors benefit at all. For this reason top-slicing has been introduced.

FUNDING ADMINISTRATIONS – A MISSED OPPORTUNITY

2.25 During the long period of reports and consultation papers which culminated in the White Paper, it was recognised that something had to be done about financing an insolvent company through an administration. In the US, the Bankruptcy Code provides for a specific form of financing known as 'debtor-in-possession' (DIP) financing, by which a new lender obtains super-priority over the assets of the company/debtor.[12] In Canada, the courts have decided that they have jurisdiction to confer such super-priority in the absence of such specific statutory provisions – making sure that such DIP finance is used judiciously and conservatively. In September 2002, the Canadian review body reported that their judges were becoming aware of the intricacies of super-priority funding applications and that a body of case-law was developing, generating debate on the subject.[13] Similar decisions have been made in Australia. In the UK, there appears to be no such judicial creativity. It is a matter for Parliament.

2.26   Anecdotally, it has been said that, during the preparation of the proposals and the Bill, more time was spent by the Insolvency Service and those whom they consulted considering the vexed question of how administrations would be funded than any other single topic. The assumption is that the topic proved too difficult because neither the White Paper nor the Bill made any provision for funding administrations. This fundamental issue was referred to only indirectly during the passage of the Bill through the Commons – in that the rationale behind continuing to allow the appointment of administrative receivers in large-scale private projects is that they rely heavily on bank 'step-in' finance to allow them to complete the work under the control of the banks where otherwise the deals would be threatened by collapse. The arguments during the passage of the Bill for widening the exemptions to the prohibition on the ability to appoint administrative receivers were based on the cost and availability of finance.[14]

2.27   As appears below, on 29 July 2002, during the Committee debates in the House of Lords, Lord Hunt wondered where the provisions for funding had gone and asked the Minister for an explanation 'as to what exactly has happened'. He introduced proposed amendments for 'super-priority funding' under the sub-heading 'Financing Administrations' in the following terms:

'FINANCING ADMINISTRATIONS

Powers of court to approve financing of companies in administration

57A (1) The administrator of a company may at any time following his appointment apply to the court for approval of the provision of super-priority financing to the company.

(2) In this section "super-priority financing" means finance provided to a company

---

12   In the absence of the floating charge, businesses generally in the US are not as heavily financed as in the UK. As a result, when DIP financing is required there may be room to add a creditor without causing severe risk to other creditors' security. This is reflected in the US legislation which requires that US businesses have that financial cushion and that the financing be shown to benefit existing creditors.

13   See pp 32–33 of the Report on the Operation and Administration of the Bankruptcy and Insolvency Act and the Companies' Creditors Arrangement Act by The Marketplace Framework Policy Branch: http://strategis.gc.ca/cilpd.

14   See Melanie Johnson during 17 June 2002 (*Hansard* Vol 387, col 79).

in administration which shall rank as an expense in the administration with priority over the claims of existing secured and unsecured creditors.

(3) The court shall not make an order granting an application for super-priority financing under this section unless it is satisfied that –

(a) the moneys to be provided will be used for expenditure necessary to –

    (i) continue the operation of the business of the company in order to meet the administrator's objectives; or

    (ii) otherwise to protect and preserve the business and assets of the company during the administration; and

(b) the secured creditors are not prejudiced by the provision of super-priority financing; and

(c) it is appropriate to make the order in the overall interests of the administration.'

2.28 It is worth quoting extensively from the debate – if only because it is all there is on this important topic:

'Lord Hunt

... It is now some time since a review was set up by agreement between the Chancellor of the Exchequer and the Secretary of State for Trade and Industry, with the following terms of reference:

"To review aspects of company insolvency law and practice in the United Kingdom and elsewhere relating to the opportunities for, and the means by which, businesses can resolve short to medium term financial difficulties, so as to preserve maximum economic value; and to make recommendations."

That was a very timely review. One of the principal areas of focus given to the review was:

"The further development of the rescue culture".

That was clearly set out as one of the review's objectives.

I have had an opportunity to examine the report of the review group, which is entitled, A Review of Company Rescue and Business Reconstruction Mechanisms. The report, which comes from the Insolvency Service, is a most interesting document.

I refer in particular to page 33, which is headed, "Financing Company or Business Rescues". The review group states its belief that the issue of financing,

"is central to any discussion of a rescue culture in the UK."

It goes on:

"Continued trading is essential for some form of going concern to emerge at the end of the process,"

just as it is essential,

"for a company to continue trading through an insolvency procedure,"

but often only if it receives access to some form of external finance.

The review group states:

"Unless that finance is available the rescue will fail, the assets will have to be sold piece-meal and the company will usually be forced into liquidation."

The review group rightly centred on the need for a special form of financing if a company was to continue as a going concern. In broad terms,

> "new secured finance is only available to support a rescue procedure in the UK to the extent that existing secured creditors agree, and/or if the company has uncharged assets (or charged assets with sufficient equity)."

We have previously been referred to the position in the United States, where, in recognition of the critical nature of post-petition funding, Chapter 11 of the US bankruptcy code creates a framework in which new lenders can be afforded an advantageous position as regards other creditors of the company.

The review group concluded that it would be wholly inappropriate to attempt to replicate Chapter 11 in the United Kingdom, where the business culture and the economic environment are quite different. But it went on to say:

> "we nonetheless thought that the basic principles underlying US practice were the most important aspect for our purposes."

The review group continued:

> "We would summarise these basic principles as follows:

The provision of additional finance to businesses in distress can be 'value-enhancing' for the business, provided it is part of a properly considered plan for financial recovery".

I could not agree more. The issue of finance and, in particular, super-priority finance in company and business rescues was, indeed, recognised as a key issue in that original report, which, I understand, was produced in May 2000.

What I cannot understand is what has happened since. The working group strongly recommended detailed consideration and wide consultation on the issue. It concluded:

> "The review group believes that there is a case for a more radical approach to company rescues giving the courts (or supporting tribunals) discretion to agree to superpriority finance within tight criteria. This would be a major change, and there would need to be detailed consideration and wide consultation. Key issues would include the development of institutions and a legal framework to support it."

The review group concluded:

> "We recommend that a debate on this proposal should begin as soon as possible."

That was in May 2000. So far as I can see, the idea has been dropped. The Bill does not provide for it anywhere, and, I say to the Minister, surely there needs to be some kind of explanation as to exactly what has happened. If an enhanced form of administration is to be used successfully as a rescue tool, I believe it is necessary to tackle the issue of funding. In future, under these changes in the Bill, funding will not necessarily be forthcoming from the party who seeks the appointment of an administrator. Therefore, it is important to have a mechanism which provides for companies having access to ongoing finance during a rescue.

... The clause that I propose provides for super-priority financing where priority is given to a lender who is prepared to put cash into a business in order to keep it going while a rescue is worked out. I believe that failure to provide for that financing during an administration under the new regime proposed by the Bill will undermine the ability of administration to operate as an effective rescue tool.

Therefore, this is not an attempt to introduce a Chapter 11-type system – far from it. Rather, I believe that the amendment provides for a key component currently missing from the Bill to facilitate properly business rescues and to give the aims which the Bill seeks to achieve a real chance of working. I beg to move.

Lord McIntosh of Haringey:

I am grateful to the noble Lord, Lord Hunt, for having given the notice that he did about the background to the amendment. Of course, we are familiar with the review of company rescue and business reconstruction mechanisms. However, I hope that the noble Lord will agree that the conclusion of the review was a good deal more tentative than one might suppose by listening to what he said. He said that they called for debate. Indeed, they did but they did not actually recommend anything. They discussed the whole issue of super-priorities, but they did not reach a concluded view. In the absence of a concluded view, we have taken a view. I agree that we have not gone for an extended debate. Perhaps we could be at fault on that, although I assure the noble Lord, Lord Hunt, that if there is to be a debate we would happily take part. I want to explain our position, which can be our contribution to the debate for the time being.

We have taken the view that the issue of whether to lend to a company that is in administration should be a commercial one, best left to the commercial judgment of the lending market. If the proposed rescue would constitute a commercially viable proposition, or if there are free assets which can be offered as collateral, then it is for a lender to decide whether or not to lend. It is not an issue, as the amendment says, for the courts to make an order granting an application for super-priority financing. We do not consider it an issue with which the courts should be equipped to deal. Perhaps the suggestion is that there are uncharged assets, which certainly is the case in the United States, but it is much more rare in corporate insolvencies in this country, where we have so many floating charges.

If the suggestion behind the amendment is that there is little or no funding available during a rescue, that is clearly not the case. In company rescues, a company's existing bankers are the most likely source of continued funding, but alternative sources of finance for companies and businesses have emerged. There is the growth of asset financing, factoring and discounting where funders may be more oriented towards the rescue environment and prepared to advance funding to companies in administration and subject to company voluntary arrangements.

We shall certainly keep the matter under review and we shall certainly participate in any debate that takes place. There will need to be a continuous review as the new provisions in the Bill take effect because they will need to be monitored. However, our present position is that the matters of funding should be left to the commercial judgment of the lending market.'

2.29 Over the next few months, the Government reflected again. The extent of the further consultation and the nature and extent of the road block are not known. Whatever the problems, the Act as passed makes no provision whatsoever for funding the new-look administrations. The Minister finally disposed of the issue in the House of Lords on 21 October 2002 in the following exchange between Lord Hunt and the Minister:

'**Lord Hunt**

... the Government's position is essentially that the decision to lend to a company should be left to the commercial judgment of the lending market, based on whether free assets are available to use as security, among other things.

However, with the greatest respect, I believe that that approach appears to misunderstand the position that many small and medium-sized companies find themselves in when facing serious problems involving insolvency. Of course, if assets are available to lend against, why would such a company seek administration at that point? The key is to give a company protection from its creditors. That is why we have the moratorium on creditor action. Then, of course, it must have the finance to carry on while a rescue plan is put into place; otherwise, in many cases, the company would not have the funds to carry on and another potentially viable business would be lost.

I understand that much of the international community still considers our insolvency system within the UK to be essentially a liquidation process. Many small and medium-sized businesses view the system in the same way – that is, as something to be avoided at all costs, often until it is too late.

I believe we are making great progress with this Bill in reforming the whole structure. But if the new administration process does not allow a business properly to restructure and to be adequately financed while it does so, we risk making no real improvements to the rescue culture and nothing much will change. That is why I make no apology for raising again the issue of financing because I believe that it needs to be considered and properly debated.

In Committee, the noble Lord, Lord McIntosh of Haringey, noted that the Government would take part in any debate on the issue. I am informed by the noble Lord, Lord Sainsbury, that some debate has taken place during the Recess. The noble Lord, Lord Sainsbury, mentioned to me a meeting with some former members of the review group on the company rescue and business reconstruction review and some United States bankers. I have not had time to speak to all the members of the review group but those members to whom I have spoken were unaware that the meeting had taken place. Following the comments of the noble Lord, Lord McIntosh of Haringey, that he or his officials would be in touch with the review group, several members have been awaiting a telephone call but have heard nothing further. The report took some degree of effort and commitment by those who participated. The group has not met since the report was presented, nor has it been asked to attend any meeting. There is need for further debate and discussion.

It may help if the noble Lord, Lord McIntosh of Haringey, could let me know who attended that meeting, the views expressed and conclusions reached. It is a vital issue which has to be considered further in order to have the positive effect on the whole rescue business that the Bill admirably seeks to achieve. I beg to move.

Lord McIntosh:

My Lords, it is a difficult and complex issue. It is true that there are some parallels with practice in the United States; but it is also true that there are differences about which we have to be careful. Yes, we debated the issue in some detail in Committee. There has been correspondence between the noble Lord, Lord Hunt, and the noble Lord, Lord Sainsbury. The noble Lord, Lord Hunt, wrote to me on the matter within the past 10 days or so. I hope that he has received the letter in which I replied to him this morning.

I go back to the origins of the issue. The noble Lord, Lord Hunt, again referred to them. The report of the joint DTI/Treasury review group, entitled A Review of

Company Rescue and Business Reconstruction Mechanisms, was published in November 2000. The review was quoted in Committee. However, as I said then, I have to record the fact that the report did not make any recommendation in relation to "super priority" financing because of the difficulty of the issue and its view that it would be necessary to have courts that were able to take largely commercial decisions to consider applications under such a procedure.

Having published its report, the work of the review group was completed. I do not know who its members were. The group does not exist at present. But it is true that the Insolvency Service has continued to draw on the expertise of members of the group. The noble Lord, Lord Hunt, raised the issue that former members of the group – I do not know which of them but I shall find out – met with US bankers to consider the issue of "super-priority" funding, but concluded only that this was a complex issue which would need careful consideration. That is, after all, what the review group said two years ago.

One major reservation on such funding for a company that is in administration is that it would essentially guarantee a return to lenders advancing funds on the basis of such priority irrespective of the commercial viability of the rescue proposals. The decision to finance such companies must be an economic one based on the viability of the company. The review group thought that that was not necessarily within the skills of the courts as presently constituted. It is not the intention of this Government that all companies should be given the chance of rescue irrespective of their viability, but rather that an administrator, on being appointed, should determine whether the company and/or its businesses can be rescued. Therefore – it is the point I made in Committee – whether to finance such a rescue should be a commercial decision, best left to the judgement of the lending market and not the court. The courts have made clear on a number of occasions, and it is generally recognised, that it is not the role of the courts to make judgements on commercial matters. That is for the parties concerned. That has been acknowledged in our discussions on other aspects of the administration process.

When considering the substance of Amendment No 217, it is difficult to see in the context of UK corporate lending, where lenders take fixed and floating charges usually over all of the property of a company, how the court could satisfy itself in relation to proposed new paragraph 57A(3)(c), where it may not make an order for super priority financing, unless satisfied that,

> "the secured creditors are not prejudiced by the provision of super-priority financing".

In practice, there may be few occasions where that could be possible.

The review group's report concluded, and former members of that group found when they subsequently met with US Bankers, that the whole issue of super priority financing is an extremely complex one, with far-reaching potential effect. Legislative changes should be proposed only following extensive consideration and wide consultation. That is not something that should be dealt with in the Bill's progress.'

2.30 The British Bankers Association (BBA) has predicted that this approach will lead to more asset-based finance and it is difficult to disagree. It is said that such finance is more expensive. And so the single most important practical question concerning administrations remains unresolved and left to the vicissitudes of 'market forces'. Perhaps Mr Mandelson saw something in Silicon Valley which turned him off DIP finance. More likely, it was considered that the US is a foreign country and that they do things differently there. Whatever the reason, these exchanges in the House of Lords are unlikely to be the last words on the topic.

POSTSCRIPT– NOMENCLATURE

2.31   The general idea is that the efficiency with which our insolvency system enables assets to be re-deployed improves overall economic performance. An efficient statutory scheme offers some security for investors and lenders alike and it also plays a role in attracting domestic and foreign investment as well as promoting enterprise and innovation. In all of this, impression plays a part. For instance, 'liquidation' is viewed negatively, signifying failure, 'administration' imports the sense of a cumbersome process, whereas expressions used in the US and Canada such as 'reorganisation' and 'debt restructure' give a more positive, dynamic message. Perhaps those considering a future raft of reforms of corporate insolvency law will consider leaving 'administrations' behind altogether.

Chapter 3

CROWN PREFERENCE – CORPORATE INSOLVENCY

'The state is not "abolished", it withers away.'
Friedrich Engels[11]

INTRODUCTION

The principles

3.1   One of the fundamental principles of insolvency law is that, as far as possible, there should be equal distribution among the unsecured creditors. Traditionally, this has not applied in respect of the Crown. Its unsecured debts are given preferential status by statute,[2] traditionally imposed on the basis of the following justifications:[3]

(a) unpaid tax is owed to the community at large and, therefore, the preference benefits the community as a whole; and
(b) unlike those who engage in business on a day-to-day basis, the Crown is an involuntary creditor.

3.2   In this way, prior to the coming into force of the EA 2002, amounts due to the Inland Revenue[4] and to HM Customs & Excise[5] were paid under the statutory scheme for insolvency after amounts secured by a fixed charge but before all other liabilities.

3.3   Not surprisingly, there has been considerable dissatisfaction with, and criticism of, the system of this 'Crown preference' (as it is known) for some time. The Cork Report described the ancient prerogative of Crown preference as unsupportable by principle or expediency and, with a few exceptions, could not stand against the powerful tide calling for fairness and reform.[6] The White Paper

---

1   *Anti-Duhring.*
2   IA 1986, s 386 and Sch 6 (debts due to Inland Revenue (Category 1), debts due to HM Customs & Excise (Category 2) and Social Security Contributions (Category 3)).
3   *Insolvency Law and Practice: Report of the Review Committee (The Cork Report)* (1982) Cmnd 8558, para 1409.
4   In respect of PAYE, income/corporation tax and National Insurance contributions in the 12 months prior to the insolvency.
5   Including VAT in the 6 months prior to insolvency.
6   The Cork Report, para 1417.

recognised the recent trend in other jurisdictions towards restricting or abolishing Crown or State preferences.[7]

3.4   Crown preference is now abolished with retrospective effect in the sense that there will be no Crown preference in any corporate insolvencies commenced after the EA 2002 has come into force. In future, there will be a small, residual category of preferential creditors (see **3.16**). The next category of creditor to be paid after the (few, if any, remaining) preferential creditors will be floating chargees. For those floating charges created after the coming into force of the relevant provisions, a part of the 'net property'[8] will be set aside (or 'top-sliced') for the benefit of unsecured creditors.[9] This top-sliced part of the net property will be known as the 'prescribed part'.

3.5   These proposals received universal support during the passage of the Bill through Parliament. However, reservations were expressed that the abolition of Crown preference would cause the historic indulgence of the Crown departments towards ailing businesses to harden into taking earlier enforcement measures.

The flaw

3.6   The concept that moneys which were formerly payable to the Crown should find their way to the unsecured creditors is excellent. For it to work in corporate insolvency, the abolition of Crown preference must be linked to the new 'top-slicing' provisions. In other words, through the mechanism of top-slicing, realisations which used to be paid to the Crown departments as preferential creditors must be channelled to the unsecured creditors.

3.7   However, as is recorded elsewhere in this book, this excellent idea has been substantially undermined by the Government's concession that debentures created prior to the coming into force of the relevant part of the EA 2002:

(a)   shall take the benefit of the abolition of Crown preference; but
(b)   shall not be subject to top-slicing.

The shareholders of the banks and other institutional lenders will intercept the moneys which the Government had promised would go to the unsecured creditors. This is a major flaw in the proposals as enacted.

The wider picture

3.8   The Government sees the abolition of Crown preference as an integral part of the scheme to rescue more companies by streamlining the administration procedure and abolishing administrative receiverships.[10] If there is no floating charge-holder, the sums released will be entirely for the benefit of the unsecured creditors. In a case where there is a floating charge created after the relevant commencement date, at least some of the benefit will filter down to the

---

7   For example, Germany and Australia; see the White Paper, para 2.19.
8   Meaning funds that would otherwise be available for the floating charge-holder.
9   As to top-slicing, see Chapter 5.
10   Department of Trade and Industry White Paper, *Productivity and Enterprise, Insolvency – A Second Chance*, July 2001, Cm 5234, para 2.19.

unsecured creditors by virtue of the 'top-slicing' provisions.[11] However, in the short-term, it is difficult to envisage existing debenture holders relinquishing their security in exchange for post-commencement security.

Explanation in Parliament

3.9   The new proposals passed from the initial draft to Royal Assent intact. There was much praise of, but very little debate on, the topic until late in the passage of the Bill. In the House of Lords on 29 July 2002, the Minister, Lord McIntosh of Haringey, gave the following explanation of the link between the abolition of Crown preference and top-slicing:[12]

> 'We announced in the White Paper, *Insolvency: A Second Chance*, that we would make provisions to ensure that the benefit of the abolition of the Crown's preferential status will go to unsecured creditors. It is, after all, they who are at the end of the queue and for whom there is often nothing left after costs and secured creditors have been paid. It is estimated that an additional £70 million per year will become available to unsecured creditors as a result of the Crown giving up its preferential status. It is only right that unsecured creditors – including those in cases in which a floating charge has been given – receive the benefit of this money. This clause achieves that promise.
>
> Therefore, in company insolvency cases where a floating charge has been given, this clause instructs the office-holder to set aside – or 'ring-fence' – a proportion of the money that he has available for the floating charge holder and to hold it for distribution to unsecured creditors.
>
> While exact figures are not available to show what the Crown gets as a result of its preferential status as a proportion of all distributions made in insolvencies, we estimate – from figures held by the Insolvency Service – that, preferentially, the Crown gets somewhere in the region of 10 per cent of all distributions – it is certainly not less than that and nor do we believe that it is as much as 20 per cent.'

Moving the goalposts – the contemporaneous decision in *Brumark*

3.10   As can be seen from Lord McIntosh's explanation, it was intended, in broad terms, that in corporate insolvencies the amount surrendered by the Crown by the abolition of Crown preference would equate with the amount channelled to the unsecured creditors by the top-slicing provisions. It is doubtful that this assumption is correct.

3.11   The White Paper was published on 31 July 2001. It followed the landmark decision of the Privy Council in *Agnew v Commissioners of Inland Revenue*[13] ('the *Brumark* decision') on 5 June 2001, which severely limited the extent to which banks could rely upon their purported fixed charges over book debts and certain other species of property. Whilst the true annual value of all fixed charge assets lost to the floating charge pool is not easily calculated, the potential economic effect of *Brumark* on the institutional secured lenders is

---

11   See para 721 of the Explanatory Notes.
12   See *Hansard*, No 178, 29 July 2002, House of Lords sitting in Committee, at cols 805 and 806.
13   [2001] UKPC 28, [2001] 2 AC 710.

enormous. There is nothing to suggest that the removal of the Crown's preferential status was a political deal to soften the impact of *Brumark* on these lenders. In reality, the proposals were tabled and passed through Parliament without catching up with the contemporaneous impact of *Brumark*.

3.12   Thus, the Government estimated that it received approximately £90 million per year preferentially from all insolvencies, and that the result of the proposal would be that some £70 million would be released to other creditors. In fact, once it is appreciated that all book debt and certain other realisations are not fixed but floating charge assets, the amounts conceded by the Government are far greater than £90 million.

3.13   Conversely, it was anticipated that the Crown would recoup a further £20 million in its capacity as an unsecured creditor in these insolvencies.[14] That figure might well be far larger once it is accepted that book debt and other realisations will not, as hitherto, be scooped by the banks and other secured lenders under their fixed charges.

A half-measure?

3.14   The problems which have given rise to the need to abolish Crown preference are rooted in the very existence of the floating charge. If the objective was to increase the assets payable to the unsecured creditors, the obvious answer for corporate insolvencies would be to abolish the floating charge. The floating charge has not always met with universal approval. As long ago as 1905, distinguished members of the judiciary were critical of the effect that the all-encompassing floating security was having on distributions:

> 'The cases are numerous in which ... if the company is wound up, there is nothing for any one but the debenture-holders.'[15]

3.15   On the other hand, the simplicity and flexibility of the floating charge has long been recognised as an important tool for finance. The power held by a floating-charge holder is a power that is envied by banks in almost all other foreign jurisdictions in which the floating charge is not recognised. The EA 2002 endorses the existence and efficacy of the floating charge. Even the Law Commission has now shirked from proposing its abolition as a security mechanism.[16]

THE IMPACT OF THE ABOLITION OF CROWN PREFERENCE

Repeal of the relevant parts of the IA 1986

3.16   The provisions are enacted in a triumph of statutory drafting that is not matched in many of the other provisions of the Act. By EA 2002, s 251(1), it is

---

14   Department of Trade and Industry, *The Enterprise Bill, Insolvency Provisions – Regulatory Impact Assessment*, para 5.29.

15   Per Buckley J in *Re London Pressed Hinge Co Ltd* [1905] 1 Ch 576 at 583.

16   *Registration of Security Interests: Company Charges and Property Other Than Land, A Consultation Paper* (July 2002).

simply stated that the relevant paragraphs of IA 1986, Sch 6[17] shall cease to have effect. The effect of this is that the other preferential debts remain. The other, non-Crown preferential debts, are:

(a) contributions to occupational pension schemes (category 4);
(b) remuneration of employees for the relevant period (category 5); and
(c) levies on coal and steel production under the European Coal and Steel Community (ECSC) Treaty (category 6).

3.17 The subrogated rights of the DTI where the Crown has made payments from the National Insurance Fund to cover all or part of any employee's preferential claims in respect of salary and wages under the Employment Rights Act 1996 (ERA 1996) will survive. This is on the basis that the Crown is not then relying upon its own preferential rights, but is stepping into the shoes of the preferential rights of the employee.[18]

3.18 Further, s 189(4) of ERA 1996 is removed. Consequently, in so far as it remains a preferential creditor on such grounds, the DTI will not be paid in priority to any remaining preferential claims of employees.[19]

Strengthening preferential claims of employees

3.19 The abolition of Crown preference will change the landscape for employees considerably. At a stroke, they will become the principal preferential creditors.[20] In cases where the business is sold by the administrator as a going concern, the Transfer of Undertakings (Protection of Employment) Regulations 1981, SI 1981/1794 (TUPE) will apply with the result that there could be no preferential claims at all. The implications of this are explored further below.

Interception of abolished 'preference' moneys by pre-commencement charge-holders

3.20 The first and most obvious impact of the new provisions is that, in a case where a bank or other lender has lent money to a company secured by a floating charge that would previously have ranked behind the Crown's preferential debts,[21] the realisations 'released' by the abolition of Crown preference will go straight to the bank. This windfall was not intended at the outset. Indeed, along with almost all other interested consultees, the Association of Business Recovery Professionals (R3) positively welcomed the perceived bonus to the unsecured creditors as proposed in the White Paper:[22]

> 'Removing Crown preference is terrific news. The change will cost the taxpayer money, but not very much. In return, unsecured creditors should get higher returns

---

17 Ie paras 1–7 which include comparatively rare claims such as landfill tax, climate change levy and car tax.
18 See para 726 of the Explanatory Notes.
19 See EA 2002, s 248(3) and Sch 17, para 49(4), together with para 726 of the Explanatory Notes.
20 The entire list of surviving preferential creditors can be found in paras 8–15A of Sch 6 to the IA 1986.
21 IA 1986, s 40.
22 *Recovery* September 2001.

and the revenue departments should take a more positive attitude to business rescues.'

3.21   In this way, banks and other secured lenders with existing floating charges not only remain in the best position to benefit from the demise of the corporate borrower – their position will be strengthened considerably when the abolition of Crown preference comes into force as part of the EA 2002. They have retained the right to appoint administrative receivers under their existing debentures yet find themselves free of the burden of the priority afforded to the Crown's preferential debts. In one swoop, the Crown has released its status directly in favour of the banks and other secured lenders. It is regrettable that the Government has allowed existing charges to intercept the benefit in this way.

3.22   It would have been a far more equitable approach to have kept the Crown preference in respect of charges created before the coming into force of the Act. That would not have prejudiced the banks (for that is the present position). The abolition of Crown preference in respect of existing charges is an unjust enrichment for the banks with no apparent justification. Further, this benefit will apply for many years to come, until such time as the present crop of debentures is exhausted and replaced by ones created after the commencement of the EA 2002.

Intervention of the rights of unsecured creditors

3.23   The intervention of the rights of unsecured creditors is best explained by returning to *Brumark*. Many of the major institutional lenders, including some of the clearing banks, have been in denial about the effect of *Brumark*. The extent to which they have persuaded the insolvency profession that *Brumark* does not mean what it says has been extreme. This has led to the issue of technical guidelines to the profession.[23] These entail a liquidator holding book debt realisations, writing first to the bank and then to the preferential creditors in order to seek agreement. In the absence of agreement, the liquidator is told to apply to court for directions. Usually, there being no prospect of a dividend for the unsecured creditors, the liquidator effectively interpleads. The point is that the principal candidates as beneficiaries of the realisations have been the bank and the Crown (ie as preferential creditor).

3.24   In future, the principal beneficiaries are likely to be the floating charge-holder and the unsecured creditors. It is not unreasonable to suppose that the court will guard more jealously the interests of the latter than those of the Crown (which has the resources to look after its own interests). Moreover, currently the compromise of such disputes involves an agreement between the representatives of the bank and the Crown. In the future, the liquidator will be a protagonist, representing the unsecured creditors against the bank.

Hardening of attitudes by the Crown departments

3.25   The third immediate impact will be upon the working capital of small businesses. The existence of the system of Crown preferences has encouraged an

---

23   See R3 *Technical Bulletins* Nos 47 (March 2002) and 50 (May 2002).

environment in which the Crown was more indulgent when collecting outstanding debts than would have been the case if it had not enjoyed such preferential status. This is an effect even recognised by the banks themselves:[24]

> 'A prominent banker, who is at pains to remain nameless ... is also worried at the impact of the abolition of Crown preference on the funding of small businesses. "In the past, things like uncollected VAT and other taxes provided working capital to small business. The VAT man and the Revenue were willing to go along with this knowing that, in the end, they had Crown preference to rely on. Not any more. They will, therefore, collect their taxes sooner. I believe it is quite a danger to small businesses".'

3.26 One effect of the removal of Crown preferences may be, therefore, that the Inland Revenue and HM Customs & Excise will not be so lenient in granting companies breathing space. Crown creditors are likely to seek to recover the outstanding debt at a much earlier stage than has been the case to date. This may, ironically, lead to more cases of insolvency rather than fewer.[25]

Company voluntary arrangements

3.27 The abolition of Crown preferences is likely to have the effect of a greater involvement of the Crown departments in company voluntary arrangements (CVAs). The Voluntary Arrangements Service, managed by the Inland Revenue on behalf of itself and HM Customs & Excise, has published criteria by which it will judge the proposals put to it.[26] Practitioners will have to bear these guidelines in mind to a far greater extent now that the Crown will be participating as an unsecured creditor in such voluntary arrangements. Whilst the abolition of Crown preference is part of the encouragement of rescue together with the increased benefit for unsecured creditors, it remains to be seen whether, in practice, the Voluntary Arrangements Service will relax its criteria.

LIQUIDATION EXPENSES – A POTENTIAL LACUNA

Administrative receiverships and liquidation expenses

3.28 One final consequence of the abolition of Crown preference relates to the manner in which 'liquidation expenses' will be met and/or provided for out of assets realised by an administrative receiver.

3.29 Floating charge-holders will retain the right to appoint an administrative receiver under pre-commencement security whilst that security continues in existence.[27] Section 40 of IA 1986 specifically provides that if a company in administrative receivership is not at the time being wound up, its preferential debts[28] shall be paid out of the assets coming into the hands of the receiver in

---

24 Willcock 'How the Banks Won the Battle for the Enterprise Bill', *Recovery* June 2002.
25 The Cork Report felt that such worries were unjustified: 'time to pay outstanding tax is allowed only in exceptional cases. Deferred payments are allowed only to businesses which are expected to survive', para 1422.
26 They are published on the Inland Revenue web-site at www.inlandrevenue.gov.uk/pdfs/cwl5.htm#6.
27 For further details, see Chapter 4 on Administrative Receiverships.
28 Defined in IA 1986, s 386.

priority to the claims for principal or interest in respect of the debenture.[29] In that event, IA 1986, s 175 stipulates the priorities, namely that the preferential debts:

(a) rank equally amongst themselves *after the expenses of the winding-up* and shall be paid in full, unless the assets are insufficient to meet them, in which case they abate in equal proportions;[30] and

(b) as far as the assets of the company available for the payment of general creditors are insufficient to meet them, have priority over claims of holders of debentures secured by, or holders of, any floating charge created by the company, and shall be paid accordingly out of any property comprised in or subject to that charge.[31] (emphasis added)

3.30 This is the route by which it is determined that liquidation expenses are payable in advance of preferential debts. IA 1986 obliges an administrative receiver to pay the preferential creditors. IA 1986, s 175 obliges an administrative receiver to pay the preferential creditors after the expenses of the winding-up. Therefore, the administrative receiver is obliged to pay, or provide for, the liquidation expenses prior to discharge of the debt due under the floating charge. This is an onerous obligation. It is a positive statutory duty placed on the administrative receiver[32] and is one that continues even if the debenture holder's debt has been discharged.[33]

The problem

3.31 The difficulty is that if there are *no preferential debts*, s 175 is not engaged and there is no statutory basis upon which liquidation expenses[34] come to be given priority. This gives rise to a practical problem which might be explained by reference to the decision of Mr Anthony Mann QC in *Re Demaglass Ltd*.

The decision in Demaglass

3.32 In two connected receiverships, an administrative receiver held £3.1 million by way of floating charge realisations. The preferential creditors were owed £1.864 million. The liquidator's principal argument was that he was entitled to all the floating charge realisations, on the basis that such realisations would in due course be applied to pay liquidation expenses. Failing that argument, the liquidator argued that he had identified sums for which he should be entitled to draw as liquidation expenses in advance of their expenditure, identifying £234,500 by way of proposed expenditure.

---

29   See IA 1986, s 40(2).

30   Ibid, s 175(2)(a).

31   Ibid, s 175(2)(b).

32   See *Commissioners of the Inland Revenue v Goldblatt* [1972] Ch 498.

33   See *Re Pearl Maintenance Services Limited* [1995] BCC 657.

34   The full meaning and impact of the phrase 'liquidation expenses' in the context of the definition of expenses of the winding-up in IR 1986, r 4.218 were considered in *Re Toshoku Finance (UK) Ltd* [2002] UKHL 6, [2002] 1 WLR 671 HL, *Re Leyland DAF Ltd; Buchler v Talbot* [2002] EWCA Civ 228, [2002] 1 BCLC 571, CA and *Re Demaglass Ltd* [2002] BPIR 1093.

3.33   It was held that the liquidator could not demand payment of the entirety of the realised sums because, among other things, IR 1986, r 4.218 was couched in past terms, and so had no application. It was also held that, as a fiduciary, the liquidator was not entitled to take the money out of the fund that he held in advance of its actually being incurred or, possibly, in advance of his becoming liable to pay them. He was not justified in requiring all the realisations to be paid over, or the sums in relation to the identified future expenses. He was entitled to an indemnity only, not payment in advance of expenditure.

The problem revisited

3.34   With the abolition of Crown preference, it is entirely possible that an administrative receiver may find himself in the position that there are no preferential creditors. A particular example may arise where there has been a speedy and successful sale of the entirety of the company's business as a going concern, such that no employees have any claims against the company. The administrative receiver may have substantial sums in hand prior to the discharge of the debenture holder's debt under the floating charge after discharge of the debenture holder's debts. In the absence of any preferential creditors, there is no priority afforded to 'liquidation expenses' such that the administrative receiver will be able to account for the entirety of the floating charge realisations to his debenture holder.

3.35   A practical problem arises: even if there are some small preferential claims, the liquidation may be in its early stages, when little or nothing might have been incurred by way of expenses of the winding-up. Typically, the liquidator might be preparing to incur legal expenses by embarking on litigation against the company's former directors (all such expenses are now likely to be within the definition of expenses of the winding-up[35]). It is difficult to see what precisely the administrative receiver should do in those circumstances. Should he simply do nothing save prolong the administrative receivership without discharging the debenture holder's debt? Should he pay the debenture holder, and hope that nothing is incurred by way of liquidation expenses in the future? Or should he require the liquidator to make a decision as to precisely what is going to happen in the liquidation?

A potential solution

3.36   The analysis in *Re Demaglass Ltd* demonstrates that, even if he knows what he is likely to do, the liquidator is not going to be in a position to request payment over to him of sums that he anticipates that he might incur by way of liquidation expenses.

---

35   See Insolvency (Amendment) (No 2) Rules 2002, SI 2002/2712, r 23, which came into force on 1 January 2003 amending IR 1986, r 4.218 so as to provide that the costs properly chargeable in relation to any legal proceedings which the official receiver or liquidator has power to bring in his own name or that of the company are payable as expenses of the winding-up. The effect of *Lewis v Commissioner of Inland Revenue* [2001] 3 All ER 499 (otherwise known as *Re Floor Fourteen Limited*) is therefore avoided.

3.37 It would seem that the only route open is that identified by the deputy judge in *Demaglass* itself. It was held that, on appropriately detailed evidence as to the proposed steps and the reason for their being taken, the liquidator might, in advance of expenditure, obtain a declaration that an anticipated future cost would, after being incurred, amount to a liquidation expense within the meaning of IR 1986, r 4.218. The administrative receiver could then retain an appropriate sum to account for the liquidation expenses to be incurred in future prior to distributing to the floating charge-holder. But, the administrative receiver would still not be protected against the incurring of other expenses beyond those covering by the prospective order, whether by way of the nature of the expense or the level of expenditure. These questions are likely to be litigated after the abolition of Crown preference.

CONCLUSION

3.38 The abolition of Crown preference should result in a substantial benefit to unsecured creditors in the statutory schemes for personal insolvency.[36] However, in corporate insolvency, the existing secured lenders (ie with pre-commencement floating charges) will receive the benefits which were intended to flow down to the unsecured creditors. It is only in corporate insolvencies where there is no floating charge, or a floating charge created after the relevant commencement date, that the unsecured creditors can expect to receive the intended benefit of the abolition of Crown preference. The means by which the Crown preference moneys are to be channelled to unsecured creditors are the new top-slicing provisions.

---

36 See Chapter 15.

Chapter 4

ADMINISTRATIVE RECEIVERSHIP

'A bank is a place that will lend you money
If you can prove that you don't need it.'
Bob Hope[1]

INTRODUCTION

Development of the administrative receivership procedure

4.1   The floating charge was first recognised by a Court of Equity in the latter part of the nineteenth century.[2] It enables a creditor to take security over all the assets of the company both present and future, including fluctuating assets. 'Receivership' is the process whereby assets which are the subject of a floating charge are realised for the benefit of the floating charge-holder. Typically, charge instruments include provision for the appointment by the charge-holder of a receiver, who is given extensive powers to manage the company's business whilst carrying out the receivership. By reason of the contractual basis of the appointment, no professional qualifications were required and the receiver was solely accountable to the charge-holder. The substance of the 'administrative receivership' procedure was, therefore, well developed prior to the 1986 legislation.

4.2   In 1982, the Cork Committee recognised the benefits of the receivership procedure, but recommended reform.[3] The recommendations included making receivers more accountable to the general body of creditors and requiring certain minimum professional qualifications for the office-holder. The Insolvency Act 1985 (IA 1985) and IA 1986 largely implemented these recommendations. The office of 'administrative receiver' was created. Such a person had to be a qualified insolvency practitioner.[4] Part III of the IA 1986 increased the reporting requirements of the administrative receiver, and therefore increased the amount of information available to all the creditors. However, the changes did not deflect the administrative receivers' primary duty away from the charge-holder. Once appointed, the control of the company was

---

1   *The Tyranny of Farms* (1959).
2   See *In re Panama, New Zealand, and Australian Royal Mail Co* (1870) LR 5 Ch App 318. The history of the floating charge is helpfully summarised by Lord Millett in *Agnew v Commissioners of Inland Revenue* [2001] 2 AC 710 (*'Brumark'*).
3   *The Cork Report*, para 110 and 495 and, generally, Chapter 8.
4   Part III of IA 1986, s 29(2).

in the hands of a single secured creditor who had little duty to consider the interests of other creditors.

4.3   The great scope for the administrative receiver to rescue an ailing company was recognised by the Cork Committee in 1982. This recognition led to the creation of the administration procedure in the IA 1985 and 1986. However, the power of the charge-holder to appoint an administrative receiver continued. If so desired, the charge-holder was able to appoint a receiver before the administrator took office, thereby frustrating any attempt to put the company into administration.

Perceived inadequacies of administrative receivership

4.4   The Minister for E-Commerce and Competitiveness (Mr Douglas Alexander), who deputised for the Secretary of State for Trade and Industry (Patricia Hewitt) during some of the debates on the Enterprise Bill, summarised the Government's reasoning behind the proposed abolition of administrative receiverships as follows:

> 'The impression left by the recession of the early 1990s is that administrative receivership was often used to pull the plug on a company with no thought given to whether, with breathing space, the company could trade out of its difficulties and survive. By prohibiting a floating charge holder from appointing an administrative receiver and ensuring that the collective administration procedure is used, we shall move firmly in favour of a procedure in which all creditors have the opportunity to participate and under which the administrator must act in the interests of all creditors.'[5]

4.5   The Government was not swayed by statistics compiled by the BBA which purported to show that 75% of cases handled by bank specialists involved the recovery of the company. Nor was it persuaded by the suggestion that the proposed changes would lead to an environment in which finance would become more expensive and less available.[6]

4.6   In essence, there were two perceived inadequacies which drove the corporate reforms which are now contained in the EA 2002. First, the Government expressed the view that the administrative receivership procedure did not provide 'adequate incentives to maximise economic value'.[7] Administrative receivers could carry out their duties without regard to other creditors' interests in circumstances when there was nothing to encourage them to try and rescue the company as a going concern. Whilst the BBA might be able to show that the banks were currently making an effort to be a contributor to the 'rescue culture', there was no guarantee that they would not change their tune during harder times. A specific legislative incentive seemed to be necessary.

---

5   See *Hansard*, Standing Committee B, Enterprise Bill, Fifteenth Sitting, 9 May 2002 at col 610.

6   Ibid, at col 608.

7   See the White Paper (Cmnd 5234), *Productivity and Enterprise: Insolvency – A Second Chance* at paragraphs 2.2 and 2.3 (which can be found at http://www.insolvency.gov.uk/5234.htm).

4.7 The second major perceived inadequacy of administrative receivership was that the administrative receiver remained substantially unaccountable to creditors other than the charge-holder in circumstances where their actions had a significant effect on those creditors' interests. An example cited in the White Paper was that an administrative receiver was entitled to consider solely the interests of his or her appointor when determining the timing of a sale of a business. An administrative receiver could sell immediately, whereas a delay in the timing of the sale could result in an increased realisation for the benefit of all creditors.[8] Thus, a new collective procedure would involve the office-holder being accountable to all the creditors, notwithstanding the fact that he had been appointed by the floating charge-holder.

Summary of the changes

4.8 The Government's solution to the perceived inadequacies was to propose the end of administrative receivership in the majority of cases, in favour of a collective administration procedure. In July 2001, it was announced that administrative receiverships were 'outdated' and were to be replaced by a new 'streamlined administration procedure'. This was to ensure that all interest groups got a 'fair say'.[9] These proposals have now been enacted.

4.9 Before considering the qualifications to this broad reform, it is worth briefly stating those matters which have not changed. The right to use floating charges as a form of security remains unchallenged.[10] In addition, no change to the right to appoint the Law of Property Act 1925 (LPA 1925) receivers has been made.[11] The change solely relates to the rights of floating charge-holders as regards the procedure by which the assets covered by the floating charge are realised.

4.10 Having considered those matters which will not change, it is worth summarising the qualifications to the general rule that an administrative receiver may no longer be appointed.

4.11 The first significant qualification to the general rule emerged in November 2001. It was announced that the prohibition would not be retrospective and would only apply to lending agreements supported by floating charges created after the commencement of the relevant provisions of the EA 2002.[12] The banking lobby had persuaded the Government that rights provided by existing debentures should not be retrospectively reduced.[13] Thus,

---

8   See *Re Charnley Davies* [1990] BCLC 760.
9   See the White Paper (Cmnd 5234), *Productivity and Enterprise: Insolvency – A Second Chance*, Foreword by the Secretary of State for Trade and Industry, The Rt Hon Patricia Hewitt MP.
10 The only in-road to the 'substantive' as opposed to 'procedural' rights of the floating charge-holder has been made by the 'top-slicing' provisions. See Chapter 5 on 'Top-Slicing'.
11 Although, notably, an administrator is now given power to oblige an LPA 1925 reciever to vacate office — see IA 1986, Sch B1, para 41(2). See Rupert Connell of Fladgate Fisher, 'Enterprising Receivers', *Recovery*, Spring 2003, pp 20–22.
12 Department of Trade and Industry (DTI) Press Release, 9 November 2001.
13 See 2.2.

s 72A(4)(a) of IA 1986[14] provides that the prohibition only applies to a 'floating charge created on or after a date appointed by the Secretary of State by order made by statutory instrument' ('post-commencement charges'). Charges created before the appointed day ('pre-commencement charges') are not caught by the new legislation. Hence, the two parallel, but separate, regimes of administrative receivership and administration will continue for the foreseeable future in so far as floating charge holders wish to continue to invoke their right to appoint an administrative receiver in respect of pre-commencement charges. The result is that the floating charge-holders have it both ways. They keep their ability to appoint administrative receivers and gain the windfall arising from the abolition of Crown preference.

4.12   The second major qualification to the general prohibition on appointment of administrative receivers is that the new administration procedure imports many of the benefits that floating charge-holders enjoyed under the administrative receivership regime. The tool of receivership is much cherished by lenders as it allows a quick and easy way of intervening in a failing company and realising their security without being troubled by other third-party interests. The ability to appoint an insolvency practitioner of the debenture holder's choice was considered to be crucial. The ability of the floating charge-holder to appoint their chosen insolvency practitioner has been included in the new administration regime. Under the new procedure, the qualifying floating charge-holder has the ability to make their own out-of-court appointment of an administrator.[15] In addition, they will be able to intervene in respect of other parties' applications in order to ensure that they have their own practitioner appointed, subject to a right of refusal by the court in the latter case.[16] The new three-pronged 'purpose' of administration also makes accommodation for the interests of the floating charge-holder by providing that where it is not reasonably practicable to save the company, or achieve a better result for the creditors as a whole than would be achieved under a winding-up, the administrator may pursue the sole objective of realising property in order to make a distribution to secured or preferential creditors.[17] It can be seen, therefore, that the new administration procedure has been fashioned, and amended, to accommodate the interests of the floating charge-holder. What the floating charge-holders lose in name, they largely recover in substance.

4.13   In conclusion, therefore, despite the fact that the general rule is that administrative receiverships will be prohibited in the future, the reforms have a subtler underlying effect. It may be better to describe the reforms as a 'transmutation' or 'merger' of the administrative receivership and administration procedures rather than as being the end of the administrative receiver-

---

14   Inserted by EA 2002, s 250.
15   IA 1986, Sch B1, paras 14–21.
16   Ibid, para 36. The only qualification in respect of intervention is that it would seem the court has a discretion to refuse such an application when the circumstances justify it: para 36(2). The ambit of this discretion remains to be properly defined and early case- law will be watched with eager interest.
17   Ibid, para 3(1).

ship procedure. It is suggested that the EA 2002 will be better understood if approached with the concept of 'transmutation' in mind.

PROSPECTIVE PROHIBITION OF APPOINTMENT OF ADMINISTRATIVE RECEIVER

The new ss 72A–72H of IA 1986

4.14 Section 250 of EA 2002 inserts a new Chapter IV (ss 72A–72H) into Part III of IA 1986. Schedule 18 to EA 2002 inserts a new Sch 2A to IA 1986. The new ss 72A–72H, together with the new Sch 2A, govern the terms of the phasing out of the administrative receivership procedure. At the time of writing it is expected that the changes will commence some time in July 2003.[18]

4.15 The prohibition of appointment of an administrative receiver in respect of post-commencement charges is provided for by s 72A(1) of IA 1986:

> 'The holder of a qualifying floating charge in respect of a company's property may not appoint an administrative receiver of the company.'

4.16 The general rule, therefore, is that a qualifying floating charge-holder (as defined in para 14 of Sch B1 to IA 1986) will not be able to appoint an administrative receiver (s 72A(1)) where the source of such power derives from an instrument created on or after the appointed date (s 72A(4)). The appointed date will be determined by order made by statutory instrument. The Government has given reassurances that the appointed date in the order will not precede the date of the order itself.[19]

4.17 Before considering the exceptions to the general rule specified in ss 72B–72G, it is worth considering how this general prohibition is likely to work in practice.

Practical implications of the prospective prohibition

4.18 There are four questions which immediately attract interest:

(a) Who will be a qualifying floating charge-holder?
(b) How will the courts determine whether the floating charge is 'created' before the appointed day, as defined in s 72A(4)(a)?
(c) How will subss (4) and (5) of s 72A be used by the Secretary of State to deal with transitional cases, and, for example, charges which secure the advancement of moneys after the appointed day?
(d) In what circumstances might the prohibition be avoided or evaded?

(1) Who will be a qualifying floating charge-holder?

4.19 This question is relatively straightforward to answer. First, we know that the intention of the legislation is to stop anyone being able to appoint

---

18 For the latest information as regards commencement, the reader is encouraged to review the information contained at the Insolvency Service's website: www.insolvency.gov.uk.

19 See *Hansard*, Standing Committee B, Fifteenth Sitting, Thursday 9 May 2002, at cols 603 and 604 and see also the DTI Press Release, 9 November 2001.

administrative receivers in respect of charges created on or after the 'appointed day'. Section 72A(4)(b) provides that the prohibition will apply in spite of an instrument which purports to empower the appointment of an administrative receiver. Secondly, there is a definition of the qualifying floating charge-holder in para 14 of Sch B1 to IA 1986.

4.20   Subsection (1) of para 14 gives the power to the holder of a qualifying floating charge to appoint an administrator. Subsection (2)(c) of the same paragraph states that a floating charge is a qualifying charge if it is created by an instrument which, amongst other things, purports to empower the holder to make an appointment which would be the appointment of an administrative receiver within the meaning of s 29(2) of IA 1986. The purpose of this drafting would appear to be twofold. It reinforces the point that post-commencement charges cannot enable the appointment of an administrative receiver. It also enables the holders of pre-commencement charges to choose to appoint an administrator instead of an administrative receiver if they so wish.[20]

4.21   In short, therefore, the legislation provides that the creation of 'old-style' charges after commencement of the Act, which seek to empower the debenture holder to appoint a receiver or manager of 'the whole (or substantially the whole) of a company's property … secured by a charge which, as created, was a floating charge, or by such a charge and one or more securities',[21] will be ineffective to enable the appointment of an administrative receiver. Instead, such provisions will be treated as empowering the appointment of an administrator.

(2) *When is a floating charge created?*

4.22   The second question is, how will the courts approach the question of whether the floating charge is 'created' before, on or after the appointed day? The better read, or, dare I say it, older, reader may recall that the determination of when a charge is 'created' attracted some judicial interest in the context of the registration requirements in the Companies Acts. The requirement of registration of floating charges was first introduced by s 14 of the Companies Act 1900. Section 95 of the Companies Act 1948 (CA 1948) provided that the charge had to be submitted for registration in the manner required by that Act within 21 days after the date of its creation in order to ensure that the charge was valid against the liquidator and any creditor of the company. To date, these provisions remain largely unchanged.[22] The wording of s 95 of CA 1948 attracted considerable case-law, particularly on the question of when the charge had been created.

4.23   In the context of s 95 of CA 1948, the date of 'creation' of a mortgage or charge is the date when the instrument is executed, or the deposit of deeds made. It is not the date on which any money is subsequently advanced or any of

---

20   See *Hansard*, Standing Committee B, Fifteenth Sitting, Thursday 9 May 2002, at col 610.
21   IA 1986, s 29(2)(a).
22   See Companies Act 1985, ss 395 and 396.

the charges subsequently issued.[23] It is the date on which the instrument is executed by the company which is important, irrespective of whether it is expressed to be a multi-party document and is not signed by the other parties until another date. Furthermore, the practice of leaving the document undated until the other parties had signed the instrument did not affect the date on which the charge was deemed to be 'created' for the purposes of s 95 of CA 1948.[24] The picture is slightly more complicated as regards the registration provisions, because once the registrar's certificate is issued such certificate is deemed to be conclusive evidence of, amongst other things, the date of creation of the charge.[25] This complication need not concern us however when construing the meaning of 'created' for the purposes of the new s 72A(4)(a) of IA 1986.

4.24   In summary therefore, it is suggested that, for the purposes of interpreting s 72A(4)(a), a charge will be deemed to have been 'created' on the day the instrument of charge is executed. Furthermore, case-law under s 95 of CA 1948 will be of assistance in determining other queries which may arise as to when a charge has been 'created', a number of which have been highlighted in the preceding paragraph.

(3) How do the transitional provisions apply?

4.25   Subsection (5) of s 72A states that an order under subs (4)(a) may:

'(a) make provision which applies generally or only for a specified purpose;
(b) make different provision for different purposes;
(c) make transitional provisions.'

Thus, the Government has a discretion as to how to implement transitional provisions relating to the prohibition.

4.26   Prior to the publication of the Enterprise Bill, in November 2001, Patricia Hewitt, the Secretary of State for Trade and Industry, stated that:

'... the insolvency law provisions will continue to apply to lending agreements supported by a floating charge where they are entered into prior to the commencement of these aspects of the Enterprise Bill.'[26]

The use of the word 'they' might be taken to suggest that both the lending and the charge must have taken place or been created prior to the appointed day. Some commentators anticipate that the transitional provisions will deal with the question of charges which secure both moneys advanced before and moneys

---

23   See *Esberger & Son v Capital Counties Bank* [1913] 2 Ch 366 (though this case appeared to overlook the effect of the issue of the registrar's certificate); see *Re CL Nye Ltd* [1971] Ch 442 and s 401(2) of the Companies Act 1985 and commentary on those matters in Lightman & Moss *The Law of Receivers and Administrators of Companies* (Sweet & Maxwell, 3rd edition, 2000) at pp 85–86).

24   See commentary on s 95 of CA 1948, and the case-law relating to the same, at pp 248–249 in *Buckley on the Companies Acts* (Butterworths, 14th Edition, 1981) at pp 248–249, where there is discussion of, amongst other things, the treatment of agreements to give security.

25   See s 401(2)(b) of Companies Act 1985 and see for example *Re CL Nye Ltd* [1971] Ch 442.

26   See Department of Trade and Industry (DTI) Press Release, 9 November 2001.

advanced on and after the appointed day.[27] However, the wording of the new s 72A(4)(a) indicates that the prohibition only applies to floating charges created on or after the appointed day. It does not seek to distinguish between old and new lending. Thus, on the face of it, new lending covered by pre-commencement floating charges will not be caught by the prohibition. This construction of s 72A(4)(a) of IA 1986 is supported by a consideration of the everyday practicalities of lending. It is difficult to see how the transitional provisions could be applied to an old debenture which is security for a fluctuating overdraft. Furthermore, it is anticipated that the parliamentary draftsman will not wish to attempt to untangle the principles relating to mixed funds and overdrawn accounts. Whilst a conclusive answer cannot be given here, it is suggested that it is most likely that fresh lending under standard pre-commencement charges will not be caught by the prohibition.

(4) How might the prohibition be avoided or evaded?

4.27   It seems likely that a general assignment of floating charges, for example in the context of re-financing, would not be caught by the wording of s 72A(3). Similarly, a subrogated charge-holder should in principle acquire the right to appoint an administrative receiver. In these circumstances, the prohibition might be avoided, notwithstanding the fact that the relevant transactions took place after the 'appointed day'.

4.28   As regards evasion of the prohibition, it would appear to be possible for a tertiary lender to incorporate a large number of companies and to create floating charges over the assets of those companies prior to the appointed day. Lenders could require, as a condition of lending, that borrowers must transfer their assets into the pre-existing corporate shells in order to obtain the benefit of having floating charges which were created before the appointed day. If the Government wishes to achieve its stated objective of a collective procedure, it is hoped that some thought is given to preventing the easy evasion of one of the stated purposes of the EA 2002. This point will have even greater importance if the lender, by continuing with pre-commencement charges, can also evade the top-slicing provisions discussed in Chapter 4.

THE EXCEPTIONS TO THE GENERAL PROHIBITION

The recognition of special cases

4.29   The Government recognised that there are a number of special cases where the administrative receivership plays a crucial role which justifies exceptions to the general prohibition:

> 'We recognise that some very specialised financing structures are used in business today for which the ability to appoint an administrative receiver is vital in order to maintain control and ensure continued cash flows or capital repayments to the appointer [sic].

---

27   See *Insolvency Law & Practice* (Tolley), Vol 18, No 2, 2002, p 41 (Editorial).

That is perceived to be necessary by City financiers and their advisors to allow these structures to raise the amounts of finance – at the sort of interest rates – that they currently raise, and which are often significantly more favourable than through traditional commercial lending.'

4.30 Where these exceptions apply, the floating charge-holder's contractual right to appoint an administrative receiver remains intact. There are six explicit exceptions to s 72A, as set out in the new ss 72B–72F, which will now be considered in turn.

First exception – capital market arrangements (s 72B)

4.31 The first exception is set out in s 72B of IA 1986. This stipulates that an administrative receiver may be appointed for arrangements which are, or form part of, 'capital market arrangements' (as defined by para 1 of Sch 2A to IA 1986) if two conditions are satisfied. First, a party[28] to the arrangement must incur or, when the agreement is entered into, expect to incur, a debt of at least £50 million under the arrangement (s 72B(1)(a)). Secondly, the arrangement must involve the issue of a 'capital market investment' (s 72B(1)(b)). A 'capital market investment' is defined in paras 2 and 3 of Sch 2A to IA 1986. It is understood that, after further consultation, it has been decided to amend these new provisions, but the precise terms of the amendment are unknown.

Second exception – public-private partnerships (s 72C)[29]

4.32 The second exception to s 72A is in respect of 'public-private partnership (PPP) projects' with 'step-in rights' (s 72C of IA 1986). A PPP project means a project where the resources are provided by both public bodies and private persons or which is designed wholly or mainly for the purpose of assisting a public body to discharge a public function (s 72C(2)).[30] The inclusion of PPPs as an exception to the prohibition came under some fire during the parliamentary debates. It was suggested that the Government had double standards; on the one hand they were taking away private lenders' rights to appoint an administrative receiver, yet on the other hand they were preserving the right to 'slash and burn with their administrative receiver'.[31] The rationale behind the inclusion of PPPs was stated to be as follows:

'Continued delivery of some public services is obviously essential, and continued recourse to administrative receivership provides for a continued exercise of step-in rights. Without recourse to administrative receivership, step-in rights could be blocked by a moratorium on administration. On that basis, we came to the view that

---

28 The definition of 'party' as defined in para 1(3)(c) of the new Sch 2A is discussed in *Hansard*, Standing Committee B, Fifteenth Sitting, Thursday 9 May 2002, at col 605.

29 For a practical account of the effect and the inter-relation of ss 72C, 72D and 72E, see Johnson and Jennings of LeBoeuf, Lamb, Greene & Macrae 'The Effect of the Enterprise Act on PFI projects' (www.llgm.com).

30 For a commentary on this definition and an insight into how this exception will operate in practice see: 'The Enterprise Act 2002 – What it means for Project Finance', *Project Finance Internatonal*, Issue 255, 11 December 2002.

31 See *Hansard*, Standing Committee B, Fifteenth Sitting, Thursday 9 May 2002, at col 609.

it was appropriate for one of the exceptions to be defined in terms of the PPP, as outlined in the drafting.'[32]

4.33   The words 'step-in rights' are used in ss 72C–72E, and are defined in para 6 of Sch 2A to IA 1986 as the conditional right of the financier of the project to step in and assume responsibility for carrying out all or part of the project. These rights are commonly taken by financiers to protect their security when a project begins to fail.

Third exception – utility projects (s 72D)

4.34   Thirdly, administrative receivers may still be appointed in respect of a project company which is a 'utility project' which includes step-in rights (s 72D of IA 1986). A utility project is one designed wholly or mainly for the purpose of a regulated business. Examples of such regulated businesses are telecommunications providers, railway operators, gas and electricity suppliers and water and sewerage undertakers. See para 10 of the new Sch 2A to the IA 1986 for a full list of such regulated businesses.

Fourth exception – large project finance arrangements (s 72E)

4.35   The fourth exception applies to project finance companies with step-in rights where the finance under the agreement will exceed, or is expected to exceed, £50 million (s 72E of IA 1986). There was some discussion in the parliamentary debates as to whether this threshold had been set too high, particularly in the context of special-purpose vehicle companies in the field of commercial property refurbishment and regeneration. The Government resisted efforts to reduce the threshold.[33] It is noteworthy, however, that there is wide discretion delegated to the Secretary of State to amend these provisions by statutory instrument, including such threshold figure, should the need arise.

4.36   Other changes were made to the initial proposals, however, which did impact on project finance arrangements. The provision on 'step-in rights' was amended during the course of the passage of the Enterprise Bill in order to cover the following situations: first, where a new company is used as a vehicle to help rescue a project which has gone wrong, and secondly, where finance is provided by way of an indemnity (for example where insurers provide insurance to the financier of the project and take step-in rights).[34]

Fifth exception – financial markets (s 72F)

4.37   The fifth exception relates to financial market charges (s 72F of IA 1986). An administrative receiver may be appointed where there is a market charge (as defined by s 173 of Companies Act 1989), a system-charge (within the meaning of the Financial Markets and Insolvency Regulations 1996, SI 1996/1469) and a collateral security charge (within the meaning of the Financial Markets and Insolvency (Settlement Finality) Regulations 1999). Changes were

---

32   See *Hansard*, Standing Committee B, Fifteenth Sitting, Thursday 9 May 2002, at col 613.
33   See *Hansard*, Monday 17 June 2002, Vol 387, No 159 at cols 67–69.
34   See *Hansard*, Standing Committee B, Fifteenth Sitting, Thursday 9 May 2002, at col 606.

made to the initial proposals to narrow the scope of this exception and, where necessary, regard should be paid to the Minister's comments on the amendments which were made.[35]

Sixth exception – registered social landlords

4.38 The sixth exception relates to lending housing associations which are registered social landlords (RSLs).

4.39 Initially this did not form part of the Enterprise Bill. Three consequences of abolishing the right to appoint administrative receivers were cited in support of making lending to housing associations an exception:

(a) the cost of borrowing would rise because lenders would re-evaluate their risk and insist on increased security;
(b) some projects may become unfundable due to their high-risk nature; and
(c) retail lenders' willingness to assist RSLs in difficulties would be curtailed because capital market lenders would still be able to step in and appoint an administrative receiver.[36]

The first and second consequences could be said to apply to a number of different lending situations.

4.40 The Government inititing the argument that the prohibition of appointment of receivers would damage this sector, the Minister reiterated the point that the changes would not affect the rights of lenders to make a floating charge, but would simply provide for its exercise through a fairer, collective framework of administration.[37] Subsequently, however, it would seem the Government was persuaded that this sector merited special protection. The reason for this 'u-turn' was expressed as follows:

> 'During the passage of the Bill concerns were expressed about the potential impact that the prohibition of the appointment of an administrative receiver would have on the social housing sector. Following constructive dialogues between officials and representatives from all parts of the sector, I am pleased to say that we were able to take on board and act upon their concerns. It was recognised that both the Housing Act 1996 – which covers England and Wales – and the Housing (Scotland) Act 2001 provide for a moratorium period which provides an alternative means to facilitate rescues and provide a stay on unilateral action by lenders when registered social landlords are in financial difficulty. The provisions apply to housing associations that are registered social landlords.'[38]

Further possible exceptions

4.41 In addition to the above express exceptions, it should be noted that the Government has left itself room for manoeuvre after the EA 2002 is brought into force. Section 72G inserts a new Sch 2A, which puts the flesh on the bones of

---

35 See *Hansard*, Standing Committee B, Fifteenth Sitting, Thursday 9 May 2002, at col 605.
36 See *Hansard*, Monday 17 June 2002, Vol 387, No 159 at col 78.
37 Amendment No 13 moved by Mr Waterson (MP for Eastbourne); see *Hansard*, Monday 17 June 2002, Vol 387, No 159 at cols 77–82.
38 See *Hansard*, Vol 391, No 198, 30 October 2002 at col 946.

ss 72B–72F, which need not be considered any further here. It also enables the Secretary of State to amend the new provisions in Chapter IV to Part III of the Act and to insert additional exceptions to s 72A. It is understood that provisions for the amendment of s 72B and the introduction of a new exception ('Urban Regeneration') are under preparation.

INTERACTION BETWEEN ADMINISTRATIVE RECEIVERSHIPS, ADMINISTRATIONS AND LIQUIDATIONS

4.42   The interaction between the various different insolvency procedures under the IA 1986 gave rise to some difficult questions of interpretation and substantial litigation. How will the new provisions of the EA 2002 affect the various interactions?

Administrative receiverships and liquidations

4.43   In simple terms, the old law as regards the interaction between administrative receiverships and liquidations remains the same. The fact that an administrative receiver has been appointed does not prevent the winding-up of the company and nor does a winding-up prevent the appointment of a receiver. The detailed examination of these provisions is outside the object and scope of this book.[39]

Administrative receiverships and administrations

4.44   Previously, where an administrative receiver had been appointed the court would not make an administration order without the consent of the holder of the floating charge, or where the validity of the administrative receiver's appointment could be challenged (s 9(3) of IA 1986). This enabled the holder of a floating charge with power to appoint a receiver to prevent the making of an administration order by putting the company into receivership after receiving notice of the administration petition. These provisions remain unchanged under the new administration procedure. A floating charge-holder must be notified of any administration application and has the ability to appoint an administrative receiver. The effect of the appointment of an administrative receiver is that an administrator may not be subsequently appointed; see Sch B1 to IA 1986, paras 17(b), 25(c), and 39.

4.45   The converse is also the case. Under the old provisions, upon the making of an administration order, an administrative receiver had to vacate office and no administrative receiver could be appointed: s 11 of IA 1986. These provisions are mirrored in the relevant parts of the IA 1986 as amended by the EA 2002, which also provide that where a company is in administration any administrative receiver is required to vacate office (para 41 of Sch B1).

---

39   See Lightman & Moss *The Law of Receivers and Administrators of Companies* (Sweet & Maxwell, 3rd edition), and in particular at p 234.

Summary

4.46   In summary, therefore, save for the changes made to exit routes from administrations (as to which, see Chapter 13), there are no great innovations or changes in respect of the interaction between the different insolvency procedures. Administrations and administrative receiverships (but not necessarily receiverships) remain mutually exclusive processes. The most significant changes relate to the rights of floating charge-holders to instigate a particular procedure, rather than the interaction of the different procedures.

THE FUTURE

4.47   In conclusion, therefore, save for the six exceptions identified above, the floating charge-holder's ability to appoint an administrative receiver in respect of post-commencement charges will be prohibited from the 'appointed day'. The appointed day will be the subject of a separate statutory instrument.[40]

4.48   The general prohibition will have a significant impact on practitioners. For most lenders the administrative receivership route was the preferred route for realising property subject to a floating charge.[41] In 2001, there were just under 2000 receivership appointments (including Law of Property Act 1925 receiverships) and just under 700 administrator appointments.[42] The statistics for 2002 follow a similar pattern. Assuming that the transitional provisions and secondary legislation do not allow any significant loopholes, over a relatively short period of time practitioners can realistically expect to see a doubling in the number of administrations.

4.49   The move away from administrative receiverships could be much quicker if the lenders voluntarily decide it is in their best interests to appoint an administrator, notwithstanding the existence of an old debenture. Some lending institutions may decide to announce, whether as a reactive measure (under pressure from customers) or as a proactive ('PR') measure, that they will agree to follow the new administration route in spite of their ability to appoint administrative receivers under old debentures. The administration route has some obvious attractions, such as immunity from winding-up and fewer problems with employees.

4.50   There is still some uncertainty, however, over whether administrators will become bogged down by wider disputes with the general body of

---

40   It is anticipated that such instrument will be published early in 2003.
41   See Table 3 in the DTI's Statistics Directorate Press Release dated 1 November 2002 (which can be found at http://217.154.27.195/sd/insolv/index.htm).
42   See the DTI Insolvency Press Notice, 3 May 2002, *Insolvencies in the First Quarter 2002*.

creditors.[43] In addition, it is not yet known how the courts will approach an intervention by floating charge-holders to have their own insolvency practitioner appointed in place of the practitioner chosen by the company or the creditor. For these reasons, it is suggested that the prudent and conservative lender, unless its hand is forced, will adopt the 'wait and see' approach in the first few months after the relevant provisions have been brought into force.

4.51   The requirement of a move towards a more collective procedure, together with the new 'top-slicing' provisions, constitute a substantial erosion of floating charge-holders' rights. Recent case-law developments concerning the payment of liquidators' expenses out of assets covered by floating charges have not been in the floating charge-holders' favour either.[44] It will be interesting to see, therefore, how far lenders are prepared to fund the new administrations.

4.52   Whilst, in the short term, floating charge-holders are to gain by the immediate abolition of Crown preference, the new finance regime is likely to take on a new colour in the medium to long term. Floating charge-holders may seek to enforce directly their security without the appointment of an administrator. There is also the danger that banks will become reluctant to lend on the security of floating charges and insist on charges over fixed assets, to the detriment of borrowers (such as the high-risk 'independent start-ups') whose assets are predominantly intangible.[45] Other potential consequences for the future include a greater inclination to raise interest rates. Irrespective of the reaction of the floating charge-holders, other modes of finance, such as factoring/discounting and the leasing/hire-purchase businesses are likely to continue to increase in importance. Some commetators are already predicting that the LPA receiver will come back into fashion.[46] Only time will tell.

---

43   By reason of the new three-pronged purpose of administrations (para 3(1) of Sch B1 to IA 1986). It is noteworthy that the Cork Committee rejected a suggestion that administrative receivers should owe duties to all the creditors, since it was predicted that the effectiveness of the floating charge would be seriously weakened, driving lenders towards fixed security; see the report at pp 106–107. Since the Cork Report the courts have recognised that the duties of the administrative receiver do extend beyond the charge-holder (see *Medforth v Blake* [2000] Ch 86), though the duties of the administrator under the new process will be entirely different in emphasis and could result in some of the adverse changes predicted by the Cork Committee.

44   *Re Leyland DAF; Buchler v Talbot* [2002] EWCA Civ 228, [2002] 1 BCLC 571, CA.

45   This danger was discussed in the Parliamentary Debates; see *Hansard*, Vol 637, No 162 at col 147.

46   See Rupert Connell of Fladgate Fisher, 'Enterprising Receivers', *Recovery*, Spring 2003, pp 20–22.

Chapter 5

TOP-SLICING

'Money, it's a crime
Share it fairly but don't take a slice of my pie.'
Roger Waters[1]

INTRODUCTION

5.1   The link between the abolition of Crown preference and the new 'top-slicing' provisions is dealt with at length in Chapter 3. In this chapter, there is an analysis of the new provisions themselves. However, it cannot be stated too often that these provisions will only bite on floating charges created after the commencement of the relevant part of the EA 2002. It is anticipated that it will take about 3–5 years before post-commencement floating charges start entering into insolvency procedures. That said, practitioners and lenders will no doubt be keen to understand how the new provisions are likely to operate with a view to giving informed advice to their clients and developing progressive 'know-how'.

Emergence of the idea

5.2   The idea that the extraordinary benefits which come to the holder of a floating charge should be diluted on formal insolvency in favour of the unsecured creditors is not new. It was proposed as long ago as 1897.[2] The idea was taken up by the Cork Committee in 1982. In the Cork Report, the Committee recommended that a fund equal to 10% of the net realisations of assets subject to a floating charge should be made available for distribution among the ordinary unsecured creditors, excluding the debenture holder.[3]

5.3   That distinguished committee presented a compelling case in favour of top-slicing. The proposals were rejected. Almost 20 years later they re-emerged, coupled with a proposal to abolish Crown preference. The top-slicing pro-

---

1   'Money' from Pink Floyd *The Dark Side of the Moon* (1973).
2   See Lord Macnaghten's comments in *Salomon v A Salomon & Co Ltd* [1897] AC 22 at 53, where he proposed giving trade creditors a limited form of preferential claim.
3   See para 1538 and following, describing it as 'the Ten Per Cent Fund'. The net assets were to be calculated after deducting the costs and expenses of realisation, the repayment of sums borrowed by the receiver for the purposes of the receivership, moneys paid in discharge or redemption of all fixed, but not floating charges which rank in priority to the floating charge, preferential debts and the costs, disbursements and remuneration of the receiver.

visions have now been enacted, and are likely to be brought into force in about July 2003.[4]

The statutory instrument

5.4   The detailed provisions setting out the relevant figures and the exact manner in which the burden of the top-slice is to be borne will be dealt with by way of statutory instrument. It is intended that this statutory instrument will be separate from the main new rules relevant to corporate insolvency. At the time of writing, only the draft statutory instrument has been circulated. The Government has stated that it intends to consult on the new provisions before they are implemented and so there may be changes to the draft instrument. However, the Parliamentary debates do provide a good indication of the Government's 'preferred option' for the shape of the secondary legislation. It remains to be seen whether consultation will result in any significant deviation from the statements made to date. For the purposes of this chapter, it is assumed that the Parliamentary explanations, when taken with the draft statutory instrument, provide a good signpost to the likely final form of the secondary legislation.

Parliamentary explanations

5.5   One of the most revealing Parliamentary statements concerning the interaction between top-slicing and the abolition of Crown preference has been reproduced at **3.9**. Following on from that statement, the Minister, Lord McIntosh, gave the following illustration of how the new provisions might work:[5]

> 'But, we would not want the costs of distribution to the unsecured creditors to outweigh the benefits of the additional money and so we propose to set the ring fence on a sliding scale with a de minimis level. We shall prescribe by secondary legislation exact figures in the light of consultation with interested parties. I believe that that was the matter about which the noble Lord, Lord Hunt, was concerned. But, for example, we might provide that the ring fence is 50 per cent of the first £10,000 available for distribution to the floating charge holder; then 10 per cent until the net property reaches the value of £1,000,000; and thereafter the figure should be reduced to 5 per cent.'

5.6   At an early point in the passage of the Bill, the Secretary of State gave the following insight into more of the proposed detail:[6]

> 'We propose that there should be a set minimum level that the prescribed part ought to reach, and below which the liquidator will not have to consider distribution unless he or she can clearly see that the benefits of such a distribution outweigh the costs ... We shall, of course, consult interested parties on the issue, but from discussions already held, we are minded to set the de minimis level of property available for distribution at £5,000.'

---

4   For the latest information as regards commencement the reader is encouraged to review the information contained at the Insolvency Service's website: www.insolvency.gov.uk/.
5   See *Hansard*, No 178, 29 July 2002, House of Lords sitting in Committee, at col 806.
6   See *Hansard*, 14 May 2002 (morning), at col 625.

5.7   It can be seen therefore that the Government has in mind that the top-slice will be set on a sliding scale with a de minimis level for the prescribed part of £5,000. The sliding scale will be set so that the de minimis level is easily reached (by setting a high initial percentage such as 50%). Indeed, these intentions are, to a large extent, carried through into the draft statutory instrument, which is discussed further below.

THE NEW LEGISLATIVE PROVISIONS

When are the top-slicing provisions applicable?

5.8   EA 2002, s 252 introduces a new s 176A into the IA 1986. The Act states that the provisions apply where a floating charge[7] relates to property of a company:

(a)   which has gone into liquidation;[8]
(b)   which is in administration;[9]
(c)   of which there is a provisional liquidator;[10] or
(d)   of which there is a receiver.[11]

On a first reading of the new s 176A(1) it might be assumed that the top-slicing provisions do not apply to the special category of cases where a floating charge holder may continue to appoint an administrative receiver in respect of a floating charge, notwithstanding the fact that the charge was created after the relevant commencement date.[12] This is an incorrect assumption. During the Parliamentary debates an amendment was proposed which would have inserted a definition of 'receiver' in the new s 176A(1) as meaning an administrative receiver.[13] The proposed amendment was rejected by the Secretary of State who stated as follows:[14]

> 'The purpose of amendments Nos 524 and 429 is to restrict the ambit of the new s 176A so that it affects only a receiver who is an administrative receiver. The amendments are unnecessary and could provide a loophole for a secured creditor to avoid the effect of the new section. Although it is accepted that the term "receiver" is broad and covers every kind of receiver appointed under a fixed or floating charge, it is clear enough that the section refers only to property that is available for distribution to the holder of a floating charge.'

It is clear, therefore, that the top-slicing provisions must be operated by all office-holders, whatever the procedure, in respect of floating charges created after the commencement of the order.

---

7   Being a charge which is a floating charge on its creation; IA 1986, s 176A(8).
8   IA 1986, s 176A(1)(a).
9   Ibid, s 176A(1)(b).
10   Ibid, s 176A(1)(c).
11   Ibid, s 176A(1)(d).
12   The six express statutory 'exceptions' to the abolition of the right to appoint an administrative receiver set out in ss 72B to 72H of the EA 2002 are discussed at **4.31–4.41**.
13   See *Hansard*, 14 May 2002 (morning), at cols 622–623.
14   See *Hansard*, 14 May 2002 (morning), at cols 624–625.

What must the office-holder do?

5.9   In the circumstances where the provisions apply, the liquidator, administrator or receiver:

(a)   must make a prescribed part of the company's net property available for the satisfaction of unsecured debts;[15] and

(b)   must not distribute that part to the proprietor of a floating charge except in so far as it exceeds the amount required for the satisfaction of unsecured debts.[16]

These provisions do not apply if and in so far as they are disapplied by a CVA in respect of the company[17] or a compromise or arrangement under IA 1986, s 425.[18] The principle is that the unsecured creditors may agree to waive the benefits to flow down from top-slicing in favour of a different arrangement. It is conceivable that interesting questions might arise if the majority of the unsecured creditors (and indeed some voting secured creditors) voted in a CVA to disapply top-slicing against the wishes of a minority. Such a decision may be susceptible to challenge on the basis that it unfairly prejudices the minority.[19]

What if top-slicing is impractical?

5.10   The provisions are also subject to the qualification that they may be disapplied where they will be of no practical use. There are two circumstances in which they can be disapplied. In the first, the discretion is vested in the office-holder. In the second, an application must be made to court. Each of the potential circumstances will now be dealt with in turn.

5.11   In the first circumstance, the top-slicing provisions shall not apply to a company if:

(a)   the company's net property is less than the prescribed minimum;[20] and

(b)   the liquidator, administrator or receiver thinks that the cost of making a distribution to the unsecured creditors would be disproportionate to the benefits.[21]

5.12   The draft statutory instrument states that the prescribed minimum will be £10,000.

5.13   There are three comments to make about the discretion of the office-holder to disapply when the prescribed minimum is not reached.

5.14   First, it is suggested that the terminology used by the Ministers in Parliament should be treated with some caution. Clearly, the Minister and the Secretary of State were talking in terms of the de miminis level for the 'prescribed part' (commonly referred to as the 'top-slice') rather than the 'net property'. A

---

15   IA 1986, s 176A(2)(a).
16   Ibid, s 176A(2)(b).
17   Ibid, s 176A(4)(a).
18   Ibid.
19   Ibid, s 6(1).
20   Ibid. s 176A(3)(a).
21   Ibid.

figure of £5,000 was quoted as regards the minimum level for the 'prescribed part' as being a starting point for consultation.[22] Therefore, if the order is to be consistent with this preliminary indication, the prescribed minimum for the net property will need to be more than £5,000 since only a percentage of this sum will be made available to the unsecured creditors. The proposed minimum of £10,000 in the draft statutory instrument is consistent with this reasoning.

5.15 Secondly, it should be noted that these provisions are cumulative; even though the net property is less than the prescribed minimum it may still be proportionate to make a distribution.

5.16 Thirdly, the ability to disapply the top-slicing provisions on the grounds of proportionality is clearly sensible. There is simply no point in making the prescribed part available to unsecured creditors if there is no practical benefit in applying the provisions. This situation could arise in circumstances where there are some floating charge recoveries but such a large number of creditors that the cost of notifying them all and administering the distribution would be excessive. A common example would be a mail order company with a substantial number of unfulfilled small orders, or a travel company that has accepted small deposits for holidays that it can no longer provide.

5.17 In the second circumstance, the net property is equal to or greater than the prescribed minimum. During the passage of the Bill the Government made it clear that it did not wish to give the office-holder the discretion to disapply the top-slicing provisions when the statutory minimum is exceeded. Where the net property available is equal to or greater than the prescribed minimum, the office-holder can apply to court for an order that the top-slicing provisions shall not apply. The ground to be satisfied is that 'the cost of making a distribution to the unsecured creditors would be disproportionate to the benefits'.[23] This will apply in circumstances where the costs of applying the provisions are of no practical benefit.[24] This part of the EA 2002 was explained by the Secretary of State in the following way:[25]

> 'I believe the provision could apply in cases where there is a huge number of unsecured creditors. In such cases, the costs of distributing the prescribed part may be disproportionate to the benefit gained from the distribution and the office holder should be able to take action to disapply this new section.
>
> In order to obtain an order under this subsection, the office holder will have to satisfy the court that the costs of distribution would be disproportionate to the benefits.'

How much is ring-fenced?

5.18 The company's 'net property' is defined as the amount of its property which would, but for the section, be available for the satisfaction of claims of holders of debentures secured by, or holders of, any floating charge created by

---

22 See the quote at 5.6.
23 IA 1986, s 176A(5)(a), (b).
24 See para 729 of the Explanatory Notes.
25 See *Hansard*, 30 October 2002, at col 947.

the company.[26] The method for calculating the 'net property' is discussed further at **5.30**.

How much is the 'prescribed part' or 'top-slice' likely to be?

5.19   The prescribed part of the company's property to be made available to the unsecured creditors will be:

(a)   set by statutory instrument[27] by the Secretary of State;[28] and
(b)   subject to annulment by a resolution of either House of Parliament.[29]

5.20   The Secretary of State is given a free rein to provide the method of calculating the prescribed amount. It can be by reference to:

(a)   a simple percentage of the company's net property;[30] or
(b)   an aggregate of different percentages of different parts of the company's net property.[31]

5.21   As can be seen from the parliamentary statements quoted at **5.5**, the Government is currently working on the basis that a sliding scale, in accordance with s 176A(7)(b), will be used. The draft statutory instrument provides for two percentages to apply in the following terms:

'The prescribed part is –

(i)   50% of an amount of a company's net property not exceeding £10,000; and
(ii)   20% of an amount of a company's net property over £10,000.'

Furthermore, the draft statutory instrument proposes a ceiling on the amount to be made available to the unsecured creditors:

'The maximum amount of the prescribed part to be made available in accordance with section 176A(2) is £600,000.'

5.22   It is believed that these percentages have been proposed in order to meet two objectives. The first is to try and maximise the number of cases when the unsecured creditors gain a 'slice of the pie'. The second objective is to seek to ensure that, across the whole of England and Wales, the moneys (believed) to be released by the abolition of crown preference will find their way to the unsecured creditors. As has already been stated, even when the effect of *Brumark* is ignored, the abolition of Crown preference will release approximately £90 million per year to unsecured creditors.[32] The vast majority of this sum will funnel into administrations and administrative receiverships; recoveries by the Crown under its preferential rights in liquidations and bankruptcies are considerably smaller. It is anticipated that the insolvency statistics will be keenly monitored over the next 3–5 years with a view to further refinement of the sliding scale percentages in order to ensure that the annual top-slice realisations equal the annual sum released by the abolition of Crown preference.

---

26   IA 1986, s 176A(5).
27   Ibid, s 176A(7)(a).
28   Ibid, s 176A(8).
29   Ibid, s 176A(7)(b).
30   Ibid, s 176A(6)(a).
31   Ibid, s 176A(6)(a).
32   DTI, *The Enterprise Bill, Insovlency Provisions – Regulatory Impact*, para 5.29.

Parties who may participate in the top-slice

5.23   The Cork Report recommended participation in the 'Ten Per Cent Fund' (the top-slicing fund) providing that:

(1) the floating charge-holder should not participate with the unsecured creditors in the 10% fund ('first limb'), unless the whole of the floating charge is surrendered or abandoned ('second limb');[33]

(2) creditors with only a fixed charge securing their debt would be entitled to participate with the unsecured creditors in so far as, after realisation, surrender or valuation of their security, there was an unsecured balance;[34] and

(3) if the debt was secured by a fixed and floating charge, no part of the debt would be permitted to participate in the 10% fund unless the floating element of the security were first surrendered or abandoned.[35]

We will now consider the extent to which the substance of these recommendations is reflected in the new statutory scheme.

5.24   The first limb of the first of these recommendations is echoed in the new provisions. As mentioned earlier, the prescribed part of the company's net property shall not be distributed to 'the proprietor of a floating charge' except in so far as it exceeds the amount required for the satisfaction of unsecured debts.[36] This suggests that, in so far as the floating charge holder suffers a shortfall, whether or not that shortfall arises as a result of the application of the top-slicing provisions, such holder will not be entitled to share in the benefit of the top-sliced part until the other unsecured creditors have been paid in full. The second limb of the first of the Cork recommendations highlighted at **5.23** has not been expressly included in s 176A(2)(b) of IA 1986. There is no reference to the floating charge-holder being able to surrender or abandon his floating charge in the primary legislation. Thus, on one interpretation of s 176A(2)(b) a person who held a floating charge at the commencement of the insolvency procedure would not be entitled to abandon his floating charge during the course of the insolvency procedure and thereby participate in the top-slice fund. However, s 176A(2)(b) prohibits a distribution of the top-slice fund to 'the proprietor of a floating charge'. It is suggested that the subsection can therefore be interpreted to allow a floating charge-holder to abandon or surrender the floating charge during the course of the insolvency procedure. If this were done, there would no longer be a 'proprietor' of a floating charge and therefore no bar to participation in the top-slice fund. It should be noted that the question of surrender or abandonment of a floating charge to enable participation in the top-slice fund will only arise for second or subsequent floating charge-holders. If there is only one floating charge-holder and he were to abandon or surrender the floating charge, then the top-slicing provisions will not apply.

5.25   As regards the second recommendation, the new legislation is drafted in a manner which reflects this recommendation. Since the prescribed part is to

33   See Cork Report, para 1544.
34   Ibid, para 1543.
35   Ibid, para 1544.
36   IA 1986, s 176A(2)(b).

be made available for the satisfaction of unsecured debts there would appear to be no reason in principle why a secured creditor could not share in such prescribed part in respect of any shortfall after realisation. By definition, the shortfall will be unsecured.

5.26   The third Cork Report recommendation highlighted at **5.23** would appear to be reflected in the new provisions since s 176A(2)(b) prohibits the distribution of the top-slice fund to 'the proprietor of a floating charge'.

Implementation

5.27   As has already been noted, the top-slicing provisions are not retrospective. They do not apply if the floating charge was created before the commencement of the first order of the Secretary of State setting out the prescribed parts of the company's property to be made available.[37] Furthermore, given the acceptance that this part of the Act should not have retrospective effect, it is anticipated that any later order increasing the prescribed part will have no effect on a floating charge created before the commencement of that later order.[38] In the same way that top-slicing does not affect pre-commencement floating charges, it is unlikely that post-commencement floating charges will be subject to more onerous obligations introduced in the amended secondary legislation. But, if the amending legislation is more beneficial to the floating charge-holders, there appears to be no reason why such amendments should not apply to those floating charges taken prior to the implementation of the later provisions. These consequences suggest that the Government ought not to set the relevant percentages too low.

PRACTICAL ISSUES ARISING

Top-slicing affects future floating charges only

5.28   After the commencement of the EA 2002, there is an immediate benefit to a bank appointing an office-holder in respect of a pre-commencement floating charge. Such an office-holder will be able to distribute to the floating charge-holder free of any Crown preferential debts yet also free of any top-slicing obligations. Until post-commencement floating charges filter through the system the banks will receive the benefit of the removal of Crown preference without the burden of top-slicing. Three scenarios are possible, therefore, which can be illustrated in tabular form:

---

37   IA 1986, s 176A(9).
38   Ibid, s 176A(10).

Period in which office-holder appointed (specifying whether appointed under pre- or post-commencement charge)	Application of the provisions
To July 2003 (under pre-commencement charge)[39]	Crown preference under IA 1986, Sch 6 applies. No top-slicing under IA 1986, s 176A.
July 2003 onwards under pre-commencement charge	No Crown preference under IA 1986, Sch 6. No top-slicing under IA 1986, s 176A.
July 2003 onwards under post-commencement charge	No Crown preference under IA 1986, Sch 6. Top-slicing under IA 1986, s 176A.

Calculation of 'net property'

5.29   The new s 176A is silent on the question of how the 'net property' is to be calculated. It does not spell out whether the top-sliced fund will be made available to pay any expenses (including remuneration) of the liquidation or administration or administrative receivership and, if so, whether such expenses will be limited to those incurred in administering the fund itself in accordance with the new provisions or will include all such expenses. In addition, the new s 176A does not deal with the question of whether or not net property is to be calculated after taking into account trading losses incurred after, for example, an administration order has been made.

5.30   The Cork Report recommended that the costs of realisation, and the costs, disbursements and remuneration of the office-holder, would be payable out of the floating charge realisations before arriving at the 'net property' figure, and thus before arriving at the part of the net property to be made available to unsecured creditors. Matters such as preferential debts would also have to be discharged. In this sense, if realisations were limited it is possible that the 'Ten Per Cent Fund' would be eaten into by the expenses of the relevant insolvency procedure.

5.31   The Secretary of State's statements in Parliament suggest that the Cork Report approach is likely to be followed when implementing the new top-slicing regime, and furthermore that trading losses will reduce the amount of 'net property' available:[40]

> 'I should like to clarify the matter of net property, so that it is clear to members of the Committee as I proceed . . . the net property is the property available for distribution to the floating charge holder and it therefore includes any trading loss if the office-holder has continued the company's trading . . . The net property is the amount available to distribute after taking into account a variety of things, such as the liability secured by a fixed charge and any preferential debt.'

---

39   This table has been prepared on the basis that the commencement of the corporate provisions of the EA 2002 will be in July 2003 and illustrates the combined operation of EA 2002, s 251(1) and IA 1986, s 176A(9).

40   See *Hansard*, 14 May 2002, Standing Committee B, at col 625.

5.32   In summary therefore, it is suggested that the net property will be calculated by the relevant office-holder at the end of the relevant insolvency procedure after deducting the costs of realisation, and the costs, disbursements and remuneration of the office-holder irrespective of whether or not those costs are directly referable to realising the property which is subject to the floating charge. In addition, subject to the question of sanction, there would appear to be no reason why the top-slice could not be used as a 'fighting fund'.[41]

5.33   In these circumstances it can be seen why the floating charge-holders were so eager to ensure that they had the ability to appoint the administrator of their choice in the new style administrations (or to apply to replace the directors' choice (say) with their own preferred insolvency practitioner). Administrators will be in a position to carry out general work for the benefit of the body of the creditors as a whole which will fall to be deducted from floating charge realisations.

5.34   Finally, it should be noted that if the Government's stated aim of seeking to ensure that moneys released by the abolition of Crown preference will find its way into the hands of the unsecured creditors is to succeed, such matters as the depletion of floating charge realisations by office-holders' remuneration and the effect of trading losses will have to be closely monitored. Such costs will lead to a reduction in the 'net property' available for the purpose of top-slicing.

Multiple floating charges

5.35   There was no consideration in Parliament as to how the impact of the top-slice should be borne in the circumstances where there is more than one floating charge. The Cork Report proposed that where there were two or more successive floating charges, the scheme should operate in such a way that it preserved the priorities of the debenture holders amongst themselves, while at the same time ensuring that the unsecured creditors received the same total benefits whether there were several such charges or only one.[42]

5.36   It is considered that the top-slicing provisions are unlikely to affect the priorities of multiple floating charge-holders; priorities between floating charge-holders will be preserved. Assuming that this to be the case it is worth considering how the new provisions would impact on the multiple charge-holder scenario. For the purposes of the following examples:

(a)   the prescribed part or top-slice will be calculated in accordance with the percentages, and the ceiling, stated in the draft statutory instrument (as to which see **5.21**);

(b)   Crown preferential creditors are shown separately (in order to compare the impact of the new provisions with the position pre-commencement);

(c)   'net property' is the position prior to consideration of Crown preferential creditors.

---

41   See **22.11**.
42   The Cork Report, para 1545.

Example 1

Floating charge 1	owed £155,000
Floating charge 2	owed £100,000
Floating charge 3	owed £60,000
Crown preferential creditors	owed £120,000
Unsecured creditors (other than Crown)	owed £150,000
Net property	£220,000
Top-slice (50% of £10,000, plus 20% of £210,000)	£47,000
Balance	£173,000.

5.37   Under the old regime, preferential creditors would be paid first, leaving the sum of £100,000 (£220,000 minus £120,000) to be paid to the holder of floating charge 1. The sum of £55,000 outstanding in respect of the floating charge 1 would be an unsecured claim, along with all the sums owed to the holders of floating charges 2 and 3. In this example there is little prospect of a recovery for the unsecured creditors.

5.38   Under the new regime, the Crown preference sums become unsecured, resulting in total unsecured sums of £270,000. Floating charge 1 will be paid £155,000. The holder of floating charge 2 would be paid £18,000 (£173,000–£155,000) (or, such holder could elect to surrender or abandon the whole of the charge and seek to claim as an unsecured creditor). The holder of floating charge 3 would get nothing (or, such holder could elect to surrender or abandon the whole of the charge and seek to claim as an unsecured creditor). The unsecured creditors would be entitled to participate in the benefit of the top-slice, namely £47,000. Thus the unsecured creditors would obtain a dividend of 17p in the £1 (47,000/270,000). This compares favourably with the 18p in the £1 obtained by floating charge-holder 2, and the zero dividend obtained by the holder of floating charge 3. Assuming floating charge-holder 3 could elect to surrender the whole of the floating charge in favour of proving as an unsecured creditor, then the dividend to unsecured creditors would be reduced to 14p in the £1 (47,000/330,000).

Example 2

Floating charge 1	owed £155,000
Floating charge 2	owed £100,000
Floating charge 3	owed £60,000
Crown preferential creditors	owed £120,000
Unsecured creditors (other than Crown)	owed £150,000
Net property	£310,000
Top-slice (50% of £10,000, plus 20% of £300,000)	£65,000
Balance	£245,000

5.39   Under the old regime, Crown preferential creditors would be paid first, leaving a balance of £190,000. Thus the holder of floating charge 1 would be paid in full. The holder of floating charge 2 would receive £35,000. The balance of £65,000 on floating charge 2 would not be paid, along with the whole of floating charge 3. These claims would become unsecured.

5.40   Under the new regime, there are no Crown preferential creditors so the sum to be paid to the floating charge-holders is £245,000. Floating charge-holder 1 is paid £155,000 (ie payment in full). The holder of floating charge 2 is paid £90,000. Floating charge-holder 3 has the ability to receive only £10,000 and in this scenario would bear the burden of the top-slice. Such 'tail end charlie' would not be entitled to participate in the top-slice of £65,000 unless it abandoned its charge completely. If floating charge 3 was not abandoned the unsecured creditors (including the Crown) would receive a dividend of 24p in the £1 (65,000/270,000). It would therefore be clearly in the interests of floating charge-holder 3 to seek to be able to participate in the top-slice fund.

5.41   What can be deduced from these simple hypothetical examples? The following matters are apparent:

(a) The impact of the top-slicing provisions only affects the first floating charge-holder in cases where the net property, minus the prescribed part, is less than the amount owed to it. Where the net property, less the prescribed part, is greater than the amount owed to the floating charge-holder, then junior floating charge-holders bear the brunt of the top-slice.

(b) In the first example the holder of floating charge 1 benefits from the abolition of Crown preferences and does not bear any of the burden of the top-slice. The positions of the holders of floating charges 2 and 3 are effectively worsened if they are not be able to surrender or abandon their charges in order to benefit from the top-slice. If the holders of junior floating charges are able to abandon their charges, then the top-slicing provisions may assist them where asset realisations are poor.

(c) In the second example, it is principally the holder of floating charge 2 who benefits. The holder of floating charge 3 also benefits in that a reasonable dividend is achieved, whether as a proprietor of a floating charge, or (if such a charge-holder abandons its security) as an unsecured creditor.

(d) In both examples the unsecured creditors do better. It is noteworthy that the adoption of the sliding scale approach yields significant returns for the unsecured creditors.

(e) It is apparent from the above analysis that there are significant benefits for floating charge-holders, especially those 'tail end charlies' who are exposed to bearing the brunt of a top-slice, who are able to continue to rely on pre-commencement floating charges. In respect of the situation when both pre- and post-commencement charges are involved, the following guidance provided by the Secretary of State should be noted:[43]

---

43   See *Hansard*, 30 October 2002, Melanie Johnson.

'Where a company has granted both pre- and post-commencement floating charges, an insolvency office holder would pay out to fixed security holders, then pay the expenses of the winding up, then pay any remaining preferential claims, then pay out to the pre-commencement floating charge holders, and then he would apply the prescribed part to the net property available to the post-commencement floating charge holders.'

Which office-holder will oversee top-slicing?

5.42   As regards the complexities of the collection of the funds created by the top-slice, the Cork Report made various recommendations as to how and by whom the task should be conducted. In essence the recommendations were as follows:[44]

(a)   where a liquidator or administrator has been appointed, he would carry out the necessary tasks;
(b)   in the absence of a liquidator or administrator, a receiver (including, but not limited to, administrative receivers) would carry out the task;
(c)   where there are two or more floating charge-holders, the receiver appointed in respect of the first in priority would perform the necessary duties;
(d)   where none of the above applied, the unsecured creditors would need to apply to court for the appointment of a special purpose administrator.

5.43   The new s 176A does not hold any clues as to which office-holder will be required to administer the top-slicing process. It is suggested that the logic of the Cork Report proposals is likely to find favour with the Government and/or the Parliamentary draftsman of the secondary legislation. In addition, the language used in the Parliamentary debates suggests that the liquidator may already be the Government's preferred choice where a liquidator has been appointed.[45]

Subordinated debt

5.44   As regards priorities of subordinated charges, the Minister, Melanie Johnson, has made the point tolerably clear:[46]

'It is not anticipated that there will be a problem with pre-commencement charges that have subordinated their claim to a post-commencement charge. They will have done so in the knowledge that they will be waiving their right not to be subject to the new s 176A.'

5.45   Thus, the proprietor of a pre-commencement floating charge will waive its right not to be subject to the top-slicing provisions if it has subordinated its rights to a post-commencement charge. However, ultimately, much will depend on the precise wording of any deed of priority. The effect could be that junior charge-holders by express subordination will be subject to top-slicing if the senior charge-holder is.

---

44   See paras 1546 to 1549.
45   See *Hansard*, 14 May 2002, Standing Committee B, at col 625.
46   See *Hansard*, 30 October 2002, Melanie Johnson.

Subrogated charge

5.46   The position is not clear as regards subrogation. After-commencement, a bank ('the second bank') might advance sums to be secured on a debenture, with the proceeds used to discharge a pre-commencement debenture held by the first bank. For some reason, the post-commencement debenture may not be enforceable, on the grounds of ultra vires or failure to comply with the formalities of execution. Nonetheless, equity may intervene and, to avoid the unjust enrichment of the company, allow the second bank to stand in the shoes of the first bank and take the benefit of its security, as if it had been kept alive and assigned to it.[47] In those circumstances, the first bank's security will not be subject to top-slicing. Will the second bank also gain such a benefit? The second bank will have anticipated that the floating charge that it was to take would be a post-commencement floating charge and therefore subject to top-slicing. The expectation would be that the second bank would then be able to rely on the rights of the first bank, subject to an obligation to be subject to the top-slicing provisions. Any other result would unjustly enrich the second bank at the expense of the company's unsecured creditors. It would mean that the second bank would receive security more beneficial than it would have anticipated and, indeed, bargained for.

Re-financing and assignment of existing securities

5.47   However, in the context of a re-financing where the second bank expressly envisaged that its facilities would be used to discharge the first bank's secured indebtedness, the second bank should avoid the argument by ensuring that the benefit of the first bank's security is assigned to it, rather than discharged. The first charge would then be expressly kept alive and the top-slicing provisions would not apply at all.

Section 196 of the Companies Act 1985

5.48   It is assumed that the appropriate amendments will be made to s 196(2) of CA 1985 to cater for the situation when the debenture-holder takes possession of property at a time when no insolvency procedure has been instigated. It is assumed, and hoped, that s 196(2) will be amended so as to ensure that, in addition to the payment of preferential debts, a top-slicing fund will be created.

Wider implications

5.49   Finally, the economic consequences are far from clear. After commencement, lenders will find that new finance offered pursuant to post-commencement charges will, to all intents and purposes, be on the basis that their security is worth less. This could lead to an increased reluctance to lend, especially for high-risk ventures with few or no tangible assets. Alternatively,

---

47   See *Boscawen v Bajwa* [1996] 1 WLR 328, *Banque Financière de la Cité SA v Parc (Battersea) Limited* [1999] AC 221, *Halifax plc v Omar* [2002] EWCA Civ 121 and *Eagle Star Insurance Company Limited v Karasiewicz* [2002] EWCA Civ 940.

such finance as is offered may become more expensive or require increased security.

CONCLUSION

5.50   Apart from the fact that pre-commencement floating charges are exempted and will therefore be insulated from these new provisions ('the flaw'), the principle of top-slicing should be embraced as a fair mechanism for ensuring that the banks and other secured lenders do not continue to scoop the pool in corporate insolvencies. It is hoped and anticipated that the statutory instrument will be framed in such a way as to ensure that the top-sliced funds will, in fact, find their way into the hands of the unsecured creditors. It can be seen that if the Government is to achieve its objective of achieving at least some return for the unsecured creditors in most cases, a sliding scale system of percentages is the best mechanism to use. Finally, the fact that top-slicing will only apply to post-commencement charges provides the most important reason why lending institutions will wish to try and hang on to pre-commencement floating charges as long as possible.

Chapter 6

ADMINISTRATION – AN OVERVIEW

'You never expected justice from a company, did you? They have neither a soul to lose nor a body to kick.'
Sidney Smith[1]

INTRODUCTION

6.1   The new code for administrations is contained in s 248 of and Sch 16 to EA 2002, introducing a new s 8 and Sch B1 which replace ss 8–27 of IA 1986. Schedule 17 of EA 2002 effects minor and consequential amendments to the IA 1986 and other legislation affected by the reforms.

6.2   However, the reforms do not affect the special administration regimes contained in the following enactments:

(a) Water Industry Act 1991, in relation to water and sewerage undertakers;
(b) Railways Act 1993 and Channel Tunnel Rail Link Act 1996, in relation to the railways industry;
(c) Transport Act 2000, in relation to air traffic services;
(d) Greater London Authority Act 1999, in relation to public-private partnership agreements;
(e) Building Societies Act 1986, in relation to building societies.

6.3   In so far as the above enactments refer to IA 1986, Part II, they continue to refer to the previous law.[2] However, this may be modified by order of the Treasury in the case of building societies or by the Secretary of State in any other case.[3]

6.4   The reforms do not currently affect the law of partnership. However, a consultation paper was issued on 28 January 2003 by the Insolvency Service asking whether the new streamlined administration process should be applied to insolvent partnerships. Partnerships currently have access to administration procedures which mirror Part II of IA 1986. Extending the new procedures to insolvent partnerships would have the advantage of allowing partnerships to utilise the new out-of-court appointments procedure providing more certain time-scales and simplification. It is not proposed that the procedures for the appointment of an administrator by the holder of a qualifying floating charge

---

1   1771–1845.
2   EA 2002, s 249(2).
3   Ibid, s 249(3).

would apply to the partnerships, because, generally speaking, partnerships do not have floating charges (the exception being agricultural floating charges).

THE NEW ADMINISTRATION REGIME

6.5 The administration procedure was introduced to insolvency law for the first time by the IA 1986. The procedure was slow to take hold in practice so that by 1991 it was reported that fewer than 2% of company failures used administration orders or company voluntary arrangements.[4]

6.6 One of the practical problems was that the success of the procedure depended on directors being proactive in identifying the warning signs of a company's impending difficulties, and then taking the initiative to consult an insolvency practitioner at a sufficiently early stage to enable a rescue package to be considered and put into effect. Many directors viewed insolvency prac- titioners as undertakers rather than rescue surgeons and were inclined to postpone the evil day. Others were too proud to seek advice in the early stages or indeed at all. Many others were fundamentally ignorant of the basics of corporate and insolvency law.[5] Most directors wittingly or unwittingly took the procrastination route, such that the average company was presented with no alternative but liquidation at the end of the day.

6.7 It has taken years for the culture of rescue to gain any real credence and, from statistics published by the Department of Trade and Industry[6] starting in 1993, the following pattern emerges:

Year	Total company insolvencies	Admin appts	CVAs	% (admin and CVA)
1993	26,316	112	134	0.93
1994	21,028	159	264	2.01
1995	18,297	163	372	2.92
1996	16,831	210	459	3.97
1997	15,272	196	629	5.4
1998	15,724	338	470	5.13
1999	16,813	440	475	5.44
2000	16,907	438	557	5.88
2001	17,551	698	597	7.38

6.8 These figures demonstrate a steady gain in popularity of the adminis- tration procedure over the last 10 years, such that now it has come to be accepted as an important tool in providing the company in financial difficulties with an opportunity to put a rescue plan to its creditors.

6.9 Broadly, the innovative effect of an administration order is that it affords the company protection from its creditors by means of a moratorium

---

4   Chris Hughes of Cork Gully writing in the *Independent* on 14 January 1992 on the Cork Report.
5   R3 research has regularly pointed to poor management as being the reason behind many business failures, such that in 1997 it published a Guide to avoiding failure entitled *The Ostrich's Guide to Business Recovery*.
6   DTI Statistics Directorate Insolvency Press Notice, dated 3 May 2002.

while attempts are being made to rescue it, or, if this is not feasible, to achieve a better result for creditors than on a winding-up. However, it has been recognised that the IA 1986 procedure was inadequate in a number of respects and that scope existed for its improvement.

PERCEIVED WEAKNESSES OF THE EXISTING REGIME

6.10   In many cases where a company found itself in financial difficulties under the previous regime, it has led as a matter of inevitability to the appointment of an administrative receiver by the company's bank or other financial supporter, which will have taken a floating charge over all of the company's assets. The holder of a floating charge[7] has been able to block the appointment of an administrator by exercising its power to appoint an administrative receiver and at the same time withholding consent to the making of an administration order.[8] The administrative receiver's primary function is to obtain repayment of the debt owed to his appointor and he owes no duty to act for the benefit of all of the company's creditors.[9]

6.11   Accordingly, the exercise of such a function with this short-sighted objective served to handicap, if not cripple entirely, the company which otherwise had a real prospect of being rescued for the benefit of the general body of its creditors, shareholders and employees.

6.12   The second weakness of the administration procedure in its original form was that it was seen to be cumbersome and not user-friendly. It involved an application to the court being made by the company or its directors on its behalf, or other interested parties.[10] Almost invariably, although it is a permissive rather than mandatory requirement,[11] such an application would be supported by a report from an independent person, usually an accountant,[12] to the effect that the appointment of an administrator for the company was expedient. This has come to be known as the rule 2.2 report. Experience has shown that the investigation preceding such a report was often unduly expensive. There was, therefore, a perceived danger that the whole application process and its

---

7   In a talk to the ILA on 'the Enterprise Bill and the Floating Charge' in October 2002, Michael Crystal QC said: 'The floating charge thus has a two-sided role in the history of "company rescue". In one sense, "company rescue" was (as the Cork Committee recognised) born with the floating charge and receivership. But it was a form of rescue that strongly favoured the debenture-holder, both substantively (in that he was entitled to the company's assets) and procedurally (in that he appointed the receiver to realise those assets for his benefit).'

8   IA 1986, s 9(2)(a) and (3).

9   See *Re Charnley Davies* [1990] BCLC 760 for a contrast of the positions of administrator and mortgagee.

10   IA 1986, s 9 lists those who might apply and this has not changed under the EA 2002.

11   IR 1986, r 2.2.

12   Although the Rules did not require the independent person to be an accountant; see IR 1986, r 2.2(2).

attendant costs were frustrating the aim of the procedure and putting it out of the reach of the smaller companies.[13]

6.13   Thirdly, the administration process, once embarked upon, was often capable of dragging on indefinitely and had no automatic end or statutory cut-off point. This was at odds with the aim of the procedure, which was to provide a temporary breathing-space for a company in trouble, and this also contributed to the reputation of the administration order as being an expensive insolvency procedure. It is fair to say, however, that some courts interpreted IA 1986, s 8(2) to require that the administration order ought to be made for a fixed period, and/or to require the administrator to report back to the court within a stated period, thereby addressing the statutory deficiency,[14] but regrettably this did not happen in every case.

6.14   Fourthly, the process of transition from administration to liquidation or dissolution was not addressed at all in the IA 1986 and it was left to the courts to make up for this deficiency.[15] This generated a substantial amount of litigation which, in turn, spawned a jurisprudence which was far from straightforward and contributed to the expense of the procedure in its unaltered form.

SUMMARY OF CHANGES

6.15   The changes heralded by the EA 2002 in relation to improving the administration regime take effect in tandem with the abolition of the administrative receivership procedure.[16] They evidence a desire to promote and diversify the use of the new administration regime and to make it the most popular insolvency procedure for the company in financial difficulty and its creditors, particularly the bank.[17] The professed objective of the Government in its White Paper, *Productivity and Enterprise: Insolvency a Second Chance*, has been:

> 'to make changes which will tip the balance in favour of collective insolvency proceedings – proceedings in which all creditors participate, under which a duty is owed to all creditors and in which all creditors may look to an officeholder for an account of his dealings with a company's assets.'[18]

---

13   A danger acknowledged by Sir Donald Nicholls V-C in his *Practice Note (Administration Order Applications: Content of Independent Reports)* [1994] BCC 35 in which he exhorted applicants to obtain from the independent person (where a report was considered necessary) a concise assessment of the company's situation and of the prospects of the statutory purpose(s) being achieved.

14   See *Re Newport County Association Football Club Limited* [1987] 3 BCC 635.

15   IA 1986, s 18, for instance, which deals with discharge of the administration order, fails to provide the court with jurisdiction to make a winding-up order. Similarly, IA 1986 failed to provide for the company to go into voluntary liquidation following discharge.

16   Which was a source of inspiration for the administration procedure in the first place: see Cork Report, Chapter 9.

17   The prohibition on appointment of administrative receivers applies to 'qualifying floating charges' as defined in para 12 of Sch B1 which are created on or after the appointed day and this will be discussed in detail below: Chapter 8.

18   Paragraph 2.5 of the White Paper.

6.16 Concern has been expressed that the opening up of the administration procedure to embrace security enforcement[19] objectives may result in a lack of focus emerging[20] in the implementation of the procedure. Whether this will, in turn, lead to the devaluation of the perceived merits of the procedure, remains to be seen.

6.17 An interesting amendment was proposed in the House of Lords to tackle the important issue of the funding of administrations by according discretion to the court to approve the provision of 'super-priority financing' to the company in administration.[21] The proposal envisaged that finance provided in such circumstances be accorded priority over the claims of existing secured and unsecured creditors. The proposal was rejected.

6.18 The success of the new regime will depend in significant measure on the attitude of the judges who will be asked to interpret it. It will also depend on the attitude of future office-holders. For example, will the courts encourage constituent groups of creditors, whose interests the administrator is charged to progress, to exercise their powers in meeting to control or veto the administrator? Or, will future voluntary administrators, called in at earlier stages than before, be disposed to retaining management in possession under their 'light touch' supervision? If so, will they become more susceptible to attack by creditor interest groups?

6.19 The following is a summary of the major attributes of the new procedure, each of which will then be discussed in detail.

New statutory purpose of administration

6.20 The purposes for which an administrator may be appointed have been subject to significant change. Instead of an applicant having to establish one or more of four statutory purposes before an administration order is made, as under the old law, there is now a hierarchical structure of objectives which every administrator exercising his functions in every administration must advance. An applicant to the court for an order must satisfy the court that 'the purpose of administration', as encapsulated in at least one of the hierarchy of objectives, is reasonably achievable. Similarly, in an out-of-court appointment, the proposed administrator must state that in his opinion the purpose of administration is reasonably achievable.[22]

6.21 The first and overarching objective in the hierarchy is that of rescuing the company as a going concern. If he thinks that this is not reasonably practicable, or if he thinks a better result for creditors as a whole would be achieved, then the next objective, that of achieving a better result for creditors as a whole than on a winding-up, must be considered. If he thinks that this is not

---

19 The enterprise reforms do not abolish the floating charge itself. Although there have been occasional calls for its abolition in the past, it is so well entrenched as a basis for corporate financing that it could not be abolished: Cork Report, para 107 referring to the Loreburn Committee in 1906.

20 Milman, Editorial (2002) *Insolvency Lawyer* 119.

21 See *Hansard*, 29 July 2002, p 786 ff.

22 IA 1986, Sch B1, para 3.

reasonably practicable and it will not unnecessarily harm the interests of creditors as a whole, then he must act so as to realise property to distribute to one or more secured or preferential creditors.

6.22   This reform clearly demands a fairly radical change of culture for the secured creditor who wishes to enforce his security in this manner and it remains to be seen whether the qualifying floating charge-holder will be prepared to embrace it or whether it will resort to other means once the facility to appoint administrative receivers no longer becomes available.

New out-of-court routes into administration

6.23   The EA 2002 now enables holders of qualifying floating charges as well as the company or its directors to appoint an administrator without going to court, upon the filing of a notice of appointment accompanied by a statement from the administrator identified therein consenting to the appointment, stating that, in his opinion, the purpose of administration is reasonably likely to be achieved. The company or its directors will need to declare that the company is or is likely to become unable to pay its debts as a precondition to the appointment of an administrator. However, the floating charge-holder who proposes an appointment is not required to demonstrate insolvency, or likely insolvency, of the company.

6.24   The court procedure to appoint an administrator remains. Company creditors, other than qualifying floating charge-holders, who wish to place the company into administration, will have to apply to the court.

Veto powers and trumping abilities of qualifying floating charge-holders and creditors

6.25   In respect of floating charges created prior to the coming into force of the EA 2002, the power of veto is retained for the appointor of an administrative receiver.[23]

6.26   Qualifying floating charge-holders (QFCHs) in relation to post-EA 2002 charges are no longer given a power of veto but instead they are given the right to apply to install their preferred administrator:

(a)   after receiving notice of court application by the company or a creditor, in which case its trumping application will be granted unless the court thinks it right to refuse the application because of the 'particular circumstances' of the case;[24]

(b)   after receiving notice of out-of-court application by company or director and before appointment is complete, by applying to the court or by appointing out of court.

6.27   The holder of any prior-ranking, qualifying floating charge may apply to court for an administrator appointed by a QFCH to be replaced by a nominee of the former.[25]

---

23   IA 1986, Sch B1, para 39(1).
24   Ibid, para 36.
25   Ibid, para 96(2).

6.28   The creditors' meeting may replace the administrator appointed by the company or its directors, where there is no holder of a qualifying floating charge in respect of the company's property.[26]

Timetable for administration

6.29   The administrator must make a statement setting out his proposals and send a copy to creditors as soon as reasonably practicable after the company enters administration and in any event within 8 weeks. The initial creditors' meeting must be held within 10 weeks.

6.30   There is an automatic end to the administration procedure after 1 year,[27] subject to extension by court order or by agreement with creditors.[28]

Creditors' meetings not always necessary

6.31   Creditors' meetings may be dispensed with in the new regime and decisions may be approved in correspondence[29] with creditors.[30]

Administrators' powers and duties increase

6.32   The powers of administrators have increased. In particular, they are now authorised to make distributions to secured, preferential and, with the leave of the court or under IA 1986, s 176A, to unsecured, creditors.[31]

6.33   In the exercise of his duties, the administrator must have regard to the interests of all creditors, even where he is appointed by a bank which formerly would have appointed him as an administrative receiver.[32] Where there are insufficient funds to pay the unsecured creditors, the administrator must not unnecessarily harm their interests.[33] He is also under a statutory duty to perform his functions as quickly and efficiently as is reasonably practicable.[34]

Cleaner and faster exit routes

6.34   There are now provisions which specifically address the transition from administration to creditors' voluntary liquidation or dissolution by the simple procedure of the administrator filing notice to the effect that the provisions of para 83 or 84 of Sch B1 apply. So, if the company cannot be rescued, the administrator will aim to achieve a better realisation of the company's assets than through immediate liquidation.

6.35   Where, after this process is complete, there are funds available for unsecured creditors, the administrator will take steps to put the company into

---

26   IA 1986, para 97.
27   Ibid, Sch B1, para 76(1).
28   Ibid, paras 76–78.
29   The nature of which is to be specified in the Regulations: see IA 1986, Sch B1, para 58.
30   IA 1986, Sch B1, para 58.
31   Ibid, paras 65 and 66.
32   Ibid, para 3(2).
33   Ibid, para 3(4)(b).
34   Ibid, para 74(2).

liquidation. Where there are no funds for unsecured creditors, he will realise assets, make payments to the secured and preferential creditors and arrange for the dissolution of the company.

Anti-abuse provisions

6.36   Paragraph 81 of Sch B1 makes provision for a creditor to apply to the court to have the administration stopped on the grounds of improper motive on the part of the applicant for an order or the appointor of an administrator.

6.37   Paragraph 74 replaces the unfair prejudice provisions of IA 1986, s 27 with the right for a creditor or member to challenge an administrator's conduct which unfairly 'harms'[35] his interests whether alone or in common with some or all of the members or creditors.

6.38   Paragraph 75 entitles an interested party to apply to the court for relief on the grounds that the administrator has misapplied property or has become accountable for property or has breached a fiduciary or other duty or has been guilty of misfeasance.

6.39   Creditors and members may apply to the court if they believe that the administrator is not performing his functions as quickly or efficiently as is reasonably practicable in the circumstances.[36]

SUMMARY

6.40   As mentioned in Chapter 11 ('Effect of adminsitration'), under the old procedure, administration was used as a 'gateway' to another insolvency process, whereas the new procedure opens up the possibility that administrations will often 'stand-alone' in the sense that the company will pass directly from administration to dissolution or that a very short, formal liquidation will take place at the end of the administration. In such cases, substantive rights will be altered within the administration by distributions to secured and preferential creditors and, with leave of the court, to unsecured creditors. This, in turn, will give rise to many considerations which were irrelevant in the old-style administrations, including rules as to dividends, set-off and priority of expenses.[37] Interesting questions will arise concerning the remuneration of the administrator in those cases which would otherwise have been an administrative receivership. The extent to which administrations take the place of CVLs remains to be seen but there is little doubt that the rules will require to be far more detailed and far-ranging than those which governed the old procedure.

6.41   Greater forethought will now be required. The greater number of ways by which the administration can be brought to an end and the new exit routes by the streamlined method of entering CVL or dissolution (see Chapter 13) will also require the administrator at a far earlier stage than under the old procedure

---

35   'Prejudice', a more familiar concept in the corporate legal field, was rejected by the House of Lords in debate on 21 October 2002 in the interests of more modern terminology.

36   IA 1986, Sch B1, para 74(2).

37   Compare IR 1986, r 4.218.

to give consideration as to how the administration is to end and the exit route. The need for this early strategic planning by the administrator emerges from the draft rules.

(a) It is likely that one of the matters to be included in the administrator's proposals is 'how it is proposed that the administration shall end. If a creditors' voluntary liquidation is proposed, details of the proposed liquidator must be provided'.

(b) If an administrator after realising assets proposes to make use of the new power to make a distribution to preferential or unsecured creditors,[38] the draft rules provide that he can do so only if such distribution 'is consistent with . . . any proposals made by him or which he intends to make'. That will require the proposals either to deal expressly with the question of distribution or at least be drafted in such a way that they do not prevent a distribution.[39]

6.42   The extent of these and other cultural changes introduced by the EA 2002 should not be under-estimated. A great deal of time and effort has been devoted to the formulation of the new regime by those steering Part 10 and the related Schedules through Parliament and to the drafting of the Rules. It is anticipated that it will soon be the turn of the practising insolvency practitioners and lawyers to consider carefully and implement the many practical implications of the changes.

---

38   Under para 65(3) with the permission of the court if it is to an unsecured creditor.
39   Although the administrator could always make use of the power under para 54 to revise his proposals, if it becomes clear at a later stage of the administration that a distribution to preferential and/or unsecured creditors was possible and desirable.

Chapter 7

ADMINISTRATION – THE NEW STATUTORY PURPOSE

'Neither do men put new wine into old bottles'
The Bible[1]

INTRODUCTION

7.1   Since the introduction in 1986 of the administration order as a formal insolvency process, there have been four disjunctive purposes for which an administration order may be made,[2] namely:

(a) the survival of the company, and the whole or any part of its undertaking, as a going concern;
(b) the approval of a voluntary arrangement under Part 1 of IA 1986;
(c) the sanctioning under Companies Act 1985, s 425 of a compromise or arrangement between the company and any such persons as are mentioned in that section; and
(d) a more advantageous realisation of the company's assets than would be effected on a winding-up.

The purposes specified in IA 1986, s 8 were all of apparently equal weight and each, on its own, could justify the appointment of an administrator. The nature and extent of those provisions created much litigation and some needless difficulties.

The new provisions set out in para 3 of Sch B1 to the IA 1986[3] fundamentally re-shape the purposes of administration. Unlike their predecessors, they are conspicuously the product of 15 years' experience, debate and reflection. In short, they reflect a 'real life' approach to the rescue of businesses in distress.

7.2   Under the new provisions, whether the appointment is in or out of court, there is a single statutory purpose for which a company may be placed into administration. As will be seen below, that single purpose comprises a hierarchy of three objectives. Before considering the component parts of the new single purpose, it is necessary first to mention the 'threshold test'.

---

1   Matthew 9:17.
2   IA 1986, s 8(3).
3   Inserted by s 248(2) of EA 2002.

THE THRESHOLD TEST: ACHIEVEMENT OF THE PURPOSE OF ADMINISTRATION MUST BE REASONABLY LIKELY

7.3   The court may make an administration order in relation to a company only if satisfied:

(a)   that the company is or is likely to become unable to pay its debts;[4] and
(b)   that the administration order is reasonably likely to achieve the purpose of administration.[5]

7.4   For out-of-court appointments of administrators, the relevant notice of appointment must be accompanied by a statement by the administrator that, among other things, in his opinion the purpose of the administration is reasonably likely to be achieved.[6]

7.5   The reference to achievement of a single statutory purpose reflects a descending hierarchy of distinct and mutually exclusive objectives introduced in para 3(1) of Sch B1 (see below).

7.6   The old threshold test as to likely achievement of the purpose of administration is retained but that likelihood is now qualified by the word 'reasonably'. It is submitted, however, that this probably adds little to the test ultimately applied under the former IA 1986, s 8(1)(b) (ie a real prospect of achieving the stated purpose).[7] 'Reasonably likely' in this context does not mean more likely than not (ie prospects of success greater than 50%).

7.7   Satisfaction of the threshold test only establishes the court's jurisdiction to make an administration order. The discretionary nature of that jurisdiction means that the lower the likelihood of achieving the purpose, the less likely it is that a court will make an order.[8]

THE NEW SINGLE PURPOSE – RESCUE OF THE COMPANY NOW THE PRIMARY OBJECTIVE

7.8   Although the debates in and out of Parliament about the structure and wording of the new single purpose were considerable and gave rise to amendments, the policy behind the introduction of the new single purpose has not changed. As a rule of thumb, the approach is that the administrator must act so as to rescue the company as a going concern unless another approach would produce a better result for creditors. In other words, emphasis is on rescue first. This has been achieved by the following means.

7.9   Paragraph 3(1) of Sch B1 provides:

---

4   IA 1986, Sch B1, para 11(a).
5   Ibid, para 11(b).
6   Ibid, para 18(3)(b) (appointment by holder of floating charge); para 29(3)(b) (appointment by company or directors).
7   See *Re Harris Simons Construction Ltd* [1989] 1 WLR 368; *Re SCL Building Services Ltd* [1990] BCLC 98; *Re Lomax Leisure Ltd* [2000] BCC 352. See further **8.13** and **8.14**.
8   Cf *Re Harris Simons Construction Ltd* [1989] 1 WLR 368; *Re Primlaks (UK) Ltd* [1989] BCLC 734.

'The administrator of a company must perform his functions with the objective of –

(a)   rescuing the company as a going concern, or

(b)   achieving a better result for the company's creditors as a whole than would be likely if the company were wound up (without first being in administration), or

(c)   realising property in order to make a distribution to one or more secured or preferential creditors.'

7.10   Reflecting the Government's stated aim of ensuring, where possible, the turnaround of companies in financial difficulty, rescue of the company as a going concern is identified as the primary (or overarching) objective of administration.

7.11   Under para 3(3) of Sch B1, the administrator must perform his functions with that objective (rescue of the company as a going concern):

'unless he thinks either:

(a)   that it is not reasonably practicable to achieve that objective, or

(b)   that the objective specified in sub-paragraph (1)(b) would achieve a better result for creditors as a whole.'

7.12   The structure of sub-para (3) was the product of amendments to the Bill agreed during its final stages in the House of Lords.[9] The provisions, as enacted, arguably enable old-style realisations of assets for the benefit of creditors to assume equal importance with the rescue of the company.[10] The word 'thinks' in sub-para (3) establishes that departure from the primary objective is now a matter exclusively for the opinion of the administrator.[11]

7.13   The administrator may perform his functions with the objective specified in sub-para 1(c) (realisation of property for distribution to secured/ preferential creditors):

'only if —

(a)   he thinks that it is not reasonably practicable to achieve either of the objectives specified in sub-paragraph (1) (a) and (b), and

(b)   he does not unnecessarily harm the interests of the creditors of the company as a whole.'[12]

Administrator to act in the interests of creditors as a whole

7.14   The administrator's performance of his functions is qualified in a number of important respects. Subject to sub-para (4) (which identifies the circumstances in which the administrator may pursue the objective in para 3(1)(c) above) he must perform his functions in the interests of the company's creditors as a whole.[13] The administrator must also perform his functions as quickly and efficiently as possible.[14]

---

9   *Hansard* (HL), 21 October 2002, vol 639, no 190 at cols 1099–1106.

10   In the course of debate Lord Hoffmann, speaking in his legislative capacity, described that as sending the wrong message to the profession.

11   See below at **7.24–7.26**.

12   IA 1986, Sch B1, para 3(4).

13   Ibid, para 3(2).

14   Ibid, para 4.

7.15   The requirement that the administrator must perform his functions in the interests of the company's creditors as a whole or, where objective (1)(c) applies, in such a way as does not harm those interests unnecessarily, is designed to underline the important difference between the role of an administrator and that of the administrative receiver (who is generally permitted to act in the exclusive interests of the appointing charge-holder).

Rescue of the company as a going concern

7.16   As originally drafted, the primary objective of administration was identified as the rescue of the company. The absence of any reference to the company's business or the company's survival as a going concern[15] left it open to contend that preservation of the company as a legal entity but with no business or assets (ie a shell company) would amount to rescue. As the continued (but bare) existence of the company could always be achieved, to construe rescue of the company in such a way would arguably be to deprive it of any real meaning.

7.17   In the course of the Bill's progress through both Houses of Parliament, the Government repeatedly recognised[16] that there was no purpose in requiring the administrator to try to rescue companies at the expense of preserving viable businesses. Although the Government expressed confidence that the courts would interpret the primary objective as meaning to rescue the company as a going concern with the whole or much of its business intact,[17] the addition of the words 'as a going concern'[18] goes some way to making that explicit.

7.18   Explanatory Notes prepared by the DTI issued after the Act received Royal Assent express the view (at para 647) that rescuing the company as a going concern is, in this context, intended to mean the company and as much of its business as possible. Whilst the Explanatory Notes do not form part of the Act and have not been endorsed by Parliament, they are likely to carry some weight when the time comes for the courts to interpret the phrase.

7.19   That the new provisions do not follow the wording of the former s 8(3)(a) of IA 1986 permits a distinctive interpretation. As a company may continue as a going concern with only part of its business intact, however, such an outcome would appear to be within the primary objective.

7.20   The primary objective may not, then, be so different from the former statutory purpose[19] of survival of the company, and the whole or any part of its undertaking, as a going concern. That purpose has in turn been described[20] as envisaging that:

> 'the company will emerge from administration with its solvency restored, or
> safeguarded at least for the short tem, and with its existing business or some part

---

15   Contrast the wording in the former s 8(3)(a) of IA 1986.
16   See the reported discussion of para 3 by Standing Committee B on 9 May 2002; *Hansard*, 17 June 2002 (HC); *Hansard*, 2 July 2002 (HL), Lord McIntosh of Haringey.
17   Ibid.
18   Introduced in the House of Lords on 21 October 2002.
19   See IA 1986, s 8(3)(a) (now repealed).
20   Fletcher, Higham and Trower *The Law and Practice of Corporate Administrations* (1994) at para 1.11.

thereof remaining intact and capable of being carried on outside a formal insolvency.'

7.21 The Explanatory Notes which accompanied the Bill as brought from the House of Commons on 19 June 2002 and those issued after the Act received Royal Assent express the view that achievement of the primary objective is most likely to involve the creditors of the company agreeing to its entry into a CVA or scheme of arrangement under s 425 of the Companies Act 1985. In that sense, the primary objective is an umbrella provision under which the first three former statutory purposes have been brought.

7.22 In those instances where break-up and sale of some or all of the company's individual businesses or assets will produce a better return for the company's creditors as a whole, achievement of the primary objective is expected by the Government[21] to yield to the next objective (better realisation than would result from a winding-up).

7.23 That does not, however, necessarily follow from the structure of para 3, which does give rise to a potential conflict in those instances where rescue of the company is reasonably practicable but is not necessarily in the interests of creditors as a whole. This may arise, for example, where an administrator is offered more for the whole business by a competitor with a special interest than the creditors would receive through a CVA.

ACHIEVEMENT OF THE PRIMARY AND SECONDARY OBJECTIVES MUST BE REASONABLY PRACTICABLE

7.24 The question of whether achievement of the primary or secondary objectives is reasonably practicable is, as noted above, to be determined subjectively by reference to what the administrator *thinks*. The adoption of that test, whilst avoiding potentially 'unhelpful and distracting arguments about whether a higher objective is practicable',[22] arguably precludes interested parties from seeking to challenge (whether under para 74 of Sch B1[23] or otherwise) the approach adopted by the administrator.[24]

7.25 The only possible grounds (identified in the Explanatory Notes to the Act: see para 648) for challenge to an administrator's decision as to the reasonable practicability of achieving the primary or secondary purposes are bad faith and irrationality. Relevant factors for any challenge will include not only the realisation of economic value but also the proposed timescale.[25]

---

21 *Hansard* (HL), Standing Committee B, Fourteenth Sitting, 9 May 2002 at col 849 (Douglas Alexander MP, Minister for E-Commerce and Competitiveness).
22 A reason advocated for a similar amendment by a member of the standing committee in the House of Commons.
23 As to which, see 0.
24 *Hansard* (HL), 21 October 2002, vol 639, no 190, at col 1103 (Lord Hoffmann).
25 This is evident from paragraph 633 of the Explanatory Notes accompanying the Bill as brought from the House of Commons on 19 June 2002.

7.26   Nevertheless, the court's traditional reluctance to gainsay (particularly with the benefit of hindsight) the commercial judgment of experienced professionals frequently exercised in difficult circumstances is well recorded.[26]

NO NEED FOR ORDER OR NOTICE OF APPOINTMENT TO IDENTIFY OBJECTIVE OF ADMINISTRATION

7.27   Importantly, there is no requirement for any order appointing an administrator or any notice of appointment (in the case of out-of-court appointments) to specify for which of the hierarchy of objectives the order or appointment is made.[27] That avoids the necessity to apply to vary any administration order (or to file any amended notice of appointment) when the original contemplated objective is subsequently considered incapable of achievement.

7.28   If the administrator thinks that none of the statutory objectives (and hence the purpose of administration) is capable of being achieved, he or she is obliged to make an application to the court for his appointment to cease to have effect.[28]

HOW WILL THE HIERARCHY OF OBJECTIVES WORK IN PRACTICE?

7.29   Some idea of how the provisions may be expected to work in practice appears from the examples considered in the Explanatory Notes which accompanied the Bill as brought from the House of Commons on 19 June 2002 and in those issued after the Act received Royal Assent.

7.30   Achievement of the primary objective (rescue of the company) may, for example, be reasonably practicable where the relevant company is beset by short-term cash-flow difficulties but otherwise trading profitably and where the company's bankers (or some other third-party funder) is willing to finance continued trading.

7.31   The position will be otherwise where there is no prospect of ongoing finance to ease cash-flow difficulties or, for example, to invest in necessary plant and machinery. The administrator in such circumstances may well conclude that disposal of the company's business as a going concern will yield more for creditors than the piecemeal disposal of the company's assets in a winding-up.

7.32   The objective of last resort (realisation of property in order to make a distribution to one or more secured or preferential creditors) is said[29] to be aimed mainly at those cases where the company is not viable and has no business which can be sold as a going concern. All that is open to the administrator is to

---

26   See, eg, *Mitchell v Buckingham* [1998] 2 BCLC 369; *Mahomed v Morris* [2000] 2 BCLC 536 and *Westpac Banking Corp v Totterdell* (1998) 17 ACLC 317.
27   Contrast the former IA 1986, s 8(3).
28   See IA 1986, Sch B1, para 79(2)(a).
29   Explanatory Notes, para 651.

dispose of the company's underlying assets to enable some distribution to secured or preferential creditors. This last objective is the one which most resembles administrative receivership in the sense that the process is likely to be driven by a secured lender, usually a bank or asset-based lender, seeking to enforce its security and minimise its exposure. The fundamental difference, of course, is that the new process will be a collective one in that the administrator will be an officer of the court owing statutory duties to unsecured creditors. In other words, although the objective will be the last resort set out in para 3(1)(c), the administrator will need to be more circumspect than his predecessor in such a situation, the administrative receiver.

CONCLUSION

7.33   It is difficult to envisage that there will be repeated the scale of the litigation fought over the last 15 years concerning the nature and extent of the old statutory purposes for administration appointments. It seems that the experience of the last 15 years has informed the drafting of the new statutory purpose and it is hoped and anticipated that they are unambiguous and workable.

Chapter 8

COURT APPOINTMENT OF ADMINISTRATORS

'Beware
Of entrance to a quarrel, but being in,
Bear't that th'opposèd may beware of thee.'
William Shakespeare[1]

PARTIES WHO MAY APPLY

8.1 An application for an administration order may be made to the court either by the company or its directors or one or more creditors of the company.[2] The justices' chief executive on behalf of a magistrates' court under s 87A of the Magistrates' Courts Act 1980, who is tasked with recovering fines imposed on a company, may apply for an administration order to be made against the company. Alternatively, an application may be made by a combination of those persons referred to above, together or separately.

8.2 The reference to 'directors' presupposes that a resolution of the board of directors has been passed. Conversely, the Act does not contemplate that a single director may apply for an order against the wishes of the majority of the board. There is no additional requirement that the company or its directors should demonstrate an interest in the outcome of the administration order before they have standing to make an administration application.

8.3 The reference to 'creditor' includes a contingent creditor and a prospective creditor.[3]

PARTIES TO BE NOTIFIED

8.4 As soon as reasonably practicable after the making of an administration application, the applicant must notify:

(a) any person who has appointed, or is or may be entitled to appoint, an administrative receiver of the company;[4]

---

1   Polonius' advice to Laertes from *Hamlet* 1:4.
2   IA 1986, Sch B1, para 12(1).
3   Ibid, para 12(4).
4   Who may then exercise its power of veto in IA 1986, Sch B1, para 39.

(b) any 'qualifying floating charge holder' as defined in para 14 to Sch B1, who is or may be entitled to appoint an administrator;[5] and

(c) such other persons as may be prescribed by the new rules. Such persons will include any Sheriff or other officer charged with executing against the company and any party who has distrained against the company or its property.

8.5   Parties to be served with the application will include:

(a) the appointer of an administrative receiver or person entitled to make such appointment;

(b) a qualified floating charge-holder (QFCH);

(c) any administrative receiver already in office;

(d) the proposed administrator;

(e) the company, if the application is made by anyone other than the company;

(f) the directors of the company, if the application is made by anyone other than the directors;

(g) any person who has presented a pending winding-up petition against the company, and a provisional liquidator appointed under a pending winding-up petition; and

(h) any Member State liquidator[6] appointed in main proceedings in relation to the company.

8.6   It will be observed that the notification provisions are mandatory and that there is no facility in the Act to dispense with notice in cases of urgency.[7] It is anticipated, however, that the rules will at the very least, as before, provide for abridgement of time for service of notice on the parties required to be served with the application. No doubt the court will also have power to direct substituted service on what might be described as 'CPR grounds'.

EFFECT OF THE APPLICATION[8]

8.7   An application, once made, may not be withdrawn without the permission of the court.[9]

8.8   When an administration application has been made and the application has not yet been granted or dismissed, or, if it has been granted, the administration order has not taken effect, there is an interim moratorium on insolvency proceedings and on other legal process.[10] This has the same ambit as the moratorium which takes effect once an administration order has been made.[11]

---

5   The floating charge-holder has then got an opportunity to exercise its powers under para 36 to apply to the court to have a different person appointed as administrator.

6   See the EC Regulation on Insolvency Proceedings 2000.

7   Although this was proposed in the White Paper.

8   For a detailed analysis, see Chapter 11.

9   IA 1986, Sch B1, para 12(3).

10   Ibid, para 44.

11   Ibid, para 44(5) simply applies the provisions of paras 42 and 43 to the interim moratorium. The effect of the moratorium is dealt with in Chapter 10.

8.9 However, if there is an administrative receiver of the company in place at the date on which the application for administration is made then the interim moratorium does not apply until his appointor consents to the making of the administration order.[12] If it does not consent to the making of the order, either before the application is made, which is when it is usual to procure its concurrence with the administration route, or subsequently, then the court must dismiss the administration application.[13] Indeed, the appointor's powers of veto apply whether the administrative receiver was appointed before or after the making of the administration application.[14] This maintains the position established in the IA 1986 which precluded the administrator and administrative receiver being in office at the same time, with the decision as to which procedure should prevail resting with the floating charge-holder.

PRE-CONDITIONS FOR MAKING THE ADMINISTRATION ORDER

8.10 There are two pre-conditions for the court's jurisdiction. If both of these are satisfied, the court then has a discretion whether to make an order. The pre-conditions will be referred to below as 'the insolvency condition' and 'the purpose condition'. They are set out in para 11 of Sch B1:

'The court may make an administration order in relation to a company only if satisfied

(a)   that the company is or is likely to become unable to pay its debts, and

(b)   that the administration order is reasonably likely to achieve the purpose of administration.'

The insolvency condition

8.11 The wording in relation to the insolvency condition is the same as under the previous regime.[15] In each case, the phrase 'unable to pay its debts' is defined with reference to the meaning given to that expression by IA 1986, s 123.[16] In other words, the court will require to be satisfied that the company is, or is likely to become, unable to pay its debts as they fall due or that the value of its assets is, or is likely to become, less than the amount of its liabilities, taking into account its contingent and prospective liabilities.[17]

8.12 As before, the focus is on the words 'only if satisfied' and 'likely'. It is suggested that the jurisdictional threshold remains the same and that the court must be convinced of insolvency or likely insolvency on a balance of probabilities.

---

12   IA 1986, Sch B1, para 44(6).
13   Ibid, para 39(1)(a).
14   Ibid, para 39(2).
15   Except the words in brackets are now in effect relegated to the Interpretations; Sch B1, para 111(1).
16   See the Interpretations, Sch B1, para 111(1).
17   IA 1986, s 123.

8.13　　Recently, the High Court has considered this wording in *Re Colt Telecom Group plc*[18] in relation to the predecessor – IA 1986, s 8(1)(a). The petitioner had argued that the words 'is or is likely to become unable to pay its debts' only require a petitioner to demonstrate a 'real prospect' that the company was likely to become insolvent in the future. On the somewhat exceptional facts of that case, Jacob J found that even if this was the test then the petitioner had failed to satisfy it. Further, he said this in relation to the standard of proof:

> 'To put a company into administration is a serious matter. Creditors, as well as the company itself, can apply. To expose the company to all the expense, danger, and problems associated with administration is a serious matter. It is most unlikely that Parliament intended this when there was a real prospect of insolvency rather than where insolvency was more probable than not.

> The experience of this case fortifies my view that it is not enough merely to show a "real prospect" of insolvency as opposed to insolvency being more likely than not. I cannot think Parliament intended that companies should be exposed to this kind of hostile proceeding where it is more likely than not that the company is not insolvent. Administration is a rescue procedure – it must be shown that rescue is probably needed before asking for a rescue team.'

8.14　　Of course, the court has to interpret in their context and apply the words of the EA 2002 and not the IA 1986. In doing so, it will heed the protestations of Millett J (as he then was) in *Re MC Bacon Ltd*[19] against the citation of cases decided under the old law. Nevertheless, it is suggested that previous cases will continue to be of some assistance where, as here, the statutory language and its context remain substantially the same.

8.15　　The holder of a qualifying floating charge who applies for an administration order is not required to satisfy the court that a company is or is likely to become unable to pay its debts – as long as the court is satisfied that the floating charge-holder is entitled to appoint an administrator under para 14 of Sch B1.[20] If the court is not so satisfied, then the applicant will of course be required to satisfy this condition.

The purpose condition

8.16　　The purpose condition is central to the object of administration. If it cannot be satisfied, a rescue or preservation of value through the process of administration is not appropriate. It is here that the statutory language has changed from that used in the equivalent pre-condition in IA 1986, s 8.

(a)　Under s 8 the court was required to 'consider' that the making of an order 'would be likely to achieve' one or more of the statutory purposes. This became the tried and tested 'real prospect' test enunciated in *Re Harris Simons Construction Limited*.[21]

18　[2002] EWHC 2815 (Ch).

19　[1990] BCC 78 at 87C–E.

20　IA 1986, Sch B1, para 35(2).

21　[1989] 1 WLR 368. In *Re Lomax Leisure Limited* [2000] BCC 352, Peter Gibson J said that this approach was 'now well established'.

(b) Under the new condition, the court must be 'satisfied' that the administration order is 'reasonably likely to achieve' the purpose of administration set out in para 3 of Sch B1.[22]

8.17 Therefore it would appear that, on the face of it, the standard of proof has been raised to some extent under the new regime. That said, it is difficult to identify the reasons why Parliament should have decided to require a higher standard than the 'real prospect' test.

8.18 There is no clue in *Hansard*, because the words of the purpose condition remained those set out in the original Bill. In other words, they are the words chosen and adopted by the Parliamentary draftsman when the legislation was first introduced to Parliament. There was no debate in either House (including Standing Committee B) which might afford an insight into why a different standard might have been intended. It is possible that the draftsman considered that the new words satisfied the modern approach of using plain English.

8.19 Had Parliament intended to introduce a full-blown balance of probabilities test, then presumably it would have used words to the effect that the order is 'more likely than not to achieve' the statutory purpose.[23] It would seem that such a test would be inconsistent with the declared objective of the reform in this area to make the procedure more accessible, as well as to make it more flexible, more effective and less onerous from an evidential perspective.[24] It would introduce an unnecessary rigidity into an area which has worked well in the past.

8.20 The correct approach might well be to conclude that, given the radical change introduced generally in relation to 'the' single purpose of administration, it is not productive to compare the new and the old regime at least in so far as the purpose condition is concerned, given the change introduced in relation to the purpose of administration. Under IA 1986, s 8, there was a disjunctive list of four purposes. Now there is a single purpose with a list of objectives to which an administrator (when appointed) in performing his functions must adhere, in desending order of priority. It is clear from the wording of para 3 that once in place the administrator has substantial control over which objective to pursue and the scope for court intervention is reduced.

8.21 Moreover, while in sub-para 11(1)(a) in relation to the insolvency condition, the reference to 'likely' is unqualified, in sub-para 11(1)(b) it is qualified by the word 'reasonably'. This suggests that a somewhat lower standard is required for the purpose condition than for the insolvency condition in that the degree of probability connoted by 'likely' must be gathered from the qualifying word 'reasonably'. It is suggested that in order to fulfil the purpose condition the applicant need only satisfy the court that there is a likelihood

---

22 IA 1986, Sch B1, para 11(b).

23 And see the reasoning of Hoffmann J in *Re Harris Simons Construction Ltd* [1989] 1 WLR 368; [1989] 5 BCC 11.

24 White Paper at paras 2.6 and 2.12. The legislation places greater emphasis on the opinion of the administrator or proposed administrator and the provision in the old rules for a report by an independent person has been dropped.

backed up by a valid reason or reasons that the statutory purpose will be achieved.[25]

8.22   To discharge this onus (ie to fulfil the purpose condition) an applicant will be required to attach to its application a written statement by the person proposed as administrator.[26] That person will be required to state that he or she believes it is reasonably likely that the order will achieve *the* purpose of administration. It is anticipated that there will be no requirement for that person to produce a comprehensive report as under the previous regime. This is perhaps understandable in the normal run-of-the-mill administration. However, in more difficult cases, or where there is reason to believe that the basis of the proposed administrator's opinion is to be contested, then presumably the court will allow, or where there is time, proceed to give directions for, more detailed evidence to be filed and served prior to the substantive hearing date.

8.23   In this context, it ought to be remembered that the proposed administrator who expresses his professional opinion in relation to the purposes of administration is an 'expert witness' within the meaning of CPR 1998, Part 35. Therefore he will be well advised to familiarise himself with and adhere to the provisons of Part 35 and the Code of Guidance on Expert Evidence of the Working Party of the Civil Justice Council. His overriding duty in providing his written statement will be to the court and this overrides any obligation to the applicant for the administration order. This inevitably places him in a position where there is a potential conflict between his duties and his personal interest, given his interest in being appointed as administrator.[27] In *Colt*, Jacob J said that even in the ordinary case a proposed administrator:

> 'must be particularly careful to be objective in giving is advice to the directors as to the need for and the purpose of an administration order. Contested petitions are significantly different. They are rare birds. I think that an insolvency practitioner asked to give expert evidence to support such a case should not propose himself as administrator. Otherwise the Court is faced with an expert giving highly contested evidence in a case where he has a direct interest in his evidence being accepted.'[28]

8.24   Further, the court will be provided with:

(a)   a statement of the company's financial position, specifying, to the best of the applicant's knowledge and belief, the assets and liabilities including contingent and prospective liabilities;

---

25   *Re Harris Simons Construction Limited* provides a helpful analysis, albeit in relation to the pre-existing legislation.

26   To be addressed in the Rules but it is anticipated that this will be in similar terms to the information required in relation to out of court appointments: see IA 1986, Sch B1, paras 18(3), 29(3).

27   As to the inadmissibility of 'expert' evidence when the expert has a personal interest in the case, see *Liverpool Roman Catholic Archdiocesan Trustees Inc v Goldberg (No 3) (Practice Note)* [2001] 1 WLR 2337.

28   It remains to be seen whether the Rules will make provision for a let-out in acute conflict cases.

(b) details of any security known or believed to be held by creditors and whether the security entitles the appointment of an administrative receiver or an administrator under para 14; if an administrative receiver has been appointed, that fact shall be stated;

(c) details of any petition presented for winding up or any other insolvency proceedings, so far as within the immediate knowledge of the applicant;

(d) any other matters which in the opinion of those intending to make the application for an order will assist the court in deciding whether to make such an order.[29]

8.25 Where the applicant is a QFCH under para 35, he must give sufficient details in the schedule of evidence in support to satisfy the court that he is entitled to appoint an administrator under Sch B1, para 14.

8.26 It is expected that in most cases the court will make an order on the basis of the proposed administrator's statement of belief coupled with the financial information establishing the company's insolvency or likely insolvency. The evidential threshold is therefore expected to be lower than under the old regime in most cases.

The residual discretion

8.27 As was the position under IA 1986, s 8, the court then retains a discretion as to whether or not to make the order.[30] Paragraph 11 of Sch B1 states 'the court *may* make an administration order ... *only if satisfied*' that the two conditions are fulfilled. So, for example, if it becomes apparent in the course of the hearing that the majority of the creditors opposed the making of the order and that, in fact, the proposals are unlikely to be approved by a creditors' meeting if an order were granted, then these considerations would militate against making the order. Similarly, if evidence is produced which demonstrates that the proposed administrator's statement of belief must have been made on a mistaken basis, then the court will be able to exercise its discretion to refuse the application or to adjourn it pending the obtaining of further evidence.

POWERS OF THE COURT

8.28 On hearing an application for administration, the court has a wide discretion and the powers in para 13(1)(a)–(d) of Sch B1 reflect those available to the court under the previous law.[31]

8.29 In addition, however, the court is now empowered to treat the application for administration as a winding-up petition.[32] The powers available to a court on hearing a winding-up petition under IA 1986, s 125 are now available to the court hearing the administration application and therefore the

---

29 To be addressed in the Rules.
30 For the operation under s 8 of the two pre-conditions followed by the discretion, see *Re Far East Abrasives* (unreported) 1 August 2002.
31 IA 1986, s 9(4) and (5).
32 Ibid, Sch B1, para 13(1)(e).

court is vested with the widest discretion to make the order it considers most appropriate to regulate the future of the company.[33]

8.30   A court may decide to treat the application as a winding-up petition if, for example, it becomes apparent from the evidence in the course of the hearing of the administration application that not only is the company hopelessly insolvent, but that the interests of creditors as a whole require an immediate investigation of its affairs by a liquidator. If this consideration outweighs any marginal advantage that a realisation of assets in administration is likely to achieve, then the court may be persuaded to pursue the liquidation route. In those circumstances, it would be likely that the court would adjourn the hearing on directions for appropriate notification to be made to the body of creditors of the deemed winding-up petition.

8.31   The court has power to make an interim order. This power enables the court, for example, to make an order in cases where urgent intervention is needed, restricting the exercise by the directors of any or all of their powers in relation to the company for the period of the interim order, or to subject the decision-making powers of the directors to the supervision of an insolvency practitioner, usually the proposed administrator, or indeed of the court itself.[34]

8.32   The Act does not provide a power to the court to appoint an interim administrator although such a power was proposed in the White Paper.[35]

SPECIAL CASES

Qualifying floating charge-holders

8.33   Where a qualifying floating charge-holder decides to apply to the court under para 35 of Sch B1 to appoint an administrator rather than to exercise its own powers to appoint, then the floating charge-holder is not required to demonstrate to the court that the company is or is unlikely to become unable to pay its debts.[36] The application must state, however, that it is being made under para 35 of the Schedule. As a further concession to the qualifying floating charge-holder (QFCH), where an application for administration is made by a different party, then the holder of the qualifying floating charge may intervene in the application and apply to have its own nominee appointed as administrator instead of the proposed administrator put forward by the administration

---

33   See also para 13(1)(f).

34   IA 1986, Sch B1, para 13(3)(a) and (b). A winding-up petitioner will also be entitled to
     apply to appoint a provisional liquidator in cases of urgency.

35   Paragraph 2.10 of the Government White Paper: *Productivity and Enterprise: Insolvency –
     A Second Chance*. The proposal was that a floating charge-holder ought to be empowered
     to make an application for an administrator without giving notice and without a r 2.2
     report in urgent cases. According to the White Paper, the court ought to have the power in
     such circumstances to appoint an interim administrator who would then have 14 days to
     report to the court as to whether an administration order ought to be made.

36   IA 1986, Sch B1, para 35(2).

applicant.[37] The court must accede to this application unless the particular circumstances of the case suggest otherwise.[38]

Applications where a company is in liquidation

Application by a QFCH

8.34   Paragraph 8(1) of Sch B1 imposes a general prohibition on the appointment of an administrator where a company is in liquidation either as a result of a resolution for voluntary winding-up or a court order for winding-up. However, there are two exceptions to this. First, if the holder of a qualifying floating charge makes an application to the court in relation to a company which is subject to a compulsory order for winding-up, and the court decides to make an administration order, then the court must discharge the winding-up order, make consequential provision to enable the administrator to take over the affairs of the company from a liquidator and in that regard shall specify which of the powers in Sch B1 are exerciseable by the administrator.[39] No such facility is accorded to a lender in place of a resolution for voluntary winding up. Instead, the lender will have to apply to the court to replace the liquidator and then persuade the liquidator that it is expedient to apply under para 38 for an administration order.[40]

Application by the liquidator of a company

8.35   A liquidator of a company in compulsory or voluntary liquidation is entitled under the Act to make an administration application.[41] If he applies and the court makes an administration order then the court must discharge any winding-up order and make consequential provision for the company's affairs to be run under administration.[42]

Applications where an administrative receiver is appointed

8.36   Where an administrative receiver has been appointed to the company, the court must dismiss any application for an administration order in relation to the company unless the party by or on behalf of whom the receiver was appointed consents to the making of the administration order.[43] The right of veto therefore remains with the appointor of the administrative receiver, whether he was appointed before the application was made or at a later stage,

---

37   IA 1986, Sch B1, para 36(1).
38   Ibid, para 36(2).
39   Ibid, para 37(3).
40   See **8.29** *et seq* for a discussion on this.
41   IA 1986, Sch B1, para 38(1).
42   Ibid, para 38(2).
43   Ibid, para 39(1)(a).

albeit in advance of the hearing before the court.[44] However, the Act abolishes the right to appoint an administrative receiver in respect of all qualifying floating charges created on or after a date appointed by the Secretary of State by order made by statutory instrument[45] and therefore it is expected that the occasions in which the right of veto is exercisable will reduce with the passage of time.

---

44   IA 1986, Sch B1, para 39(2). In the consultation exercise that preceded the Act, the banks indicated that they were not prepared to surrender their existing rights under existing debentures. They alleged that there would be a breach of Art 1 of the First Protocol (right to protection of property) in relation to the existing debentures, were Parliament to expropriate their proprietary right to appoint a receiver. Whatever the merits of this argument, Ms Hewitt on behalf of the Government conceded it on 9 November 2001.

45   IA 1986, s 72A, as introduced by EA 2002, s 245.

Chapter 9

APPOINTMENT OF ADMINISTRATORS BY FLOATING CHARGE-HOLDER

'A lawyer with his briefcase can steal more than a hundred men with guns.'
Mario Puzo[1]

INTRODUCTION

9.1   Paragraphs 14–21 of Sch B1 to the IA 1986, as inserted by the EA 2002, contain the provisions detailing the out-of-court route into administration for the holder of a floating charge.

9.2   These provisions are pivotal to the stated intention underlying the EA 2002 that 'administrators will in future be appointed in situations that would have been dealt with through administrative receivership'.[2] They provide the mechanism most likely[3] to be used by banks and other lenders ('the lender') who hold a floating charge and who otherwise would have looked to appoint an administrative receiver to realise their security.

9.3   The diagram overleaf summarises the requirements and procedures for an out-of-court appointment by a floating charge-holder.[4]

9.4   Where the debenture has been granted by a company prior to the commencement of the EA 2002 and the day appointed by the Secretary of State under s 72A(4) of the IA 1986 (as inserted by the EA 2002), the lender will still be able to appoint an administrative receiver to recover and realise its security. The same is not prohibited by the EA 2002. Section 72A only prohibits[5] the appointment of an administrative receiver by the holder of a qualifying floating charge (as defined in para 14, ie a lender who is entitled to appoint an administrator out of court under para 14) and only where the floating charge was created after the appointed day.

9.5   As regards lenders who have pre-EA 2002 debentures and thereby the ability to choose whether to appoint an administrative receiver or appoint an administrator out of court under para 14,[6] there are substantial advantages to

---

1   *The Godfather* (1969).
2   EA 2002, Explanatory Notes, para 643.
3   Save in respect of lenders who hold pre-EA 2002 debenture, who retain the ability to appoint an admnistrative receiver – see **9.4** and **9.5**.
4   The diagram is an amended version of Annex F to the EA 2002 Explanatory Notes.
5   Subject to the exceptions set out in IA 1986, ss 72B–72G as amended.
6   Which they have the power to do, pursuant to IA 1986, Sch B1, para 14(2)(c).

FLOATING CHARGE-HOLDER

- Must have qualifying floating charge/s.
- Charges must be enforceable on date of appointment.
- Company not in liquidation and no provisional liquidator appointed.
- Administrative receiver not in office.

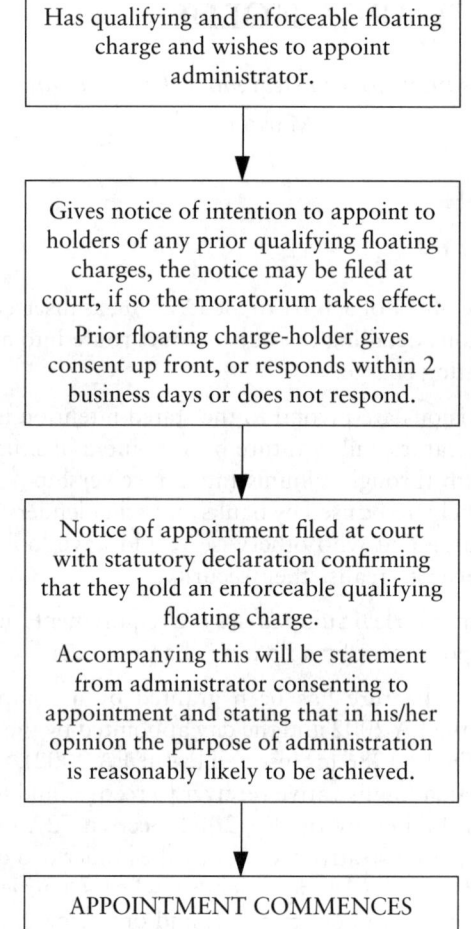

Has qualifying and enforceable floating charge and wishes to appoint administrator.

Gives notice of intention to appoint to holders of any prior qualifying floating charges, the notice may be filed at court, if so the moratorium takes effect.

Prior floating charge-holder gives consent up front, or responds within 2 business days or does not respond.

Notice of appointment filed at court with statutory declaration confirming that they hold an enforceable qualifying floating charge.

Accompanying this will be statement from administrator consenting to appointment and stating that in his/her opinion the purpose of administration is reasonably likely to be achieved.

APPOINTMENT COMMENCES

the lender in having the old debenture and opting for the administrative receiver route for realisation of its security:

(a) speed and ease of appointment;[7]
(b) choice of administrative receiver and difficulty for the company, its directors or other creditors to remove him;

---

7   There is no need to comply with the notice requirement to any prior floating charge-holder under para 15(1) and the formality requirements for the appointment of an administrator set out in para 18.

(c) ability to appoint an administrative receiver notwithstanding the liquidation of the company, whereas a lender cannot appoint an administrator out of court under para 14 where the company is in voluntary or compulsory liquidation;[8]

(d) control by the lender after appointment of the administrative receiver, compared to an administrator who will be an officer of the court and acting in the interests of creditors as a whole;

(e) administrative receiver's primary duty is to serve the interests of the lender and obtain payment of the lender's secured debt. His duties to other creditors are severely limited.[9]

9.6 The stated aim of the EA 2002 was to turn administration into the 'remedy of choice for maximising value' for lenders.[10] Only time will tell as to whether lenders will embrace the new regime and:

(a) take new security to replace their pre-EA 2002 debentures for existing customers; or

(b) if they retain their old security and have the choice, decide to appoint administrators rather than administrative receivers.

There appears to be little incentive in the EA 2002 for lenders to relinquish the advantages and control they have via administrative receivership. The only real motivation for lenders is as regards publicity and being seen to embrace the new administration regime as part of the rescue culture. Whilst there has been over the last few years from certain lenders in certain circumstances a reluctance to appoint administrative receivers where they have not been invited to do so by the company (and sometimes to support an administration petition by the directors or company) it remains to be seen whether this trend will continue.

POWER TO APPOINT

9.7 The holder of a qualifying floating charge in respect of a company's property may appoint an administrator under para 14(1) of Sch B1 to the IA 1986 without having to make an administration application to court. The mechanism for appointment is slightly more complex and burdensome than the requirements for the appointment of an administrative receiver but, overall, should enable lenders to make an appointment speedily and cheaply. It is certainly quicker and cheaper than the old procedure for appointment of an administrator (which in any event was not used directly by lenders) and the new procedure for an administration application to the court.

9.8 In order to come within para 14(1) and have the power to appoint an administrator out-of-court, the lender must have a floating charge:

(a) which 'qualifies' by satisfying one of the conditions set out in para 14(2); and

---

8   IA 1986, Sch B1, paras 8 and 37.
9   See *Re B Johnson & Co (Builders) Ltd* [1955] 2 All ER 775; *Cuckmere Brick Co v Mutual Finance Ltd* [1971] 2 All ER 633; *Medsforth v Blake* [1999] 3 All ER 97; *Insolvency – A Second Chance*, Cm 5234, paras 2.2, 2.3, Annex C, C15–C21.
10 *Insolvency – A Second Chance*, para 2.6.

(b) the floating charge and/or other security held by the lender must extend over the whole or substantially the whole of the property of the company by satisfying one of the conditions set out in para 14(3).

9.9   A floating charge 'qualifies' for the purposes of para 14(1) if it is created by an instrument which:

(a) states that para 14 applies to the floating charge;
(b) purports to empower the holder of the floating charge to appoint an administrator of the company;
(c) purports to empower the holder of the floating charge to make an appointment which would be the appointment of an administrative receiver within the meaning given by s 29(2) of IA 1986; or
(d) purports to empower the holder of a floating charge in Scotland to appoint a receiver who on appointment would be an administrative receiver.

9.10   Paragraph 14(2)(a) anticipates that lenders will amend their existing standard form of debentures to be used for new customers after the EA 2002 is brought into force, to remove the references to a power to appoint an administrative receiver and replace the same with a power to appoint an administrator and an express reference to the power to appoint the same out of court under para 14.

9.11   Paragraph 14(2)(b) deals with those debentures which have been amended to refer to a power of the lender to appoint an administrator but do not specifically refer to para 14.

9.12   Paragraph 14(2)(c) covers two situations. First, it allows a lender who has a debenture which pre-dates the coming into force of the EA 2002 to appoint an administrator out of court, if the lender wants to do so, rather than exercising his right to appoint an administrative receiver. Secondly, if a debenture is entered into after the coming into force of the EA 2002 in a standard form which has not been amended by the lender (either because the lender has not got round to amending the same or because by error an old-form debenture has been used) and which still refers to the power to appoint an administrative receiver, the lender may likewise appoint an administrator out of court.

9.13   In order to satisfy the 'property' requirement under para 14(3), the lender must hold one or more debentures of the company secured:

(a) by a qualifying floating charge which relates to the whole or substantially the whole of the company's property;
(b) by a number of qualifying floating charges which together relate to the whole or substantially the whole of the company's property; or
(c) by charges and other forms of security which together relate to the whole or substantially the whole of the company's property and at least one of which is a qualifying floating charge.

9.14   The property requirement under para 14(3) is to be contrasted with s 29(2) of IA 1986, where an administrative receiver is defined as:

'(a)   a receiver or manager of the whole (or substantially the whole) of a company's property appointed by or on behalf of the holders of any debentures of the company secured by a charge which, as created, was a floating charge, or by such a charge and one or more other securities; or

(b)   a person who would be such a receiver or manager but for the appointment of some other person as the receiver of part of the company's property.'

9.15   Whilst there are similarities between the two provisions (eg the reference to the 'whole (or substantially the whole) of a company's property'), there are differences too. The most obvious difference between para 14(3) and s 29(2) is that para 14(3) looks to the debenture or debentures held by the lender prior to appointment and whether the same cover, either separately, together or along with other forms of security, the whole or substantially the whole of the company's property. Section 29(2), by contrast, looks at the matter after the appointment has occurred and the extent of the property over which the receiver and manager has been appointed.

9.16   The wording of s 29(2) and its focus on the extent of the property over which the receiver and manager was appointed led to controversy as to whether a lender could appoint an LPA 1925 receiver over real property under the fixed charge contained within the debenture without such receiver being held to be an administrative receiver.[11] Given the formality requirements for the appointment of an administrator, it appears that lenders can now safely appoint an LPA 1925 receiver[12] without his being held to be an administrator. There will still be a risk of such an LPA 1925 receiver being held to be an administrative receiver where the debenture is granted prior to the appointed day. However, for debentures after the appointed day this uncertainty will be removed.[13]

RESTRICTIONS ON POWER TO APPOINT

Notice to holder of prior floating charge

9.17   If there is a prior qualifying floating charge (ie it satisfies para 14(2)) to that held by the lender, then the lender may not appoint an administrator under para 14, unless he has given at least 2 business days' written notice to the prior charge holder.[14] This enables the prior qualified floating charge-holder (QFCH) to consider appointing an administrator[15] itself, which it may wish to do, in order to choose who should be appointed as administrator. This introduces

---

11   *Meadrealm Ltd v Transcontinental Golf Construction Ltd* (unreported, 29 November 1991 (Vinelott J)) held that the lender could appoint an LPA receiver; see discussion Lightman & Moss, *The Law of Receivers and Administrators of Companies*, 3rd Edn, para 1–007 (Sweet & Maxwell, 2000); cf Doyle *Administrative Receivership: Law and Practice*, para 1.7.

12   In appropriate cases, eg where the principal assets of the company are real property or a property development.

13   See Rupert Connell of Fladgate Fisher, 'Enterprising Receivers', *Recovery*, Spring 2003, pp 20–22.

14   IA 1986, Sch B1, para 15(1).

15   Or administrative receiver if the prior floating charge holder has a pre-EA 2002 debenture.

potential for delay in the lender's appointment[16] but, in practice, it is likely that the prior QFCH[17] will consent to an immediate appointment if it does not want to make an appointment.

9.18   A floating charge is treated as 'prior' if:

(a) it was created first; or
(b) it is to be treated as having priority in accordance with an agreement to which the holder of each floating charge was party (ie there is a priority agreement between the charge-holders).[18]

Floating charge must be enforceable at time of appointment

9.19   Paragraph 16 of Sch B1 to IA 1986 provides that an administrator may not be appointed under para 14 while a floating charge on which the appointment relies is not enforceable. Although no definition is given as to the circumstances in which a floating charge is 'not enforceable', the Explanatory Notes to EA 2002 state that in the context of para 16, 'enforceable' means that 'the floating charge holder is entitled to call in their security'.[19]

9.20   The debenture and other security documents, together with any underlying loan agreements, will have to be considered as to the terms upon which the lender is entitled to call in its security and exercise its remedies.[20]

No incumbent provisional liquidator, administrative receiver or administrator

9.21   An administrator cannot be appointed by a lender if a provisional liquidator has been appointed by the court or there is an administrative receiver of the company appointed and still in office[21] or the company is already in administration.[22]

If company is already in liquidation

9.22   If the company is already in voluntary liquidation or subject to a winding-up order by the court, then an administrator may not be appointed, apart from in the circumstances set out in paras 37 and 38 of Sch B1 to IA

---

16   If the prior QFCH insists on having 2 business days' notice and refuses to consent. The delay in such cases may be even longer if the notice by the lender has to go out on or covers non-business days, eg weekends, bank holidays, Christmas or New Year.
17   If it is a primary lender.
18   IA 1986, Sch B1, para 15(2).
19   Paragraph 658 of the Explanatory Notes.
20   See Lightman & Moss *The Law of Receivers and Administrators of Companies*, 3rd Edn (Sweet & Maxwell, 2000), paras 4–033–4–047 for a detailed consideration as to the circumstances in which administrative receivers can be appointed, construction of the debenture and whether there must be a demand as a pre-requisite to any appointment; see also Doyle *Administrative Receivership: Law and Practice*, para 7.3.
21   IA 1986, Sch B1, para 17.
22   Ibid, para 7.

1986.[23] A lender therefore cannot appoint an administrator out of court where the company is already in voluntary[24] or compulsory liquidation.

Company in compulsory liquidation

9.23   Where a company is already subject to a compulsory winding-up order and the restriction in para 8(1)(b) of Sch B1 applies, then para 37 of that Schedule enables the lender to make an administration application to the court.

9.24   Although the point is not expressly dealt with in the EA 2002,[25] it appears that if such an administration application is made by a lender, then the compulsory liquidation of the company will be suspended and the incumbent liquidator prevented from carrying out any of his functions pending the outcome of the administration application. Paragraph 44(5) provides that where an administration application has been made but not granted or dismissed or the administration order has not yet taken effect, then the provisions in paras 42 and 43 shall apply (ignoring any reference to the consent of the administrator). Paragraph 43(6) provides that:

> 'No legal process (including legal proceedings, execution, distress and diligence) may be instituted or continued against the company or property of the company except … (b) with the permission of the court.'

The compulsory winding-up would appear to be a 'legal process' and thereby be caught by the interim moratorium.[26]

9.25   On an administration application by a lender where the company is already in compulsory liquidation, the court may make an administration order under para 13 of Sch B1. Presumably, in the exercise of the court's discretion under para 13, the court will need to be persuaded by the lender that the purpose under para 3 (or at least one of the three objectives thereunder, eg realising property in order to make a distribution to the lender and/or other secured or preferential creditors) is reasonably likely to be achieved. Furthermore, the court is likely to require some evidence as to why it is believed that an administration order is likely to be a better collective insolvency process than a compulsory liquidation.

9.26   If the court is persuaded to make an administration order on the application of the lender, then:

> '(a) the court *shall* discharge the winding-up order,
> (b) the court *shall* make provision for such matters as may be prescribed,
> (c) the court may make other consequential provision,
> (d) the court *shall* specify which of the powers under [Schedule B1] are to be exercisable by the administrator, and
> (e) [Schedule B1] shall have effect with such modifications as the court may specify.'

---

23   IA 1986, Sch B1, para 8.
24   Be that a members' or creditors' voluntary liquidation (ie whether the liquidation is an insolvent liquidation or not).
25   Cf para 44(7)(d) as regards the carrying out of the functions of an administrative receiver where an administration application is made.
26   As to the interim moratorium, see **11.3–11.5**.

9.27   Under Sch B1, para 37(3)(b), the rules will probably provide for such matters as:

(a) the costs of the petitioning creditor;
(b) the expenses and remuneration of the liquidator and whether there is to be a charge on the insolvent estate for the same;
(c) the handing over of assets and records from the liquidator to the administrator;
(d) an indemnity for the liquidator;
(e) the release of the liquidator; and
 (f) the submission or a receipts and payments account by the liquidator.

9.28   It is not clear what provisions are contemplated as being required to be made by court order to Sch B1 or to the powers of the administrator. This may depend upon the stage reached by the liquidator in dealing with the liquidation of the company and which of the objectives set out in para 3 of Sch B1 to IA 1986 are achievable.

Company in voluntary liquidation

9.29   If the company is in voluntary liquidation, a lender is prohibited by para 8(1)(b) from appointing an administrator out of court under para 14. Furthermore, the lender cannot apply by way of administration application for an administrator to be appointed where the company is in voluntary liquidation. Paragraph 8(2) states that para 8(1) (ie where the company is in voluntary liquidation) is subject to para 38, whereas para 8(3) states that para 8(2) (ie where the company is in compulsory liquidation) is subject to paras 37 and 38. Thus, the lender cannot apply under para 37 for an administration order. Paragraph 38 provides that the liquidator of a company may make an administration application and thus the voluntary liquidator is the only person who can make an administration application in respect of a company that is in voluntary liquidation.

9.30   If the lender is dissatisfied with the actions of the voluntary liquidator or wishes to have an administrator rather than a voluntary liquidator dealing with the company, then the lender must apply under s 100 of IA 1986 within 7 days of the date on which the creditors of the company nominate a liquidator to the court for an order for a particular liquidator nominated by the lender to be appointed as voluntary liquidator. EA 2002, Sch 17, para 14 inserts a new sub-para (4) to s 100 of IA 1986, which reads:

> 'The court shall grant an application under subsection (3) made by the holder of a qualifying floating charge in respect of the company's property (within the meaning of paragraph 14 of Schedule B1) unless the court thinks it right to refuse the application because of the particular circumstances of the case.'

9.31   Once the lender has obtained an order appointing his choice of liquidator as voluntary liquidator it would then be up to the lender to persuade the voluntary liquidator to make an application under para 38 for an administration order.

9.32 The above appears to be an unduly cumbersome way by which a lender might obtain the appointment of an administrator where the company is in voluntary liquidation. It is not at all clear why it was considered necessary to prevent a lender making an administration application where the company was in voluntary liquidation and yet allow such an administration application to be made where the company was in compulsory liquidation.

9.33 The above restrictions are a significant disadvantage to the lender compared with its ability to appoint an administrative receiver out of court after the company has gone into liquidation. There is now the possibility of directors of a company placing the company into voluntary liquidation with their choice of liquidator and, if they have the support of unsecured creditors for the liquidator, the lender will be forced:

(a) to make an application to impose his chosen liquidator; and then
(b) to persuade that liquidator himself to make an administration application.

9.34 This area has obviously caused concern because the draft Rules are in the process of being revised to provide additional protection to a lender with a qualifying floating charge. It is understood that Part 4 of IR 1986 will be amended to provide for notice to be given to a lender of a s 98 meeting for the lender to have a right to attend and vote at that meeting as regards the person to be appointed as voluntary liquidator without giving up its security. This may provide some additional protection to the lender, however it remains at risk because:

(a) a voluntary liquidator appointed by the company may apply to the court under s 166(2) of IA 1986 for leave to sell the business and/or assets of the company prior to the s 98 meeting (ie a *Centrebind*[27]). It may be that the IR 1986 are amended to provide that notice must be served on a QFCH where any such application is made;
(b) even though the lender may have notice of the s 98 meeting and may be allowed to vote at the meeting as regards the choice of liquidator without being required to give up its security, it may still be outvoted by the other creditors. One might therefore have the situation in which the liquidator appointed by the other creditors at a s 98 meeting sought to sell the business and/or assets of the company, prior to the lender being able to issue or have heard its application under IA 1986, s 100 to replace the liquidator.

NOTICE OF APPOINTMENT OF ADMINISTRATOR

9.35 IA 1986, Sch B1, para 18(1) requires a notice of appointment in prescribed form[28] to be filed by the lender at court in respect of the appointment of the administrator, along with such other documents as may be prescribed.[29]

---

27 *Re Centrebind Ltd* [1967] 1 WLR 377.
28 IA 1986, Sch B1, para 18(5) – the prescribed form will be included with a set of forms enacted by statutory instrument.
29 Such further documents will be set out in the rules as and when these are enacted by statutory instrument. Probably these will include the administrator's statement under IA 1986, Sch B1, para 18(3) and any written consent by prior floating charge-holder.

9.36   The notice of appointment must include a statutory declaration by or on behalf of the lender that:

(a) the lender is the holder of a qualifying floating charge in respect of the company's property;
(b) each floating charge relied upon in making the appointment is or was enforceable on the date of the appointment of the administrator; and
(c) the appointment of the administrator is in accordance with Sch B1.[30]

It is probable that a prescribed form for the statutory declaration will be prescribed by statutory instrument, in which case the statutory declaration must be in that prescribed form.[31]

9.37   The statutory declaration must be made during the prescribed period.[32] The period presumably will be a short period (probably 5 days) prior to the notice of appointment being filed at court.

9.38   Care will obviously be required in the preparation and accuracy of the statutory declaration, given that an offence is committed by the person making the statutory declaration if he makes a statement which is either false or which he does not have reasonable grounds to believe is true.[33]

9.39   The notice of appointment must identify the administrator who is to be appointed and must be accompanied by a statement by the administrator:

(a) that he consents to the appointment;
(b) that, in his opinion, the purpose of administration is reasonably likely to be achieved; and
(c) giving such other information and opinions as may be prescribed.[34]

9.40   The requirement for a statement by the administrator is another potential complication and possible delay for a lender compared with the speed and ease of appointment of an administrative receiver. The question arises as to the extent of the investigation into the company's affairs and consideration as to the likelihood of the hierarchical purpose that will be required to be carried out by the administrator prior to his being able and willing to provide such an opinion.

9.41   Whilst an administrative receiver may have prior knowledge of a company's financial position and prospects, for example, where his firm has been brought in by the lender as investigating accountants prior to the administrative receivership, there is no requirement for the prospective administrative receiver to have carried out any investigations into the company or to have formed an opinion as to the likelihood of any particular strategy being successful. The lender is simply left to consider its own commercial considerations and adequacy of its security prior to deciding whether to appoint an administrative receiver.

---

30   IA 1986, Sch B1, para 18(2).
31   Ibid, Sch B1, para 18(5).
32   Ibid, para 18(6). Probably the prescribed period will be no earlier than 5 days before filing.
33   Ibid, para 18(7).
34   Ibid, para 18(3).

9.42   In contrast to an administrative receivership, an insolvency practitioner considering accepting an appointment as administrator by a lender out of court is likely to require access to the financial records of the company along with an opportunity to discuss the position with the company directors, prior to his being in a position to be able to form an opinion as to the likelihood of the purpose of the administration being achieved.

9.43   It may be that the investigatory work necessary to provide such an opinion is very modest. Paragraph 18(3)(b) only states that 'the purpose of administration' is reasonably likely to be achieved. The purpose of the administration is in effect defined by the hierarchical three objectives set out in para 3(1)(a)–(c). Arguably, therefore, the proposed administrator may be able to say that he does not have to investigate or form an opinion as to whether the objectives of rescuing the company or a better result for creditors as a whole are likely to be achieved. He may only have to investigate and form an opinion as to whether the objective in para 3(1)(c) (ie realising property to make a distribution to the lender) can be achieved. If it can, then the purpose of the administration can be achieved and said to be likely. If this argument is correct, then little investigatory work will be required and proposed administrators will readily provide the statement required under para 18(3)(b).[35]

9.44   However, if it is not permissible to interpret 'the purpose of administration' under IA 1986, Sch B1, para 18(3)(b) such that the objectives set out in Sch B1, para 3(1)(a)–(c) can be read disjunctively, then the task of the proposed administrator will be far more onerous. If the proposed administrator has to form an opinion as to whether the objectives in para 3(1)(a) or (b) are likely to be achieved, then considerable investigation may be required before the proposed administrator is willing to provide a statement of opinion.

9.45   It is submitted that the court will probably construe para 18(3) and the objectives set out in para 3(1) in a disjunctive fashion, given that it refers to the single 'purpose' of the administration, which may be achieved by satisfying one of the objectives set out in para 3(1)(a)–(c), rather than referring to the objectives or one or more of the objectives set out in para 3 being achieved. This construction would be in keeping with the objectives of the EA 2002, by providing a low threshold for the appointment of an administrator out of court or the making of an administration order under para 11, whilst subjecting the appointed administrator to the obligation to attempt to achieve the objectives in a hierarchical fashion. However, if that is the correct construction, then the requirement for a statement of opinion from the administrator under para 18(3)(b) serves little practical purpose bar adding to the cost of the procedure. It will surely be rare for an administrator who is to be appointed by a lender to form the opinion that the limited objective contained in para 3(1)(c) is unlikely to be achieved.

---

35   It is understood the Rules are likely to be in accordance with this limited obligation on the proposed administrator and, that little investigatory work will be required. The statement is likely to be in a prescribed form which may simply have a box to be ticked confirming that the administrator believes that it is reasonably likely that the purpose of the administration will be achieved.

9.46   The proposed administrator will, of course, be concerned, in providing his statement of opinion, as to the possibility of an action for breach of statutory duty or negligence being brought against him by creditors or shareholders of the company, should the administration prove unsuccessful. This area is likely to be tested in the courts.

9.47   Given the possibility of challenge by disgruntled creditors prior to the interpretation of the EA 2002 being tested in the courts, it would be prudent for any administrator to record and retain notes as to the basis upon which the statement of opinion was formed.

Out-of-hours appointments

9.48   The time at which the notice of appointment under para 18 is filed at court is important because para 19 provides that the appointment of the administrator takes effect when the requirements of para 18 are satisfied. Thus, the administrator's powers can only be exercised after that time. Furthermore, the moratorium under para 43 applies when the company is 'in administration', which is defined in para 1(2) as being 'while the appointment of an administrator has effect'.

9.49   In addition, where a QFCH seeks to appoint an administrator and there is a prior qualifying floating charge, he must give 2 business days' written notice to that prior charge-holder. If the prior charge-holder does not consent (such that there can be an immediate appointment by the QFCH) and a notice of intention to appoint has to be served, then for the interim moratorium under para 44(2) to have effect, such notice of intention to appoint must be filed at court.

9.50   The question arises as to what happens where the lender seeks to make the appointment or give notice of intention to appoint an administrator outside the normal court hours. The situation will be covered by the Rules, which will probably provide a mechanism whereby:

(a) the lender may file a notice of appointment or notice of intention to appoint out of normal business hours;

(b) the notice will have to be faxed to a central fax machine (probably in the Royal Courts of Justice);

(c) the appointer will be required to ensure that a record of the time and date of the fax transmission is recorded;

(d) the appointment will take effect from the date and time indicated on the fax transmission report;

(e) the notice of appointment or intention to appoint will be required to specify the court to which the hard copies will be supplied and a copy of the fax transmission will be sent by the Court Service to that local court;

(f) the statutory declaration on the notice of appointment will include a statement that the appointer has in his possession all those documents required by the IA 1986 and IR 1986 for the making of the appointment;

(g) the appointer will be required to make a further statutory declaration confirming the details of the out-of-hours appointment, giving reasons for the filing of the same out of hours and an explanation as to why it would have been damaging to the company and/or its creditors to have waited until normal court business hours;

(h)   the appointer will be required to take a copy of the above statutory declaration, transmission report and other documents required under para 18 to the local court on the next business day that the court is open. If those requirements are not fulfilled within the time provided, then the appointment of the administator will cease to have effect.

COMMENCEMENT OF ADMINISTRATION

9.51   The appointment of the administrator out of court by the lender takes effect when the requirements for filing the notice of appointment and other documents under para 18 are complied with.[36]

9.52   The question arises as to what happens if the requirements of para 18 have not been complied with (eg a failure to include a statement of opinion by the administrator or statutory declaration or a failure to use the prescribed forms). If the formalities required by para 18 have not been complied with, is the purported appointment of the administrator of no effect?

9.53   Paragraph 18 must be read in conjunction with paras 21 and 104. Paragraph 21 sets out the power of the court to order an indemnity in favour of the purported administrator where 'the appointment is discovered to be *invalid*'. Paragraph 104 which is headed 'Presumption of validity' states that 'An act of the administrator of a company is valid in spite of a defect in his appointment or qualification'.

9.54   These provisions suggest a distinction between:

(a)   an invalid appointment where the purported appointment of the administrator is of no effect; and

(b)   an appointment where there has been some defect in the appointment or qualification of the administrator, where notwithstanding the defect, the appointment is effective.

A similar distinction was drawn in respect of the appointment of administrative receivers by IA 1986, ss 34 and 232.

9.55   It is submitted that, if the formality requirements of para 18 are not complied with strictly in accordance with para 18, there will be a defect in the appointment, but that such defect will not invalidate the appointment of the administrator. The administrator would, in those circumstances, be entitled to rely upon para 104 in respect of any challenge by a third party. If, however, the lender did not have power to appoint an administrator under para 14 or the debenture was void ab initio, then the purported appointment would not be valid or effective.[37] In that case, the administrator would be liable to the company as a trespasser.

---

36   IA 1986, Sch B1, para 19.
37   Cf the position of an administrative receiver: see Lightman & Moss *The Law of Receivers and Administrators of Companies*, 3rd edn (Sweet & Maxwell, 2000) paras 4–052, 4–056.

NOTIFICATION OF APPOINTMENT

9.56   The lender is required by para 20(a) to notify the administrator and prescribed persons[38] as soon as reasonably practicable after the relevant documents are filed under para 18. An offence is committed by the lender if there is a failure to so notify.[39]

INDEMNITY

9.57   If the appointment of the administrator by a lender under para 14 is invalid,[40] as distinct from defective, the court may order the lender to indemnify the person purportedly appointed as administrator against any liability which arises solely by reason of the appointment's invalidity.[41]

EFFECT OF ADMINISTRATOR APPOINTED BY LENDER

9.58   An administrator appointed by a lender out of court under para 14 is in exactly the same position as an administrator appointed by the court or by the company or its directors. He is an officer of the court[42] and must perform his functions with the objectives set out in para 3. The administrator owes a duty to the creditors as a whole and not just to the appointing lender.

9.59   The company is treated as 'in administration' while the appointment of an administrator has effect.[43] The moratoriums under paras 42 and 43 on insolvency proceedings and other legal process therefore bite. As regards any winding-up petition that has been issued but unheard by the time the appointment takes effect, such petition is suspended whilst an administrator appointed by a lender under para 14 is in office.[44] It should be noted that notwithstanding that the appointment of the administrator is made by the lender out of court, such appointment will cease to have effect at the end of the period of 1 year under para 76 of Sch B1 to IA 1986.

---

38   To be stated in the Rules – presumably such persons to include the Registrar of Companies and the company.
39   IA 1986, Sch B1, para 20(b).
40   As to which, see **8.51**.
41   IA 1986, Sch B1, para 21(2). The provision is similar to IA 1986, s 34 as regards invalid appointments of administrative receivers.
42   Ibid, para 5.
43   Ibid, para 1(2)(a).
44   Ibid, para 40(1)(a) – as opposed to the winding-up petition being dismissed where an administration order is made by the court.

Chapter 10

APPOINTMENT OF ADMINISTRATORS BY THE COMPANY OR DIRECTORS

'In a free society the State does not administer the affairs of men. It administers justice among men who conduct their own affairs.'

Walter Lipman[1]

INTRODUCTION

10.1   The EA 2002 seeks to make corporate rescue more flexible, less onerous and allows for out-of-court appointments. In essence, this means that the company or its directors can place the company into administration without a court hearing. In order to achieve recognition in Europe under the EC Regulation on Insolvency,[2] the new-style out-of-court administrator will be an officer of the court.

10.2   Directors or companies using the out-of-court route will need to give notice to any qualifying floating charge-holder (QFCH). There will be a notice period during which the QFCHs may either agree to the proposed appointment or appoint an alternative administrator, although the moratorium will take effect immediately the notice of intention is filed at court. If the QFCH does not respond to the notice of intention to appoint, the company's or directors' appointee will take office after the notice period has expired and a notice of appointment is filed at court.

10.3   The directors/company wishing to appoint an administrator will need to demonstrate that it is, or is likely to become, unable to pay its debts and that notice has been given to the QFCH and any others entitled to notice. Other creditors can only apply for administration through the courts.

10.4   The administrator takes office when the notice of appointment is filed with the court, identifying the administrator and including a statement from the administrator consenting to the appointment. Attached to this will be a statutory declaration stating that the application meets the necessary requirements.

10.5   There are limited anti-abuse provisions in that the out-of-court route will not be available to a company if the directors have put the company into

---

1   US editor and writer (1889–1974) *An Enquiry into the Principles of a Good Society.*
2   Council Regulation (EC) No 1346/2000 of 29 May 2000 on Insolvency Proceedings which came into force on 31 May 2002.

administration during the previous 12 months or it has been subject to a moratorium in respect of a failed CVA under Sch A1 to IA 1986 in the previous 12 months or if a winding-up petition has been presented or a winding-up order made or a resolution for voluntary winding-up has been passed.

EMERGENCE OF THE OUT-OF-COURT ROUTE

10.6   This is a radical new move. Whilst the provisions for out-of-court appointments by QFCHs are at least reminiscent of administrative receiverships, there has been no out-of-court remedy for the company or its directors which did not involve consultation with the unsecured creditors.

10.7   It is unsurprising, therefore, that the original proposals of the Government did not include 'out-of-court appointments'. Instead, those original proposals were for a court-based administration procedure with a new concept, the 'interim administrator', to cater for urgent applications, pre-packaged sales, etc. In this way, the idea was that the private and out-of-court appointments of administrative receivers (ie by banks and other secured lenders under their security) would be replaced by new-look administrations commenced by court proceedings – the private appointment for private purposes would be replaced by a collective court process. Commentators and consultees reacted to the White Paper by suggesting that the courts would not cope with such a workload. It was said that the floodgates would open, paralysing the courts' lists.

10.8   The point was made forcefully in the House of Commons during the second reading of the Bill on 10 April 2002. However, by that time, the opposition had failed to notice that the Bill as published contained provisions for out-of-court appointments. The Minister, Melanie Johnson, responded:[3]

> '[Concerns have been] raised about the work load in the courts. I reassure the House that the intention in company insolvencies is to disengage from active involvement of the courts except in cases where there is dispute or complexity ... in future, both floating charge holders and the company itself will be able to appoint an administrator without a court hearing. The administrator will have extensive powers to deal with cases quickly without reference to the courts.'

10.9   The principle is that nothing which the company or directors may achieve out of court should prejudice the holder of a floating charge. In the House of Lords, the Minister, Lord McIntosh, summarised the position as follows:

> 'A company has to give five days' notice to floating charge holders before appointing an administrator. That allows the floating charge holder the opportunity to appoint his own choice of administrator if he so decides. Before appointing, the floating charge holder will have to give notice to the holder of any prior charges.'

---

3   10 April 2002, col 114.

THE COMPANY OR ITS DIRECTORS RESOLVE TO APPOINT OUT OF COURT

10.10   Where it is the company seeking to appoint an administrator, a resolution in a general meeting will be required. Alternatively, the consent of all shareholders should be given before the appointment process is started. Where the directors seek an appointment, they should be careful to ensure that a resolution of the board is passed. If this cannot be achieved by securing a formal resolution of the board of directors, then the agreement of all directors should be obtained prior to the commencement of the appointment process. Once a resolution has been passed, all the directors will be under a duty to take all necessary steps to give effect to the resolution. After the resolution, any one director will have the authority to implement the appointment process on behalf of all directors.[4]

THE TWO-STAGE PROCESS

10.11   In general, there are two stages to the out-of-court appointment process. The exception arises where there is no person entitled to appoint an administrative receiver or where there is no QFCH. In these circumstances, the requirements of para 28 to Sch B1 do not apply and, save for ensuring that a statutory declaration that complies with para 27 can be made, stage one is obviated.[5]

10.12   In all other circumstances, the appointee, after the necessary resolutions have been passed, must serve a notice of intention to appoint an administrator. After a period of time has elapsed and a notice of appointment has been served on all relevant parties, including the court, an appointment may take effect.

Stage one

10.13   A notice of intention has to be served on:

(a) the court;[6]

(b) any person who is entitled to appoint an administrative receiver under an old charge or by reason of one of the exceptions set out in EA 2002, ss 72B–72G;[7]

(c) any and all qualifying floating charge-holders and any other person who may be prescribed by the Rules.[8]

10.14   The Rules are likely to include a requirement to serve:

(a) any sheriff charged with execution or other legal process against the company;

---

4   *Re Equiticorp International plc* [1989] BCLC 597.
5   IA 1986, Sch B1, para 30.
6   Ibid, para 27(1). The requirement is to serve the court as soon as is reasonably possible.
7   Ibid, para 26(1).
8   Ibid, para 26(2).

(b) any person who, to the applicant's knowledge, has distrained against the company or its property; and

(c) the directors and company itself (whichever is not making the appointment).

10.15   The notice of intention to appoint must be in the prescribed form and must identify who the proposed administrator will be.[9] The prescribed form will alleviate difficulties of form and enable compliance. The disclosure of the proposed administrator allows the QFCH to make an informed decision as to whether or not to oppose the application. A period of notice has to elapse before the second of the two stages. The period of notice is specified to be a minimum of 5 *business* days. The period is intended to strike a balance between the need to allow a person notified to take stock and decide what to do on the one hand and allow for an appointment to take place quickly on the other.

10.16   The company or its directors are under an obligation to file a copy of the notice of intention to appoint *as soon as is reasonably practicable* together with any document accompanying it[10] and a statutory declaration.[11] It is anticipated that the documents will include either a resolution of the company which agreed to appoint the administrator (where it is the company that is making the appointment) or a copy of the minutes from the meeting recording the decision of the directors to appoint (where the appointment is made by the directors).

10.17   The accompanying statutory declaration must state:

'(a) that the company is or is likely to become unable to pay its debts,

(b) that the company is not in liquidation, and

(c) that so far as the person making the application is able to ascertain, the appointment is not prevented by paragraphs 23 to 25 [to Schedule B1], and

(d) to such additional effect, and giving such information, as may be prescribed.'[12]

10.18   It is anticipated that the person who makes the statutory declaration should be the same person who completes the notice of intention to appoint. It is important that the information contained in the statutory declaration is as up to date as possible. In order to achieve this, it will have to be made within a short period before filing. It is thought that an appropriate period would be no more than 5 days before the notice of intention is filed at court.

10.19   The requirement to state that the company is, or is likely to become, unable to pay its debts is peculiar to an appointment made by the company or its directors. A QFCH does not have to make such a declaration but, in contrast, has to declare that the debenture relied on in making the appointment is (or was) enforceable on the date of the appointment.[13]

10.20   The EA 2002 provides that it is an offence to make a false statutory declaration, or make a declaration which the maker does not reasonably believe

---

9   IA 1986, para 26(3)(a) and (b).

10   Ibid, Sch B1, para 27(1)(b).

11   Ibid, para 27(2).

12   Ibid, para 27(2).

13   Ibid, para 18(2)(c).

to be true.[14] It is uncertain how the courts will determine the test for the defence (reasonably believing the statutory declaration to be true) to a false (inaccurate) statutory declaration. It may be that the courts will apply (what is known as) an objective/subjective test. If the declaration is false, the party signing the declaration will have to show that he reasonably believed its contents to be true and accurate. In making the determination the court may have regard to the basis upon which be believed the document to be accurate and not false. If no reasonable person with his knowledge and armed with the information he had at the time would have signed the declaration stating the contents to be true then the court will be likely to find against him.

10.21   Reference may be made to the common-law test involved for recovery of misdirected funds in the field of dishonest accessory liability. In that context, the House of Lords[15] has recently decided that the test for dishonesty is an objective/subjective test identical to that applicable in criminal law in *R v Ghosh*:[16] was the conduct dishonest by the ordinary standards of reasonable and honest people and was the defendant aware that what he was doing was dishonest by those standards?

The interim period and the moratorium

10.22   In general, there will be an interim period of 5 working days between stage one and stage two. During this time, the floating charge-holders will be able to make a decision as to whether or not they consent to the proposed appointment. Thus, the floating charge-holder may give express consent within 5 business days of service of the notice. It is anticipated that many floating charge-holders will not reply within this period. The process should not fail for want of a response so, in these circumstances, consent will be presumed.

10.23   Although the obligation on the company or its directors is to file the various stage one documents mentioned above as soon as reasonably practicable, it will be important to file as soon as possible. This is because an interim moratorium is imposed as soon as the notice of intention is filed with the court under para 27(1) to Sch B1.[17]

10.24   It is intriguing that an out-of-court appointment can have such a far-reaching effect on proceedings in court. As appears in Chapter 11, the effect of the interim moratorium will be that:

(a)   no resolution may be passed for the winding-up of the company;
(b)   no order may be made for the winding-up of the company;[18]
(c)   no step may be taken to enforce a security over the company's property;
(d)   no step may be taken to repossess goods in the company's possession under a hire-purchase agreement;
(e)   a landlord may not exercise a right of forfeiture by peaceable re-entry in relation to premises let to the company; and

---

14   IA 1986, para 27(4)(a) and (b).
15   *Twinsectra v Yardley* [2002] 2 All ER 377.
16   [1982] QB 1053.
17   IA 1986, Sch B1, para 44(4) – for a detailed discussion on the moratorium.
18   Ibid, para 42.

(f) no legal process may be instituted or continued against the company or property.[19]

10.25   There is no doubt that there is scope for abuse here and equally no doubt that the court will have jurisdiction to restrain in an appropriate case a threatened use of the out-of-court procedure for a collateral purpose. An interim moratorium will not provide protection from a hostile winding-up petition where it is presented on public interest grounds[20] or pursuant to the Financial Services and Markets Act 2000.[21] Further, the administrator (when appointed) or the court may give permission to any creditor seeking to enforce security or quasi-security rights (such as a hire-purchase agreement or landlord covenants) or to a creditor wishing to continue any other legal process. The prohibition on a landlord to exercise a right of forfeiture is consistent with s 9 of the Insolvency Act 2000 which amended ss 10 and 11 of IA 1986, bringing the restriction within the list of court-controlled actions.

10.26   The date that the notice of intention is filed with the court is important for another reason. The ability of a company or its directors to appoint an out-of-court administrator is limited in time. To be effective, the duration of the interim moratorium will last until the appointment of an out-of-court administrator takes place but, if an appointment has not taken place within 10 *business* days from the date of filing a notice of intention, an administrator cannot be appointed and the interim moratorium will lapse.[22] This is a strict time-limit. If no appointment takes place within 10 business days, the company or its directors will have to start the procedure again by re-serving a notice of intention to appoint and will have to make fresh declarations.

10.27   It follows from the above that an appointment may not be made unless a notice of intention to appoint has been properly served and filed, the prescribed 5 days' notice has elapsed, and the necessary documents have been filed with the court within 10 business days.[23] The exception to the expiration of the 5-day rule is where each person to whom notice has been given under para 26(1) of Sch B1 has consented in writing to the making of the appointment.[24]

Stage two

10.28   The second stage of the appointment process has procedural similarities to the first. The company or its directors have to file with the court the following documents:

(a) a notice of appointment;
(b) such other documents as may be prescribed;[25] and
(c) a statutory declaration.[26]

---

19   IA 1986, para 43.
20   Ibid, s 124A.
21   Financial Services and Markets Act 2000, s 367.
22   IA 1986, Sch B1, para 28(2).
23   Ibid, para 28(1).
24   Paragraph 30 expressly states that para 28 does not apply.
25   IA 1986, Sch B1, para 29(1)(a) and (b).
26   Ibid, para 29(2).

10.29   The appointment will take effect from the date and time that the notice of appointment is filed (ie stamped) at the court. The notice of appointment must be in the prescribed form and identify the administrator. Again, the prescribed form is intended to add ease to the procedure. The notice has to be accompanied by a statement from the administrator:

(a) stating that he consents to the appointment;
(b) stating the purpose of the administration is likely to be achieved; and
(c) providing any other information that may be prescribed.[27]

10.30   The first requirement needs no further discussion. As regards the second requirement, how far the administrator will have to inquire or investigate in order to satisfy himself that the purpose of the administration can be achieved is an open question. It is expected that most out-of-court administrators will only be invited to act shortly before a notice of intention to appoint is served – the restricted time-frame will, itself, preclude a proposed administrator from being fully informed about the affairs of the company.

10.31   There can be little doubt that the legislature intended a proposed out-of-court administrator to make brief inquiries only, thereby enabling appointments to be made quickly and cost-efficiently. To assist the proposed administrator, the EA 2002 provides that he will usually be entitled to rely upon information provided by the directors of the company.[28] Nevertheless, the administrator's reliance cannot be blind. If he has reason to believe that the information provided by the company or its director(s) is inaccurate, he will not be entitled to rely upon it.[29] When making his statement, an insolvency practitioner should have regard to the comments made by Jacob J in *Re Colt Telecom Group plc*[30] regarding his duty to consider any conflict of interest and state the basis on which he forms any opinion.

10.32   The statutory declaration has to be made by the person appointing (whether that be the company or the directors) and within the prescribed period.[31] The purpose of this declaration is to provide the court with evidence that the appointment has been properly made and is in accordance with the statutory requirements. This compliance declaration must include the following:[32]

(a) that the company or its directors (whoever appoints) is entitled to appoint;
(b) that the appointment is in accordance with Sch B1 to EA 2002;
(c) that, as far as the person appointing can ascertain, the statements made and information given in the statutory declaration filed with the notice of intention to appoint remain accurate.[33]

10.33   Where there is no person who has to be served with a notice of intention (ie no person entitled to appoint an administrative receiver and no

---

27   IA 1986, para 29(3).
28   Ibid, Sch B1, para 29(4).
29   Ibid, para 29(4).
30   [2002] EWHC 2815.
31   IA 1986, Sch B1, para 29(6).
32   Ibid, para 29(2).
33   Ibid, para 27(2).

QFCH) the appointee will not be able to declare that the statements made and information filed with the notice of intention was and remains accurate for the simple reason that he does not have to serve a notice of intention. Instead, the appointee only files a notice of appointment at court together with a statutory declaration stating that the application meets the criteria set out in para 27.

10.34   Once the above documents have been filed with the court by the appointee and the notice of appointment has been sealed, the administrator and such other person as may be prescribed must be informed as soon as reasonably practicable that the requirements of para 29 are satisfied. The person appointing commits an offence if he fails to comply with this requirement.[34]

10.35   The EA 2002 provides that it is an offence to make a false statement in the compliance declaration in the same way as it is an offence if a false statement is made in the statutory declaration that accompanies the notice of intention to appoint.[35] The same defence is available.

10.36   If, for any reason, the para 22 out-of-court appointment is discovered to be invalid, the court may make an order that the person appointing indemnify the proposed administrator.[36]

ANTI-ABUSE PROVISIONS

10.37   The limited anti-abuse provisions restrict the ability of the company or its directors from appointing an administrator in the following circumstances:

(a)   where the company has been in administration or subject to a moratorium in respect of a failed company voluntary arrangement (under Sch A1 to IA 1986) during the preceding 12 months;[37]

(b)   when it is unable to show that it is or is likely to become unable to pay its debts as they fall due;[38]

(c)   when the company is subject to an outstanding winding-up petition;[39]

(d)   when the company is in liquidation;[40]

(e)   where there is an administration application which is not yet disposed of;[41] or

(f)   where an administrative receiver is in office.[42]

SUBORDINATION

10.38   The power of the company or its directors to appoint an out-of-court administrator is subordinated to the power given to a QFCH. If a QFCH rejects

---

34   IA 1986, para 32(b).
35   Ibid, Sch B1, para 29(7).
36   Ibid, para 34.
37   Ibid, paras 23(2) and 24.
38   Ibid, para 27(2)(a).
39   Ibid, para 25(a).
40   Ibid, para 25(2)(b).
41   Ibid, para 25(b).
42   Ibid, para 25(c).

the proposed administrator within the 5 days between stage one and stage two, the company or its directors will not be able to make a valid appointment and the rules relating to notification will not take effect. Further, a QFCH may appoint its own administrator (without recourse to the court) at any time before the requirements of para 29 are satisfied.[43] The effect of such an appointment will be to trump the company/directors' attempt to appoint an administrator.

10.39   The power of a company or its directors to appoint using the court process is also subordinated to a QFCH which may intervene in the court proceedings and seek to appoint its own specified insolvency practitioner as administrator. Where the QFCH intervenes, the onus will be on the company or its directors to persuade the court that it is not right to appoint the person specified by the QFCH. It is expected that this would be a reasonably difficult hurdle for the company or its directors to jump. Further, a creditors' meeting may seek to substitute an administrator appointed by the company or its directors.[44]

CONCLUSION

10.40   Directors and companies will welcome their new ability to appoint an administrator of their choice without making an application to the court. If appointed, a company/director-nominated administrator may be more susceptible to giving consent to the directors to exercise management powers (Sch B1, para 64). The ability to appoint is not without its difficulties and subject to the greater right of a QFCH to appoint its specified insolvency practitioner, defeating the company/director application. Furthermore, the strict time-limits will have to be observed.

10.41   In the long term, it is hoped that the interaction between these powers of the company/directors and those superior powers of the floating chargeholder will result in less hostile appointments as the various interested parties are given notice and consult.

---

43   IA 1986, para 33.
44   Ibid, Sch B1, para 97.

Chapter 11

EFFECT OF ADMINISTRATION

'For this relief much thanks. 'Tis bitter cold, And I am sick at heart.'
William Shakespeare[1]

INTRODUCTION

11.1   The most commonly used description of the old administration procedure was that it operated as a 'breathing-space'. The analogy was appropriate in that the company was allowed to 'breathe' for a short period by virtue of the support given by a statutory moratorium imposed on its advancing creditors. Under the old procedure, administration was merely a 'gateway' to another insolvency process (usually either a CVA and/or liquidation) from which, eventually, an insolvent company would go to its long home. Now, there are 'stand-alone' elements to the revamped administrations. So, for instance, there will be many cases where it will be clear from the proposals (or even from the outset) that it will be intended that the company should pass directly from administration to dissolution or that a very short formal liquidation should take place at the end of the administration. In such cases, it is not apt to regard the administration simply as a 'breathing space' between distress and a full-blown insolvency process. It is not difficult to envisage circumstances in which the court might more readily lift the statutory moratorium in such cases. Perhaps an important issue will be *when* to lift the moratorium rather than *whether* to do so. The relevance of these considerations is that some of the jurisprudence which has developed in relation to the statutory moratorium under the old scheme for administrations will not necessarily apply to the new model introduced by the EA 2002. The points raised and comments made in this chapter ought to be read in that context, namely that the 'effect' of the moratorium is broadly similar under the old and new schemes (ie creditors' rights outside of the scheme are frozen), but the circumstances in which the court might lift the moratorium and bless proceedings or other enforcement by a particular creditor or creditors are likely to differ in some cases.

11.2   That said, the statutory moratorium still creates a procedural bar on enforcement of claims against the company by its creditors for the purpose of facilitating a rescue or preservation of value. Without it, the administration procedure would be of little use in the majority of cases in which the creditors

---

1   *Hamlet* 1:1.

would indulge in a free-for-all and destroy or diminish the value of the business before it could be rescued.

11.3   The moratorium is one of the key differences between administrative receivership and administration. In administrative receivership, the appointing debenture-holder does not need a moratorium because the appointment itself is a private act and the floating charge has crystallised with the result that the assets on appointment belong in equity to the debenture-holder (in other words, they are no longer available to the other creditors in a free-for-all).

11.4   As we have seen, the appointment of an administrative receiver will not be an available remedy in respect of floating charges created after the coming into force of the relevant provisions of the EA 2002. Therefore, in the vast majority of cases where there is no pre-commencement floating charge, the only formal rescue procedure available will be the 'new-look' administration.[2]

11.5   There are many differences between the old and the new administration regimes, but the statutory moratorium is retained largely in the same form. This is reinforced by the policy of using the same – or at least very similar – statutory language as that used in the old provisions of the IA 1986. Nevertheless, there are significant changes to the definitions of the freezing mechanisms and, to take account of the fact that there will now be out-of-court appointments, the events that trigger the moratoriums have changed. Equally, it is foreseeable that the new ability to trigger a moratorium without a court order might be abused and that a creditor wishing to enforce against a company might well apply for an injunction to restrain out-of-court appointments which are designed to freeze creditors' rights for a foreign or collateral purpose.

The moratorium when the company is 'in administration'

11.6   The moratorium applies when the company is 'in administration'; this is deemed to take effect when the administrator is appointed. In the case of an appointment by the company or the directors, the appointment takes effect when the requirements set out in para 29 are met.[3] Where the administrator is appointed out of court by the qualifying floating charge-holder ('QFCH'), the appointment takes effect when the requirements set out in para 18 are met.[4]

11.7   The new route to administration, the out-of-court appointment by the QFCH is, by its nature, not subject to the court process and therefore it will be vital to be able to ascertain precisely when a company is deemed to have entered into administration. The court has the power to order an indemnity in favour of the administrator against the appointer in the event that the appointment of the administrator is deemed to be invalid.[5]

---

2   It is assumed that the new, improved CVA route under the IA 2000 will not usually be attractive or practicable in most cases.
3   IA 1986, Sch B1, para 31.
4   Ibid, para 19.
5   Ibid, para 21. However, the acts of the administrator may be deemed to be valid in spite of a formal defect in appointment.

11.8 These formalities could present problems for a QFCH who was seeking to appoint an administrator out of court hours, for example, late on a Friday afternoon or over a weekend. It has now been confirmed that the forthcoming Insolvency Rules will provide that there will be a dedicated central fax number to which the details of the appointment may be sent. The acknowledgement which then follows will incorporate the date and time of receipt, such information representing the date and time of appointment.[6]

THE EXTENT OF THE MORATORIUM

11.9 The new provisions that deal with the effect of the administration replace in their entirety the former ss 10 and 11 of IA 1986, and are now to be found in paras 40–45 of Sch B1. They are similar to the previous provisions and they provide for:

(a) dismissal of pending winding-up petitions;[7]
(b) dismissal of administrative or other receiver;[8]
(c) moratorium on insolvency proceedings;[9]
(d) moratorium on other legal process;[10] and
(e) interim moratorium.[11]

WHEN DOES THE INTERIM MORATORIUM APPLY?

11.10 The interim moratorium applies pending the company going into administration. More specifically, it applies:

(a) when an administration application has been made but not yet granted or dismissed;[12]
(b) when an application has been granted, but the administration order has not yet taken effect;[13]
(c) where the notice of intention is filed by the QFCH, from the time the copy of the notice of intent to appoint has been filed until either the appointment of the administrator takes effect, or 5 business days elapse without the administrator having been appointed;[14]
(d) where the notice of intention is filed by the company or its directors, from the time the copy of the notice of intent to appoint has been filed until either the appointment of the administrator takes effect, or 10 business days elapse without the administrator having been appointed.[15]

---

6   This was announced by the Government during the passage of the debate in the Lords: *Hansard* (HL), 21 October 2002, col 1112.
7   IA 1986, Sch B1, para 40.
8   Ibid, para 41.
9   Ibid, para 42.
10 Ibid, para 43.
11 Ibid, para 44.
12 Ibid, para 44(1)(a).
13 Ibid, para 44(1)(b).
14 Ibid, para 44(2), when required to do so by para 15.
15 Ibid, para 44(4).

11.11   During the relevant interim period, the provisions of para 42 (imposing a moratorium on insolvency proceedings) and para 43 (imposing a moratorium on other legal processes) automatically apply and the creditors' rights are frozen as against the company.[16] If, however, an administrative receiver is already in place, then the interim moratoriums do not apply until the person on whose behalf the receiver was appointed has consented to the making of the administration order[17] and thereby indicated his support for the administration process.

11.12   The reason for this is clear. It stops an applicant invoking the protection of the interim moratorium and preventing the creditors from exercising their rights in circumstances where there is no real prospect of the administration becoming effective because of the failure to obtain the consent of the pre-commencement debenture-holder. It preserves the rights of the charge-holder. This is the same as the effect of s 10(3) of the old IA 1986.

11.13   The old s 10(2) allowed a creditor to present a winding-up petition after the presentation of the petition for an administration order, but before the order was made or dismissed. The reasoning was that a winding-up petition was a class remedy that was designed to protect the general body of creditors. This express provision has been omitted from the new Act and the moratorium on instituting legal processes, as provided by para 43(6), now prevents a creditor from pursuing this course of action.

11.14   By way of compensation for the removal of this right, the court has the power to treat the administration application as a winding-up petition under para 13(1)(e)[18] without the need for a winding-up petition having first been filed. This is an innovation introduced by the new provisions. Previously, the court could only make a winding-up order where a petition had been presented.[19] A creditor may be given permission[20] to make such an application at the hearing of the application for an administration order. In accordance with many elements of the new administration regime, this new power is intended to speed the process up and reduce costs by removing unnecessary procedural formalities and the need for further hearings.

11.15   Under the old law, if a winding-up petition was presented under s 10(2), but the administration order (for whatever reason) was not granted, the commencement of the liquidation was back-dated to the date of the filing of the winding-up petition,[21] thus preserving those remedies available to the liquidator that were dependent upon the date of the presentation of the winding-up petition.[22] Under the new para 13(1)(e), the winding-up order will be deemed effective as at the date upon which the administration order was made.[23]

---

16   IA 29086, Sch B1, para 44(5).
17   Ibid, para 44(6).
18   IA 1986, Sch B1. This may be done of the court's own motion.
19   IA 1986, s 124.
20   IR 1986, r 2.9(1), which will probably be carried across in the new rules.
21   IA 1986, s 129(2).
22   For example, transactions at an undervalue, preferences, avoidance of floating charges and property dispositions post-petition.
23   IA 1986, s 129(1A), inserted by EA 2002, Sch 17, para 16.

11.16   However, none of the statutory moratoriums operates to prevent:

(a) the presentation of a winding-up petition under s 124A of IA 1986 (a petition in the public interest);[24]
(b) the presentation of a winding-up petition under s 367 of the Financial Services and Markets Act 2000 (a petition by the Financial Services Authority);[25]
(c) the appointment of an administrator by a QFCH;[26]
(d) the appointment of an administrative receiver of the company;[27] or
(e) the carrying out by an administrative receiver (whenever appointed) of his functions.[28]

It will be noted that none of these actions requires the permission of the court.

MORATORIUM ON INSOLVENCY PROCEEDINGS WHILST THE COMPANY IS 'IN ADMINISTRATION'

11.17   Whilst a company is 'in administration':[29]

(a) no resolution may be passed for the winding-up of the company;[30]
(b) no order may be made for the winding-up of the company[31] save on the hearing of:

  – a winding-up petition presented under s 124A of IA 1986 (a petition in the public interest);[32] or
  – a winding-up petition presented under s 367 of the Financial Services and Markets Act 2000 (a petition by the Financial Services Authority).[33]

If a public-interest petition is presented or the Financial Services Authority presents a petition and this comes to the attention of the administrator, the administrator must apply to the court for directions.[34]

---

24 IA 1986, Sch B1, para 44(7)(a).
25 Ibid.
26 IA 1986, Sch B1, para 14, pursuant to IA 1986, Sch B1, para 44(7)(b).
27 Ibid, para 44(7)(c).
28 Ibid, para 43(7)(d).
29 Ibid, para 42. As referred to at **10.5**, this is applicable whilst an interim moratorium is in place: IA 1986, Sch B1, para 44(5).
30 Ibid, para 42(2). This covers both creditors' and members' voluntary liquidation: *Re Paramount Airways Ltd* [1990] BCC 130; *Biosource Technologies Inc v Axis Genetics plc (in administration)* [2000] 1 BCLC 286.
31 IA 1986, Sch B1, para 42(3).
32 IA 1986, Sch B1, para 42(4)(a).
33 Ibid, para 42(4)(b).
34 Ibid, paras 42(5) and 63. As referred to at **10.5**, this is applicable whilst an interim moratorium is in place: IA 1986, Sch B1, para 44(5).

MORATORIUM ON OTHER LEGAL PROCESSES

11.18   Whilst a company is 'in administration',[35] except with the consent of the administrator or the permission of the court:

(a)   no step may be taken to enforce security over the company's property;[36]
(b)   no step may be taken to repossess goods in the company's possession under a hire-purchase agreement;[37]
(c)   a landlord[38] may not exercise a right of forfeiture by peaceable re-entry in relation to premises let to the company;[39] and
(d)   no legal process[40] (including legal proceedings, execution, distress and diligence) may be instituted or continued against the company or property of the company.[41]

These follow the old provisions of ss 10 and 11 of IA 1986. The wording of this new provision is more straightforward and it will hopefully be easier to comprehend and apply.

EFFECT ON A PENDING WINDING-UP PETITION

11.19   Upon the making of an administration order, a petition for the winding-up of the company shall be dismissed.[42] However, upon the appointment of an administrator out of court by a QFCH under s 14, the winding-up petition is merely suspended.[43] The 'suspension' of a winding-up petition is novel; the reasoning behind its introduction is that a creditor may not extinguish the class remedy by a unilateral act.

11.20   The concept of suspending the winding-up petition was introduced as a safeguard against abuse of the out-of-court appointment process. Clearly, there is potential scope for manipulation of the appointment process by those who wish to gain the protection offered by the moratoriums for purposes contrary to those expressed in the Act.

11.21   For example, following the presentation of a winding-up petition to the court, a director (who is also the QFCH) could appoint an administrator out of court, activating the moratoriums. It is, of course, open to the creditors to apply to the court to discharge the administration order. As the winding-up

---

35   Or whilst an interim moratorium is in place: IA 1986, Sch B1, para 44(5).
36   IA 1986, Sch B1, para 43(2).
37   Ibid, para 43(3). This has an extended meaning and includes a conditional sale agreement, a chattel leasing agreement and a retention of title agreement: IA 1986, Sch B1, para 111(1).
38   This includes any person to whom rent is payable: IA 1986, Sch B1, para 43(8).
39   IA 1986, Sch B1, para 43(4).
40   This is construed widely, covering arbitration (*Re Paramount Airways Ltd* [1990] BCC 130), adjudication proceedings under the Housing Grants Construction and Regeneration Act 1986 (*A Straume (UK) Ltd v Bradlor Developments Ltd* [2000] BCC 333) and criminal proceedings under the Environmental Protection Act 1990 (*Environment Agency v Clark* [2000] BCC 653).
41   IA 1986, Sch B1, para 43(6).
42   IA 1986, Sch B1, para 40(1)(a).
43   Ibid, para 40(1)(b).

petition is only suspended, the court can terminate the administration and move straight to winding-up without further delay and costs. The ease with which the court can oversee a jumping of horses can also be seen in the streamlined exit routes introduced for creditors' voluntary liquidation and dissolution.[44]

11.22   There may well be a delay between the out-of-court appointment and the subsequent winding-up of a company and, thus, there are provisions to validate any disposition of property by the administrator during this period. The EA 2002 amends IA 1986, s 127[45] so that it does not apply in respect of anything done by the administrator of a company whilst the winding-up petition is suspended.

11.23   However, the EA 2002 does not make any reference to the manner in which dispositions that are entered into between the presentation of the winding-up petition and the appointment of the administrator are to be treated in the event that the court subsequently makes a winding-up order on the previously suspended winding-up petition. No doubt the court will be required either to validate the dispositions retrospectively (whether in whole or in part) or, possibly, to disapply the effect of s 127 in relation to such dispositions.

VACATION OF OFFICE BY ADMINISTRATIVE OR OTHER RECEIVER

11.24   When an administration order takes effect,[46] any administrative receiver of the company shall vacate office.[47] This is a mandatory consequence of the making of an administration order. Any other receiver of the company shall vacate office if required to do so by the administrator.[48] This provision is couched in the same terms as that providing for the dismissal of the administrative receiver.

11.25   In either case, the remuneration of the person vacating office shall be charged on and paid out of the property of the company that was in his custody or control immediately before he vacated office.[49] Remuneration includes expenses properly incurred and any indemnity to which he is entitled.[50] Importantly for the receiver vacating office, the express provision that the charge for his remuneration has priority over the security held by the person on whose behalf he was appointed is preserved,[51] although such payment is subject to the moratorium imposed by para 43. Upon vacating office in these circumstances, the administrative receiver and receiver are released from having to take any

---

44   The members also have the option to apply to the court to discharge the administration order.
45   IA 1986 by EA 2002, Sch 17, para 15.
46   Ie according to the terms of the order itself (contrast **9.51**).
47   IA 1986, Sch B1, para 41(1).
48   Ibid, para 41(2).
49   Ibid, para 41(3)(a).
50   Ibid, para 41(4)(a).
51   Ibid, para 41(4)(b).

further steps under ss 40 and 59 of IA 1986 (duties to pay preferential creditors).[52]

PAYMENT BY ADMINISTRATORS FOR USE OF GOODS OR PREMISES

11.26 The former moratorium provisions gave no guidance as to the circumstances in which a secured creditor (including, for example, a landlord or an owner under a hire-purchase agreement) might be given leave to repossess his goods or property. Often such a creditor will be content simply to receive payment for use of his property during the administration period.

11.27 The former provisions were silent on how to approach this question. A practice grew up which involved the creditor applying to court for leave to repossess in the hope and expectation that the court would refuse leave, but on terms that the administrator should meet the payments accruing for use of the property *during* the administration. This was unsatisfactory – not least of all because it gave rise to uncertainty and often necessitated a court application. Each side might accuse the other of adopting a ransom position. Attempts were made to introduce clauses during the passage of the Bill to render the position more certain.

11.28 First, there was an amendment tabled during the Committee debates in the Commons during the afternoon on 9 May 2002. The Government was asked to consider the introduction of the following proposed new clause suggested by the Finance and Leasing Association:

> 'Where the goods are used by the administrator to continue running the business, the administrator must make payments to the owner of the goods under the terms of the hire-purchase agreement.'

10.29 The rationale for this proposal was expressed by the opposition as follows:

> '. . . if the administrator is using goods under a hire purchase agreement – a company might hire equipment to produce its goods, vans for distribution and so on – the owner of the goods should continue to receive payment under the terms of the agreement. The administrator should not delay disposing of the goods if they are not in use and payments are not being made under the agreement. The amendment is designed to reflect the ruling in the case involving Atlantic Computer Systems plc in 1992. The Minister will be familiar with its terms and will be able to tell us about it. The point needs to be made clear in the Bill, and that is the purpose of the amendment...The market value of equipment will not in all cases compensate the lender for the goods on hire. The re-hire value is often worth more than the market value and where the equipment is still within its basic life expectancy, the lender will seek to re-hire in order to capitalise on its investment. The court should be able to use its discretion in such cases, hence the amendment.'

11.30 The Government spokesman of the day, Douglas Alexander, responded that the amendment:

---

52   IA 1986, Sch B1, para 41(3)(b).

'[The proposed amendment] would provide that where the administrator used hire purchase goods in order to continue running the business, he or she would have to make payments to the owner of the goods under the terms of the hire purchase agreement. However, that situation is better dealt with by existing provisions in insolvency law, which have been incorporated into the schedule. If the owner of the goods is not being paid for their use, paragraph 41(3) provides that he or she may ask the administrator to return them; if that is not granted, he or she may go to court to seek permission to repossess the goods.

Case-law sets out a number of principles for the courts to follow in deciding such cases; in particular, administration for the benefit of unsecured creditors should not be conducted at the expense of those who have proprietary rights over goods. But the courts are also required to weigh the legitimate interests of the owner of the goods against those of the company's other creditors. In doing so, they should take into account, among other things, the prospects for the success of the administration. We want the courts to continue to be free to carry out this balancing act on a case-by-case basis.'

11.31 The proposed amendment of the Finance and Leasing Association was rejected. The question was subsequently re-visited in the House of Lords. The point was raised and rejected in Committee and then again during the debate on 20 October 2002 when Lord Hunt for the opposition introduced the following proposed provision:

'Where the goods are used by the administrator to continue running the business, the administrator must make payments to the owner of the goods under the terms of the hire-purchase agreement.'

11.32 Lord Hunt explained:

'If the administrator uses any goods under a hire purchase or lease agreement the owner of the goods should continue to receive payment under the terms of the agreement. The administrator should not delay disposing of the goods if they are not in use and payments are not being made under the agreement. The amendment reflects the ruling in *Re Atlantic Computer Systems plc (1)* [1992] 1 All ER 476. On the face of the Bill that will bring clarity to administrators and lenders.'

Lord McIntosh gave[53] the Government's reasons for rejecting the clause as follows:

'I understand the concerns of the Finance and Leasing Association. We have considered carefully the views expressed to us, but as I explained in Committee, the Government do not want to amend the current legislation. Clearly, where assets that are subject to such an agreement continue to be used during the administration, the hire purchase companies would suffer a loss through lack of payment during that period. But the purpose of administration is to provide a breathing space in which to put forward rescue proposals or proposals for improving the outcome for creditors. It would not be right to allow such proposals to fail as a result of a legal requirement to continue making payments of this kind throughout such a breathing space, as suggested by Amendment No 220.

The Bill as drafted does not make a change in the existing law. It replicates existing provisions whereby it falls to the courts to resolve the difficult act of balancing the

---

53 *Hansard* (HL), 21 October 2002, col 1119.

interests of the hire purchase creditor, and their need for continuing payments, and the interests of the general body of creditors which requires that the breathing space is sufficient for workable proposals to be developed and implemented.

We believe that existing case law on the ability of creditors to enforce their rights during the moratorium will continue to be fully relevant to the hire purchase provision in the revised administration procedure. It remains the Government's view that the courts are best placed to resolve such matters on a case-by-case basis, taking full and proper account of the facts of each case.'

11.33   This was an opportunity missed. On each occasion, the Government's objection was justified because the proposed amendments sought to introduce a new *right* to be paid. This would have created a super-priority for the leasing creditors and landlords and others within the administration. What was required was a statutory set of criteria to be taken into account by an administrator when considering whether to make payment and, if so, how much. In fact, as appears below, the problem might have been eased indirectly by creating wider powers to make payments.

WIDER POWERS TO MAKE PAYMENTS DURING THE MORATORIUM

11.34   As has already been mentioned, a creditor who continues to supply during the administration or whose property or goods are used for the purpose of the administration will seek payments from the administrator. In para 66 of the new Sch B1 to EA 2002 re-phrases the administrator's powers to make payments. On first reading, it would appear to extend the former power as provided pursuant to para 13 of Sch 1 to IA 1986. Paragraph 13 of Sch 1 was couched in objective terms:

'Power to make any payment which is necessary or incidental to the performance of his functions.'

The new para 66 provides:

'The administrator of a company may make a payment otherwise than in accordance with paragraph 65 or paragraph 13 of Schedule 1 if he thinks it likely to assist achievement of the purpose of administration.'

This introduces a lower threshold for the exercise of the power than previously. Now it is a question of what, subjectively, the administrator 'thinks' is likely to assist rather than an objective test.

11.35   In the House of Lords, the Minister explained the rationale behind the widening of the powers as follows:

'... the administrator will continue to be able to make payments, by virtue of para 13 of Sch 1 to the Insolvency Act 1986, to one or more creditors in respect of debts that were owed at the date of administration as well as expenses and liabilities that arise during the course of the administration, where such payments are necessary or incidental to the performance of his duties ... the amendment will allow the administrator to make payments that he believes are likely to assist the achievement of the purpose of administration. That will involve the administrator using his commercial judgment. Examples of such a situation could be payment of outstanding debts to the supplier of equipment that requires regular safety inspections and maintenance or payment to the franchisor of a franchise business to enable necessary goods to be supplied. Payments such as those would need to be made out of the standard order of priority and to a specific creditor or creditors, rather than by way of distribution to creditors generally.'

11.36 During the passage of the Bill through the Commons, concerns were raised[54] that this proposed provision might lead to abuse and the administrator being held to ransom. For example, a belligerent unsecured creditor might be paid in preference to a reasonable person of moderate dealings in order to facilitate the smooth running of the administration process.

11.37 As the wording expressly stipulates that the administrator must believe that the distribution will assist the purpose of administration, such attempted abuse is unlikely to be successful. It is difficult to see why this – rather limited – extension of the administrator's power to make payments will impact upon his exercise of judgment.

11.38 Even before the new regime was introduced, the courts had considerable experience of dealing with applications brought by secured creditors, such as landlords or lessors of goods under a hire-purchase agreement for repossession or payment of rent. The factors that the administrator must give weight to when considering such applications by secured creditors will remain unchanged by the introduction of the new administration process.

LIFTING THE MORATORIUM

11.39 General guidance in giving leave to proceed against the company in administration was provided by the Court of Appeal in *Re Atlantic Computer Systems plc*.[55] It is clear that the Government does not intend that the new provisions should alter the law in this respect. As mentioned at **11.1**, this appears to have been achieved in so far as the *imposition* of the moratorium is concerned, but it is doubtful whether applications for leave or permission to lift the moratorium will be approached in the same way in a new-style 'stand-alone' administration. Nevertheless, the guidance provided by the Court of Appeal in *Atlantic Computers* is likely to remain useful – especially for those new administrations bearing the hallmarks of the old administrations (ie providing a breathing space and gateway to another insolvency process).

11.40 The criteria may be summarised as follows.

(a)   The burden is on the party seeking leave to make out his case to be given leave.

(b)   The prohibition in s 11(3)(c) and (d)[56] is intended to assist the purpose for which the administration order was made. If granting leave to the lessor or hirer of goods is unlikely to impede achieving the purpose of administration, leave ought to be granted.

---

54   *Hansard*, Vol 391, no 198, 30 October 2002, col 951.
55   [1992] 1 All ER 476.
56   Now re-enacted as IA 1986, Sch B1, paras 43(2), (3) and (6).

(c)   In other cases, the court must conduct an exercise balancing the legitimate interests of the lessor against those of the other creditors of the company. This must not be a mechanical exercise and the court must exercise its judicial judgment; having regard to the parties' interests and all the circumstances of the case. The purpose of the power to give leave is to relax the prohibition where it would be inequitable for the prohibition to apply.

(d)   In conducting this exercise, great importance will be given to the lessor's proprietary interests. The underlying principle is that an administration for the benefit of the unsecured creditors should not be conducted at the expense of those who have proprietary rights, save to the extent that this is unavoidable (and then only acceptable to a strictly limited extent).

(e)   It will normally be sufficient if the lessor can show that refusal of leave would lead to a significant loss. For these purposes loss comprises any kind of financial loss, direct or indirect, including loss by reason of delay, and may be extended to cases other than financial loss. However, even if this is shown, leave will not be granted where it would cause substantially greater loss to others, or loss which is out of all proportion to the benefit.

(f)   In assessing these respective losses, the court will have regard to: the financial position of the company; its ability to pay the rental arrears and continuing rentals; the administrator's proposals; the period for which the administration order has been in force and is expected to remain so; the effect on the administration if leave were given; the effect on the applicant if leave were refused; the end result which the administration is seeking to achieve (that is, the stated purpose); the prospect of that result being achieved and the history of the administration thus far.

(g)   Consideration of these factors will require the court making an assessment based upon probability, including virtual certainties and remote possibilities.

(h)   The list is not intended to be exhaustive and the conduct of the parties involved may well be a material consideration. A lessor is advised to make his position clear to the administrator at the beginning of the administration and, if it becomes necessary, to apply to the court promptly.

(i)   These considerations are also relevant not only to the decision whether or not to grant leave, but also to a decision to impose terms where leave is granted.[57]

---

57   As in the old s 11, IA 1986, Sch B1, para 43 does not give any express power to the court to impose terms where leave is refused. It is submitted, however, that since the new paragraphs are drafted in similar terms to the old, the court retains the discretion. Under the old law, it could do so either directly, pursuant to ss 17 and 14(3) or under its general control of the administrator as an officer of the court. These sections are reproduced in the new Act at paras 68(2), 63 and 5 (the latter is now specifically provided by statute); or indirectly by granting that leave will be granted *unless* the administrator complies with prescribed steps: [1992] 1 All ER 476, 543F–H.

(j) These observations were stated to apply to a lessor of land or owner of goods seeking to repossess because of non-payment, but a similar approach should be taken on other applications to enforce security. These other applications will require a consideration of whether or not the applicant is fully secured or not (if he is, delay is likely to be less prejudicial).

(k) The court should avoid adjudicating on the existence, validity and nature of the security that the applicant is seeking to enforce. At this stage, the court need only satisfy itself that the applicant has a seriously arguable case.

11.41   The *Atlantic Computers* guidelines have been consistently applied by the courts in assessing whether or not leave ought to be given. *Atlantic Computers* represents an attempt to balance the interests of individual creditors against the purpose of administration and the interest of the creditors as a whole. The difficulty lies in the practical application. Creditors, particularly those exercising proprietary rights (especially ongoing payments such as those pursuant to leases and hire-purchase arrangements), will want to establish their rights in the administration at an early stage. Yet courts discouraged early applications under the old s 11.[58] It is to be hoped that these practical difficulties experienced under the old law will cease but, in the absence of any statutory intervention, it appears that the old practice and procedure are likely to remain.

PUBLICITY

11.42   As a postcript, it is worth mentioning that one (very public) effect of administration is the routine alteration of all company documents generated during the administration. While a company is in administration, every business document issued by or on behalf of the company or by the administrator must state:

(a) the name of the administrator; and
(b) that the affairs, business and property of the company are being managed by him.[59]

If the administrator, an officer of the company or the company itself authorises or permits a contravention of this section without reasonable excuse, he commits an offence.[60]

---

58   *Re City Logistics Ltd* [2002] 2 BCLC 103. In *Re Atlantic Computer Systems plc*, Nicholls LJ indicated that creditors should make their position clear to the administrator at an early stage and if necessary, apply to the court promptly. In *Re City Logistics*, Lloyd J remarked upon the 'slightly desultory correspondence' that had passed between the parties, which may in part explain the court's reasoning.
59   IA 1986, Sch B1, para 45(1).
60   Ibid, para 45(2).

11.43   A business document is defined as an invoice, an order for goods and services and business letters:[61] documents provided to third parties. These publicity provisions are designed to protect those dealing with the company whilst in administration. Hence, even if a business document does not appear to fall within the categories provided by the Act, it is suggested that it is prudent business practice to treat it as if included in the requirements of para 45(1) where reasonably practicable to do so.

---

61   IA 1986, Sch B1, para 45(3). There are, of course, other 'business documents' such as business cards which are not specifically identified; however, it is suggested that those to whom para 45(2) applied ought to make every reasonable effort to ensure all documents supplied to third parties carry the prescribed information.

Chapter 12

CONDUCT OF ADMINISTRATIONS

'We are unprofitable servants: we have done that which was our duty to do.'
The Bible[1]

INTRODUCTION

12.1   This chapter deals with the conduct of the administration, whether the administrator is appointed out of court or by the court.

12.2   The general provisions regarding conduct of the administration under the new administration procedure remain largely the same as those under the old administration procedure. However, there are some amendments, some innovation and some changes required by reason of the change of the statutory purpose and use of the administration procedure to replace administrative receiverships. Those changes are highlighted below.

12.3   The detailed provisions concerning conduct of an administration are to be found in the new Sch B1 to IA 1986, inserted by EA 2002, s 248 and Sch 16; and in rules which have not yet been finalised. References in this chapter to individual paragraphs are to Sch B1 unless it is indicated otherwise. In order to ease understanding of the changes to the administrator's function, there is also consideration of the draft rules. However, it must be noted that there is no certainty that the promulgated rules will be the same as the draft version.

STATUS AND GENERAL DUTIES OF ADMINISTRATOR

Status

12.4   The administrator is an officer of the court, whether appointed by court order or out of court by a floating charge-holder or the directors or company. As an officer of the court, he is subject to the directions of the court, although the same are limited by para 68(3) of Sch B1. Further, as an officer of the court he is also subject to the rule in *Re Condon, ex parte James*[2] whereby an officer of the court is required to do the fullest equity.[3]

---

1   Luke 17:10.
2   (1874) 9 Ch App 609.
3   See *Re Clark (A Bankrupt)* [1975] 1 WLR 559 as regards interpretation of the principle and Fletcher, Higham and Trower, *The Law & Practice of Corporate Administrations*, paras 5.31–5.32 as regards application in practice to administrators. See also *Re Japan Leasing (Europe) plc* [1999] BPIR 911.

12.5   In exercising his functions under Sch B1 to IA 1986, the administrator acts as the company's agent.[4] Similar provision was made by IA 1986, s 14(5) under the old administration procedure, although in that section the administrator was only 'deemed' to act as the agent of the company, whereas under para 69 there is no reference to 'deemed' agency and the administrator 'acts as its agent'.

12.6   The administrator will therefore not be personally liable on any contract or obligation that he enters into on behalf of the company. An administrative receiver by contrast, notwithstanding his deemed agency under IA 1986, s 44(1)(a) is, by virtue of s 44(1)(b), personally liable on any contract entered into by him in the carrying out of his functions, except in so far as the contract otherwise provides.

12.7   Third parties dealing with an administrator in good faith and for value need not inquire whether the administrator is acting within his powers[5] (eg in entering into a sale transaction).

The administrator's general duties

12.8   Paragraphs 67 and 68 of Sch B1 set out the administrator's general duties. Under para 67, the administrator shall, on his appointment, take custody or control of all the property to which he thinks the company is entitled.

12.9   Paragraph 68(1) provides:

'subject to sub-paragraph (2) (directions by the court), the administrator of a company shall manage its affairs, business and property in accordance with –

(a)   any proposals approved by the creditors under paragraph 53,

(b)   any revision of those proposals which is made by him and which he does not consider substantial, and

(c)   any revision of those proposals approved by the creditors under paragraph 54.'

12.10   Paragraph 68(1) must be read along with para 64, which provides:

'(1)   A company in administration or an officer of a company in administration may not exercise a management power without the consent of the administrator.

(2)   For the purpose of sub-paragraph (1) –

(a)   "management power" means a power which could be exercised so as to interfere with the exercise of the administrator's powers,

(b)   it is immaterial whether the power is conferred by an enactment or an instrument, and

(c)   consent may be general or specific.'

12.11   The management and control of the company and its property are thus taken away from the board of directors of the company under para 64 and the administrator takes control of the same under para 68.

12.12   The directors of the company, however, remain in office, albeit in a twilight world, where they cannot exercise any management powers without the

---

4   IA 1986, Sch B1, para 69.

5   Ibid, para 59(3).

consent of the administrator. If they have employment contracts, they will remain employed unless their contracts are terminated by the administrator. Depending upon the needs of the administration, the administrator may utilise the management services of the incumbent directors and grant consent under para 64, although such consent may be limited as to what the directors are permitted to do (eg if the company is to continue to trade), the directors (or some of them) may be retained and given the day-to-day management function by the administrator, albeit that financial and management control may be retained by the administrator.

Management in accordance with proposals

12.13   The administrator is required by para 68(1) to manage the company in accordance with approved proposals, subject to any insubstantial revisions by the administrator and any other revisions approved by the creditors. The contents of proposals will be considered below. Suffice to say at this stage that such proposals must be drafted so as to cover proposed actions by the administrator.

Management in accordance with court directions

12.14   Paragraph 68(1) is stated to be subject to sub-para (2), namely:

'If the court gives directions to the administrator of a company in connection with any aspect of his management of the company's affairs, business or property, the administrator shall comply with the directions.'

Sub-paragraph (3) sets out restrictions upon the ability of the court to give directions to the administrator:

'The court may give directions under sub-paragraph (2) only if –

(a)   no proposals have been approved under paragraph 53,
(b)   the directions are consistent with any proposals or revision approved under paragraph 53 or 54,
(c)   the court thinks the directions are required in order to reflect a change in circumstances since the approval of proposals or a revision under paragraph 53 or 54, or
(d)   the court thinks the directions are desirable because of a misunderstanding about proposals or a revision approved under paragraph 53 or 54.'

12.15   Paragraph 68(3)(b) coupled with para 68(1) indicate that prime control in determining what the administrator should do as regards management of the company rests with the creditors of the company and that the court should not give directions contrary to proposals or revisions approved by the creditors.

12.16   Paragraph 68(3)(c) and (d) deals with situations where there has been a change of circumstances since approval of the proposals/revised proposals or some misunderstanding concerning the same. The court may decline to give directions under those sub-paragraphs if it is feasible to hold a creditors' meeting to consider revisions to the proposals. An administrator might however seek directions of the court if there was not sufficient time or funds available to hold a creditors' meeting or the change of circumstances or misunderstanding was not sufficiently serious as to require a creditors' meeting (and cost of calling the same[6]) and could be dealt with most effectively by court order.

Management prior to initial creditors' meeting

12.17   Given that the administrator is required under para 68 to manage the company in accordance with proposals or revised proposals and pursuant to para 68(2) in accordance with the directions of the court, which can include, under para 68(3)(a), directions given where no proposals have been agreed, what can the administrator do prior to approval of his proposals by creditors? Is he free to exercise his powers or does he need to obtain directions from the court prior to exercising them?

12.18   One of the areas that was uncertain and resulted in litigation under the old administration procedure was the position of the administrator and exercise of his powers prior to the holding of the initial creditors' meeting and approval of his proposals. The issue arose in particular where the administrator wished to sell the business and assets (or part thereof) of the company prior to the holding of the initial creditors' meeting. It was not clear whether the administrator:

(a)   could not sell the assets prior to the initial creditors' meeting;

(b)   could sell assets provided the same did not amount to the entire or substantially the entire assets of the company, such that there would be nothing for the creditors to consider at the initial creditors' meeting, thereby potentially frustrating the purpose of the Act in giving the creditors the opportunity to consider proposals;

(c)   was required to obtain the leave of the court prior to the initial creditors' meeting if the administrator wished to exercise his power of sale.

12.19   The differing views of judges at first instance[7] culminated in a full and reasoned judgment by Neuberger J in *Re T & D Industries plc*,[8] in which the judge, having reviewed the earlier first instance cases, concluded that:

(a)   IA 1986, s 17(2)(a), which provided that the administrator should manage the company 'at any time before proposals have been approved ...', in accordance with any directions given by the court' did not cut down the administrator's powers under IA 1986, s 14.

(b)   Thus, the administrator was entitled to exercise the power of sale in respect of the company's assets prior to the creditors' meeting under IA 1986, s 24 to consider his proposals unless the administration order itself provided otherwise.

(c)   The administrator did not therefore need to apply to the court for directions allowing him to exercise any of his powers prior to the creditors' meeting.

---

6   Even if the same were held by correspondence under para 58.

7   *Re Charnley Davies Ltd* [1990] BCC 605; *N S Distribution Ltd* [1990] BCLC 169; *Re Consumer & Industrial Press Ltd (No 2)* (1988) 4 BCC 72; *Re Harris Bus Co Ltd* [2000] BCC 1151.

8   [2000] 1 WLR 646, [2000] 1 BCLC 471, [2000] BCC 956.

(d) It was, however, suggested that, where an administrator proposed to exercise his powers by way of sale, he should attempt to formulate his proposals and call a creditors' meeting as soon as reasonably practicable (rather than leaving it to the end of the period in which such a meeting could be called) and possibly asking the court to direct that such meeting be held at short notice.

(e) Alternatively, if the above were not possible, then the administrator should at least seek to consult, in the time available prior to the sale having to be completed, with the major creditors of the company.

12.20   Although the case is only a first instance decision, given the full and reasoned judgment, it has been followed by insolvency practitioners as regards the exercise of their powers, notwithstanding the differing views expressed in earlier cases and the absence of Court of Appeal authority.

12.21   It is submitted that the position of the administrator under the new administration procedure will be the same, namely that he will be entitled to exercise his powers under paras 59–64 of Sch B1 prior to the initial creditors' meeting and without having to obtain the directions of the court under para 68. The reasoning, in particular the practical points referred to by Neuberger J in his judgment, appear to have equal application to the new administration. The guidance given by the judge to seek a direction to call the initial creditors' meeting at short notice, or, if that is not possible, to seek the views of the major creditors of the company, has equal application under the new administration procedure.

12.22   It is convenient to mention here a related point[9] where the administrator has managed to sell the business and assets of the company prior to the holding of an initial creditor's meeting. In *Re Charnley Davies Business Services Ltd*,[10] it was held that where the purposes for which the administration order was made had either been achieved or could no longer be achieved, then a creditors' meeting to consider proposals by the administrator could not be held because there were no proposals which could sensibly be considered. The administrator could not hold a meeting simply to report to the creditors what had happened or to propose that the company petition for its winding-up or to approve his remuneration, as those were not purposes set out in IA 1986, s 8. The administrator was therefore under an obligation to apply back to the court for discharge of the administration order.

12.23   The change in statutory purpose under the new administration procedure (by para 3) calls into question whether, in similar circumstances, under the new procedure the administrator would be able to call an initial creditors' meeting and would have to apply to court under para 79. It is submitted that the administrator can probably hold an initial creditors' meeting and is not required (but might consider it appropriate) to apply to discharge the

---

9   The point is covered in more detail in Chapter 13 relating to exit routes from administration.
10   (1987) 3 BCC 408.

administration. That result follows from the change in statutory purpose. Whereas the last-resort statutory purpose in s 8(3)(d) was 'a more advantageous *realisation* of the company's assets than would be effected on a winding up', under para 3(1)(b), the secondary objective is stated to be '*achieving a better result* for the company's creditors as a whole than would be likely if the company were wound up'. That purpose might still be achieved where distribution was made by the administrator or the administrator wished to rely upon the shortcut method of placing the company into voluntary liquidation under para 83. Furthermore, even if the assets had been sold, the third objective in para 3(1)(c) is for the administrator to make distribution to secured or preferential creditors and until this is done the statutory purpose continues.

Liabilities and challenges to administrator's conduct

12.24   Liabilities and challenges to an administrator's conduct can be summarised as follows.[11]

(a) As an agent of the company, the administrator probably owes fiduciary duties to the company to act and exercise his powers in good faith, for the purposes of the company and the administration, not to make any secret profit from his position and not to place himself in a position of conflict.

(b) As a professional, he owes a duty to the company to exercise reasonable skill and care in the conduct of the administration.

(c) Given that the administrator is under specific statutory duties, a claim might lie against the administrator for breach of one of those duties, although a claimant would have to establish that the specific statutory duty was imposed for the benefit of a particular class of which the claimant forms part.

12.25   What should be highlighted, however, are the changes made under the new administration procedure, in particular:

(a) the new statutory purposes contained within para 3(1) and the duty of the administrator to perform his functions with the objective stated;

(b) the duty on the administrator under para 3(2) to perform his functions in the interests of the company's creditors as a whole. This particularly emphasises the different position of the administrator (even where appointed by a floating charge-holder) from that of an administrative receiver;

(c) the entirely new statutory duty imposed by para 4 to perform his functions as quickly and efficiently as is reasonably practicable.

12.26   Paragraph 75 introduces a new statutory procedure for obtaining redress against an administrator. It enables the court to examine the conduct of an administrator or person who purports to be an administrator[12] on the application of the official receiver, the administrator of the company, the

---

11   A detailed examination of the same is outside the scope of this book. See Fletcher, Higham and Trower, ch 5.
12   IA 1986, Sch B1, para 75(1).

liquidator of the company, a creditor of the company or a contributory of the company.[13]

12.27   The application must and can only be made on the grounds that the administrator:

(a) has misapplied or retained money or other property of the company;
(b) has become accountable for money or other property of the company;
(c) has breached a fiduciary or other duty in relation to the company; or
(d) has been guilty of misfeasance.[14]

12.28   The court may, at the conclusion of such examination, order the administrator to:

(a) repay, restore or account for money or property;
(b) pay interest;
(c) contribute a sum to the company's property by way of compensation for breach of duty or misfeasance.

12.29   The inclusion of the express statutory procedure for complaint, coupled with the new purposes and new duties upon administrators and potential tensions between secured and unsecured creditors are likely to result in a greater number of actions being brought against administrators than was the case under the old administration procedure.

Challenge to administrator's conduct of company

12.30   Paragraph 74 enables a creditor or member of the company to apply to the court on the grounds that:

(a) the administrator is acting or has acted so as unfairly to harm the interests of the applicant (whether alone or in common with some or all other members or creditors); or
(b) the administrator proposes to act in a way which would unfairly harm the interests of the applicant (whether alone or in common with some or all other members or creditors);[15] or
(c) the administrator is not performing his functions as quickly or as efficiently as is reasonably practicable.[16]

12.31   The court is given general power in dealing with the application by para 74(3) to:

'(a) grant relief,
(b) dismiss the application,
(c) adjourn the hearing conditionally or unconditionally,
(d) make an interim order,
(e) make any other order it thinks appropriate.'

Paragraph 75 provides a clear statutory route by which disgruntled creditors and contributories can seek redress from the insolvency court dealing with the

---

13   IA 1986, Sch B1, para 75(2).
14   Ibid, para 75(3).
15   Ibid, para 74(1).
16   Ibid, para 74(2).

administration, rather than having to rely upon general principles for the duties of administrators and remedies available. As such, it is likely to encourage claims against administrators, which otherwise might not have been pursued.

12.32   Paragraph 74(4) sets out specific orders that the court may make to:

'(a) regulate the administrator's exercise of his functions,
(b) require the administrator to do or not do a specified thing,
(c) require a creditors meeting to be held for a specified purpose,
(d) provide for the appointment of an administrator to cease to have effect,
(e) make consequential provision.'

12.33   The power to make an order under para 74 can be exercised whether or not the action complained about is within the administrator's powers and can relate to a sale of charged or hire purchase notwithstanding that the administrator obtained an order under para 71 or 72.[17]

12.34   The power to grant relief is, however, limited by para 74(6) which provides that an order may not be made if it would impede or prevent the implementation of:

(a) a voluntary arrangement approved under Part I of IA 1986;
(b) a compromise or arrangement sanctioned under CA 1985, s 425;
(c) proposals or a revision approved under para 53 or 54 more than 28 days before the day on which the application for an order under para 74 is made.

12.35   Paragraph 74 largely repeats the protection afforded by IA 1986, s 27. The most significant changes are:

(a) That the ground of challenge under para 74(1) is 'unfairly to harm the interests of the applicant', rather than 'unfairly prejudicial', which was used in s 27, which removes reliance on cases decided under CA 1985, s 459 and s 27 as to the interpretation of those words.

(b) Paragraph 74(2) introduces a new means of complaint in respect of an administrator who fails to comply with his new duty under para 4 to perform his functions as quickly and efficiently as is reasonably practicable.

12.36   The Explanatory Notes to EA 2002 at para 694 provide some guidance as regards para 74(2):

'The use of the expression "reasonably practicable" conveys the idea that one administration may be very different from another, where it may be practicable to act within a short time in the administration of a simple, small company, that may be entirely impracticable in the case of a large complicated case. Furthermore the courts would be unlikely to entertain claims under this provision relating to trivial delays or that are frivolous or unavoidable or cause no harm.'

12.37   Whilst such guidance may provide some comfort for insolvency practitioners, they will have to wait and see what challenges are made and whether the court is sympathetic to the speed with which they conduct administrations (particularly after the initial flurry of activity around the appointment and any sale of the business and assets). They will also no doubt

---

17   IA 1986, Sch B1, para 74(5).

find out whether their successful pleas to increase the duration of the administration to 1 year under para 76 and the time for calling an initial creditors' meeting to 10 weeks under para 51(2) were worth the imposition of the duty under para 4, which was enacted as a quid pro quo.

NOTIFICATION OF ADMINISTRATION

Disclosure of administration on face of company's business documents

12.38 It is important for those dealing with the company in administration (including members of the public, trade customers and suppliers) to know that the company is in administration, in particular if they are ordering goods or services from the company and paying a deposit or supplying goods or services to the company on credit.

12.39 Paragraph 45 of Sch B1 to IA 1986 provides that whilst a company is in administration, every 'business document' issued by or on behalf of the company must state:

(a) the name of the administrator; and
(b) that the affairs, business and property of the company are being managed by him.[18]

12.40 'Business document' is defined by para 45(3) as meaning an invoice, order for goods or services and a business letter.

12.41 The definition of 'business document' is not all-encompassing but merely specifies two specific categories of document and 'business letters'. It does not include a catchall, along the lines of 'any document issued by the company in connection with its business'. Thus, for example, order acknowledgements, receipts for cash or goods, advertisements on behalf of the company and written contracts (as distinct from mere orders) do not appear to be covered.[19]

12.42 A prudent administrator may, however, take steps to ensure that all business documents produced by the company clearly refer to the company being in administration, the name of the administrator and that he acts as agent for the company and without personal liability.

12.43 The administrator, an officer of the company and the company itself commit a criminal offence if without reasonable excuse they authorise or permit a contravention of para 45(1).[20]

---

18 IA 1986, Sch B1, para 45 substantively repeats IA 1986, s 12, the wording merely being set out in a more easily understood manner. Similar notification has to be given by a receiver (IA 1986, ss 39 and 64) and a liquidator (s 188).

19 Written contracts, leases, transfers of land and similar documents may be excluded on the basis that the other contracting party is likely to be well aware that the company is in administration and because such documents would normally be drafted to accurately define the company entering into the agreement via the administrator as agent.

20 IA 1986, Sch B1, para 45(2).

Announcement of administrator's appointment

12.44   Paragraph 46 of Sch B1 to IA 1986[21] requires the administrator as soon as reasonably practicable to:

(a) send a notice of his appointment to the company;[22]
(b) publish a notice of his appointment in the manner prescribed by the Rules;[23]
(c) obtain a list of the company's creditors and send a notice of his appointment to each creditor of whose claim and address he is aware.[24]

12.45   The administrator must also send a notice of his appointment:

(a) to the Registrar of Companies before the end of the period of 7 days beginning with the appropriate date specified in para 46(6);[25]
(b) to such other persons and within such period (beginning with the appropriate date specified in para 46(6)) as are prescribed by the Rules.[26]

12.46   Paragraph 46(6) provides that the date from which the periods referred to at **12.44** run are:

(a) in the case of an administrator appointed by the court, the date of the administration order;
(b) in the case of an administrator appointed under para 14 by a qualifying floating charge-holder, the date on which the administrator receives notice under para 20; and
(c) in the case of an administrator appointed by the company or directors under para 22, the date on which the administrator receives notice under para 32.

12.47   The court is given power by para 46(7) to direct that the requirement for the administrator to send a notice of his appointment to creditors under para 46(3)(b) or a notice to the persons prescribed by the Rules under para 46(5) shall either:

(a) not apply, or
(b) shall apply but with a different period for compliance substituted.

The ability of the administrator to apply to the court for directions under para 46(7) would therefore cover:

---

21   Under the old administration procedure IA 1986, s 21 dealt with these matters.
22   IA 1986, Sch B1, para 46(2)(a).
23   Ibid, para 46(2)(b) – the Rules will probably require the advertisements to be placed in the *London Gazette* and another newspaper which is likely to come to the notice of the company's creditors.
24   Ibid, para 46(3)(a) and (b).
25   Ibid, para 46(4).
26   Ibid, para 46(5) – the Rules will probably not fix a specific time frame but provide that the persons be notified as soon as reasonably practicable. The persons to be notified will probably be: (a) any sheriff charged with execution against the company's property; (b) anyone who has distrained against the company's property and where the administrator is appointed by the court; (c) any person who has appointed or entitled to appoint an administrative receiver; (d) any administrative receiver; (e) any petitioner who has presented a winding-up petition; and (f) any provisional liquidator.

(a) applications for an extension of time where there has been a failure by the administrator to serve the prescribed notice in time or failure to serve the same on all of those upon whom the notice should be served; and

(b) cases where the costs of serving a notice of appointment on creditors would be prohibitive. Often these are companies dealing with large numbers of members of the public where deposits or payments in advance are made or there are on-going commitments by the company (eg holiday companies, furniture retailers, mobile-phone operators, satellite or cable television suppliers). Rather than simply dispensing with personal notification of creditors by post under para 46(3)(b), the court may well require notification to be given to a large class of creditors (eg members of the public) by more extensive advertisement than is otherwise required under para 46(2)(b).

12.48 A notice under para 46 must be in prescribed form and contain the prescribed information.[27] Failure by an administrator without reasonable excuse to comply with the requirements of para 46 is a criminal offence.[28]

STATEMENT OF AFFAIRS

12.49 Paragraphs 47 and 48 of Sch B1 to IA 1986 set out the procedure for the administrator to obtain a statement of affairs for the company. It substantively reproduces the requirements under the old administration procedure of s 22 of IA 1986. The main differences are:

(a) the time within which the administrator must serve a notice requiring production of a statement of affairs has been changed from forthwith to as soon as reasonably practicable;

(b) the statement of affairs must be verified by a statement of truth under the Civil Procedure Rules 1998, rather than by way of affidavit;

(c) the time within which the statement of affairs must be produced has been reduced from 21 days to 11 days.[29]

12.50 Paragraph 47(1) imposes an obligation on the administrator as soon as reasonably practicable after his appointment to serve on one or more of the relevant persons a notice in prescribed form[30] requiring that person to provide the administrator with a statement of affairs.

12.51 The 'relevant persons' who can be served with such a notice and are obliged to produce a statement of affairs are set out in para 47(3) as:

'(a) a person who is or has been an officer of the company;

(b) a person who took part in the formation of the company during the period of one year ending with the date on which the company enters administration;

(c) a person employed by the company during that period;

(d) a person who is or has been during that period an officer or employee of a company which is or has been during that year an officer of the company.'

---

27 IA 1986, Sch B1, para 46(8) – to be set out in the Rules.
28 Ibid, para 46(9).
29 A somewhat odd number of days to have chosen.
30 To be dealt with by the Rules.

12.52   References to 'employed' and 'employee' under para 47(3) include employment through a contract of employment and a contract for services[31] (eg under a consultancy agreement).

12.53   Paragraph 48(1) requires the person served with a notice under para 47 to submit the statement of affairs to the administrator before the end of the period of 11 days beginning with the day on which he received notice to do so.

12.54   The administrator has power to revoke a para 47 notice[32] (eg if the statement of affairs has already been produced by another person upon whom a para 47 notice had been served or because the administrator is satisfied that the person upon whom a notice was served is unable to produce a statement of affairs). The administrator may also extend time within which the statement of affairs has to be produced, both before and after the expiry of the initial time-limit.[33]

12.55   If the administrator refuses to exercise his power of revocation or extension of time under para 48(2), then the person required to produce the statement of affairs may apply to the court under para 48(3), which may exercise the same powers as the administrator of revocation and extension.

12.56   Failure without reasonable excuse to comply with a requirement under para 47(1) is a criminal offence. It is not clear whether a failure by the administrator to serve a notice under para 47 is covered by this offence.[34]

THE ADMINISTRATOR'S PROPOSALS

Introduction

12.57   The administrator's proposals are important because he is obliged under para 68(1) to manage the company's affairs, business and property in accordance with such proposals and administration is supposed to be under the control of the creditors.

12.58   It might, therefore, be thought that proposals put forward by an administrator would be detailed and set out a clear strategy and course of action the administrator seeks to pursue in respect of the business and assets of the company. However, from the administrator's point of view he will wish to

---

31 IA 1986, Sch B1, para 47(4).
32 Ibid, para 48(2)(a).
33 Ibid, para 48(2)(b).
34 Ibid, para 48(4) refers to 'A person'. There is no reference to 'the administrator or a person ...'. Furthermore, the words '... comply with a requirement under paragraph 47(1)' might refer back to the requirement imposed upon the recipient of a notice from the administrator – '... the administrator ... shall by notice ... *require* one or more relevant persons ...'. However, the word 'requirement' is used in other sub-paras which create offences (eg para 46(9)) and appears to be used in a general manner to include all obligations under a paragraph. It would therefore be prudent for an administrator to work on the basis that he might be covered by the offence if he fails to serve a notice under para 47(1).

retain maximum flexibility as regards his actions. He will not wish to be constrained by the proposals and para 68(1) to particular courses of action or to have to go back to a further creditors' meeting to obtain revisions to those proposals under para 54.

12.59 Under the old administration procedure, the practice was therefore adopted in the majority of cases of the administrator only including extremely general and wide proposals, which left the administrator with as much freedom as possible (eg to manage the company to achieve the stated statutory purpose, to continue to trade if considered appropriate and to cease to trade if considered appropriate, to sell the assets and business of the company by such means and at such value as the administrator considers appropriate and upon achieving the statutory purpose to place the company into voluntary liquidation with the administrator appointed as liquidator).

12.60 Save in a minority of cases (usually large administrations) the creditors were content to accept such bland and unspecific proposals, leaving the matter to the professional judgement of the administrator, in an effort to keep costs to a minimum.

12.61 It is probable that the administrator under the new administration procedure will continue to put forward only general proposals, for the reasons that applied under the old administration procedure.

12.62 However, creditors under the new administration procedure may seek to require greater detail from administrators and, if they do not receive it, seek to put forward modifications to the proposals under para 53(1)(b). This may occur because:

(a) of the greater number of administrations that are likely to occur, not least because of the abolition of administrative receiverships in respect of debentures granted after the coming into force of the EA 2002;

(b) the ability of the company and directors to appoint an administrator out of court may give creditors a greater concern to tie down the administrator as regards his proposals if the administrator remains the one appointed by the directors or company;

(c) the new statutory purpose under para 3 and the hierarchical objectives under para 3(1) coupled with the obligation on the administrator to perform his functions in the interests of the creditors as a whole may give rise to conflicts between secured and unsecured creditors and differing views as to what can be achieved and whether the same is in the interests of the creditors as a whole.

For example, issues may arise as regards the timing of a sale of the business or assets of the company; the length of any marketing period; whether trading should or can continue (if there is funding); whether time and money should be spent on obtaining planning permissions prior to sale or carrying out repairs or completing development/improvement works. The unsecured creditors may well want consideration of such issues and proposals which set out a clear course of action, which is in the interests of the creditors as a whole, rather than the strategy of the administration being dictated by the secured creditors. If the proposals are merely general ones, there may be a risk that the administrator will treat the administration as an administrative receivership (by another name) for the benefit of secured creditors.

12.63   The precise contents of the proposals will vary from case to case, dependent upon the time within which they are produced, information available to the administrator and proposed strategy of the administrator for the conduct of the administration.

12.64   The administrator is required by para 49(1) of Sch B1 to produce a written statement of his proposals for achieving the purpose of the administration. Such proposals must be produced as soon as reasonably practicable and in any event within 8 weeks of the company entering administration.[35]

12.65   The proposals must deal with specified matters,[36] which will be set out in the Rules. If the administrator does not think that the objective set out in para 3(1)(a) (rescue of company as going concern) or 3(1)(b) (better result for company's creditors as a whole) can be achieved, then his proposals must explain why he has reached that conclusion.[37]

12.66   It is likely that the proposals will be required by the Rules to set out details as to how it is proposed that the administration will end, and in particular if a voluntary liquidation is proposed, who the liquidator is to be. It may also have to state whether the administrator proposes to make a distribution to unsecured creditors (assuming funds allow) or whether that will be dealt with in any subsequent liquidation.

12.67   It should be noted that where the administrator seeks to dispense with the holding of an initial creditors' meeting under para 52 (payment in full, no distribution to unsecureds or only para 3(1)(c) objective can be achieved), then he must include a statement in the proposals under para 52 to that effect.[38]

12.68   A para 52 statement by the administrator in his proposals is of great importance because of its consequences.

(a)   An initial creditors' meeting does not have to be held by the administrator. The creditors therefore lose their automatic right to have such a meeting and for them to consider and vote on the administrator's proposals or put forward modifications. Instead, it requires a creditor or creditors holding 10% of the debts of the company to requisition an initial creditors' meeting, at those creditors' risk as to costs of such meeting.

(b)   Even if an initial creditors' meeting is requisitioned by creditors, if a para 52(1)(b) statement has been made, then the draft Rules provide that the secured creditor will be entitled to vote at that meeting on the proposals put forward by the administrator, without deducting the value of the secured creditor's security.

---

35   IA 1986, Sch B1, para 49(5).
36   Ibid, para 49(2)(a).
37   Ibid, para 49(2)(b).
38   Ibid, para 52(1).

(c) The draft Rules contemplate that if a para 52(1)(b) statement has been made by the administrator in his proposals, then the administrator's remuneration is to be fixed by the secured creditors and a majority of the preferential creditors (if they are to receive any distribution).

12.69 The para 52 statement procedure is therefore potentially open to abuse by administrators who wish to conduct, in effect, administrative receiverships for the benefit of secured creditors under an administration. That is particularly so given that all that is required for the inclusion of a para 52(1)(b) statement in the proposals is that the administrator subjectively 'thinks' that there will be insufficient property to enable a distribution to unsecured creditors.

12.70 Furthermore, there is no express statutory provision whereby that para 52(1)(b) statement can be removed from the administrator's proposals or set aside, thereby setting aside the consequences that follow from such statement (as set out above). It may be that the court will be prepared to entertain an application by unsecured creditors challenging the inclusion of such a statement and direct the administrator that such statement should be removed from the proposals, if the court is satisfied that such statement ought not to have been included or ought not now to remain in the proposals.

12.71 Strangely, there also does not appear to be any means by which the administrator himself can remove a para 52 statement from his proposals and thereby disapply the consequences of such a statement, if the administrator subsequently formed a different view after further investigation or on the emergence of further evidence or assets or a reduction in the claims of secured or preferential creditors.

12.72 The proposals may include:

(a) a proposal for a company voluntary arrangement; or

(b) a proposal for a compromise or arrangement with creditors under s 425 of the Companies Act 1985.[39]

Protection for secured and preferential creditors

12.73 Paragraph 73(1) provides that an administrator's proposals[40] may not include any action which:

'(a) affects the right of a secured creditor of the company to enforce his security,

(b) would result in a preferential debt of the company being paid otherwise than in priority to its non-preferential debts, or

(c) would result in one preferential creditor of the company being paid a smaller proportion of his debt than another.'

12.74 The restrictions on proposals contained within para 73(1) do not apply to:

(a) action to which the relevant creditor consents;

---

39 IA 1986, Sch B1, para 49(3).

40 Which, by para 73(3), includes any statement of revised proposals or modifications to proposals.

(b)   a proposal for a voluntary arrangement under IA 1986, Part I although the same is without prejudice to IA 1986, s 4(3);

(c)   a proposal for a compromise or arrangement to be sanctioned under CA 1985, s 425.

12.75   A copy of the proposals must be sent by the administrator to:

(a)   the Registrar of Companies;

(b)   every creditor of the company of whose claim and address he is aware;

(c)   every member of the company of whose address he is aware.

The administrator must send the proposals:

(a)   as soon as is reasonably practicable after the company enters administration, and

(b)   in any event, before the end of the period of 8 weeks beginning with the day on which the company enters administration.

12.76   The 8-week period for preparation of the proposals and sending a copy to the registrar, creditors and members can be varied under para 107 of Sch B1. Paragraph 107 allows the court, on the application of the administrator, to extend the period. Such an extension can be made more than once and even after the expiry of the period.[41]

12.77   Although not expressly referred to in para 49, the 8-week time period can also be extended by the administrator himself provided he has the requisite consent.[42] The provisions as to what amounts to 'consent' are set out in para 108(2)–(4).[43] Such consent can only be used to extend a period once, the extension can only be for a maximum of 28 days, it cannot be used to extend a period which has already been extended by the court and cannot be used to extend a period after expiry of that period.[44] Given those limitations and the cost of obtaining the requisite consent from creditors, such power of extension by consent is unlikely to be used by administrators and an application to the court preferred.[45]

12.78   Rather than serving members personally with a copy of the proposals, the administrator is allowed to publish a notice[46] undertaking to provide a copy of the proposals free of charge to any member of the company who applies in writing for the same.[47] This power is useful where there are large

---

41   IA 1986, Sch B1, para 107(2).

42   Under para 108.

43   Usually the consent of each secured creditor and 50% of unsecured creditors (disregarding the debts of any creditor who does not respond to an invitation to give consent) or, if the administrator has made a statement under para 52(1)(b) that there are insufficient assets to make a distribution to unsecured creditors (apart from by virtue of s 176A(2)(a) but the administrator thinks that a distribution may be made to preferential creditors, the consent of 50% of preferential creditors.

44   IA 1986, Sch B1, para 108(5).

45   The power of extension under para 108 might be used where the unsecured and preferential creditors are not going to receive a distribution and thus where the administrator only needs to obtain the consent of the secured creditors.

46   In a manner to be prescribed by the Rules.

47   IA 1986, Sch B1, para 49(6), which is similar to the old administration procedure under IA 1986, s 23(2).

numbers of members (eg public limited companies) and the potential cost of supplying copies of the proposals greatly outweighs the cost of advertising.

12.79   Unfortunately, there is no provision for the administrator to publish a notice of undertaking to provide a copy of the proposals to creditors. This would have been useful in cases with large numbers of creditors. Often these are companies dealing with large numbers of members of the public where deposits or payments in advance are made or there are on-going commitments by the company (eg holiday companies, furniture retailers, mobile phone operators, satellite or cable television suppliers). The copying, postage and staff time costs in serving copies of the proposals on a large number of creditors can be extremely large.

12.80   Notwithstanding the failure to include an express dispensation provision in the EA 2002,[48] the practice developed under the old administration procedure (in cases where there were large numbers of creditors) of the administrator applying to the court for directions dispensing with the require-ment to serve copies of the proposals on all creditors and instead for advertisements to be placed informing creditors that a copy of the proposals could be obtained free of charge from the administrator or his solicitors. In appropriate cases the court was usually prepared to take a pragmatic approach and give such directions under s 14(3) of IA 1986 (see now para 63 of Sch B1 to IA 1986).[49]

12.81   The administrator commits a criminal offence if he fails without reasonable excuse to comply with para 107(5) by serving the proposals within the time stated.

The initial creditors' meeting

12.82   The administrator must (save in the circumstances mentioned below) summon an initial creditors' meeting and must send creditors an invitation to it with the statement of proposals under para 49(4)(b).[50] The purpose of the initial creditors' meeting is for the administrator to present his proposals to the creditors and for the creditors to approve, modify or reject those proposals.[51]

12.83   The initial creditors' meeting must be held:

(a)   as soon as reasonably practicable after the company enters administration, and

---

48   There will probably be no express dispensing power in the Rules.
49   A similar approach is adopted by the court in company liquidations to documents or notices that have to be served on large numbers of creditors (eg the voluntary liquidators of ITV Digital plc (formerly ONdigital 1998 plc) were required under IR 1986, r 4.49, to serve a copy or summary statement of affairs plus a report of the s 98 meeting on creditors. They were allowed by the court instead to advertise in the *Radio Times*, offering to supply copies to those creditors who requested the same. The court tends to have regard to the factors referred to under IR 1986, r 4.47(2), which gives a dispensation power to the court in respect of the official receiver's reporting duties when acting as liquidator (ie the cost of carrying out the duty, the amount of assets available, the extent of the interest of creditors or contributories or any particular class of them).
50   IA 1986, Sch B1, para 51(1).
51   Ibid, paras 51(3) and 53.

(b) in any event, within the period of *10 weeks*, beginning with the date on which the company enters administration.

The period is therefore somewhat shorter than the 3 months required under the old administration procedure by IA 1986, s 23.

12.84   The period within which the initial creditors' meeting is to be held can be extended:

(a) by the court on the application of the administrator under para 107;
(b) by the administrator with the consent of the creditors under para 108(1),[52] subject to the limitations contained in para 108(5).[53]

Dispensing with the initial creditors' meeting

12.85   Paragraph 52(1) of Sch B1 to IA 1986 provides that:

'Paragraph 51(1) shall not apply where the administrator's statement of proposals states that the administrator thinks –

(a)   that the company has sufficient property to enable each creditor of the company to be paid in full,
(b)   that the company has insufficient property to enable a distribution to be made to unsecured creditors other than by virtue of section 176A(2)(a), or
(c)   that neither of the objectives specified in paragraph 3(1)(a) and (b) can be achieved.'

Paragraph 52(2) further provides that:

'But the administrator shall summon an initial creditors' meeting if it is requested –

(a)   by creditors of the company whose debts amount to at least 10% of the total debts of the company,
(b)   in the prescribed manner, and
(c)   in the prescribed period.'[54]

12.86   The above provisions are rather oddly drafted, for the following reasons.

(a) It is clear from para 52(2) that the intention of para 52(1) is that where one of the circumstances set out in para 52(1)(a)–(c) is satisfied, then no initial creditors' meeting is summoned or held.

(b) However, para 52(1) does not disapply the entirety of para 51 but merely the obligation under para 51(1) to include an invitation to the initial creditors' meeting with the copy of the proposals sent to creditors. In particular, the obligation on the administrator under para 51(3) to 'present

---

52   Usually the consent of each secured creditor and 50% of unsecured creditors (disregarding the debts of any creditor who does not respond to an invitation to give consent) or, if the administrator has made a statement under para 52(1)(b) that there are insufficient assets to make a distribution to unsecured creditors (apart from by virtue of s 176A(2)(a)) but the administrator thinks that a distribution may be made to preferential creditors, the consent of 50% of preferential creditors.
53   Only one extension; extension limited to 28 days; cannot extend period already extended by the court; cannot extend after expiry of period.
54   The manner and period to be set by the Rules.

a copy of his statement of proposals to an initial creditors' meeting' remains. Presumably, para 52(2) and (3) must be construed as having no application if para 51(1) is disapplied by para 52.

(c) Presumably, if para 52 applies then para 53 is also disapplied.

(d) The result on first reading is a rather curious situation in which proposals have been prepared by the administrator[55] but (assuming there is no request for an initial creditors' meeting under para 52(2) by creditors) such proposals are never considered, approved, modified or rejected by any creditors.

(e) The fact that the administrator's proposals are not approved by an initial creditors' meeting means that the proposals themselves carry no weight, the administrator is not required to conduct the administration in accordance with the proposals he has put forward and he is under no duty to manage the affairs, business and property of the company in accordance with those proposals under para 68(1). The administrator is therefore left to perform his functions in accordance with the objective set out in para 3 and subject to the direction of the court under para 68(2).

(f) However, it is understood that the new rules will cover the above lacuna by providing that where an initial creditors' meeting has not been called by the administrator because of a statement under para 52(1), then the administrator's proposals are deemed to have been approved by the creditors.

(g) The legislative intent behind para 52 was no doubt aimed at attempting to save time and costs in not holding an initial creditors' meeting in circumstances where it was considered that there was little point in such a meeting being held. Whilst no doubt laudable, such costs savings could have been achieved by the use of correspondence instead of a creditors' meeting under para 58.

(h) Whilst in practice a number of creditors' meetings under the old administration procedure were not in fact attended by creditors or their personal proxies (as distinct from proxies being given to the chairman), the requirement for such a meeting to be held in all cases and the ability of all creditors[56] to attend provided an important safeguard for the administration procedure. Whilst an administrator might anticipate (depending upon the type of case) that no creditors would actually attend the meeting, he had to work and prepare his proposals and preparation for the meeting on the basis that creditors might attend.

(i) Under the new procedure and para 52, the administrator has the initial control as to whether an initial creditors' meeting is to be held.[57] He determines whether it is to be held and can decide that such meeting will not take place. Furthermore, such decision is based upon the administrator's

---

55 It is clear that proposals still have to be prepared by the administrator even if para 52 applies, not least because para 52 can apply only if the administrator states in his proposals that one of sub-paras (a)–(c) of para 52 applies.

56 Irrespective of the amount of their claim.

57 Subject to requisition of a meeting by 10% of the creditors under para 52(2).

subjective assessment as to whether any of the circumstances under para 52(1)(a)–(c) applies. Unfortunately, this power is ripe for abuse.

12.87   The underlying rationale (cost saving and little useful purpose being served in holding a meeting) for not requiring an initial creditors' meeting (and thereby not requiring any approval of the administrator's proposals by any creditors of the company) is also somewhat questionable if one examines the individual circumstances under para 52(1)(a)–(c).

(a) As regards para 52(1)(a), whilst it is not often that there will be a solvent administration in which it is anticipated that all creditors will be paid in full, in such cases there may still be reason for an initial creditors' meeting, for example:

   (i)   the creditors may have views as to the manner in which assets are realised, notwithstanding that the administrator at that stage 'thinks' that there is sufficient property to enable creditors to be paid in full,

   (ii) the administrator's belief that creditors may be paid in full may prove incorrect because of error on his part, assets not realising as much as anticipated or assets thought to belong to the company proving to belong to third parties. It appears that the administrator in those circumstances is entitled to continue with his proposals which are deemed to have been accepted even though there has been a material change,[58]

   (iii) even if it is reasonably believed that there will be payment in full to creditors, there may be issues arising as regards proposals and the manner in which assets are realised because of potential conflicts with the company's directors or shareholders who would be entitled to the return of the company or any surplus after payment of the creditors and the costs of the administration.

(b) As regards para 52(1)(b), even if unsecured creditors will not receive any distribution and therefore have no interest in the proposals, preferential creditors and secured creditors may have a substantial interest in the proposals.

(c) As regards para 52(1)(c), even if the administrator is reduced to the objective in para 3(1)(c), there may be a number of interested secured and preferential creditors.

12.88   Paragraph 52(2) does provide a means for a creditor whose debt is 10% of the total debts of the company or a group of creditors with total debts amounting to 10% to requisition a meeting.[59] However, the onus is entirely upon them to do so. They must act swiftly to make such a request (and possibly gather together support to give them 10%) as the prescribed period is likely to be

---

58   The creditors here would have to rely upon the administrator considering that he is under an obligation to refer the matter to a creditors' meeting or to the court.

59   It appears that a creditor holding less than 10% of the total debts of the company and who cannot gather together other creditors to bring the total debt up to 10% is powerless as regards requesting an initial creditors' meeting, although he may be able to mount a claim under para 74 if his interests will be unfairly harmed by the administrator's proposals.

short.[60] Furthermore, it is likely that any such requesting creditor will be required under the rules to pay for the cost of summoning the meeting (albeit the meeting of creditors may resolve that such costs be paid as an expense of the administration), which will obviously act as a substantial disincentive for creditors to make such a request.

Business at the initial creditors' meeting

12.89   The initial creditors' meeting to which the administrator's proposals are presented shall consider the proposals and the creditors may:

(a) approve the proposals;
(b) approve the proposals but with such modifications as may be agreed and put forward by the creditors, provided the administrator consents to such modifications; or
(c) reject the proposals.[61]

12.90   The Rules will set out in detail the procedure and provisions as to voting entitlement at such meeting, which will probably follow substantially the old procedure under rr 2.18–2.28 of IR 1986.

12.91   After the conclusion of the initial creditors' meeting, the administrator must, as soon as reasonably practicable, report any decision to the court, registrar of companies and such persons as may be prescribed by the Rules.[62] An offence is committed by the administrator if he fails without reasonable excuse to do so.[63]

12.92   If the creditors fail to approve the administrator's proposals at the initial creditors' meeting, then upon receiving the administrator's report under para 53(2), the court may:

(a) provide that the appointment of the administrator shall cease to have effect from a specified time;
(b) adjourn the hearing conditionally or unconditionally;
(c) make an interim order;
(d) make an order on a petition for winding-up suspended by virtue of para 40(1)(b);
(e) make any other order (including an order making consequential provision) that the court thinks appropriate.

12.93   In those rare cases where the administrator's proposals are rejected,[64] it may be prudent for the administrator to issue an application for directions to

---

60   It is understood that the same is likely to be 10 days.
61   IA 1986, Sch B1, para 53. Although rejection of the same is not mentioned in para 53, such power arises by implication from the paragraph and the use of the word 'may', as regards approval or approval with modification.
62   Ibid, para 53(2).
63   Ibid, para 53(3).
64   The same is unlikely given the power of the creditors to put forward modifications, although the administrator might decline to consent to the same. It is also likely that there will be power to adjourn the initial creditors' meeting (although probably only once and for a limited period), which would enable proposals to be reconsidered and further evidence obtained.

the court or obtain a hearing date for the court to consider the administrator's report and consider exercising its powers under para 55(2), notwithstanding that he is under no express obligation to do so. Alternatively, if the case is straightforward, the administrator may suggest in his report or a covering letter the directions under para 55(2) that he considers it would be appropriate for the court to give.

12.94   Notwithstanding the methods to avoid having to hold an initial creditors' meeting (eg dispensation with the same by the administrator including in his proposals a para 52(1) statement) or to hold the same by correspondence under para 58, it is possible that the initial creditors' meetings will in fact take on a far greater significance than it has under the old administration procedure.

12.95   In particular, the initial creditors' meeting appears to be the likely initial forum in which creditors will wish to consider whether:

(a) the administrator is correct in his subjective assessment that the objective in para 3(1)(a) or (b) cannot be achieved;

(b) the proposals by the administrator (particularly if appointed out of court by a floating charge-holder) take into account the obligation of the administrator to perform his functions in the interests of the creditors as a whole.

12.96   Thus issues may arise as regards the timing and method of sale of assets. For example, there may be a dispute between the secured creditors, who might wish to see an early sale because they are covered by their security and wish to obtain early repayment, and the unsecured creditors, who might wish to have a sale delayed for an improvement in the market or to allow a longer exposure to the market or advertising campaign. In a development site there may be disputes as to whether the development should be continued (and if so how the same can be funded) or sold on in its current uncompleted state.

12.97   An interesting aspect will be the entitlement to vote of secured creditors at the initial creditors' meeting. The draft Rules provide that in the normal case of an initial creditors' meeting, a secured creditor will only be able to vote in respect of the balance of his debt after deducting the value of his security. If he holds full security, then he will not be able to vote. If all the secured creditors were likewise fully secured, it would leave the control as to what proposals were adopted entirely in the hands of the preferential and unsecured creditors.

12.98   The only exception contemplated by the Rules to the above normal voting procedure is where the administrator has made a statement under para 52(1)(b) and the initial creditors' meeting has been requisitioned under para 52(2). In that case the secured creditor is entitled to vote for the full value of his debt without deducting the value of the security. However, even in that instance and even though the administrator thinks that no distribution will be made to unsecured creditors, the unsecured creditors may have voting control of the meeting and be able to dictate what actions should be taken by the administrator.

12.99   In addition, as mentioned above under 'proposals', under the new administration procedure creditors may seek to exercise a greater influence by putting forward modifications to the proposals that seek to set out in more detail the actions to be taken by the administrator.

Revision of administrator's proposals

12.100 If an administrator's proposals have been approved by an initial creditors' meeting, the proposals may be revised[65] by the administrator. If such revisions are not substantial, then the administrator may make such revisions without referring the same to the creditors for approval. It should be appreciated, however, that if there are revisions needed to the proposal, even though they are not considered by the administrator to be substantial, such revisions need to be recorded in writing by the administrator as revisions. Quite apart from possible challenge by creditors if the administrator acts outside the terms of the original approved proposals, para 68(1)(b) imposes a duty on the administrator to manage the company's affairs, business and property in accordance with 'any revision of those proposals which is made by him and which he does not consider substantial'.

12.101 Where the administrator thinks that the revisions are substantial then the administrator is required to obtain the approval of the creditors.[66] If the revisions are substantial, the administrator must summon a meeting of creditors,[67] send a statement in prescribed form of the proposed revision with a notice of the meeting to each creditor[68] and member[69] of the company and present a copy of the statement of proposed revisions to the creditors' meeting.[70]

12.102 The decision as to whether the revisions are 'substantial' is a matter for the subjective assessment of the administrator. Presumably, in assessing whether the revisions are substantial, the administrator should assess whether it is likely that the creditors would have reached a different view on the initial proposals or possibly wished to have put forward proposed modifications had the revised proposals been put to them at the initial creditors' meeting or were now put to them at a further creditors' meeting. If they would, then the administrator should probably refer the proposals to the creditors, particularly given that such creditors' meeting could be dealt with by correspondence under para 58.

12.103 The proposed revisions are considered by the creditors' meeting and either approved, approved with modifications (provided the administrator consents to the same) or rejected.[71] The administrator must then as soon as

---

65 And presumably altered.
66 IA 1986, Sch B1, para 54(1) and (2).
67 Ibid, para 54(2)(a).
68 Ibid, para 54(2)(b).
69 Ibid, para 54(2)(c). There is power of the administrator to give the notice to members by advertisement in prescribed manner under para 54(3) and (4), rather than by personally serving each member.
70 Ibid, para 54(2)(d).
71 Ibid, para 54(5).

reasonably practicable report the decision of the creditors' meeting to the court, registrar of companies and such other persons as may be prescribed.[72]

12.104   If the administrator's proposed revisions are not approved by the creditors, then upon receiving the administrator's report under para 54(6) the court may make an order under para 55(2).

Creditors' meetings by correspondence

12.105   An innovation in the new administration procedure is that para 58 enables the administrator to obtain the approval of his proposals[73] via correspondence with the creditors, rather than by calling and holding an initial creditors' meeting. Such correspondence will have to be sent in accordance with the Rules and subject to any prescribed condition. Such Rules will no doubt provide a timescale for responses from the creditors, an ability for the creditors to request further information and that if there is a breakdown in attempting to deal with the matter by correspondence (eg no responses or objections by creditors to a meeting not being held), then the administrator should summon a creditors' meeting in traditional form.

12.106   'Correspondence' is defined in para 111(1) as including 'correspondence by telephonic or other electronic means'. Thus, the progressive insolvency practitioner will be able to conduct such meetings by email, fax or telephone, provided the procedure to be set out in the Rules is followed. If those means are adopted, procedures will have to be put in place by the administrator to ensure that there is a clear documentary record of the electronic or telephonic correspondence, so that the same can be proved if challenged.

12.107   Whilst para 58 may prove useful (and no doubt highly attractive to the administrator) in smaller cases and for creditors' meetings after the initial creditors' meetings (eg to approve revisions or the administrator's remuneration where there is no creditors' committee), it may take some time before creditors will generally be prepared to accept the same in place of a physical initial creditors' meeting.

Further creditors' meetings at instance of creditors or court

12.108   Paragraph 56(1) requires the administrator to summon a meeting of creditors if:

---

72   IA 1986, Sch B1, para 54(6). An offence is committed if the administrator fails without reasonable excuse to do so: para 54(7).

73   Or revisions or in fact anything that otherwise would be required or permitted by or under Sch B1 to be done at a creditors' meeting – para 58(1). Although para 58(1) refers to 'creditors' meeting' and it might be suggested that the same did not cover the 'initial creditors' meeting' under para 51, 'creditors' meeting' is defined in para 50(1) as 'a meeting of creditors of a company summoned by the administrator'. It therefore appears to cover the initial creditors' meeting. It is understood that the Rules will in fact make it obvious that correspondence under para 58 can be used instead of holding an initial creditors' meeting.

(1) he is requested in the prescribed manner by a creditor or creditors holding 10% of the total debts of the company to do so;[74] or

(2) the court directs him to do so.

Creditors' committee

12.109   As with the old administration procedure, provision is made in para 57 for the creditors' meeting to establish a creditors' committee[75] to carry out the functions conferred on it by or under the IA 1986. The wording of para 57(2) makes it clear that the committee is only entitled to exercise such functions as are conferred on the committee by or under the IA 1986. It is not therefore possible for the creditors' meeting to delegate to the creditors' committee functions that are required to be performed by the creditors' meeting under the IA 1986, unless the IA 1986 states that such function can be carried out by creditors' committee. This removes the uncertainty that existed under the old procedure in s 26 where the wording was ambiguous and might have been interpreted as allowing delegation by the creditors' meeting.[76]

12.110   One of the major functions of the creditors' committee under the old administration procedure was to agree the basis and amount of remuneration for the administrator. It is likely that such function will also be given to the creditors' committee under the new Rules, save where the administrator has made a statement under para 52(1)(b) (ie the company has insufficient property to enable a distribution to be made to unsecured creditors other than by virtue of s 176A(2)(a)), in which case the administrator's remuneration can be approved by the secured creditors and (if a dividend is payable to preferential creditors) 50% of the preferential creditors.

ADMINISTRATOR'S POWERS

12.111   The administrator's general powers in connection with the company and its assets are set out in paras 59–64 of Sch B1. They largely replicate the general powers under the old administration procedure contained within s 14 of IA 1986. The differences are highlighted below.

12.112   The administrator's powers are subject to two limitations:

(a) the powers given to the administrator are given for the purpose of the administration as set out para 3 and the administrator must perform his functions (and thereby exercise powers conferred on him) with the objective of:

   (i) rescuing the company as a going concern, or

---

74   This is a new power given to creditors which they did not have under the old administration procedure.

75   IA 1986, Sch B1, para 57(1).

76   See Sealy and Milman *Annotated Guide to the Insolvency Legislation*, 6th edn (Sweet & Maxwell, 2002), p 88.

(ii) achieving a better result for the company's creditors as a whole than would be likely if the company were wound up (without first being in administration, or

(iii) realising property in order to make a distribution to one or more secured or preferential creditors.

The administrator is not entitled to exercise his powers for purposes other than those set out in para 3.

(b) As the powers are conferred on the administrator as agent of the company, the administrator therefore has no power to commit the company to an ultra vires act (ie an act outside the scope of the objects clause in the company's memorandum of association).[77]

12.113   Paragraph 60 provides that the administrator has the powers expressly specified in Sch 1 to IA 1986. Schedule 1 to IA 1986 remains unamended by the EA 2002. The powers set out in Sch 1 are those that were applicable to administrators and administrative receivers, namely:

'1.   Power to take possession of, collect and get in the property of the company, and, for that purpose, to take such proceedings as may seem to him expedient.

2.   Power to sell or otherwise dispose of the property of the company by public auction or private auction or private contract ...

3.   Power to raise or borrow money and grant security therefor over the property of the company.

4.   Power to appoint a solicitor or accountant or other professionally qualified person to assist him in the performance of his functions.

5.   Power to bring or defend any action or other legal proceedings in the name and on behalf of the company.

6.   Power to refer to arbitration any question affecting the company.

7.   Power to effect and maintain insurances in respect of the business and property of the company.

8.   Power to use the company's seal.

9.   Power to do all acts and to execute in the name and on behalf of the company any deed, receipt or other document.

10.   Power to draw, accept, make and endorse any bill of exchange or promissory note in the name and on behalf of the company.

11.   Power to appoint any agent to do any business which he is unable to do himself or which can more conveniently be done by any agent and power to employ and dismiss employees.

12.   Power to do all such things (including the carrying out of works) as may be necessary for the realisation of the property of the company.

13.   Power to make any payment which is necessary or incidental to the performance of his functions.

---

77   *Re Home Treats Ltd* [1991] BCLC 705.

14.   Power to carry on the business of the company.

15.   Power to establish subsidiaries of the company.

16.   Power to transfer to subsidiaries of the company the whole or any part of the business and property of the company.

17.   Power to grant or accept a surrender of a lease or tenancy of any property of the company, and to take a lease or tenancy of any property required or convenient for the business of the company.

18.   Power to make any arrangement or compromise on behalf of the company.

19.   Power to call up any uncalled capital of the company.

20.   Power to rank and claim in the bankruptcy, insolvency, sequestration or liquidation of any person indebted to the company and to receive dividends, and accede to trust deeds for the creditors of any such person.

21.   Power to present or defend a petition for the winding-up of the company.

22.   Power to change the situation of the company's registered office.

23.   Power to do all other things incidental to the exercise of the foregoing powers.'

12.114   The above powers are largely self-explanatory and given that they have not been changed by the EA 2002, reference should be made to any of the standard texts for commentary thereon.

12.115   In addition to the above specified powers, para 59(1) contains an extremely wide general power enabling the administrator to:

'do anything necessary or expedient for the management of the affairs, business and property of the company.'

The wording has in fact been widened from the old general power contained in s 14(1) of IA 1986 by the inclusion of the words 'or expedient', such that an act which does not fall within the express powers referred to below can now be done by the administrator, even if the same cannot be shown to be necessary, which was a somewhat high hurdle.

12.116   The general power contained within para 59(1) is not to be narrowly construed by reason of any provision in Sch B1 which expressly permits the administrator to do a specified thing; see para 59(2), which states that any provision in Sch B1 which expressly permits the administrator to do a specific thing is without prejudice to the generality of para 59(1). This would appear to include para 60 (and the specified express powers contained in Sch 1)[78] and the other express powers of the administrator set out in paras 61–63, 65–66 and 70–72.

Power to remove and appoint directors

12.117   The administrator may remove a director of the company and also appoint a director of the company, whether or not such appointment is to fill a

---

78   As was the position under the old administration procedure and the wording of IA 1986, s 14(1)(b).

vacancy on the board.[79] Whilst during the administration the powers of management of directors cannot be exercised without the consent of the administrator,[80] a director might purport to exercise powers on behalf of the company and seek to interfere with the administrator. Paragraph 61 enables the administrator to remove such a director. Notwithstanding para 64, since the directors remain in office during the administration and in some cases (particularly trading administrations) the administrator may continue to use the management services of the incumbent directors and give consent under para 64, the administrator may be dissatisfied with the conduct or performance of a director and use para 61 to remove such director and appoint a new director.

Power to call meetings of creditors or members

12.118   The administrator is given power to call a meeting of members or creditors of the company under para 62. The power replicates that under the old administration procedure contained in s 14(2)(b). The administrator might for example need to call a meeting of members if it appeared that there would be a surplus after payment of creditors and the expenses of administration. The members in those circumstances would need to be consulted by the administrator as to the conduct of the administration. Another example would be where the administrator proposed to sell assets of the company to a company connected with one of the directors, which would require shareholder approval under CA 1985, s 320 (see *Demite Ltd v Protec Health Ltd*,[81] as the exception contained within s 321(2)(b) relates only to liquidators and does not cover sales by receivers, administrative receivers or administrators).

Power to apply for directions

12.119   Paragraph 63 enables the administrator to apply to the insolvency court dealing with the administration for directions in connection with his functions. The power replicates that contained under the old administration procedure in s 14(3) of IA 1986 and is similar to the power available to a liquidator under s 168(3) of IA 1986.

12.120   However, the directions that may be given by the court to the administrator on such an application are now restricted by para 68(3),[82] which provides that the court can give directions under para 68(2) (and presumably therefore also on any application by the administrator to court under para 63) only if:

(a)   no proposals have been approved under para 53;
(b)   the directions are consistent with any proposals or revision approved under
      para 53 or 54;

---

79   IA 1996, Sch B1, para 61; the power replicates the power under the old administration
     procedure contained in IA 1986, s 14(2)(a).
80   Ibid, para 64.
81   [1998] BCC 638.
82   There was no equivalent express restriction under the old administration procedure.

(c)   the court thinks the directions are required in order to reflect a change in circumstances since the approval of proposals or a revision under para 53 or 54; or

(d)   the court thinks the directions are desirable because of a misunderstanding about proposals or a revision approved under para 53 or 54.

12.121   Paragraph 68(3) could be applied by the court restrictively (eg because directions can be given 'only' if one of (1)–(4) applies and because of the reference to 'consistent' in para 68(3)(b) rather than 'not inconsistent'). However, it is likely that the court will adopt a benevolent and expansive construction of para 68(3)[83] and the directions which it may give to its officer, in a similar fashion to that displayed under the old administration procedure.

Power of distribution

12.122   Paragraph 65(1) enables the administrator to 'make a distribution to a creditor of the company'. Any such distribution is subject to s 175 of IA 1986 (ie payment of preferential debts in priority), which shall apply to a distribution under para 65 as it applies to a winding-up.[84]

12.123   The administrator can make a distribution to secured creditors or preferential creditors without any consent being obtained from the court. This power is obviously required in view of the abolition of administrative receivership in respect of new debentures, the power of appointment of an administrator at the instance of a qualifying floating charge-holder (QFCH) in order to realise its security and the objective in para 3(1)(c). No consent from the court was required for an administrative receiver to make distributions to secured and preferential creditors and thus none is required for an administrator to do so under the new administration procedure.[85]

12.124   In addition, the administrator is also given power under para 65(3) to make a distribution to an unsecured creditor but only if the administrator obtains permission from the court.

12.125   It is understood that the new rules will make extensive provision as to distributions to be made by an administrator, in effect incorporating the relevant equivalent provisions in respect of distributions by liquidators. They will probably also state that distributions can only be made by an administrator both to preferential creditors and unsecured creditors if such distributions are consistent with the proposals made by him. Thus, if the administrator's proposals state that it is proposed that the administration shall end by placing the company into voluntary liquidation after realisation of assets, then the administrator would not be able to make a distribution to preferential creditors

---

83   Probably construing para 68(3)(c) and (d) as enabling and clarifying that the court can intervene and give directions in those circumstances, rather than the same being construed as restrictive of the circumstances in which the court may intervene and give directions.

84   IA 1986, Sch B1, para 65(2).

85   An administrator under the old administration procedure was of course not appointed to realise assets subject to security and could not do so except with the leave of the court under s 15 of IA 1986, s 15(6) providing for the discharge of the sums secured.

or unsecured creditors, unless he revised the proposals under para 54. If an administrator is at the time of preparation of his proposals (and on the information then available to him) able to envisage a distribution to preferential creditors and an application to the court for permission to make a distribution to unsecured creditors, then it would be prudent to include reference to such distribution in his proposals.

12.126   The power contained in para 65 to make distributions to preferential creditors and (with permission of the court) to unsecured creditors raises the interesting question as to whether the new administration procedure will be used by insolvency practitioners in place of voluntary liquidation. In particular, it might be used not only to realise assets[86] but also to effect distribution of the realisations, without the need to place the company into voluntary liquidation under para 83.

12.127   It might also be attractive for directors of a company to place the company into administration with a view to distribution in the administration rather than placing the company into voluntary liquidation for reasons such as those given below.

(a) There would be no need for the directors to submit themselves to a s 98 meeting and possibly hostile questioning;
(b) There would be likely to be adverse publicity at the time of liquidation, whereas in an administration they would be seen to be doing all that director could to assist a company in trouble with the assistance of 'recovery' specialists.
(c) References to the administration of a company might attach less stigma to a director's career history than if his company has been subject to a liquidation.
(d) The director would be able to avoid the restriction on the re-use of a prohibited company name in a successor business under IA 1986, s 216 (which only applies to insolvent liquidations).

12.128   However, the use of the new administration procedure as a general replacement for voluntary liquidation and use of the power of the administrator to apply to the court for permission to make a distribution to unsecured creditors in general cases may not be warmly received by the court for the following reasons.

(a) The administrator is not given a general power to make distributions to creditors without the need for an application for permission to the court. That is to be contrasted with s 143(1) which provides that the function of a liquidator is 'to secure that the assets of the company are got in, realised and *distributed* to the company's creditors ...' Sch 4, Part III, para 13 provides that the liquidator has 'power to do all such things as may be necessary for winding up the company's affairs and distributing its assets' and r 4.180(1) of IR 1986, which requires the liquidator to declare and distribute dividends whenever he has funds in his hands to do so.

---

86   Assuming no chance for rescuing company as a going concern.

(b) The power conferred under para 65(1) is simply that, and does not impose an obligation; nor is it framed as a power to make distributions to creditors but a distribution to '*a* creditor'.

(c) Paragraph 83 provides a shortcut method for the administrator to place the company into voluntary liquidation and applies where an administrator thinks that:

    (i)   the total amount which each secured creditor of the company is likely to receive had been paid to him or set aside for him; and

    (ii) a distribution will be made to unsecured creditors of the company.[87]

(d) The explanatory notes to the EA 2002 at para 700 and the diagram at Annex H clearly contemplate that the exit route from administration where assets have been realised sufficient to enable a distribution to be made to unsecured creditors should be by way of voluntary liquidation by notice under para 83. Paragraph 700 states:

'Paragraph 83 allows the administrator to end the administration and convert the proceedings into a voluntary winding-up. This *will occur* if the preferential and secured creditors have been paid all they are likely to receive (or such has been set aside for them), and there is money available for the unsecured creditors.'

(e) The agreement of creditors' proofs and distribution to unsecured creditors can easily and more appropriately be done by a voluntary liquidator, rather than by the administrator. There is no reason why an administrator should generally be allowed to undertake such tasks, where the assets of the company have been realised, whilst under the protection of the administration moratorium.

(f) The automatic end of the administration under para 76 is 1 year, beginning with the date on which the appointment of the administrator takes effect. The proposed period of administration was extended following representations made during the passage of the Enterprise Bill but not to enable the administrator to deal with the acceptance of proofs and payment of dividends to unsecured creditors. The underlying parliamentary intention appears to have been to keep the period of administration as short as possible.

12.129 The above points are likely to have a bearing upon an application by an administrator seeking permission to allow distributions to unsecured creditors in general. It is submitted that permission should not be granted for the administrator to make such distributions unless the administrator can justify why the normal course of a voluntary liquidation under para 83 is inappropriate.

12.130 Quite apart from the above points and whether the court under para 65(3) will in general grant permission (or only in special cases), from the

---

87   Although para 83 does not require the administrator to exercise the power to place the company into voluntary liquidation where the circumstances set out in para 83(1) are satisfied. Paragraph 83(3) states that 'The administrator *may* send to the registrar of companies a notice that this paragraph applies'.

administrator's point of view there are substantial advantages to him in not taking on the responsibility of dealing with proofs and distributions whilst acting as administrator:[88]

(a) he is subject to the express misfeasance provisions of para 75;
(b) he is subject to the express statutory duty contained in para 4 to perform his functions as quickly and efficiently as is reasonably practicable.

Payment otherwise than by way of distribution

12.131   Paragraph 66 of Sch B1 enables the administrator to make a payment otherwise than in accordance with para 65 or para 13 of Sch 1 if he thinks it likely to assist the achievement of the purpose of the administration. It is not clear what payments are intended to be covered by para 66 and which fall outside para 13 of Sch 1 and para 65 of Sch B1. It might cover a payment to an existing creditor of the company in respect of an existing debt otherwise than by way of pari passu distribution or payment of a sum to that creditor prior to the declaration of any dividends, which the administrator considers is necessary for the administration in order, for example, to obtain some services, goods or co-operation from that creditor which would otherwise not be forthcoming.

Power to deal with property which is subject to a floating charge

12.132   The administrator may dispose of or take action relating to property which is subject to a floating charge.[89] If he disposes of the property, then the holder of the floating charge is entitled to the same priority in respect of acquired property as he had in respect of the property disposed of.[90]

12.133   This enables the administrator, for example, to dispose of property which is subject to a floating charge[91] where the administrator is attempting to sell the business of the company as a going concern and does not have time to obtain the consent of the floating charge-holder, cannot locate the floating charge-holder or the floating charge-holder has refused consent to the sale. Consent of the court is not required. The floating charge-holder will, however, have priority on any proceeds of sale from the charged property. It is not clear whether the reference to having 'priority' as regards any acquired property or proceeds refers to the preservation of priority as regards other charge-holders or whether it refers to priority as regards payment from those proceeds. If the latter, it is not clear whether the floating charge-holder is entitled to be paid from the sale proceeds in priority to preferential creditors. Paragraph 691 of the Explanatory Notes to EA 2002 suggests that the floating charge-holder is

---

88   The administrator will be the liquidator by default under para 83(7)(b) and in any event is likely to be nominated by the creditors, so he has little to fear by placing the company into voluntary liquidation.
89   IA 1986, Sch B1, para 70 which substantively replicates IA 1986, 15(1), (3) and (4) under the old administration procedure.
90   Ibid, para 70(2). 'Acquired property' is defined by para 70(3) as property of the company which directly or indirectly represents the property disposed of.
91   Which is defined in para 111(1) as 'a charge which is a floating charge on its creation', irrespective of any subsequent crystallisation.

entitled to be paid in priority to any preferential creditors' claim: '... the floating charge-holder has first call on the proceeds of sale'.[92]

Power to deal with property which is subject to a fixed charge

12.134   The administrator may apply to the court for an order enabling him to dispose of property which is subject to a fixed charge as if it were not subject to the security.[93] Again, this provision is likely to be used where the administrator cannot obtain the co-operation of the fixed charge-holder, cannot locate the charge-holder or cannot do so within the time available to the administrator to sell the business as a going concern.

12.135   An order can only be made by the court on the application of the administrator and where the court considers that the disposal of the charged property would be likely to promote the purpose of the administration in respect of the company.[94] If the administrator is seeking to sell the business of the company as a going concern and the charged property is required by the purchaser or if the charged property is included is likely to result in a greater overall sale price for the business, then that condition is likely to be satisfied.

12.136   Where the court makes an order under para 71, then there shall be included in the order a condition that there be applied by the administrator towards discharging the sums secured by the charge:

(a) the net proceeds of disposal of the property; and
(b) any additional money required to be added to the net proceeds so as to produce the amount determined by the court as the net amount which would be realised on a sale of the property at market value.[95]

Market value is defined in para 111(1) as being the amount which would be realised on a sale of the property in the open market by a willing vendor.

12.137   If the property to be disposed of is subject to two or more securities, then the condition under para 71 as regards the application of the sale proceeds applies to all the securities and the moneys are applied in the order of priority of the securities.[96]

12.138   The administrator is required to send a copy of any successful order under para 71(1) to the Registrar of Companies[97] and commits an offence if he fails without reasonable excuse to do so.[98]

---

92   However, see the discussion as regards IA 1986, s 15(3) and (4) under the old administration procedure in Sealy and Milman, op cit, p 72.
93   IA 1986, Sch B1, para 71 which substantively replicates the power under IA 1986, s 15(1)–(8) as regards fixed charges under the old administration procedure.
94   Ibid, para 71(2).
95   Ibid, para 71(3).
96   Ibid, para 71(4).
97   Ibid, para 71(5).
98   Ibid, para 71(6).

Power to deal with hire-purchase property

12.139   The administrator may apply to the court for an order allowing him to dispose of goods which are in the possession of the company under a hire-purchase agreement as if the rights of the owner under the agreement were vested in the company.[99] A 'hire-purchase agreement' is defined by para 111(1) as including a conditional sale agreement, a chattel-leasing agreement and a retention of title agreement. The circumstances in which an order can be made by the court, conditions to be attached to such order, obligation to send a copy of any successful order made to the Registrar of Companies and offence for failure to do so are the same as those that apply under para 71 to the disposal of property which is subject to a fixed charge.[100]

REPLACEMENT OF ADMINISTRATOR

Resignation of administrator

12.140   An administrator is only allowed to resign in the circumstances prescribed by the Rules,[101] which are likely to be:

(a) if he has ceased practising as an insolvency practitioner;
(b) if there has arisen a conflict of interest or change of personal circumstances, which precludes him or makes impracticable the further discharge of his duties;
(c) if the court grants permission on such other ground as it sees fit.

12.141   In order to resign the administrator must serve written notice on the court if appointed by it and, otherwise, on the person appointing him (ie floating charge-holder, directors or the company).[102]

Removal from office by court

12.142   Paragraph 88 enables the court to remove the administrator from office. No circumstances are stated, but it is likely that the court would only do so on sufficient cause being shown, applying by way of analogy the cases concerning the removal of liquidators and trustees in bankruptcy.

Ceasing to be qualified

12.143   The administrator shall vacate his office if he ceases to be qualified to act as an insolvency practitioner in relation to the company. He is required to give notice of that fact to the court if appointed by the court, and otherwise to the person appointing him.[103]

---

99   IA 1986, Sch B1, para 72, which replicates the power under IA 1986, s 15, which was extended to hire-purchase agreements by s 15(9).
100   Ibid, para 72(2)–(5).
101   Ibid, para 87(1).
102   Ibid, para 87(2).
103   Ibid, para 89(2). Failure to do so without reasonable excuse is an offence under para 89(3).

Filling vacancy in office of administrator

12.144   Paragraphs 91–95 set out the procedure for filling a vacancy in the office of administrator arising from the death, resignation, removal under para 88 or vacation of office under para 89 of the administrator.[104] The procedure varies depending upon the mode of appointment of the departed administrator.

(1) Where appointed by court by administration order

12.145   The court may make an order appointing an administrator on the application of the creditors' committee, the company, the directors, a creditor or a joint administrator. However, it can only do so at the instance of the company, directors or a creditor if:

(a)   there is no creditors' committee;
(b)   the court is satisfied that the creditors' committee or a remaining joint administrator is not taking reasonable steps to make a replacement; or
(c)   the court is satisfied that for another reason it is right for the application to be made.[105]

(2) Where appointed under para 14 by floating charge-holder

12.146   The floating charge-holder is entitled to appoint the replacement.[106]

(3) Where appointed under para 22(1) by the company

12.147   The company may appoint the replacement; however, the consent of each person who is the holder of a qualifying floating charge must be obtained, failing which permission must be obtained from the court.[107]

(4) Where appointed under para 22(2) by the directors

12.148   The directors of the company may appoint the replacement; however, the consent of each person who is the holder of a qualifying floating charge must be obtained, failing which permission must be obtained from the court.[108]

12.149   There is a residual power of the court under para 95 to appoint a replacement administrator on the application of the creditors' committee, the company, the directors of the company, a creditor or a joint administrator, if the court is satisfied that:

(a)   the person who otherwise would be entitled to make such appointment under paras 92–94 is not taking reasonable steps to make a replacement; or

---

104 IA 1986, Sch B1, para 90.
105 Ibid, para 91.
106 Ibid, para 92.
107 Ibid, para 93.
108 Ibid, para 94.

(b)   that for another reason it is right for the court to make the replacement.

Substitution of administrator by prior floating charge-holder

12.150   The holder of a prior qualifying floating charge may apply to the court to replace an administrator appointed under para 14 by the holder of a qualifying floating charge.[109] A floating charge is treated as 'prior' if it was created first or is to be treated as having priority in accordance with an agreement to which the holder of each floating charge was party.[110] Since this paragraph does not give the prior floating charge-holder a right to appoint a substitute, presumably the prior floating charge-holder must establish some grounds relating to the conduct of the incumbent administrator to justify its replacement. The requirement to show grounds is sensible, because the prior floating charge-holder would have been served with notice of intention to appoint the incumbent administrator under para 15(1)(a) prior to his appointment and thereby could himself have appointed his own choice of administrator.

Substitution of administrator appointed by company or directors at instance of creditors' meeting

12.151   If an administrator is appointed by the company or its directors under para 22 and there is no holder of a qualifying floating charge in respect of the company's property, then a creditors' meeting can substitute the administrator with a person chosen by the creditors.[111] The new administrator's written consent to act must be presented to the creditors' meeting before the replacement is made.

Discharge from liability on vacation of office

12.152   Where a person ceases to be the administrator of a company (whether he vacates office, is removed from office or his appointment ceases to have effect because of the ending of the administration under paras 76–85), the administrator is discharged from liability in respect of any action of his as administrator by para 98(1).

12.153   The discharge takes effect:

(a)   in the case of an administrator who dies, on the filing with the court of notice of his death;
(b)   in the case of an administrator appointed out of court under para 14 or 22 at a time appointed by resolution of the creditors' committee or, if there is no committee, by resolution of the creditors; or
(c)   in any case, at a time specified by the court.[112]

In the case of (b), if the administrator has made a statement under para 52(1)(b), a resolution shall only be taken as passed if approved by:

---

109   IA 1986, Sch B1, para 96(1) and (2).
110   Ibid, para 96(3).
111   Ibid, para 97(1) and (2).
112   Ibid, para 98(2).

(a) each secured creditor; or
(b) where the administrator has made a distribution to preferential creditors or thinks that a distribution may be made to preferential creditors, then by each secured creditor and by 50% of the preferential creditors.[113]

12.154   Paragraph 98(4) provides that:

> 'discharge—
> (a) applies to liability accrued before the discharge takes effect, and
> (b) does not prevent the exercise of the court's powers under paragraph 75.'

12.155   Paragraph 98 replaces the discharge provisions contained in IA 1986, s 20(2) and (3). Section 20(2) contained wider wording in that it referred to 'all liability both in respect of acts or omissions of his in the administration and otherwise in relation to his conduct as administrator', whereas para 98 only refers to 'any action of his as administrator'.

12.156   There remains uncertainty as to the effect of the release from liability granted by para 98, given that the same does not prevent the court exercising its powers under para 75 in respect of claims brought against the administrator.

Charges and liabilities on vacation of office

12.157   Where a person ceases to be the administrator of a company (whether he vacates office, is removed from office or his appointment ceases to have effect because of the ending of the administration under paras 76–85), then para 99 applies as regards charges and liabilities.

12.158   Paragraph 99(3) provides that the former administrator's remuneration and expenses shall be:

(a) charged on and payable out of property of which he had custody or control immediately before the time that he ceases to be the company's administrator; and
(b) payable in priority to any security to which para 70 applies.

12.159   That sub-paragraph substantively reproduces s19(4) of IA 1986 so the position will remain the same as under the old administration procedure.

12.160   The administrator's remuneration is otherwise not referred to in the EA 2002. Provision for the same will be made in the rules, the provisions under the old administration procedure which is likely to repeat, save that where the administrator has made a statement under para 51(1)(b), a resolution for approval of his remuneration by the creditors' meeting will be treated as passed if the same is approved by:

(a) each secured creditor; or
(b) if the administrator has made a distribution to preferential creditors or thinks that a distribution may be made to preferential creditors:

    (i)   each secured creditor; and
    (ii) preferential creditors whose debts amount to more than 50% of the preferential debts of the company.

---

113 IA 1986, Sch B1, para 98(3).

12.161   Paragraph 99(4) provides:

'A sum payable in respect of a debt or liability arising out of a contract entered into
by the former administrator or a predecessor before the administrator ceases to be
company's administrator shall be—

    (a)   charged on and payable out of property of which the former administrator had
           custody or control immediately before he ceases to be the company's
           administrator, and
    (b)   payable in priority to any charge arising under sub-paragraph (3).'

12.162   Paragraph 99(4) substantively reproduces IA 1986, s 19(5) so the
position will remain the same as under the old administration procedure. This
still leaves unresolved the issues surrounding administration expenses, including
liabilities arising under pre-administration contracts (eg rental payments and
hire charges): see, for example, *Re Salmet International Ltd.*[114]

12.163   Paragraph 99(5) deals with contracts of employment and states that
sub-para (4) shall apply to a liability arising under a contract of employment
which was adopted by the administrator or a predecessor before he ceased to be
the company's administrator. For that purpose:

(a)   action taken within the period of 14 days after the administrator's
       appointment shall not be taken to amount or contribute to the adoption of
       a contract;
(b)   no account shall be taken of a liability which arises, or in so far as it arises,
       by reference to anything which is done or which occurs before the adoption
       of the contract of employment; and
(c)   no account shall be taken of a liability to make a payment other than wages
       or salary.

12.164   Paragraph 99(6) states that 'wages or salary' in sub-para (5)(c)
includes:

'(a)   a sum payable in respect of a period of holiday (for which purpose the sum
        shall be treated as relating to the period by reference to which the entitlement
        to holiday accrued),
   (b)   a sum payable in respect of a period of absence through illness or other good
        cause,
   (c)   a sum payable in lieu of holiday,
   (d)   in respect of a period, a sum which would be treated as earnings for that period
        for the purposes of an enactment about social security, and
   (e)   a contribution to an occupational pension scheme.'

12.165   Paragraph 99(5) and (6) substantively reproduces the IA 1986,
s 19(6)–(10), which were introduced by the IA 1994 in the light of *Powdrill v
Watson; Re Paramount Airways Ltd (No 3)*.[115] The position remains the same
as under the old administration procedure.[116]

---

114   [2001] BCC 796.
115   [1994] BCC 172.
116   See Sealy and Milman, op cit, pp 80–82.

Chapter 13

ENDING THE ADMINISTRATION AND EXIT ROUTES

'Our life is frittered away by detail ... Simplify, simplify.'
Henry David Thoreau[1]

INTRODUCTION

13.1   After 15 years' experience of the administration process, the insolvency profession can testify that, at a practical level, one of the more irritating deficiencies of the 1986 legislation was its failure to provide procedures for coming out of administration. Until now, the profession had grown accustomed to referring to the troublesome procedures for coming out of the old administrations as 'exits'.

13.2   As part of the quest to modernise statutory language, the old English 'end' or 'ending' has been adopted in the EA 2002 to describe compendiously the various routes out of the new administration procedure. In this chapter, 'exits' (a term not used in the EA 2002) are referred to as a sub-group of the wider group of 'endings'.

13.3   'Exits' connote a positive act by the administrator to send the company to its long home and will be mentioned first. After a brief description of the old procedures, consideration will then be given to the broader group of 'endings'.

Summary of new exit routes

13.4   The EA 2002 has clarified and simplified the exit routes. The major innovations are as follows.

(a) Convert to CVL – allowing the administrator to end the administration and convert the insolvency proceedings into a creditors' voluntary winding-up in circumstances where the secured and preferential creditors have been paid all they are likely to receive (or such has been set aside for them) and there is money available for the unsecured creditors.

(b) Straight to dissolution – the administrator may take steps to dissolve the company where the company has no further assets available for distribution. The company will be dissolved at the expiration of 3 months of the registration of a notice sent by the administrator to the Registrar of Companies.

---

1   1817–1862.

13.5   Under the old procedure (see below), where an administrator sought to discharge the administration order and place the company into compulsory or voluntary liquidation, the process was over-complicated and fraught with technical hurdles. This, in turn, involved a waste of time and money in applications to the court at the expense of the creditors. Experience and judicial comment have long indicated the need for more streamlined exit routes from administration. With the new emphasis in the EA 2002 on administration as the preferred rescue procedure, it is both timely and fitting that the EA 2002 should introduce improved procedures for exiting administration.

13.6   The stated aims behind the new administration procedure are speed and economy and the principal exit routes under the new procedure are:

(a)   CVA – where there has been a rescue, the principal exit route is a creditors' voluntary arrangement (CVA) or s 425 of CA 1985 arrangement;

(b)   CVL – where there has been a better realisation of assets and there are sufficient realisations to enable payment to the secured and preferential creditors and a dividend to unsecured creditors, then the principal exit route is a creditors' voluntary liquidation (CVL);

(c)   dissolution – where assets have been realised to enable a distribution to secured creditors and possibly preferential creditors but there will be no dividend available to unsecured creditors, then the principal exit route is dissolution of the company.[2]

The old procedure – ending the administration

13.7   Under the old administration procedure, given that all administrations were commenced by an administration order made by the court, there was only one means by which the administration could come to an end, namely by an order of the court.

13.8   In cases where the administration order was granted only for a specified period,[3] then the administration could come to an end by effluxion of time under the original order, if no application was made by the administrator to extend the administration. In those cases where an administration order was made but it was not limited to a specified time[4] and in those cases where the administration order was for a specified period, then the administration could be brought to an end by an application by the administrator to court for the discharge of the administration order under s 18(1) of IA 1986. The administrator was under a duty by s 18(2) of IA 1986 to apply for the discharge of the administration order if:

---

2   See Explanatory Notes, Annex H and paras 700–701.

3   Which some judges favoured in order for the judge to retain control of the administration, progress therein and obtain reports back from the administrator.

4   Which other judges favoured in order to keep costs to a minimum and in reliance on the administrators as officers of the court bringing the matter back to court as speedily as possible if the objective of the administration was achieved, could no longer be achieved or there was a material change in circumstances from when the order was made which might justify the discharge of the administration.

(a) it appeared to the administrator that the purpose or each of the purposes specified in the administration order had been achieved; or

(b) it appeared to the administrator that the purpose or each of the purposes specified in the administration order was incapable of achievement;[5] or

(c) the administrator was required to make such an application by a meeting of the company's creditors summoned for the purpose.

13.9   Under the old procedure the court could also discharge the administration order:

(a) under s 24(5) of IA 1986, following a report by the administrator that his proposals had not been accepted by the creditors' meeting;

(b) under s 27(4) of IA 1986, if the company's affairs, business and property were being managed by the administrator in a manner which was unfairly prejudicial to creditors or members or some part of the same.

The old procedure – exit routes

13.10   The exit routes for the company in practical terms following an order of the court discharging the administration order were not expressly set out. In general the exit routes were as follows.

(a) A compulsory winding-up order. This was on the petition of the administrator presented in reliance on the power given to the administrator under Sch 1, para 21 od IA 1986 and r 4.7(7)(a) of the IR 1986.[6] The application for discharge of the administration order under s 18 of IA 1986 is contained within the winding-up petiton.[7] This exit route tended to be used for unsuccessful[8] administrations where there were insufficient assets in the hands of the administrator to warrant a voluntary winding up and where the administrator was unwilling to act as liquidator.

(b) A CVL. This exit route tended to be used where there had been a better realisation of assets than on a liquidation and there were sufficient assets for distribution to preferential and unsecured creditors. The major advantage of the voluntary liquidation route was the saving in costs because the

---

5   *Re Charnley Davies Business Services Ltd* (1987) 3 BCC 408 being an example in which the discharge application was made where one of the purposes was achieved and the other stated purpose could no longer be achieved.

6   The draftsman of the IA 1986 having omitted to include the administrator as a person entitled to present a petition for winding-up in s 124 of IA 1986.

7   IR 1986, r 4.7(7). By r 4.7(9) such winding-up petition is treated as a petition filed by contributories and therefore Chapter 4 of IR 1986 applied to it. There was therefore no requirement for the petition to be advertised and the court would give directions for the conduct of the petition under IR 1986, r 4.23(1). In practice and in order to save time and costs, the winding-up petition by the administrator was often simply made returnable at the time of issue before the judge (rather than having an initial directions hearing before the registrar or district judge with the petition then being adjourned to the judge) so that the administration order could be discharged and winding-up order made on the return day (para 5.1(7) of the Practice Direction: Insolvency Proceedings now requires petitions to discharge an administration order and to wind up to be made direct to the judge).

8   Although there might have been a return to secured creditors and/or a marginally better realisation of assets than in a liquidation, albeit no likely dividend to unsecured creditors after the costs of the administration.

voluntary liquidator was not obliged to pay moneys into the Insolvency Services account and therefore the ad valorum fee would not be payable. However, there were substantial complications with using this exit route, as set out below.

(c) A CVA.

(d) The sanction of a compromise or arrangement under s 425 of CA 1985.

THE NEW PROVISIONS – 'ENDING ADMINISTRATION' – EIGHT WAYS TO LEAVE ADMINISTRATION

13.11   Under the new procedure there are now eight means by which the appointment of the administrator can cease to have effect and thereby for the company to cease to be in administration.[9] These are:

(a) under para 76 by effluxion of time;
(b) under para 79 by court order on the application of the administrator;
(c) under para 80 by notice filed by the administrator where the purpose of the administration has been sufficiently achieved;
(d) under para 81 by court order on the application of a creditor where there has been an improper motive in the appointment of the administrator;
(e) under para 82 by court order where there has been a winding-up order made in the public interest;
(f) under para 82 by notice filed by the administrator to place the company into CVL;
(g) under para 84 by notice filed by the administrator to dissolve the company;
(h) under para 55(2) by court order where there has been a failure of the creditors to agree the administrator's proposals or revisions to proposals;[10]
(i) under para 74(4)(d) by court order where there has been unfair harm to creditors or members by the administrator's actions.[11]

'AUTOMATIC END'

Effluxion of time

13.12   By para 76(1) the appointment of an administrator shall automatically cease to have effect at the end of the period of 1 year, beginning with the date on which the appointment takes effect.

---

9   The change in the wording away from the 'discharge of the administration order' to 'the appointment of an administrator shall cease to have effect' is required because of the ability to appoint an administrator out of court. Para 1(2)(b) provides that the company is 'in administrtion' while the appointment of an administrator of the company has effect and para 1(2)(c) provides that the company ceases to be in administration when the appointment of an administrator of the company ceases to have effect.
10   See **12.91–12.93** and **12.104**.
11   See **12.30–12.37**.

13.13   The Enterprise Bill had proposed an automatic end to the administration after 3 months. However, following strong lobbying,[12] the Act in its enacted form has extended the period for automatic end to 1 year.[13]

13.14   It should be noted that the automatic end of the administrator's appointment applies irrespective of whether the administrator was appointed by the court, or out of court by a QFCH under para 14 or by the directors or company under para 22. It will therefore be imperative that this date is diarised by administrators, particularly those appointed by a QFCH who still regard themselves as adminstrative receivers, by another name.

13.15   It should also be emphasised that the automatic end of the administrator's appointment applies, even if the administrator has made a statement in his proposals under para 52(1)(b) and he is only pursuing the objective under para 3(1)(c) of realising property in order to make a distribution to one or more secured creditors.

Extension of period

13.16   The automatic end of the administrator's appointment under para 76(1) is subject to the power to extend the period of 1 year under para 76(2).

Extension by creditors

13.17   The administrator's term of office can be extended by the consent of the creditors. It can be extended for a specified period not exceeding 6 months.[14] However, the creditors cannot extend the term of office by consent:

(a) more than once;
(b) after an extension has been granted by the court; or
(c) after the expiry of the term of office.[15]

13.18   The 'consent' of creditors is in general defined as the consent of:

(a) each secured creditor of the company, and
(b) if the company has unsecured debts, creditors whose debts amount to more than 50% of the company's unsecured debts, disregarding the debts of any creditor who does not respond to an invitation to give or withhold consent.[16]

13.19   However, where the administrator has made a statement in his proposals under para 52(1)(b) (insufficient property to allow distribution to unsecured creditors), then consent means:

(a) the consent of each secured creditor, or

---

12 By the insolvency profession, R3, the BBA, the FLA and the CBI.
13 Although with the introduction of the express statutory duty on the administrator under para 4 to perform his functions as quickly and efficiently as is reasoanbly practicable, as a quid pro quo.
14 IA 1986, Sch B1, para 76(2)(b).
15 Ibid, para 78(4).
16 Ibid, para 78(1).

(b) if the administrator thinks that a distribution may be made to preferential creditors, the consent of:

  (i)   each secured creditor, and
  (ii) preferential creditors whose debts amount to more than 50% of the preferential debts of the company, disregarding debts of any creditor who does not respond to an invitation to give or withhold consent.[17]

13.20   The consent of creditors may be obtained by the administrator in writing or at a creditors' meeting.[18] If consent is obtained, then the administrator is required to file a notice of the extension at court and notify the Registrar of Companies.[19]

Extension by the court

13.21   The court may extend the term of office of the administrator and duration of the administration on the application of the administrator for a specified period under para 76(2)(a). There is no restriction on the period by which the court may extend the term of office.

13.22   An extension by the court may be made:

(a) where the term of office has already been extended by the creditors by consent, or
(b) where the term of office has already been extended by the court.[20]

13.23   However, an extension cannot be granted by the court after the expiry of the administrator's term of office.[21] There is therefore no jurisdiction for the court to extend retrospectively the term of office if the term has already expired. This highlights the importance of diarising the automatic end-date, to ensure that any application to extend time is issued and heard prior to the expiry of the period.

13.24   If the court grants an extension, then the administrator is required to notify the Registrar of Companies of the extension as soon as reasonably practicable.[22]

13.25   There may be a number of reasons why it is necessary for the administrator to seek an extension of the 1-year period, for example because:

(a) the administration is large and has proved complicated and/or technical – this may include difficulties in agreeing proposals, the terms of a CVA or s 425 arrangement or getting in and realising assets;

---

17   IA 1986, para 78(2).
18   Ibid, para 78(3).
19   Ibid, para 78(5). The administrator commits an offence if he fails without reasonable excuse to comply with para 78(5): para 78(6).
20   Ibid, para 77(1)(a).
21   Ibid, para 77(1(b).
22   Ibid, para 77(2). The administrator commits an offence if he fails to do so without reasonable excuse: para 77(3).

(b) the administration may include continued trading;

(c) the administration may include continued development of a property or building site, works of renovation or repair/impovement to property or the obtaining of planning permission;

(d) the administrator may be pursuing litigation (eg clawback litigation against directors or connected companies), which has not yet reached trial;

(e) there may be delays in agreeing creditors claims if the administrator is proposing to make a distribution to creditors.

13.26   The following factors may be relevant to the court's discretion and consideration of the reasons given by the administrator for seeking the extension:

(a) the new administration procedure has the stated aim of being streamlined, short, inexpensive and temporary;

(b) the new procedure includes an automatic end after 1 year, from which it may be inferred that Parliament intended in normal cases that administrations would be completed within this period. That can be contrasted with there being no automatic end date for administrations under the old procedure or for administrative receiverships;

(c) para 4 provides that the administrator must perform his functions as quickly and efficiently as is reasonably practicable. The court must consider whether the administrator has in fact fulfilled that duty or if the reason for the requested extension is due to failure by the administrator to progress the administration expeditiously;

(d) whether the remaining matters that need to be dealt with by the administrator could more appropriately be dealt with if the company was in a CVL or compulsory liquidation (eg distributions to unsecured creditors, investigations into the conduct of directors, investigations into possible recovery proceedings, the conduct of litigation). Linked to this is whether the company requires the continued protection of the moratorium on insolvency proceedings and other legal process.

13.27   It is certainly not safe to assume that the court will look favourably on applications for extensions in run-of-the-mill administrations.

COURT ENDING ADMINISTRATION ON APPLICATION OF ADMINISTRATOR

13.28   The court can order that the appointment of the administrator shall cease to have effect and the administration end from a specified time, on an application to the court by the administrator under para 79(1).

13.29   An administrator is required by para 79(2) to make an application under para 79(1) to bring his appointment to an end if:

(a) he thinks the purpose of the administration cannot be achieved in relation to the company;

(b) he thinks the company should not have entered into administration; or

(c) a creditors' meeting requires him to make an application under this paragraph.

13.30 IA 1986, Sch B1, para 79(1)(a) mirrors the obligation under s 18(2)(a) of IA 1986;[23] however, given the expansion of the statutory purpose by para 3(1)(b) and (c), it seems unlikely that an application under para 79(1)(a) would be common place.[24] The only circumstance would appear to be where no distribution could be made even to a secured creditor (eg because there were no assets realised or any realisations would be used in meeting the administrator's remuneration).

13.31 IA 1986, Sch B1, para 79(1)(b) would appear to cover situations where the company is solvent and the administration procedure is not required by the company. It would also cover the situation where the administrator formed the view that a QFCH did not have the power to appoint an administrator (eg because its floating charge was void or not enforceable).

13.32 IA 1986, Sch B1, para 79(1)(c) will cover a situation where the creditors consider that it is not in their interests for the administration to continue. In theory, this could be used by unsecured creditors to force a company out of administration (eg where the administrator was appointed by a QFCH) and into liquidation, if they did not perceive any benefit accruing to them from the administration and provided they held a majority of the debt (including any ability of the QFCH to vote without surrendering its security by reason of a para 52(1)(b) statement by the administrator in his proposals). The creditors might, for example, prefer an investigation into the directors' conduct of the company by the official receiver.

WHERE OBJECTIVE ACHIEVED ON ADMINISTRATION ORDER GRANTED BY COURT

13.33 In addition to the circumstances set out in para 79(2), an administrator appointed by the court is also required by para 79(3) to apply to the court under para 79(1) if he thinks that the purpose of the administration has been sufficiently achieved.

13.34 That would cover situations where there has been a rescue and turnaround of the company, which is able to survive and be returned to the control of the directors. It would also cover a rescue where a CVA was approved or a s 425 arrangement sanctioned.

13.35 IA 1986, Sch B1, para 80 referred to below covers the equivalent situation where the purpose of the administration has been achieved but the administrator was appointed out of court by a QFCH or the company/directors.

13.36 On an application under para 79(1), the court is given power to:

(a) adjourn the hearing conditionally or unconditionally;
(b) dismiss the application;
(c) make an interim order;

---

23   See, for example, *Re Charnley Davies Business Services Ltd* (1987) 3 BCC 408.
24   Although see *Re Carter Commercial Developments Ltd* [2002] BPIR 1053.

(d) make any order it thinks appropriate (whether in addition to, in consequence of or instead of the order applied for).[25]

TERMINATION OF OUT-OF-COURT ADMINISTRATION WHERE OBJECTIVE ACHIEVED

13.37   IA 1986, Sch B1, para 80 provides the means of terminating an administration where the administrator was appointed out of court by a QFCH under para 14 or the company/directors under para 22 and the administrator thinks that the purpose of the administration has been sufficiently achieved.

13.38   In those circumstances, the administrator may file a notice in the prescribed form with the court and the Registrar of Companies[26] and the administrator's appointment will cease to have effect once those notices are filed.[27]

13.39   It should be noted that the administrator is not obliged to use the para 80 route for ending the administration. He may consider that putting the company into a CVL under para 83 or dissolving the company under para 84 is the more appropriate route.

13.40   If the administrator files a notice under para 80(2), then he is required by para 80(4) to send a copy of the notice to every creditor of the company of whose claim and address he is aware. IA 1986, Sch B1, para 80(5) provides that the Rules may provide a means whereby the administrator can advertise within a prescribed period such a notice, which includes an undertaking to provide a copy of the notice to any creditor who applies in writing for the same.[28]

IMPROPER 'MOTIVE'

13.41   IA 1986, Sch B1, para 81(1) gives the court power to provide for the appointment of an administrator to cease to have effect at a specified time, on the application of a creditor of the company.

13.42   Such application can only be made if it alleges (and presumably the court is satisfied that) there was an improper motive:

(a) in the case of an administrator appointed by an administration order, on the part of the applicant for the order; or
(b) in any other case, on the part of the person who appointed the administrator.

13.43   On such an application the court may:

(a) adjourn the hearing conditionally or unconditionally;
(b) dismiss the application;
(c) make an interim order;

---

25   IA 1986, Sch B1, para 79(4).
26   Ibid, para 80(2).
27   Ibid, para 80(3).
28   The administrator commits an offence if he fails without reasonable excuse to comply with para 80(4).

(d) make any order it thinks appropriate (whether in addition to, in consequence of or instead of the order applied for).

13.44   As regards what amounts to an 'improper motive' the court is likely to be guided by *Re Dianoor Jewels Ltd* [2001] 1 BCLC 450.[29] However, it should be noted that the relevant test under this paragraph is improper 'motive' rather than an improper 'purpose'. This may give greater scope for challenge as it concentrates on the motivation of the applicant/appointer, which may prove easier to establish than an improper 'purpose', where the respondent could claim to have a number of purposes, some of which were legitimate.

PUBLIC INTEREST WINDING-UP

13.45   Where a winding-up order is made against the company on a petition presented under:

(a) IA 1986, s 124A (public interest), or
(b) Financial Services and Markets Act 2000, s 367 (petition by the Financial Services Authority),

or a provisional liquidator is appointed on such a petition, then that order may provide that the appointment of the administrator shall cease to have effect or that such appointment shall continue.[30]

13.46   The court may also make an order that if the administrator is to remain in office, his powers are to be restricted or modified.[31]

13.47   Such order will presumably take into account the reasons for the petition, the administrator's proposals and whether the public interest is best protected by leaving the administrator in situ or removing him and leaving the matter to the liquidator or provisional liquidator.

CREDITORS' VOLUNTARY LIQUIDATION

The old procedure – the problems

13.48   The IA 1986 did not contain any express provision allowing a company to enter into voluntary liquidation following the discharge of an administration order by the court, despite the fact that in many cases a voluntary liquidation was preferred to a compulsory liquidation by the creditors. Opting to exit administration and enter into a CVL created two particular problems.

Transition from administration to winding-up

13.49   First, there was the practical difficulty of the transition from administration into voluntary liquidation since the old s 11(3)(a) forbade the passing of a resolution to wind up the company whilst it was still in administration. This was generally overcome by making the discharge out of

29   See also *Re Ross (A Bankrupt) (No 2)* [2000] BPIR 636; *Hicks v Gulliver and Another* [2002] BPIR 518.
30   IA 1986, Sch B1, para 82(1)–(3).
31   Ibid, para 82(4).

administration conditional upon the passing of a resolution for the winding-up of the company or by directing that the order for discharge not be drawn until copies of the resolution had been lodged with the court.

13.50 Secondly, some preferential creditors would be disadvantaged by reason of the application of s 387(3)(a) or (c) where a different 'relevant date' for the purposes of the winding-up applied. In a voluntary liquidation, they are ascertained as at the date of the resolution to wind up and they would be in a worse position than if there was a compulsory liquidation. There was a considerable amount of litigation on how these problems could practically be overcome.[32]

13.51 Furthermore, a voluntary liquidation is the significantly cheaper option of the two and there will consequently be more funds available for distribution amongst the unsecured creditors. These points clearly created a conflict between their interests and those of the creditors who were preferential creditors as at the time of the administration order.[33]

The new procedure

CVL by notice

13.52 The new scheme eliminates these difficulties in two ways. First, exit into a CVL will now take place automatically upon the registration of the requisite notice with the Registrar of Companies.[34] Secondly, the Act empowers the administrator to make distributions to preferential and secured creditors without the need to apply to the court for directions, thereby reducing costs.[35] The administrator may also make a distribution to unsecured creditors, but for this, he will require the permission of the court.[36]

13.53 The streamlined nature of the new procedure was highlighted by Lord McIntosh of Haringey in the Lords:[37]

> 'The potential for a company to move directly into a creditors' voluntary liquidation from administration is new and is introduced by paragraph 83 of Schedule B1 ... This will facilitate, for example, distributions to unsecured creditors.

---

32 See *Re Powerstore (Trading) Ltd* [1998] BCC 305; *Re Philip Alexander Securities and Futures Ltd* [1998] BCC 819; *Re Mark One (Oxford Street) plc* [1998] BCC 984; *Re Norditrak (UK) Ltd* [2000] 1 WLR 343; *Re Wolsey Theatre Co Ltd* [2001] BCC 486; *Re UCT (UK) Ltd* [2001] Ch 436. *Re Mark One (Oxford Street) plc* [1998] BCC 984 finally settled the matter. Jacob J held that the court had power to order that the administrator make payments to preferential creditors as if the voluntary liquidation were a compulsory one, or alternatively, that the payment of the funds to the future liquidator by the administrator was to take the form of a trust. He identified the source of this power as derived from ss 14(3) and 18(3) of IA 1986 and the court's inherent power to control an administrator in his capacity as an officer of the court.

33 Although the abolition of Crown Preference will reduce the number of preferential creditors.

34 IA 1986, Sch B1, para 83(6).

35 Ibid, para 65. The Act specifically applies s 175 of IA 1986 (payment of preferential debts) in relation to this exercise of the administrator's powers.

36 Ibid, para 65(3).

37 *Hansard* (HL), vol 639, 21 October 2002, col 1124.

...

We have provided that certain requirements necessary where a company goes directly into voluntary liquidation will not be necessary or appropriate where a company moves from administration into creditors' voluntary liquidation. These matters include the requirement to publish a notice of the resolution to wind up, to hold a meeting of creditors, to lay a statement of affairs before the creditors and appoint a liquidator. This latter requirement is addressed specifically by paragraph 83. The others will have already been undertaken as part of the administration process. There is no value in repeating them simply for the purpose of the creditors' voluntary liquidation.

In addition, the possibility of a declaration of solvency has no place in this procedure. Where a creditors' committee has already been formed in administration, it will continue to exist as if it were a liquidation committee.'

Repetition of needless formalities has no place in this procedure.

13.54   If the administrator thinks that the company should exit administration and move into a CVL because there will be funds to distribute to unsecured creditors, he may send a notice to this effect to the Registrar of Companies.[38] Before the administrator can use this provision, he must believe that:

(1)   the total amount which each secured creditor is likely to receive has been paid to him, or that sum has been set aside for him;[39] and

(2)   a distribution will be made to unsecured creditors, if there are any.[40]

If the administrator files such a notice with the Registrar of Companies, he must, as soon as is reasonably practicable, file a copy of the notice with the court and send a copy to every creditor of whom he is aware.[41]

Appointment of liquidator

13.55   Once this notice is registered, the administrator's appointment shall cease and the company will be wound up as if a s 84 resolution for voluntary winding-up had been passed on that day.[42] The creditors thereafter have the power to appoint a liquidator,[43] but, in the absence of any such appointment, the administrator will automatically be appointed liquidator.[44]

13.56   Paragraph 58[45] provides that any action which is required or permitted to be taken at a creditors' meeting may be done in correspondence between the administrator and the creditors, including the requirement to hold the meeting itself;[46] again, providing that the process is as quick and cheap as possible.

---

38   IA 1986, Sch B1, para 83(3).
39   Ibid, para 83(1)(a).
40   Ibid, para 83(1)(b).
41   Ibid, para 83(5).
42   Ibid, para 83(6).
43   Ibid, para 83(7)(a).
44   Ibid, para 83(7)(b).
45   Ibid.
46   Ibid, para 58(3).

13.57 The new legislation provides either that the creditors may nominate a liquidator or the administrator is *automatically* appointed by default. Presumably, the proposal for the CVL will nominate the creditors' chosen liquidator.

13.58 There is no specific provision as to what will occur in the event that the creditors fail to nominate a liquidator and the administrator, for whatever reason, does not wish to continue his involvement with the company as liquidator.

13.59 It seems unlikely that the administrator will be required to become liquidator against his wishes; further, it is sometimes the case that the administrator is not appointed liquidator for other practical reasons such as complaints from creditors about the administrator's conduct of the administration.

13.60 The administrator can, of course, still put the company into compulsory liquidation, as opposed to taking advantage of the new statutory exit routes. In this way, the liquidator is appointed in the conventional manner and the issue of the administrator's appointment in that role can be avoided.

13.61 It is to be noted that para 83 specifically disapplies or amends a number of existing sections under Part IV of IA 1986, most of which are rendered superfluous by the introduction of the automatic exit route:

(a) gazetting of the resolution to wind up the company[47] does not apply;

(b) commencement of the voluntary winding-up shall be calculated as if reference to the time of the passing of the resolution for the voluntary winding-up of the company were reference to the beginning of the date of registration of the notice;[48]

(c) the statutory declaration of solvency[49] does not apply;

(d) the requirement of a creditors' meeting,[50] a directors' statement of affairs[51] and an appointment of a liquidator does not apply;[52]

(e) commencement of the winding-up by the court shall be calculated as if reference to the time of the passing of the resolution for the voluntary winding-up of the company were reference to the beginning of the date of registration of the notice;[53]

(f) any creditors' committee which is in existence immediately before the company ceases to be in administration shall continue in existence after that time as if appointed as a liquidation committee under s 101.[54]

Effect of new procedure

13.62 The practical outcome of this new scheme will be that voluntary liquidation will largely replace compulsory liquidation as an exit route for

---

47 IA 1986, s 85.
48 Ibid, s 86.
49 Ibid, s 89.
50 Ibid, s 98.
51 Ibid, s 99.
52 Ibid, s 100.
53 Ibid, s 129.
54 Ibid.

administration. Since a CVL will occur as a matter of course on the filing of the requisite notice, it is unlikely that an administrator would go to the extra effort and expense of a compulsory winding-up, especially now, as the right of preferential creditors to be paid during the course of the administration itself has been expressly provided for,[55] so there are few practical advantages left in taking that route.

13.63   Although these new provisions in the EA 2002 will cause an increase of voluntary, as opposed to compulsory, liquidations, that is not to say that they will disappear. There are, and will remain, circumstances where a compulsory liquidation is the preferred route. For example, where a company has no further funds from which to pay a liquidator because it is in a compulsory liquidation, the official receiver will be appointed, in the absence of any other nominees, and the costs of the liquidation will be met from State funds. Likewise, where the directors (or other officers of a company) are accused of misfeasance, the cost of investigating such allegations will initially be met by the public purse through the medium of a compulsory liquidation. Equally, an administrator might take the view that the official receiver would be the best person to report on the directors under the directors' disqualification legislation.

DISSOLUTION

13.64   If the administrator concludes that there will not be funds available from which to make a distribution to creditors, he may take steps to dissolve the company.

13.65   The EA 2002 adapts the existing statutory framework for dissolution by bypassing the need to enter first into voluntary liquidation. A company without assets can simply pass unimpeded out of administration into dissolution as it would normally do from voluntary liquidation to dissolution. It is effectively a fast-track process.

13.66   The administrator is required to file a notice to that effect with the registrar of companies.[56] Once that notice is filed, his appointment ceases.[57] As soon as is reasonably practicable,[58] the administrator must also file a copy of that notice with the court[59] and send one to every known creditor.[60] The statute expressly provides that, 3 months after the filing of the notice, the company is deemed to be dissolved,[61] although the administrator – or any other interested party – may apply to the court to extend, suspend or disapply that provision.[62] If

---

55   And of course, the number of preferential creditors will also be reduced by the new legislation.
56   IA 1986, Sch B1, para 84(1). The court has the power to disapply that requirement under para 84(2).
57   Ibid, para 84(4).
58   This will probably be defined in the new Insolvency Rules.
59   IA 1986, Sch B1, para 84(5)(a).
60   Ibid, para 84(5)(b).
61   Ibid, para 84(6).
62   Ibid, para 84(7).

such an application is made, the administrator must, as soon as is reasonably practicable, notify the Registrar of Companies.[63]

13.67   The reason for the 3-month delay following exit from administration into dissolution is that the process takes place automatically on the filing of the notice with the Registrar of Companies and before any creditors (or any other interested person) have been notified. The EA 2002 does not afford them the opportunity to intervene before this application. Any objections they may have to the dissolution will necessitate making an application under this section to extend or suspend the 3-month period.

13.68   There are important reasons why the period prior to the dissolution taking effect may need to be extended or suspended. A dissolved company cannot sue or be sued and it may be that the administrator, or an interested party, wishes to defer the dissolution for this purpose; alternatively, it may subsequently be discovered that a dissolved company has assets which were previously untraced.

13.69   It will still be possible to resurrect the company after dissolution by having that dissolution declared void under s 651 of IA 1986, but obviously it is cheaper and easier, if possible, simply to delay the dissolution instead.

---

63   IA 1986, para 84(8).

Part 2

PERSONAL INSOLVENCY

Chapter 14

INTRODUCTION TO PERSONAL INSOLVENCY

'There's no accounting for laws. Or the changes wrought by men and time.
For nearly eight years the only way to get a divorce in our state was to have
your spouse convicted of a felony or caught in an act of adultery. And I had
made a good living off these antiquated divorce laws. Then the state
legislature, in a flurry of activity at the close of a special session, put me out
of business by civilising those divorce laws ... I spent the next two days
sulking in my office ... considering the prospects for my suddenly
very dim future.'
James Crumley[1]

THE END OF BANKRUPTCY AS WE KNOW IT?

14.1   The reforms of personal insolvency law embodied in the EA 2002 represent the Government's attempt to bring our antiquated bankruptcy laws up to date with economic reality. The reforms have not been well received by those many insolvency practitioners and lawyers who have been making a living out of the law and practice of bankruptcy. Many consider that it is the end of the road for them. This is because they perceive that the new reforms limit the involvement of the private sector.

(a) In future, 9 out of 10 bankrupts will make only one visit to the official receiver's office and, without further investigation, obtain their discharge within about 6 months of the bankruptcy order.

(b) The remaining 1 out of 10 bankrupts will be targeted by the Government as candidates for the new bankruptcy restriction orders (BROs), a process to be directed and managed by the Government, not the private sector.

(c) The official receiver will be able to act as nominee and supervisor in respect of new fast-track post-bankruptcy IVAs.

(d) Even in cases where a private sector appointment of a trustee in bankruptcy is made, the trustee will only be able to apply to sell the matrimonial home (often the only valuable asset in the estate) on certain conditions, namely that he does so within 3 years, that the home exceeds a minimum value and that he can demonstrate that the creditors will receive something out of the proceeds.

---

1   *The Wrong Case* (1975).

14.2   In truth, although only time will tell, it is unlikely that the prospects are as bleak as the private sector fears. Early discharge will have no bearing on the vesting of assets in the trustee in bankruptcy. All that has happened is that the law of bankruptcy has been re-addressed in the light of the following factors:

(a)   changed economic conditions; and

(b)   the fundamental objects of bankruptcy.

14.3   A review of the objects of bankruptcy against the changed economic conditions of the twenty-first century has revealed the fact that it is no longer appropriate to lump together all bankrupts and to stigmatise them in the same way. A brief look at each of these two factors is worthwhile for the purpose of understanding the new reforms. First, there are the economic conditions and 'consumer debt'.

CHANGED ECONOMIC CONDITIONS – BALLOONING CONSUMER DEBT

14.4   Consumer debt in Britain is now reaching £900 billion. In one sense, this is a meaningless figure but, in an era when Britain's manufacturing industry appears to be in terminal ill-health, it is consumerism which keeps the economy afloat. At the end of the century, everyday spending by families topped £500 billion a year, compared with around £150 billion in 1951. The average household now spends 3.5 times as much in real terms as it did 50 years ago. However, a much greater proportion of that figure is now funded by credit. The removal of legal curbs on borrowing money and increasing earnings means consumer debt is nearly double that of the late 1980s when high levels of borrowing contributed to recession.

14.5   In turn, it is not an exaggeration to say that consumer credit is keeping the economy afloat. It is difficult to overstate the growth in consumer credit in the last 20 years or its effect on the economy. The credit institutions are the life-blood of modern consumerism to an extent that could not have been imagined when the Consumer Credit Act was passed in 1974 or the Insolvency Act was passed in 1986. In November 2002, the Deputy Governor of the Bank of England, Mervyn King, unveiled his quarterly inflation report. As the *Daily Telegraph* reported,[2] he was at pains to emphasise that 'looks deceive':

> 'Consumer debt and the house price boom are feeding off each other. The lowest base rate since the Beatles were topping the charts has made servicing debts cheap, especially mortgages.
>
> But the *housing market simply isn't up to coping with the demand*. Planning restrictions and the red tape smothering the building industry mean the supply of new houses is about 50,000 a year fewer than required, so there is a shortage of homes. The result is a housing bubble, as our ultra-modern mortgage market collides with the ancient planning system.
>
> This, in turn, is *encouraging people to run up debts*. First-time buyers have to pull out all the stops to pay for somewhere to live. While those who have already got

---

2   'The end of the best of all worlds', *Telegraph Money*, 16 November 2002.

their own place are borrowing against the rising value to pay for a day at Bluewater or the Metro Centre, a new holiday or some refurbishments.

Consumer debt is one of the great phenomena of our strangely anti-Victorian times. Just about every borrowing record is being smashed, month by month. Britons *have added to their debts* at a rate of 14pc in the last year, faster than any other nation. Total net lending to individuals is now over £800 billion, up by more than £100 billion in 12 months. Those with credit cards have now accumulated average debts of over £1,200. Sometimes they pay them off each month, but, according to the Bank of England, they usually wait for over 5.5 months before doing so, half as long again as they did five years ago.

Merrill Lynch, the investment bank, reckons British households have more debts than any other country. In the last year, the Citizens Advice Bureau has dealt with 1m cases of bad debts, mostly among young people who have recently suffered some disaster or other, like a divorce.'

14.6 So the bankruptcy debts of 2003 are not the bankruptcy debts of 1914 or even 1986. Correspondingly, the characteristics of the typical debtor have also changed. English bankruptcy legislation was originally developed to resolve business failures. Thus, in 1914 (and even 1986) most bankruptcies, though not all, resulted from business activities. Consumer credit was not widely available. With the growth of consumer credit, many of the administrative procedures and requirements of bankruptcy need to be changed in order to streamline the system. Before mentioning the different categories of bankrupts, it is necessary to recall the objects of bankruptcy.

THE OBJECTS OF BANKRUPTCY

14.7 What are the objects of bankruptcy and how should they be applied to this unsustainable boom in consumer debt? The ever-accelerating rate of change in the last 20 years has been such that it is no longer fashionable to look very far back in time in order to assess where we have reached. Nevertheless, David Graham QC[3] has reminded us that, at least as far as the development of the law of bankruptcy is concerned, whilst history may not repeat itself, it does have a rhythm. This is especially so in the context of the radical reforms brought in by the EA 2002. In 1832, Robert Eden described[4] what he considered to be the nature and purpose of bankruptcy law. In his view, the chief aim of every system should be to combine and regulate two great objects:

'The first is the distribution of the effects of the debtor in the most expeditious, the most equal and the most economical mode.

The second object is the liberation of his person from the demands of his creditors when he has made a full surrender of his property.'

14.8 170 years later, it might fairly be said that these two great objects have informed and driven the Government's reforms of personal insolvency law. The pursuit of these has led the Government to consider the proper approach to the

---

3   See David Graham QC 'The Development of English Bankruptcy Law' (2002) 11
     International Insolvency Review 97.
4   Eden *A Digest of the Bankruptcy Law* (1832).

fact that there are different types or categories of bankrupt. Now, the largest category might be described as the 'consumer bankruptcies', in which the debtor has scant or no assets and low (if any) income. The position is the same in the US, Australia and Canada. In this category, there is usually no question of dishonesty in the old-fashioned sense. Creditors take little interest because the prospects of a return are slim. This form of categorisation is relatively unsophisticated. Again, history is informative.

DIFFERENT TYPES OF BANKRUPTS

14.9   In 1697, Daniel Defoe,[5] drawing on his own experience of the debtors' prison, identified four types of bankrupts:

(1) The honest debtor who fails by visible necessity, losses, sickness, decay of trade or the like.

(2) The knavish, designing, or idle, extravagant debtor who fails because either he has run his estate in excesses, or on purpose to cheat and abuse his creditors.

(3) The debtor exposed to a moderate creditor who seeks but his own, but will omit no lawful means to gain it, and yet will entertain reasonable and just arguments and proposals.

(4) The debtor who is compelled to face the rigorous severe creditor who values not whether the debtor be honest man or knave, able or unable, but will have his debt, whether owing or not, without mercy and compassion but full of ill language, passion and revenge.

14.10   In 2002, commentators and Parliamentarians alike largely agreed that it was appropriate to distinguish between categories of bankrupts and that a 'one size fits all' approach was no longer justified. Predictably, there was much debate as to where the boundaries lay and the treatment which each category should receive. Credit card bankrupts are not generally serial fraudsters or reckless businessmen and the Government considered that it is antiquated and wrong in principle to label them as 'undischarged bankrupts' together with all the stigma which attaches to that expression. Further, prior to the coming into force of the EA 2002, there an estimated 267 restrictions on a bankrupt's freedom. Only culpable individuals ought to be subjected to special restrictions which come with bankruptcy.

14.11   It is in this area that one can begin to see the unlikely link between 'bankruptcy' and 'enterprise'. In the admirable Consultation Paper, *Bankruptcy – A Fresh Start*,[6] the Government set out its new agenda by distinguishing between culpable and non-culpable bankrupts. The implication was that consumer debtors inhabited the 'non-culpable' pigeon hole:

---

5   *An Essay Upon Projects.*
6   Produced by the then Secretary of State, Stephen Byers MP in March 2000 (http://www.insolvency.gov.uk/introduction/freshstart/foreword.htm).

'2.1   In a world in which the general availability of credit is taken for granted, indeed in which generally available credit is seen as a principal motor of economic growth, this advice, so well known a generation or two ago, now seems hopelessly out of date. The use of credit is a fact of everyday life and so, therefore, is the risk that some credit will fail to be repaid. It is also the case that in the overwhelming majority of cases credit advanced *is* repaid, whether by businesses or by consumers. The responsible use of credit is, therefore, a phenomenon which should be encouraged whilst recognising that even the most responsible user may, through force of circumstance, be unable to fulfil a bargain honestly entered into. The unexpected loss of employment or of a market, a period of ill health or the need to give up paid employment in response to a change in family circumstances, the failure of a major customer, these are all familiar occurrences that can often lead to financial difficulty and, in some cases, to insolvency. For a small minority of individuals insolvency is the result of conduct, which at best has been irresponsible, or, at worst, simply dishonest. Current (and past) bankruptcy law and practice seems to many to be predicated on the reverse assumption ...

7.1   The idea that bankruptcy might represent *"an easy solution for those who can bear with equanimity the stigma of their own failure"* seems at considerable odds with present day reality. Despite that, it is clearly one that any proposal for reform of the law relating to personal insolvency must ensure does not become reality. Nor should any changes to the system serve to encourage individuals not to pay their debts when, with a little effort, payment, in full or in part, could be made. However the experience of official receivers is that the vast majority of people who become bankrupt become so from necessity not choice, that they will have made very considerable efforts to avoid becoming bankrupt and that they will have dealt responsibly with their creditors. For many individuals bankruptcy represents a personal tragedy, the last act in a series of events that have led to financial disaster. For many others there is still an element of shame in being unable to pay their debts.'

14.12   The problem of categorisation and differentiation was explored by Mr Nigel Waterson for the Opposition during the morning debate in Standing Committee B on 14 May 2002. Mr Waterson moved an amendment which was designed to introduce statutory definitions of the categories of bankruptcy and bring some certainty to the debate. As with every other of his amendments, it was not carried. But it is interesting to see that he moved closer to Daniel Defoe in that he identified at least a third category of bankrupt, 'the pathological optimist':

'The Under-Secretary has a fond notion, which I think is a massive problem with the clause, that there are two rather simple categories: culpable and non-culpable bankrupts. They are, first, the bad-luck bankrupts, who through no fault of their own, or even an inability to foresee what might happen as the hon gentleman suggested, find themselves facing insolvency, and, secondly, the bad guys – the rogues or the reckless. Those are difficult definitions; much of our debate will be sterile because we do not know how those definitions are to be given flesh in practice.

I made a point on Second Reading, to which we will come in more detail, that there are actually at least three categories. There are the rogues or the reckless, the bad-luck bankrupts, as the Under-Secretary calls them, and what I call the pathological optimists, who get up every morning fully intending to make the world a better place, and are not crooked in any sense, just wildly incompetent. They leave as much of a trail of devastation behind them as the Maxwells or the Lakers. Those distinctions are difficult to make. The Under-Secretary went to some length, showing a certain sensitivity, to deny the US provenance of the changes and suggested that somehow a convergence with the US was going on. We shall consider that in more detail.

I simply do not accept what the Under-Secretary says about the problems of defining business versus consumer bankrupts. There will be marginal cases, but it seems to me that someone cannot make up the fact that they have been in business simply as a way of getting into the other category. The only real justification, the whole case for the clause, is to encourage entrepreneurs, although I do it a disservice by summarising it quite that shortly. There is absolutely no place in the legislation for helping people with what are primarily consumer-debt bankruptcies.

The only difference between myself and the Under-Secretary is the problem of definition. If she does not like the way in which we, or the Consumer Credit Association, have defined things, let her Department bring the battery of intellect that it has at its disposal to work on the issue. It is not a question of principle that divides us; it is simply a matter of practical drafting.'

14.13   In the event, although the distinction between the culpable and the non-culpable is at the heart of the reforms, the EA 2002 does not expressly distinguish between the different categories. That exercise is left to the official receiver at the first meeting with the bankrupt. In his discretion, he will decide which bankrupts to investigate and which to recommend for early discharge.

CONSEQUENCES OF THE NEW REFORMS

14.14   It is widely accepted that the new pain-free regime will cause the number of annual bankruptcies to rise considerably. Predictions vary wildly. Lobby groups from the consumer credit industry introduced chilling statistics[7] showing the exponential rise in consumer bankruptcies in the US. This was pithily summarised by Mr Waterson during the morning session in Standing Committee B on 14 May 2002[8] when he read the following extract from a letter from Patrick Boyden, a partner in PricewaterhouseCoopers:

'... most bankruptcies are the result of consumer credit, not failed enterprises. ... Warning should be heeded from America, where a more friendly attitude towards consumer debt has led to a bankruptcy rate which is about 10 times the rate in the UK in relation to population.'

14.15   During seminars on the EA 2002,[9] Mr Boyden's former colleague, Steve Hill,[10] made a rational (if extreme) case for suggesting that, if it were permissible to draw a parallel with the US experience, these new provisions of the EA 2002 could be the cause of the next recession.

---

7   During a period of economic growth, bankruptcies increased in the US from 700,000 in 1990 to 1.2 million in 2000. In Canada, the total number of filings with the Office of trhe Sueprintendent of Bankruptcy, Canada have increased from less than 10,000 in 1971 to almost 100,000 in 2001.

8   Column 644.

9   'Insolvency and the Enterprise Act 2002' Seminars on 26/27 November 2002 (Jordans).

10   Now of Moon Beever, Solicitors.

14.16   There are many unknown factors. Perhaps one of the most worrying of those factors is the alternative market for dealing with consumer debt. In one sense there is a public interest in having a court-based statutory scheme for managing the debts of an insolvent individual. But another by-product of the explosion in consumer credit is the rapid growth of debt management companies – many of which are dressed-up debt sharks. These out-of-court procedures are preferred by the majority of insolvent individuals to formal IVAs or bankruptcy. During a recent debate in the House of Commons on the Financial Services Industry, Paul Flynn MP described this alternative market as follows:[11]

> 'Let us start with the bottom feeders in the murky pond of the financial services industry: debt management companies and non-status lenders. Debt management companies infest daytime television with advertisements that promise that all one's debts can be rolled up into one manageable payment and that, somehow, the burden and anxiety of debt can be magicked away. Debt management companies take on the debts, routinely add 15% to the total debt and then pocket a whole month's repayments. Then, with one exception – Firstplus is a reasonably efficient firm – they are inefficient when it comes to paying the debts on time. They actually increase the debt and lengthen the period of indebtedness. Even more damaging is the impression they give that, by going along to such a company, debts can be magicked away. That encourages people who are not in serious debt to take on debts in the belief that, if they get into serious trouble, they need only phone the nice people on the television, who will solve all their problems for them.

> There is no painless escape from debt. The average adult in Britain is now a record £3,000 in debt, and that figure is growing rapidly. In the past year alone, it has risen by 12% to a massive £130 billion,[12] and I believe that the activities of debt management companies have played a significant part in that increase. Good advice on debt is available free from citizens advice bureaux or the Foundation for Credit Counselling. Debt management firms say that their job is loan consolidation, but it is not; it is debt multiplication.'

14.17   It is difficult to predict whether the growth of these companies with their extra-curial care will continue. If it does, this is likely to dilute considerably the predicted surge in the annual number of bankruptcy orders.

14.18   The socio-economic considerations touched upon in this introduction are heavily influenced by the American experience. In a simplistic sense, there is a spectrum. At one end, we find the Continental (civil code) countries where the moral element is strong with an emphasis on repayment without much concern for rehabilitation. At the other end, there is the US Bankruptcy Code – the home for the last 100 years of the 'fresh start'. A closer study reveals that each of the systems has its problems. The Continentals are busy trying to liberalise their personal insolvency laws and the Americans are taking radical steps to tighten theirs – almost to the point of removing the 'fresh start' approach.

---

11   *Hansard*, 11 June 2002, col 208WH (ttp://www.parliament.the-stationery-office.co.uk/pa/cm200102/cmhansrd/cm020611/halltext/20611h02.htm).

12   Not to be confused with the total consumer debt of individuals (including mortgages) which stands at nearly £900 billion.

ON THE REBOUND – THE LATEST CHAPTER OF THE AMERICAN EXPERIENCE

14.19 For present purposes, there are some aspects of American society which are replicated in the UK and some which are not. The activities of the credit industry are similar, if more sophisticated in the US. However, the anti-abortion debate is on a different scale, leading to an unexpected intervention in creditor legislation. Starting with the credit industry, according to one report[13]

> '... credit card companies and even big automakers have been lobbying for reform and contributing to Republican candidates. MBNA American Bank, a large issuer of credit cards, was the single largest contributor to Bush's campaign in the last election.'

14.20 Turning to the anti-abortionists, on 1 March 2001 a Bill to reform the fresh start provisions of the Bankruptcy Code passed the House of Representatives. A similar Bill passed the Senate on 15 March 2001. Its provisions represented a package of pro-creditor and anti-abuse reforms, including the introduction of means testing of bankrupts and the repayment of credit card debts incurred during the 3 months leading to bankruptcy. At the time of writing, the Bill was held up in November 2002 by the anti-abortion lobby in a way which simply could not happen in the UK. Nevertheless, the following colourful CNN report[14] on an earlier stalling discloses both the differences and the similarities between the US and the UK. It also reveals how the US is on the reobund from the place to which the UK is presently destined:

> 'A coalition of anit-abortion Republicans forced what could be a fatal delay of a landmark House-Senate bankruptcy agreement that would have made it tougher for Americans to dissolve debt. The House was expected to pass the compromise bankruptcy legislation Friday night before leaving for the summer, but it hit a snag after an argument rose among Republicans over an abortion provision in the Bill. The Bill will now have to wait until after Congress returns from its summer recess, congressional aides said. The sticking point was a provision that would prohibit people who attack or block access to abortion clinics from declaring bankruptcy to avoid paying court-ordered fines.
>
> Rep Henry Hyde of Illinois, one of the leading anti-abortion Republicans in the House, had fought to curb or kill that provision, and went along with the bankruptcy deal only after Senate Democrats agreed to limit the measure to people who intentionally or knowingly violate the law.
>
> But a group of anti-abortion Republicans, led by GOP Rep Chris Smith of New Jersey, objected to Hyde's deal with Senate Democrats, delaying the floor movement until September ...
>
> The bankruptcy bill has been in the mix for five years, coming close several times but never able to cross the final hump. If the House had passed the bill, the Senate would have taken it up next, and President Bush already has indicated that he would sign it
> ...
> Consumer groups said the legislation was so unfriendly to financially strapped Americans they might start flooding into bankruptcy court now to avoid the new rules.

---

13   CNN.com, 'Senate marches toward sweeping bankruptcy overhaul', 15 March 2001.
14   'Abortion Spat Delays Bankruptcy Bill', 27 July 2002:
     http://www.cbsnews.com/stories/2002/07/26/politics/main516481.shtml.

"To Joe Blow, I'd say be very careful about unsecured debt, about credit cards, and tell your family that if they're in financial trouble, they should think about declaring bankruptcy sooner rather than later," said Travis Plunkett of the Consumer Federation of America.

But banking and business groups insisted that most Americans should never even have to think about the legislation, which took almost five years to reach the point where the GOP-controlled House, the Democrat-controlled Senate and the White House are all ready to sign on.

"The bankruptcy system is still going to continue to be there for most Americans. Nothing is going to change", American Bankers Association spokeswoman Catherine Pulley said. "The bill is only going to affect Americans who can afford to pay their bills back, but choose not to".

Personal bankruptcy filings rose 15 per cent last year, federal officials reported in April. There were 1.5 million bankruptcy filings in the US Bankruptcy Courts in the 12 months that ended 31 March, the most recent data available.

Personal bankruptcy accounts for about 97 per cent of that, officials said.

Seven out of every ten consumer bankruptcy filings come under Chapter 7 of the US Bankruptcy Code, which allows people to escape paying any of their credit-card and other debts. Filings under Chapter 13 force people to repay debts over time in accordance with a court-appoved plan. The legislation applies a new standard if a debtor is found to have sufficient income to repay at least 25 percent of the debt over five years or has at least the median income for his or her state. Then, the debtor would automatically be forced into a Chapter 13 repayment plan ...

Credit card companies and banks have complained for years about the rise in Chapter 7 filings, which forces them to eat billions of dollars in losses a year from bankrupt consumers, Pulley said.'

14.21   If the American experience is anything to go by, it would appear that the new reforms of our personal insolvency law should be regarded as the beginning of a new journey. Perhaps we can bear in mind the US experience when planning the route.

ON THE REBOUND – RETRENCHMENT IN AUSTRALIA

14.22   Meanwhile, the Australians have been on a similar journey. There, the number of bankruptcies has increased dramatically from 7,500 in 1986/87 to over 24,000 in 2001/02. In 1996, the Australians introduced a 6-month bankruptcy period for certain debtors below a certain income and debt threshold. A series of Government reports concluded that there was widespread abuse of the system at many levels. Early discharge had become the most common reason for dissatisfaction. The conclusion was that bankruptcy had become too easy. From 5 May 2003, the Bankruptcy Legislation Amendment Act 2002 (Aus) will come into force. The new legislation will remove a bankrupt's rights to apply for early discharge – the full 3-year period will be reinstated. There will be new powers to reject debtors' petitions and objections to discharge will be made easier.[15] It should not be assumed that the Australians have completed their retrenchment.[16]

---

15   See http://www.itsa.gov.au/aghome/commaff/itsa/frame.bankreforms.html.
16   See Murray 'Major bankruptcy reform in Australia', *Insol World*, First Quarter 2003.

Chapter 15

CROWN PREFERENCE – PERSONAL INSOLVENCY

'A dog starv'd at his master's gate Predicts the ruin of the State'
William Blake[1]

INTRODUCTION

15.1   Much of what was said in Chapter 3 about the abolition of Crown preference as regards corporate insolvency applies equally to personal insolvency. The historical justification for it, the criticism and the ethos behind its abolition are all the same. The Crown has decided to give up the benefit of its exalted status in a step towards the more equal distribution of assets. Thus the vast majority of its previously preferential debts will filter down for the benefit of unsecured creditors generally, many of which will be small businesses.

REPEAL OF THE RELEVANT PARTS OF THE IA 1986

15.2   The abolition is effected by the same provisions that deal with the corporate insolvencies. By EA 2002, s 251(1), it is simply stated that the relevant paragraphs of IA 1986, Sch 6[2] shall cease to have effect. The effect of this is that the other preferential debts remain. The other, non-Crown preferential debts, are:

(1)   contributions to occupational pension schemes (category 4);
(2)   remuneration of employees for the relevant period (category 5); and
(3)   levies on coal and steel production under the European Coal and Steel Community (ECSC) Treaty (category 6).

15.3   The subrogated rights of the Department of Trade and Industry where the Crown has made payments from the National Insurance Fund to cover all or part of any employee's preferential claims in respect of salary and wages under the Employment Rights Act 1996 will survive. This is on the basis that the Crown is not then relying upon its own preferential rights, but is stepping into the shoes of the preferential rights of the employee.[3]

---

1   'Auguries of Innocence'.
2   Ie paras 1–7 which include comparatively rare claims such as landfill tax, climate change levy and car tax.
3   See para 726 of the Explanatory Notes.

15.4 Further, s 189(4) of the Employment Rights Act 1996 is removed. Consequently, in so far as it remains a preferential creditor on such grounds, the DTI will not be paid in priority to any remaining preferential claims of employees.[4]

15.5 These provisions are predicted to come in to force in June/July 2003, alongside all the provisions affecting corporate insolvency and in advance of the personal insolvency reforms which will come into force in around April 2004.

COMPARISON

15.6 The major difference in respect of personal insolvency is that there are no top-slicing provisions, as, save for one instance,[5] individuals do not grant floating charges. Therefore, there is no reason to ensure that a prescribed part of the floating charge realisations should be ring-fenced for the benefit of the unsecured creditors. The direct effect of this is that the benefit will accrue to the remaining preferential creditors (such as they are; principally, employees) and thereafter to the unsecured creditors. The issues of the benefits to the banks, and the exact extent of that benefit post-*Brumark*, simply will not arise.

EFFECT OF ABOLITION

15.7 As with corporate insolvencies, one of the most immediate effects for debtors will be the hardening of attitudes of the Crown departments. They are likely to be far less indulgent when collecting outstanding debts, thereby reducing the working capital for small businesses.[6]

15.8 This, consequently, is also likely to mean that the Crown departments will have a more active involvement in the consideration of IVAs.[7]

CONCLUSION

15.9 Due to the lack of involvement of the banks and other financial institutions as floating charge-holders, the impact of the abolition of Crown preference in personal insolvency will be more directly beneficial to the general body of unsecured creditors. In one sense the other unsecured creditors will not benefit in full because they will now participate cheek by jowl with the full amount of the Crown debt as an unsecured creditor. The abolition of Crown preference will have a far more wide-ranging effect in corporate insolvencies than in personal insolvencies. Whilst the intention to benefit unsecured creditors is admirable, only time will tell to what extent it will result in greater dividends being distributed to those creditors.

---

4   See EA 2002, s 248(3) and Sch 17, para 49(4), together with para 726 of the Explanatory Notes.
5   The exception being agricultural floating charges granted under the Agricultural Charges Act 1928.
6   This is dealt with in more detail in relation to corporate insolvency: see **3.25** and **3.26**.
7   This also dealt with in more detail in relation to corporate insolvency; see **3.27**.

Chapter 16

AUTOMATIC DISCHARGE

'One must have some sort of occupation nowadays. If I hadn't my debts I shouldn't have anything to think about.'

Oscar Wilde[1]

INTRODUCTION

16.1 Under the new provisions, it is anticipated that the vast majority of bankrupts will obtain their discharge in less than 6 months. The social and political implications of this should not be underestimated. More specifically, for many private sector insolvency practitioners, this new regime will spell the end of an era. This is, not least of all, because it is envisaged that for about 90% of all bankrupts the process will involve one meeting at the official receiver's office followed by discharge on the filing of the requisite papers by the official receiver. Whilst it should not be forgotten that even for these 'quick and easy' bankruptcies, certain legal consequences of bankruptcy will continue after discharge, it is difficult not to conclude that the reduction of the bankruptcy period from 3 years to 6 months or less will alter fundamentally attitudes towards, and the economic effect of, bankruptcy. Before turning to these new provisions, it is worth briefly recalling that it was only comparatively recently that the concept of automatic discharge was introduced.

BACKGROUND TO AUTOMATIC DISCHARGE

16.2 The Insolvency Act 1976, which came into force in October 1977, introduced the notion of automatic discharge. The period for automatic discharge was 5 years from the commencement of the bankruptcy order. The intention was:

> 'in part to reduce the number of persons at large in the population whose undischarged status exposes them to the illegal incurring of credit and to the commission of other offences under the Bankruptcy Acts; and in part to obviate the necessity of maintaining "open" large numbers of bankruptcy files where the bankrupt has not chosen, or would not wish, to apply for his discharge, or is precluded from so going by a "sine die" order.'[2]

16.3 The idea of automatic discharge was therefore novel. Prior to 1976, the onus had been on the bankrupt to apply to the court for discharge. Many

---

1   *A Woman of No Importance* (1893).
2   *Williams and Muir Hunter on Bankruptcy*, 19th Edn at p 139.

bankrupts failed to do so. The reason for the failure to apply was that most bankrupts were either ignorant of the procedure or did not want to attend open court, which would attract publicity.[3] Nevertheless, the changes introduced by the Insolvency Act 1976 meant that only in the most basic bankruptcies would the bankrupt escape the clutches of a bankruptcy order after 5 years. Taking into account the competing arguments as to whether automatic discharge was a good or bad thing, the Cork Committee Report (1982) recommended that the onus should always be upon the bankrupt to apply for his discharge and prove that his discharge was warranted. The escape for those ignorant of the procedure (it was recommended that the hearing be in chambers so as to limit publicity) was to be an automatic review by the court 5 years after the date of the bankruptcy order. However, the automatic review recommendation was not to impede a bankrupt from making an application for his discharge at an earlier date, provided that it was not within 12 months of the bankruptcy order. Under the recommendations, creditors would be given a voice at the hearing for discharge.

16.4   However, these recommendations were largely ignored and the changes made by the IA 1986 have meant that the majority of bankrupts have been able to look forward to an automatic discharge on the third anniversary of the making of a bankruptcy order.[4] Further, Parliament wanted to make a distinction between those bankrupts whose bankruptcy debts were high and those whose debts were low (presumably because they were considered to be less of a danger to the general public if debts were low). Thus, in the case of summary administration (that is where the debtor owed £20,000 or less), the period of bankruptcy was reduced and automatic discharge provided on the second anniversary of the date of the bankruptcy order.

16.5   Parliament recognised then, as it does now, that there may be circumstances where automatic discharge would not be appropriate or beneficial to the public. The official receiver (and only the official receiver) was given power under the IA 1986 to apply to the court to stop the 3-year automatic discharge period from running in various circumstances, the most common of which was where the bankrupt failed to comply with his obligations under the IA 1986.[5] It was curious that Parliament did not think it appropriate to empower a trustee to make an application to stop time running as it is usually a trustee who deals with the more difficult bankruptcies and has the personal experience of the bankrupt's behaviour.

16.6   In one sense, 'automatic discharge' after 3 years was therefore not bestowed as of right and was not universal, in that the bankrupt had to comply with his statutory obligations. There was also special treatment for those who were subject to a criminal bankruptcy order[6] or who had been an undischarged bankrupt at any time in the period of 15 years ending with the commencement of the bankruptcy. In such cases, Parliament thought that the courts should have

3   *Insolvency Law and Practice: Report of the Review Committee*, chaired by Sir Kenneth Cork (1982) Cmnd 8558 (The Cork Report), paras 605 *et seq*.
4   IA 1986, s 279(2)(a).
5   IA 1986, s 279(3).
6   Ibid, s 264(1)(d).

control over discharge and so the bankrupt had to make an application for an order of the court to discharge.[7] For these 'repeat bankrupts', the IA 1986 provided for a minimum period of bankruptcy so that an application for discharge could not be made until the end of the period of 5 years beginning with the commencement of bankruptcy.[8]

Political will to liberalise the bankruptcy regime

16.7   The question of discharge from bankruptcy is at the heart of the fundamental changes heralded by those parts of the Act which deal with personal insolvency. The White Paper[9] (published in July 2002) developed proposals contained in the Insolvency Service consultation paper, *Bankruptcy – A Fresh Start*, published in April 2000 and set out the Government's proposal, stating that its aim was to:

> '... strengthen competition and the powers of consumers by ... transforming our approach to bankruptcy ... our "Fresh Start" proposals for personal bankruptcy are based on the recognition that honest failure is an inevitable part of a dynamic market economy. Our radical liberalisation of the bankruptcy regime will mean a fresh start for many, backed by a very tough regime for those whose conduct of their financial affairs is irresponsible or reckless.'[10]

16.8   The philosophy is based on the belief that most bankruptcies are caused either by factors outside the control of the bankrupt or by an error of judgment. According to this view, the majority of bankrupts are honest and prepared to take business risks in order to increase their wealth. Therefore, the entrepreneurs should not be penalised but valued by society as they generally promote wealth creation. A different approach is adopted if it is found that a bankrupt is one of the small minority of bankrupts who has conducted his financial affairs in an 'irresponsible or reckless' manner. That minority apart, it is thought that to put an honest business risk-taker in the 'sin bin' for 3 years is a waste of a national resource. Such people should be allowed to rejoin the business community in a short period of time:

> '... it is the nature or risk-taking that, on occasions, there will be failure. But in a society which is genuinely enterprising the cost of failure must not be so high that it acts as a deterrent to economic activity.'[11]

16.9   There appears to be a genuine political drive behind these new provisions to exploit rather than waste entrepreneurial spirit.[12] The economy in mainland Europe, with many State-owned enterprises, is often thought to be different from that of Great Britain, which is more aligned to the enterprise culture of the US. It is interesting to note that small business, with fewer than 10

---

7   IA 1986, s 279(1)(a).

8   Ibid, s 280(1).

9   *Productivity and Enterprise Insolvency – A Second Chance* (Cm 5234).

10   As to the meaning of 'irresponsible or reckless' see **19.1**. In essence, the BRO procedure is modelled on the procedure applicable to the disqualification of directors under the Company Directors Disqualification Act 1986, s 6.

11   The White Paper.

12   Statistics provided to the House of Lords by the Law Society and the lending banks in *Royal Bank of Scotland v Etridge (No 2)* [2001] 4 All ER 449.

employees, comprise about 95% of all businesses in England and Wales and these small business are responsible for nearly one-third of all employment.

NEW 1-YEAR PERIOD

16.10   However, some time is needed to investigate the bankrupt's state of affairs and the causes of his or her bankruptcy. Time is required to establish whether the bankrupt conducted his financial affairs in an 'irresponsible or reckless' manner. The Insolvency Service has decided, and Parliament has agreed, that the right balance is struck by reducing the period of bankruptcy, in straightforward cases, by two-thirds. Thus, the Act has replaced s 279 of IA 1986 with a new section which provides for automatic discharge after 1 year from the date of the bankruptcy order.

16.11   The reduction in time before automatic discharge will mean that an official receiver's office will be put under a time pressure. Within a short period, the official receiver will have to ascertain whether the bankrupt's failure to pay his creditors was:

(a) as a result of conducting his affairs in an irresponsible or reckless manner; or

(b) merely a vicissitude of business life where honest behaviour led to misfortune.

The official receiver's office will inevitably deal with a high percentage of consumer bankruptcies and these should be less demanding in terms of time. In the case of business bankruptcies, if the official receiver, having made the appropriate investigations, considers that the bankrupt's financial failure is as a result of irresponsible or reckless behaviour then he may apply for a bankruptcy restriction order (BRO) or an interim BRO (see Chapter 19 for an in-depth discussion). The effect of a BRO or interim BRO is to impose certain conditions as if he were an undischarged bankrupt (see **19.56**). The White Paper envisaged that only 10% of all bankrupts will be subjected to a BRO.

One year is a maximum period

16.12   The reforms go much further. Although s 279, as amended, now stipulates that a bankrupt will be discharged at the end of the period of 1 year beginning with the date on which the bankruptcy commences;[13] this is in fact a maximum period. Controversially, the effect of the new provisions will be that very many bankruptcies will result in an earlier discharge than 12 months. The period may be made shorter if, before the end of 12 months, the official receiver files with the court a notice stating that an investigation of the conduct and affairs of the bankrupt under IA 1986, s 289 is either unnecessary or has been concluded. Thus, the official receiver has discretion whether or not to make an investigation into the affairs and dealings of the bankrupt. In the event that the official receiver files a discharge notice prior to the expiration of 12 months, the

---

13   EA 2002, s 250(1) provides that 'the following shall be substituted for section 279 of the Insolvency Act 1986'.

bankrupt will be free of the bankruptcy regime although not for all purposes (see below).

16.13 Therefore the official receiver and his staff will, within a relatively short period, have to decide whether the bankrupt's affairs require investigation and, following an investigation, whether an application to the court should be made for an interim BRO or full BRO. There can be little doubt that the Insolvency Service will want to ensure that the process under which the official receiver will decide these issues is effective, consistent and cost-efficient. There can also be little doubt that the success of the new regime will depend upon the ability of the official receiver to identify and investigate those whose conduct has been culpable or irresponsible. It is hoped that the offices of the official receiver will have adequate resources for this purpose.

16.14 The concept of early discharge has not had universal approval. During the passage of the Bill through Parliament there were many objectors to the notion that a bankrupt could be discharged within the 12-month period. In particular:

(a) an amendment was tabled to ensure that 12 months would be a fixed minimum duration; there would be no early discharge;

(b) the objectors feared that 'serial bankrupts' would abuse the system;

(c) they also feared that early discharge would have a negative effect on the cost of and even the availability of credit;

(d) the possibility of early discharge was said to render IVAs otiose;

(e) concern was also expressed that an early discharge would be a disincentive to co-operate fully with the official receiver once a notice had been filed;

(f) questions were raised as to whether the official receiver would have adequate (ie additional) resources to make proper investigations and deal with the inevitable flood of bankrupts seeking early discharge.

16.15 A practical difficulty may arise as a result of different regional centres having different resources and expertise, leading to a disparity in the treatment of bankrupts who will be more likely to have an early discharge in one area than in another. Thus, a non-culpable bankrupt may be discharged after 50 weeks have elapsed since the date of the bankruptcy order in Southampton, but the same bankrupt would be discharged within 16 weeks in Newcastle, or vice versa. In a different context, the US has found that regional differences have led to a reduction in the availability of credit for those who need it most. In Texas, a bankrupt's home and up to $30,000 are exempt from his estate. In Connecticut, all the debts have to be repaid in full. The result has been an inevitable movement of the improvident to Texas to take advantage of its generous laws. In Texas, the availability of business credit has been greatly reduced. It is to be hoped that similar disparities will not result in this country.

Eight-week bankruptcies

16.16 The possibility of being discharged before the 12-month period led one speaker in the House of Lords to comment that being a bankrupt is now dangerously close to being 'pain free'. Indeed, the bankruptcy period could be very short: the changes could result in someone filing for his own bankruptcy and being discharged 8 weeks later.[14] Whether or not the experience of being bankrupt for the honest man is 'pain free', the Centre For Economic and Business Research paints a bleak picture. It warns that the reduction in the duration of a bankruptcy will directly lead to a 53.5% increase in the number of bankruptcies (an increase of 13,000). This, in turn, will lead to the loss of £180 million from the gross domestic product. The effect is said to be an estimated £76 million extra cost each year, which will be borne by unsecured creditors and may lead to up to 170,000 individuals being excluded from the credit market. The real concern is that consumers rather than entrepreneurs will take advantage of the short discharge period.

16.17   With radical change, there often come predictions of bleak conse-quences and it is likely that these forebodings of the Centre For Economic and Business Research are too dramatic. The economy has a curious way of adapting to circumstances and the credit industry is particularly flexible.[15]

16.18   Furthermore, some bankrupts will be subject to a BRO and remain subject to restrictions for longer periods, as will those who have been adjudicated bankrupt within the previous 15 years. This may help to deter a serial bankruptcy culture. Further, although discharged from bankruptcy, a former bankrupt may feel its effect for years afterwards (see below). Regardless of the concerns expressed in relation to early discharge, the Government was not persuaded to fix a minimum term. The reality is that the assets of a bankrupt are to be made available to his creditors and this will not be a 'pain-free' experience for the majority.

DISCHARGE IN PRACTICE

16.19   So, how will the typical bankruptcy procedure operate in practice? The Insolvency Service envisages that all bankrupts will be interviewed and an enquiry made into the facts of each case. Where the initial inquiry shows that further investigation is unnecessary, the official receiver will report to the creditors and to any trustee that he proposes to give notice to the court that the bankrupt be discharged in less than 12 months. Otherwise, the official receiver may investigate further to see whether there are grounds for a BRO or criminal prosecution. Once the official receiver has notified creditors of any proposal to allow discharge in less than 12 months, the creditors will have a period of time (28 days is suggested by the Insolvency Service) in which to provide information to the official receiver showing why the bankrupt should not be so discharged.

16.20   If there are no objections, the official receiver will file a notice at court at the end of the prescribed period. The date of filing of that notice will be the date of discharge. Where objections are received, the official receiver will delay filing at court a notice of entitlement to early discharge until the objections

---

14   A remark made by Lord Hunt to the House of Lords on 21 October 2002. Lord Hunt was concerned that by creating a possibility of early discharge (earlier than 12 months) the Government may be creating a 'rogue's charter'.

15   Note the American experience where there are credit card companies which have made a speciality out of advancing credit to newly-discharged (ie debt-free) bankrupts.

have been dealt with. If the official receiver does not file a notice for early discharge, discharge will happen automatically after a year, unless otherwise suspended.

16.21 A bankrupt will be entitled to information regarding the progress of the official receiver's investigations. But a bankrupt is not able to direct the official receiver to file a notice of early discharge if investigations appear to have come to an end. Under the old (ie unamended) s 279 of IA 1986, the official receiver was entitled to apply to suspend the period of 3 years after which automatic discharge took effect. In making that decision (and it is submitted in making the decision to file a notice of early discharge) the official receiver performs a public law function and neither s 303(1) nor s 303(2) of IA 1986 gave the court jurisdiction or power to give directions to the official receiver as to his exercising of his public law functions. An aggrieved bankrupt can, however, apply for judicial review if the application is made within the strict time-limits. The decision not to give direction to the official receiver may be reviewed in light of the Human Rights Act 1998.

Negating the stigma

16.22 The Government made it clear in the White Paper that it wanted to change the general public's perception of bankruptcy. What, in fact, the Government asks is that a distinction be drawn between the dishonest or irresponsible bankrupt who should be stigmatised as such and the honest and 'above-board' bankrupt who should perhaps be viewed as having been unlucky on one occasion. The White Paper expressed it as follows:

> 'Bankruptcy law in this country treats everyone subject to it in the same way irrespective of whether the bankrupt was dishonest or irresponsible or whether his failure was honest and above-board. There are numerous other enactments that impose restrictions, prohibitions or disqualifications on bankrupts solely on the basis of the existence of the bankruptcy proceedings. This automaticity of approach may be capable of justification in some cases but requires a belief in the proposition that the debtor, by becoming bankrupt, is not someone in whom society can have trust or confidence. This approach takes no account of the risks that are an everyday part of business life, and warrants substantial re-appraisal.'

16.23 The White Paper recognised a raft of restrictions imposing practical difficulties upon the bankrupt and contributing towards a general slur upon his character. The prohibitions identified in the White Paper were:

(a) acting as a director or in the management of a limited company without the court's permission;

(b) obtaining credit above a prescribed limit (currently £250) without disclosing the bankruptcy;

---

17 *Hardy v Focus Insurance Co Ltd* [1997] BPIR 77.

18 Above.

19 Gearty and Davies *Insolvency Practice and the Human Rights Act 1998: A Special Bulletin* (Jordans, 2000), p 43.

20 Paragraph 1.21 of the White Paper.

(c) carrying on business in a different name from that in respect of which the bankruptcy order was made without revealing the earlier (or 'bankruptcy') name.

16.24   In order to eliminate the stigma attached to bankruptcy these prohibitions should therefore be relaxed, but the relaxation of some prohibitions will be dependent upon many and various Government departments.[21] Therefore, the Act provides a structure enabling the Government, through its various departments, to alter the restrictions placed on bankrupts. Accordingly, Government departments are given a broad discretion to apply restrictions on a case-by-case basis. In addition, the Act provides for removal of the restrictions preventing bankrupts from acting as a justice of the peace, from sitting and voting in either House of Parliament or being a member of a local authority. For justices of the peace, the Lord Chancellor retains discretion about a person's eligibility, while Members of Parliament or local authorities will not be eligible to sit and vote if subject to a BRO.[22]

16.25   Whether the reduction in the duration of the bankruptcy period coupled with the relaxation of prohibitions, and a movement away from punishment, lead to a different perception of bankruptcy is questionable. The principle is that culpable and irresponsible bankrupts will be called to account. It is their affairs and conduct which will attract most of the official receiver's attention. A non-culpable bankrupt will still have to provide an explanation as to how it was that he became bankrupt. But for the latter category, bankruptcy may also be viewed as an opportunity to regularise that person's financial affairs. Indeed, in Canada, the bankrupt receives debt counselling and it is not impossible to imagine the introduction of similar provisions here. After all, advice which might prevent a debtor/bankrupt from becoming serially improvident is consistent with the policy that non-culpable bankrupts should be put back on the road as soon as reasonably practicable.

THE BANKRUPT POST-DISCHARGE

16.26   The bankrupt will still feel the effect of the bankruptcy order after his discharge. An income payment order (IPO) or income payment agreement (IPA) will usually remain in force for a period of up to 3 years from the date of the IPO/IPA irrespective of discharge. This promotes the philosophy that those who can pay should pay. Bankrupts will therefore be bound to make affordable contributions towards their debts.

16.27   In addition, the general law relating to the post-bankruptcy period remains largely unaltered. For instance, s 364 of IA 1986 confers upon the court the power to make an order for arrest and the power can extend beyond discharge.[23] Likewise, s 366 of IA 1986 provides the court with jurisdiction to

---

21   These are dealt with in more detail in Chapter 19.
22   For a more detailed consideration of the restrictions and prohibitions affecting bankrupts, see Chapter 20.
23   *Oakes v Simms* [1997] BPIR 499.

order a bankrupt to attend for private examination. The corresponding section under the Bankruptcy Act 1914 was in very similar terms and it was held by the Court of Appeal to apply after discharge as well as before it.[24] The power remains unlimited, applicable any time after the bankruptcy order has been made and is not affected by discharge.[25] Further, applications under ss 303 and 363 of IA 1986 may be made after the discharge in relation to acts done or omitted while the bankruptcy order subsists.[26]

16.28   Also, post-discharge, the bankrupt will remain liable for those debts that survive the discharge process. As a general rule, the bankrupt is released from bankruptcy debts.[27] There are a number of debts from which the bankrupt is not discharged, and these remain unaffected by the EA 2002. They are:

(a) any debt which the bankrupt incurred in respect of any fraud or fraudulent breach of trust to which he was a party;[28]
(b) fines imposed for an offence or liability under a recognisance;[29]
(c) liability to pay damages for negligence, nuisance or breach of statutory, contractual or other duty, to pay damages under Part 1 of the Consumer Protection Act 1987, in either case being damages in respect of personal injuries to any person;[30]
(d) liability arising under any order made in matrimonial proceedings;[31] and
(e) other bankruptcy debts, not being debts provable in the bankruptcy, which might be prescribed.[32]

Student loans

16.29   The class of debts that survive bankruptcy is likely to be expanded to include liability under student loan arrangements. Historically, it was thought that:[33]

(a) loans governed by the Education (Student Loans) Act 1990 were not released upon discharged from bankruptcy;
(b) whereas loans covered by the Teaching and Higher Education Act 1998 and the Education (Student Support) Regulations 1999, which came into force on 3 March 1999, were released upon discharge.

---

24 *Re Poulson* [1934] Ch 45.
25 *Oakes v Simms* [1997] BPIR 499.
26 *Engel v Peri* [2002] BPIR 961.
27 IA 1986, s 281(1).
28 Ibid, s 281(3); see *Masters v Leaver* [2000] BPIR 284, CA; *Mander v Evans* [2001] 1 WLR 2378; *Woodland-Ferrari v UCL Group Retirement Benefits Scheme* [2002] EWHC 1354 (Ch), [2002] 3 WLR 1154.
29 Ibid, s 281(4).
30 Ibid, s 281(5)(a); see *Woodley v Woodley (No 2)* [1994] 1 WLR 1167, CA; *Wehmeyer v Wehmeyer* [2001] BPIR 548; and *Cartwright v Cartwright* [2002] EWCA Civ 931, [2002] BPIR 895.
31 Ibid, s 281(5)(b) and (8). For example, confiscation orders under the Criminal Justice Act 1988, the Drug Trafficking Offences Act 1986 and the Proceeds of Crime Act 2002.
32 Ibid, s 281(6).
33 See Dear *Insolvency Practitioner Millennium Edition*, Chapter 17, Article 7 available at www.insolvency.gov.uk/information/dearip/dearipmill/chapter 17.htm.

However, following reconsideration of these matters in the context of the EA 2002, the Insolvency Service has revised these views. It is now thought that all student loans outstanding at the date of the bankruptcy order, regardless of whether they were made under the 1990 Act or the 1998 Act, are provable in bankruptcy and so are released upon discharge from bankruptcy.[34]

16.30   The Government's response to this was swift, acting to close this loophole. The Department for Education and Skills has announced that it will prevent student loans forming part of the bankrupt's estate and prevent their release upon discharge, in order to reflect the non-commercial nature of the loans.[35] Insolvency lawyers might take the view that the proposed amendments will actually create a loophole, for the benefit of the Student Loans Company Ltd, rather than close one. Nonetheless, whatever the political rights or wrongs of funding education in this way, since student loans are advanced at preferential interest rates and on beneficial repayment terms, there is some justification for their being treated differently from commercial loans.[36]

16.31   Until the proposed amendments are introduced, it would seem that any student made bankrupt whilst the balance of his student loan remains outstanding will be released from the liability to repay it upon discharge. It remains to be seen whether there are any students who, post-bankruptcy order, have continued to make payments to the Student Loan Company Ltd on the basis of the previous understanding of the law. They may stand some chance of recovering those payments, as having been made under a mistake of law.[37]

EXCEPTIONS TO AUTOMATIC DISCHARGE

16.32   In common with the position prior to the coming into force of the EA 2002, there are exceptions to the automatic discharge provisions.

16.33   First, if the official receiver makes an application to the court within the 12-month period demonstrating (to the satisfaction of the court) that the bankrupt has failed to comply with an obligation[38] imposed by the IA 1986, then the court may order that the 12-month automatic discharge period be suspended either for a specific time or until the bankrupt fulfils a specified 'condition'.[39] As noted above, the old s 279(3) of IA 1986 had a similar provision in that the court could stop the running of the 3-year automatic discharge period if the bankrupt failed to comply with his obligations. In such circumstances, conditions could be

---

34   See Dear *Insolvency Practitioner Millennium Edition*, Chapter 17, Article 19, also available
      at www.insolvency.gov.uk/information/dearip/dearipmill/chapter 17.htm.
35   See DfES White Paper, *The Future of Higher Education*, January 2003, Cmnd 5735 at
      para 7.54.
36   IA 1986, new s 279(4).
37   For an interesting analysis of the problems in Canada regarding repayment of student loans,
      see the Office of the Superintendent of Bankruptcy Personal Insolvency Task Force, Final
      Report, Chapter 2, available at
      http://strategis.ic.gc.ca/epic/internet/inbsf-osb.nsf/vsGeneratedIngerE/h_br01225e.html.
38   See *Kleinwort Benson Limited v Lincoln City Council* [1999] 2 AC 349, HL.
39   IA 1986, new s 279(3).

imposed before the time began to run again. Thus, the language in the new s 279 is similar to the provisions being replaced. There is, however, at least one practical difference. Now, both the official receiver and the trustee in bankruptcy may apply for time to stop running, whereas previously only the official receiver had standing to make such an application.[40] The Act provides that the term 'condition' shall include a condition requiring that the court be satisfied of something.[41] This leaves the court with a wide discretion to require a bankrupt to fulfil a judicially imposed duty in connection with his bankruptcy obligations. Nevertheless, the effect of suspending discharge on an individual may be far reaching and should not be underestimated. It has been observed that the power vested in the official receiver to suspend discharge is a 'great power': see *Ernst Abraham Siewsertsz Van Reesema v official receiver.*[42]

16.34 Secondly, Parliament has retained the provisions concerning those bankrupts who have been adjudicated bankrupt as a result of criminal proceedings and those who are repeat bankrupts. Thus, automatic discharge will not apply if the individual is made bankrupt on a petition made pursuant to s 264(1)(d) of IA 1986; or where the bankrupt has been an undischarged bankrupt at any time in the period of 15 years ending with the commencement of the bankruptcy order.[43]

16.35 There will, inevitably, be cases where the 12-month period is about to expire and the official receiver is faced with a decision whether to allow the bankrupt automatic discharge, seek an order for suspension (if the circumstances are appropriate) or make an application for an interim BRO or BRO. In circumstances where there is some evidence that a bankrupt has failed to disclose surplus income that should be available to his creditors or that the court is satisfied that it is otherwise appropriate, the language of the new s 279 may permit the official receiver to apply successfully for an interim order extending the time prior to discharge.[44] There is no express provision in the Act allowing for a conditional discharge – unlike that provided by s 26 of the Bankruptcy Act 1914.[45]

16.36 The absence of an express provision permitting conditional discharge does not by itself mean that a conditional discharge cannot be made. In a different context, the courts have power, in appropriate circumstances, to make a conditional annulment order notwithstanding that s 282 of IA 1986 does not contain an express provision providing the court with the jurisdiction to make such an order.[46]

16.37 The EA 2002 will not prevent a bankrupt from applying to have his bankruptcy order annulled pursuant to s 282(1)(a) (if at any time it appears to

---

40   *Hardy v Focus Insurance Co Ltd* [1997] BPIR 77.
41   IA 1986, s 279(5).
42   (1983) 50 ALR 253, 260.
43   IA 1986, s 279(6).
44   *Jacobs v The official receiver* [1998] BPIR 711.
45   Cf Bankruptcy and Insolvency Act (Can), s 172(2); Bankruptcy Act 1966 (Aus), s 149s(1) Part VII.
46   *Engel v Peri* [2002] BPIR 961.

the court that on any grounds existing at the time the order was made, the order ought not to have been made)[47] or pursuant to s 282(1)(b) (where the bankruptcy debts and expenses have been paid, or secured for to the satisfaction of the court).[48]

TRANSITIONAL PROVISIONS

16.38   The provisions for automatic discharge contained in the IA 1986 shall not apply to a person who has been made bankrupt before the commencement of the Act and remains undischarged at the commencement of the EA 2002 ('a pre-commencement bankrupt').[49] A pre-commencement bankrupt shall be discharged at whichever is the earlier of the following:

(a)   the end of the period of 1 year, beginning with the commencement of the EA 2002 (thereby immediately bringing into effect the 12-month period); or
(b)   the end of the relevant period applicable to the bankrupt (ie under the old s 279(1)(b) of IA 1986), as it had effect prior to the commencement of the Act.[50]

Those who are adjudicated bankrupt after the commencement of the EA 2002 benefit from the new automatic discharge provisions and (if the official receiver makes a decision that they are non-culpable bankrupts) can look forward to an early discharge. Consistent with the approach taken in relation to culpable bankrupts, the new provisions continue any order made pursuant to the old s 279(3) of IA 1986 in respect of pre-commencement bankruptcies[51] but allow for an application to be made to vary or revoke such an order.[52]

16.39   Different provisions apply to the second-time pre-commencement bankrupt. An order made pursuant to IA 1986, s 280(2)(b) (an order of court discharging a person absolutely) or IA 1986, s 280(2)(c) (discharge subject to conditions with respect to any income which may subsequently become due or with respect to any property devolving upon him or acquired by him after discharge), shall continue unaffected by the implementation of the EA 2002.[53] If no court order has been made, the second-time pre-commencement bankrupt will be deemed to be discharged either at the end of 5 years from the commencement of the Act[54] or at such earlier time as the court may order, after the commencement of the Act, on an application made under s 280 of IA 1986.[55]

16.40   The transitional provisions do not inhibit a person from contesting a bankruptcy order or from seeking to pay the bankruptcy debts and expenses. The transitional provisions will not apply to those who were made bankrupt on

---

47   See Briggs and Sims 'Escaping Bankruptcy-Applications to Annul' [2002] *Insolvency Lawyer* Feb, Issue 1.
48   IA 1986, s 279(7).
49   EA 2002, Sch 19, para 3.
50   Ibid, para 4(1)(a) and (b).
51   EA 2002, Sch 19, para 4(2)(a).
52   Ibid, para 4(2)(b).
53   Ibid, para 5(3).
54   Ibid, para 5(4)(a).
55   Ibid, para 5(4)(b).

a petition under s 264(1)(d) of IA 1986 (criminal bankruptcy); the bankrupt will still need to apply to the court for a discharge order pursuant to s 280 of IA 1986.[56]

CONCLUSION

16.41   The new s 279 of IA 1986 reduces the automatic discharge period from 3 years to 1 year. The official receiver is charged with the responsibility of investigating each bankruptcy (although he has a discretion not to investigate). He must reach a decision as to whether the bankrupt is culpable or irresponsible or whether he is non-culpable. If the bankrupt is non-culpable, he may be discharged within a very short period. For such bankrupts, bankruptcy should be viewed as an opportunity to regularise his financial affairs, and an opportunity for the creditors to receive a distribution from the orderly realisation of his assets.

16.42   Notwithstanding early discharge for the majority (estimated at 90% of all bankrupts), in theory at least, the effect of the bankruptcy order may be felt for years after. In reality, the vast majority of the 90% will be in and out of bankruptcy in a matter of months with little or no adverse residual consequences. It is doubted that the credit industry will refuse to extend them credit after discharge.

16.43   If, however, the bankrupt is categorised as culpable or irresponsible the official receiver may apply for an interim BRO or BRO. The courts retain a power to extend the period before discharge if the circumstances are special. The exceptions to automatic discharge remain as before.

16.44   At **14.19–14.22**, reference was made to the US and Australian experiences. In each of those jurisdictions the Government is responding to criticism that bankruptcy is too easy and the discharge period too short. The new reforms in Australia seem to be particularly relevant. In 1996, they introduced a 6-month period for small bankruptcies. As from 5 May 2003, they will revert to the full 3-year period. The main reason for this reversal of policy was a public perception of widespread abuse of a bankruptcy system which had become too quick and easy, such that debtors were queuing up to present their own petitions. The new reforms include a power to reject debtor's petitions. It remains to be seen whether the Government will be forced to bring the 'pain' back into our system in due course or whether the BRO system will remove the need to do so.

---

56 EA 2002, Sch 19, para 6.
57 See **14.19–14.21**.

Chapter 17

THE BANKRUPT'S HOME

'In delay there lies no plenty'
William Shakespeare[1]

INTRODUCTION

17.1 During the passage of the Enterprise Bill through Parliament, amendments were tabled to relieve bankrupts and their families from the perceived injustices which can arise when a trustee in bankruptcy seeks to realise the bankrupt's interest in the matrimonial home years after his discharge. New provisions have now been passed in the EA 2002 to provide for the bankrupt's interest to revert to the bankrupt after 3 years if no action is taken by the trustee during that period to realise that interest. Special provisions have also been introduced in relation to 'low-value' homes.

The old law

17.2 Under the former regime, all of the bankrupt's estate permanently vests in the trustee in bankruptcy pursuant to IA 1986, s 306. The bankrupt's estate includes all property belonging to or vested in the bankrupt at the commencement of the bankruptcy, save for some limited exceptions, such as tools, books and vehicles used by the bankrupt in his employment or business, personal items such as clothing, bedding, furniture, and household equipment necessary for satisfying the basic domestic needs of the bankrupt and his family.[2] Thus, the bankrupt's interest in the matrimonial home, or the former matrimonial home, vests permanently in his trustee.

17.3 In the past, trustees have not taken steps to realise the estate's interest in the matrimonial home where there has been no equity, or only a small amount of equity, in the property. In recent times, property values have risen sharply, creating generous amounts of equity available for the satisfaction of the bankruptcy debts where previously there was no such equity, or no equity worth pursuing. Consequently, trustees have taken steps to realise their interest in the matrimonial home, in some cases many years after the discharge of the bankrupt.

---

1   *Twelfth Night* 2:3.
2   IA 1986, s 283.

The problem

17.4 During the debate on 17 June 2002 in Standing Committee B, the Members appeared to be heavily influenced by a letter received from 'an anonymous insolvency practitioner' who had also worked for the Insolvency Service. He indicated that, in his experience, insolvency practitioners were most commonly appointed as trustees in bankruptcy when it became known that the bankrupt and/or his wife wished to sell their home. This was often years after the bankruptcy, in circumstances where there had been negative equity at the time of bankruptcy but a sharp rise in the property market during the years after discharge. A simple letter of request to the official receiver for consent to the sale had resulted in the appointment of a private insolvency practitioner. The subsequent tensions and disputes were considered to be unfair to the family wishing to sell the property.

17.5 Typically in such cases, the bankrupt has remained in the property, meeting the mortgage payments of interest and capital and maintaining the property. In the meantime, the value of the trustee's interest in the property has risen by reason of the general inflation of property prices and by reason of the bankrupt's payments towards the mortgage debt, and the bankrupt's general care and maintenance of the property. The trustee may nevertheless realise the estate's interest in the property. The perceived inequities of the situation are as follows.

(a) Perhaps many years after the discharge of the bankrupt, the trustee may take the advantage of any increase in value of the property, notwithstanding the fact that the property has been retained at the expense of the bankrupt (by payment of mortgage instalments and general care and maintenance of the property).

(b) In the past, many bankrupts have mistakenly presumed that once the trustee had taken a decision not to realise the estate's interest in the property, the decision would not be reviewed and reversed at some unspecified time in the future. In some cases, the bankrupt has not only continued to make the mortgage repayments, but also made significant improvements to the property.

(c) There is no certainty as to time. Realisation of the matrimonial home is an open-ended process and there is no time after which the bankrupt and his family can confidently presume that the trustee will not attempt to realise the estate's interest in the property.

(d) In many cases, the appointment of a trustee many years after the discharge of the bankrupt is triggered by the bankrupt taking steps to sell or re-mortgage the matrimonial home. The trustee then proceeds to realise the estate's interest in the property, in the course of which the trustee generates significant fees which are satisfied upon the realisation of the estate's interest in the property. There is a perception that the appointment of trustees in such circumstances is a tawdry, fee-generation process only benefiting the trustee and his professional advisers, particular where the equity in the property is modest.

(e) The open-ended possibility that the trustee may elect at some arbitrary time in the future to realise the estate's interest in the matrimonial home adds significantly to the burden and stigma of bankruptcy and is incompatible with the concept of a 'fresh start'.[3]

The existing jurisprudence has not developed sufficiently to provide a remedy for many of the perceived inequities.[4]

LATE EMERGENCE OF NEW PROVISIONS

17.6 Despite the known injustices in this area of bankruptcy law, the Government's original proposals did not include any proposed reforms. During the Committee stages in the House of Commons, the MP for South Ribble, Mr David Borrow, tabled his own clause to deal with the problem. This was as a result of representations made by the Insolvency Practice Council,[5] the Bankruptcy Advisory Service[6] and the Association of Business Recovery Professionals.[7] The Government accepted that reform was necessary and produced its own new clause on 17 June 2002. After further amendments and debate, the clause became uncontroversial.

THE NEW PROVISIONS

17.7 As a result, the EA 2002 now tackles the perceived injustices by:

(a) introducing the requirement that the trustee must take certain steps to realise the bankrupt's interest in a matrimonial home or former matrimonial home within a specified period, after which the property re-vests in the bankrupt (new s 283A of IA 1986);[8]

(b) wholly excepting 'low-value' matrimonial or former matrimonial homes from realisation by the trustee (new s 313A of IA 1986);[9] and

---

3   See, in general, Official Report Standing Committee B, 16 May 2002, 714.

4   Some solutions may be provided by the doctrine of equitable accounting (eg *Re Pavlou* [1993] 1 WLR 1046), the rule in *Ex parte James* (1874) LR 9 Ch App 609, recently applied in *Green v Satsangi* [1998] BPIR 55, the application of resulting trusts (eg *Foskett v McKeown and Others* [1997] 3 All ER 392), and the potential impact of the Human Rights Act 1998 on the bankrupt's home (see, for instance, Gearty and Davies *Insolvency and the Human Rights Act 1998* (Jordans, 2000) at p 41). A detailed discussion of the extent and the limitations of these potential remedies are beyond the scope of this book.

5   The Council's view was summarised as follows : 'It is accepted there are many different circumstances affecting the value of the equity and the potential value of the bankruptcy estate. When should a decision be taken on realisation? At present some of the variations do not seem to be soundly based.'

6   They reported : 'We continue to hear from people who were bankrupt some years ago and who have taken steps to secure their home from any actions by their official receiver/trustee in bankruptcy. Now years later, they find that the property has increased in value and their regular mortgage repayments have reduced the borrowing, putting substantial equity in the property for the official receiver/Trustee to claim.'

7   Who commented : 'This is the concern, which has been identified ... about variations in practice between trustees in bankruptcy in how they deal with the matrimonial home, and a perceived unfairness in selling the home many years after the bankrupt's discharge.'

8   EA 2002, s 261(1).

9   Ibid, s 261(3).

(c) amending IA 1986, s 313 (charge on bankrupt's home) so that, where a charging order is placed on the bankrupt's matrimonial home or former matrimonial home, the bankrupt stands to take advantage of any increase in value of the property after the date that the charge is imposed.[10]

In general, the amendments are intended to:

(a) provide certainty as to the time-scale within which the matrimonial homes may be realised by the trustee and thereby strike a fairer balance between the interest of the creditors and the interests of the bankrupt and his family;

(b) support the concept of a 'fresh start' after the expiry of the 'use it or lose it' period; and

(c) help reduce the stigma of bankruptcy.

It is worth noting at the outset that the amendments and additions to the IA 1986 only affect matrimonial homes, or former matrimonial homes occupied by the bankrupt's estranged spouse or former spouse. Otherwise, the familiar regime of permanent vesting in the trustee under the IA 1986 is unaffected.

The 'use it or lose it' rule

17.8   New s 283A(1) and (2) of IA 1986 provides that the bankrupt's interest in a dwelling-house which at the date of the bankruptcy was the sole or principal residence of:

(a) the bankrupt,

(b) the bankrupt's spouse, or

(c) a former spouse of the bankrupt,

shall cease to be comprised in the bankrupt's estate and shall vest in the bankrupt at the end of the period of 3 years, beginning with the date of the bankruptcy. The property vests in the bankrupt (and the trustee is consequently divested) automatically without any conveyance, assignment or transfer.[11] Of course, in those intervening 3 years, the property remains part of the bankrupt's estate under the familiar provisions of IA 1986, s 283 and vests in the trustee pursuant to IA 1986, s 306. The trustee is likely to make the usual entries at HM Land Registry against the property, and take the usual steps to protect the trustee's interest in respect of unregistered land.

17.9   It is envisaged that new rules will provide that, where the trustee has made an entry at HM Land Registry showing the trustee's interest in the property, the trustee will be obliged to make the necessary applications to HM Land Registry in order to show the re-vesting of property in the bankrupt, and to inform the bankrupt of the re-vesting. Similarly, where the property is

---

10   EA 2002, s 261(2).

11   IA 1986, s 283A(2)(b). The property vests in the bankrupt in exactly the same manner as property first vests in the trustee under IA 1986, s 306. An amendment to s 307 (after-acquired property) by EA 2002, s 260(4) introduces a new subsection, s 307(2)(aa), preventing the trustee acquiring property which re-vests in the bankrupt as after-acquired property.

unregistered, it is envisaged that new rules will provide for the trustee to issue a certificate to the bankrupt conclusively proving that the property has re-vested in the bankrupt.

17.10   It is noteworthy that, potentially, an interest in more than one dwelling may be caught by s 283A. For instance, if a bankrupt has an interest in three properties, one occupied by the bankrupt, the other by an estranged spouse, and the third by a former spouse, each interest may re-vest in the bankrupt after the expiry of 3 years from the date of bankruptcy. Indeed, it may be the case that the bankrupt has more than one former spouse. On the other hand, the definition does not encompass a property occupied by an estranged cohabitee/partner, even if there are children of the relationship living with and cared for by the estranged cohabitee/partner.

17.11   It is envisaged that new rules under s 283A(8) and (9) will provide for the trustee to give a written notice to the bankrupt identifying any property which is 'use it or lose it' property within the meaning of IA 1986, s 283A. Such a notice provision will help crystallise any dispute concerning the qualification of any particular interest in property as 'use it or lose it' property under s 283A. The rules will provide a mechanism for resolving any dispute as to whether any given property qualifties for protection under s 283A, and possibily provide the the compensation of a bankrupt when the trustee has taken an inappropriate position in relation to the selection of 'use it or lose it' property.

17.12   During the 3-year, 'use it or lose it' period, the trustee may prevent the property vesting in the bankrupt at the expiry of the period by taking one of five prescribed steps towards realising the interest:

(1) by the trustee realising the interest in the property: obviously, if the trustee realises the value of the interest by sale the property will not vest in the bankrupt;[12]

(2) by the trustee applying for an order for sale in respect of the dwelling-house:[13] IA 1986, s 335A applies so that, where the application is made after a period of 1 year beginning with the vesting of the bankrupt's estate in a trustee, the court will assume that the interests of the bankrupt's creditors outweigh all other considerations unless the circumstances of the case are exceptional;

(3) by the trustee applying for an order for possession of the dwelling-house:[14] IA 1986, s 336 applies so that where the application is made after a period of 1 year beginning with the vesting of the bankrupt's estate in a trustee, the court will assume that the interests of the bankrupt's creditors outweigh all other considerations unless the circumstances of the case are exceptional;

(4) by the trustee applying to the court for a charge on the property for the benefit of the bankrupt's estate pursuant to IA 1986, s 313:[15] s 313 (charge on bankrupt's home) is itself amended so that it is consistent with the 'use it or lose it' principle. However, it is worth noting that the amendments to

---

12   IA 1986, s 283A(3)(a).
13   Ibid, s 283A(3)(b).
14   Ibid, s 283A(3)(c).
15   Ibid, s 283A(3)(d).

s 313 retain the condition precedent that the trustee is, for any reason, unable for the time being to realise the property. The option of a charging order remains the option of last resort except in exceptional circumstances.

(5) by the trustee and the bankrupt agreeing that the bankrupt shall incur a specified liability to his estate (with or without interest from the date of the agreement) in consideration of which the interest mentioned in s 283A(1) shall cease to form part of the estate.[16]

Discussion

17.13   The proposed agreement between the trustee and the bankrupt raises some interesting points. This step appears to envisage an agreement whereby the bankrupt agrees to incur a liability to be met at some specified date in the future by the means of a single payment or by instalments. There do not appear to be any restrictions within the IA 1986 upon the length of time that the bankrupt and the trustee may agree to defer payment, or the amount of interest that may be charged.[17] There is no particular formality required by s 283A, but the agreement would appear to be an agreement for the sale or other disposition of an interest in land.[18] In those circumstances, it would be good practice to ensure that any such agreement complied with the provisions of s 2 of the Law of Property (Miscellaneous Provisions) Act 1989,[19] at least until the formality requirements under this subsection are clarified by the courts.

17.14   When considering an agreement under s 283A(3)(e), the trustee will also have to consider to what extent the funds offered by the bankrupt might be recovered by the trustee in any event under an income payments order/agreement or as after-acquired property. If the proposal is for the bankrupt to utilise the bankrupt's income to purchase the estate's interest in the property, the trustee should consider whether the estate should take the benefit of that income for 3 years by means of an income payments order/agreement *and in addition* realise the estate's interest in the property. In the usual course it may not be appropriate to enter into a s 283A(3)(e) agreement unless the purchase is being funded by a third party, borrowing from a third party by the (discharged) bankrupt, income received by the bankrupt after the completion of a suitable 3-year income payment order/agreement and/or a windfall to the bankrupt which is not after-acquired property within the meaning of IA 1986, s 307.

---

16   IA 1986, s 283A(3)(e).

17   There is a risk that, where payment is deferred and the amount of credit is less than £25,000, the agreement may be a regulated consumer credit agreement within the meaning of the Consumer Credit Act 1974. Unless and until agreements by trustees are exempted from regulation under the Consumer Credit Act 1974 pursuant to s 16 of that Act, trustees should take care that the agreement is framed in such a way so as to avoid the provisions of the Consumer Credit Act 1974.

18   It may be arguable that the agreement under s 283A(3)(e) is an agreement concerning statutory vesting, rather than an agreement concerning a sale or other disposition of an interest in land.

19   A contract for the sale or other disposition of an interest in land can only be made in writing and only by incorporating all the terms which the parties have expressly agreed in one document, or, where contracts are exchanged, in each, and must be signed by or on behalf of each party to the contract.

17.15   The creditors' committee may also have a role to play in determining the balance between a s 283A(3)(e) agreement and/or an income payments order/agreement. The creditors' committee may prefer the trustee to enter into a lump-sum s 283A(3)(e) agreement at the expense of a lengthy income payments order/agreement so that the creditors receive a significant lump sum early in the bankruptcy.

17.16   Where the trustee makes an application for sale or for possession (see above) which is dismissed, the interest to which the application relates shall cease to be comprised in the bankrupt's estate and shall automatically vest in the bankrupt, unless the court otherwise orders.[20] There is no suggestion in the Act when it might be appropriate for the court to order that the interest should not cease to form part of the estate and should not vest in the bankrupt. No doubt it would be appropriate for the court to order otherwise where there is some prospect of the trustee successfully realising the interest by applying for a charging order under IA 1986, s 313.

17.17   It is envisaged that, where the trustee takes a step which results in the interest in the property re-vesting in the bankrupt (ie a sale to the bankrupt, an agreement under s 283A(3)(e), the completion of a charging order or an unsuccessful application for possession order or order for sale), then new rules will provide for the trustee to make all necessary applications to HM Land Registry to show the re-vesting of the property in the bankrupt, and in the case of unregistered land, to issue the bankrupt with a certificate conclusively proving that the property has re-vested in the bankrupt.

Exceptional cases

17.18   The court may substitute a longer period for the 3-year 'use it or lose it' period under s 283A(2) in such circumstances as the court thinks appropriate, or in prescribed circumstances.[21]

17.19   It is unclear from the Act when it might be appropriate for the court to substitute a longer period. No doubt, inefficiency by the official receiver and/or the trustee will not excuse a failure to take an appropriate step within the 3-year 'use it or lose it' period. An extension might be appropriate where the bankrupt has voluntarily vacated the property and the sale of the property is delayed beyond the 3-year 'use it or lose it' period, despite the reasonable efforts of the trustee. An extension might also be appropriate where an application for sale and/or possession has been made within the 3-year 'use it or lose it' period but, at the hearing of the application, after the expiry of the 'use it or lose it' period, the application is dismissed on exceptional grounds. It might be appropriate in those circumstances for the court to substitute a longer period which has a connection to the duration of the exceptional circumstances, or to allow the trustee to make an application for a charging order.

17.20   Subsection (7) makes provision for rules to prescribe a shorter 'use it

---

20   IA 1986, s 283A(4).
21   Ibid, s 283A(6)(a), (b).

or lose it' period in certain circumstances. At the date of writing there does not appear to be any immediate intention to utilise this power in the proposed rules.

Evasion

17.21   Where the bankrupt fails to inform the trustee or the official receiver of his interest in a property before the end of 3 months ending with the date of the bankruptcy, the running of the 3-year 'use it or lose it' period is postponed to the date upon which the trustee or official receiver becomes aware of the bankrupt's interest.[22]

TRANSITIONAL PROVISIONS

17.22   The 'use it or lose it' provisions in respect of interests in the sole or principal residence of the bankrupt, his spouse or a former spouse apply to bankrupts who are adjudged bankrupt before the commencement of s 261(1) of EA 2002. In such cases, the interest in the property re-vests in the bankrupt after the expiry of a 3-year transitional period running from the commencement of s 261(1) of EA 2002. During the transitional period, the trustee may prevent the property re-vesting in the bankrupt by taking one of the prescribed steps under IA 1986, s 283A(3) (ie realising the interest, applying for an order for sale, applying for an order for possession, applying for a charging order under s 313 or reaching an agreement that in consideration of a specified liability the interest shall cease to form part of the estate).[23]

17.23   The provisions in respect of dismissal of applications for sale or possession (s 283A(4)), evasion (s 283A(5)), substitution of a longer 'use it or lose it' period (s 283A(6)), rules for shorter 'use it or lose it' period (s 283A(7)), and other subordinate legislation (s 283A(8), (9)) all apply, with any necessary modifications, to transitional cases.[24] For example, in transitional cases the reference in s 283A(2) to the 'use it or lose it' period of 3 years commencing with the date of the bankruptcy shall be construed as a reference to the transitional 'use it or lose it' period of 3 years from the date of commencement of EA 2002, s 261(1).[25]

Low-value homes

17.24   A new IA 1986, s 313A provides that where property comprised in the bankrupt's estate consists of an interest in a dwelling-house which at the date of the bankruptcy was the sole or principal residence of:

(a) the bankrupt,
(b) the bankrupt's spouse, or
(c) a former spouse of the bankrupt,

and the trustee applies for an order for sale of the property, or an order for possession of the property, or an order for a charging order under IA 1986,

---

22   IA 1986, s 283A(5).
23   EA 2002, s 260(8), (9).
24   Ibid, s 260(10).
25   Ibid, s 260(10)(a)–(c).

s 313, then the court shall dismiss the application if the value of the interest is below an amount prescribed for the purposes of s 313A.[26] Section 313A(3) envisages rules requiring the court to disregard certain matters in ascertaining the value of the property thereby simplifying the valuation process. As yet, there is no indication what might be disregarded under the rules.

17.25 The title to s 313A, 'Low-value home: application for sale, possession or charge', is misleading. It is worth noting that the provisions relate to the value of the bankrupt's interest in the home, rather than the value of the home in which the bankrupt has an interest. If the bankrupt has a relatively small interest in the matrimonial home, that interest may qualify for protection under s 313A, even if the property as a whole is relatively valuable and the spouse/former spouse might reasonably be expected to be able to raise the modest sum required to purchase the estate's interest. In those circumstances, the provisions of s 313A may appear to be a gift to the bankrupt and his family rather than serving any particular social purpose.

17.26 To date, there is no indication of whether the new set of rules consequential upon the EA 2002 will prescribe a threshold value under s 313A and, if so, what the threshold might be. Unless and until a threshold value is prescribed, s 313A is ineffective and useless. The huge disparity of property prices across the UK will mean that any single threshold value may prove to be a blunt instrument.

17.27 It may be that the rules will provide a more sophisticated definition of 'the amount prescribed for the purposes of this section'.[27] Rather than prescribe a threshold figure (ie £5,000, £10,000, etc), it is thought that the rules may provide a formula which defines the amount prescribed by reference to the net recovery that the creditors might reasonably expect to receive from the realisation of the interest in the property, after the deduction of the trustees' fees, costs and expenses, etc from the gross proceeds. The section would then operate to cure the perceived mischief of trustees realising interests in matrimonial homes merely as a fee generation and collection exercise.[28] How such a concept would operate in practice will depend largely upon the detail of any future rules.

17.28 It is not yet clear whether the rules will prescribe a simple threshold figure, or attempt a more sophisticated approach. Although a simple threshold figure may prove to be a blunt instrument in some circumstances, it nevertheless has the benefit of being ascertained and certain, where any more sophisiticated

---

26 IA 1986, s 313A(1), (2). IA 1986, ss 384 ('Prescribed' and 'the Rules') and 418 ('Monetary limits (bankruptcy)') are also amended to include reference to the new s 313A and this new prescribed amount (see EA 2002, s 260(5), (6)).

27 IA 1986, s 313A(2).

28 Such a formulation of the rules may have changed the result in *Trustee of the estate of Eric Bowe v Bowe* [1997] BPIR 747 where it was held, per Jonathan Parker J that: (1) the bankrupt's creditors have an interest in an order for sale being made notwithstanding that the entirety of the bankrupt's share in the net proceeds of sale of the property might be swallowed up in defraying the expenses of the bankruptcy, as it was in the interests of the creditors that the expenses of the bankruptcy be discharged so far as possible out of the assets of the bankrupt; and (2) the fact that the entirety of the net proceeds of sale would be swallowed up in paying the expenses of the bankruptcy was not an exceptional circumstance for the purpose of IA 1986, s 336(5).

approach opens up the prospect of litigation between the trustee and the bankrupt concerning the application of that definition to the particular circumstances of the case.

17.29   It is worth noting that low-value property is not excluded from the bankrupt's estate from the outset, although the relevant low-value interest is 'use it or lose it' property under s 283A(1). If the trustee does not make an application for sale, possession or a charging order under s 283A(3) (for instance, because the interest in the property is undoubtedly within the low-value threshold and therefore the application is bound to fail) the property will re-vest in the bankrupt upon the expiry of the 3-year period under s 283A(2) (or upon the expiry of the 3-year transitional period in respect of pre-commencement bankruptcies). This treatment of low-value property has some interesting ramifications.

17.30   For instance, despite the provisions of s 313A, it may be nevertheless possible to enter into an agreement under s 283A(3)(e) (an agreement whereby the bankrupt incurs a specified liability in consideration of which the property ceases to form part of the bankrupt's estate) in respect of a low-value interest, even though an application for sale, possession or a charging order would be dismissed. This appears to be consistent with the possible intent of this section to cure the perceived mischief of trustees realising interests in low-value homes as a fee generation and collection exercise, because the costs of any such agreement are likely to be small compared to the costs of applying for sale, possession or a charging order. However, where an application for sale, possession or a charging order would be dismissed on the 'low-value' ground, there is no incentive for the bankrupt to enter into such an agreement, and a well advised bankrupt may refuse to entertain such an agreement.

17.31   Furthermore, it appears possible that a relevant interest may qualify as a low-value home at the beginning of the 3-year period, but may have increased in value towards the end of the 3-year period so that it no longer qualifies for protection. In those circumstances, an application for sale, possession or a charging order heard at the beginning of the period would be dismissed under s 313A(2), but a later application might be successful. Where an application is dismissed pursuant to s 313A(2), the trustee needs to consider applying for a direction under s 283A(4) if there is a prospect that the property will increase beyond the low-value threshold before the expiry of the 3-year 'use it or lose it' period. Furthermore, where a trustee takes a decision not to make an application on the basis that the property is a low-value property, that decision may need to be revisited a short time before the expiry of the 3-year 'use it or lose it' period so that an application may be issued if the value of the property has increased beyond the low-value threshold.

Amendments to IA 1986, s 313 (charge upon bankrupt's home)

17.32   Under the former regime, the court imposed a charge on the bankrupt's home for the benefit of the bankrupt's estate 'up to the value from time to time of the property secured'.[29] This leaves the property encumbered

---

29   See IA 1986, s 313, unamended by the EA 2002.

with the entire bankruptcy debt and costs to the full value of the property from time to time. The bankruptcy estate thereby took the advantage of any increase in value of the property after the date of the charge and this former approach is inconsistent with the 'use it or lose it' concept and the idea of a 'fresh start'. The new regime dispenses with the concept of the value of the property secured, and introduces the new concept of a charge enforceable 'up to the charged value from time to time'.[30] The 'charged value' is defined by a new s 313(2A)[31] as the amount specified in the charging order as being the value of the bankrupt's interest in the property at the date of the order plus interest from the date of the order at the prescribed rate. The concept of 'charged value' puts the value of the bankrupt's interest in the property squarely in issue upon the application and plainly the value will have to be agreed or determined by evidence. On the other hand, under the concept of 'charged value' the bankrupt stands to take the benefit of any increase in value of the property over and above the prescribed rate of interest.

17.33 A new s 313(2B) envisages rules requiring the court to disregard certain matters in ascertaining the value of an interest in the property, thereby simplifying the valuation process. As yet, there is no indication what the rules may prescribe. The intent is that the determination of the value of the bankrupt's interest will simply be a matter of applying the bankrupt's interest (expressed as a proportion of the property as a whole, eg 10%, 50%, etc), to the value of the property, without taking any account of the possible difficulties in obtaining an order for sale, etc against co-owners, spouses, etc. Presumably these 'disregards' rules will be identical or similar to any rules made under s 313A(3) (low-value homes). It appears likely that any rules made under s 313(2B) will inform any agreement made pursuant to s 283A(3)(e) as to the quantum of the specified liability incurred by the bankrupt in consideration of the bankrupt's interest in the matrimonial or former matrimonial home shall cease to form part of the bankrupt's estate.

17.34 IA 1986, s 313(4) provides that s 3(1), (2), (4)–(6) of the Charging Orders Act 1979 applies to charging orders made under s 313. Section 3(5) of the Charging Orders Act 1979 provides that the court may vary or discharge a charging order on the application of the debtor or any person interest in the property to which the order relates. A new subs 313(5) provides that an order under s 3(5) of the Charging Orders Act 1979 may not vary the charged value specified in the charging order under s 313(2A).

17.35 It is envisaged that new rules will require applications for charging orders in respect of dwelling-houses to be served on any spouse or former spouse occupying the dwelling, and for the joinder of any other person with an interest in the property to the application. It is likely that the rules will require the trustee to identify the extent of the bankrupt's interest in the property and also state the amount outstanding to unsecured creditors at the time of the application. It is likely that the new rules will provide a mechanism for ascertaining the 'chargeable value', possibly including the appointment of a

---

30   EA 2002, s 260(2)(a), amending IA 1986, s 313(2).
31   Inserted by EA 2002, s 260(2)(b).

joint expert valuer. It is envisaged that the rate of interest specified by the rules in relation to charges under s 313 will be the Judgement Act 1838 rate from time to time.

DISCHARGE

17.36   Under IA 1986, s 332(2) the trustee shall not summon a final meeting of creditors (that is, to consider his release) where a house is unrealised unless he has either:

(a) obtained a charging order under s 313; or
(b) the court has refused to make such an order; or
(c) the Secretary of State has certified that it would be 'inappropriate or inexpedient' to make such an application.

17.37   It has been suggested in the past[32] that it may be 'inappropriate or expedient' to apply for a s 313 charging order where there are no funds in the estate, and even if there are funds, it is arguably more appropriate to give them to the creditors rather than to risk them on an application under s 313, and that the trustee can protect his interest by making an appropriate registration at HM Land Registry or Land Charges Registry.

17.38   Plainly the 'use it or lose it' provisions mean that doing nothing will result in the property re-vesting in the bankrupt and the trustee can no longer simply register his interest and wait until the passage of time has rendered it economic to realise the bankrupt's home. In those circumstances it is difficult to imagine circumstances where it might be 'inappropriate or expedient' to fail to take steps to realise the bankrupt's home, if only to obtain a s 313 charging order.

17.39   However, s 332(1)(a) provides that the restrictions upon calling a final meeting of creditors (to consider the release of the trustee) apply where:

> '... there is comprised in the bankrupt's estate property consisting of an interest in a dwelling house which is occupied by the bankrupt or by his spouse or former spouse...'

17.40   It appears at least arguable that where the 3-year 'use it or lose it' period has expired, and the property has re-vested in the bankrupt pursuant to s 283A of IA 1986, then the bankrupt's interest in the property is no longer comprised in the bankrupt's estate within the meaning of s 312(1). In those circumstances, it appears that the trustee would be entitled to call a meeting under s 331 after the expiry of the 3-year 'use it or lose it' period, even if the trustee's own inactivity had resulted in the property re-vesting in the bankrupt. What the creditors would make of such an omission is another matter entirely.

---

32   For instance, Steven Hill 'Charge on bankrupt's home – s 313 IA 1986' (1990) *Insolvency Law & Practice* Vol 6, p 12.

Chapter 18

INCOME PAYMENTS ORDERS AND AGREEMENTS

'Expenditure rises to meet income.'
C Northcote Parkinson[1]

INTRODUCTION

18.1   The bankruptcy regime may be understood as a balance struck in the public interest between competing interests. On the one hand, there is the interest of the creditors in recovering the bankrupt's assets and obtaining satisfaction, and on the other the interest of the bankrupt in being relieved from the demands of the creditors, maintaining a minimum standard of living and dignity, and being rehabilitated.

18.2   In general terms, the bankruptcy regime holds the balance by thinking in terms of 'selling up' the assets of the bankrupt at the commencement of the bankruptcy and dividing the proceeds between the creditors (see, in general, IA 1986, s 283(1)). Consequently, the income of a bankrupt does not vest automatically in his trustee in bankruptcy, but may vest in the trustee under the provisions of s 310 of IA 1986.[2]

18.3   Under the former regime, a trustee in bankruptcy could only obtain a portion of the bankrupt's income by making an application to the court. The procedure involves issuing an application, giving notice to the bankrupt, and preparing and serving a short statement of the grounds of the application. The rules provide that the notice given to the bankrupt must inform the bankrupt that, unless at least 7 days before the date fixed for the hearing he sends to the court and to the trustee written consent to an order being made in the terms sought, he is required to attend the hearing and that, if he attends, he will be given an opportunity to show cause why the order should not be made or, if made, not in the terms sought by the trustee.[3] If the bankrupt does not provide written consent the trustee is obliged to attend court. In many cases, the bankrupt does consent to an income payment order (IPO), but the trustee must nevertheless issue the application and serve the bankrupt according to the rules.

---

1   *The Law and the Profits* (1960).
2   See, in general, Miller 'Income Payment Orders' (2002) *Insolvency Law & Practice*, Vol 18, No 2.
3   IR 1986, r 6.189.

This formal procedure is often costly in comparison to the usually modest sums recovered by the trustee under an income payments order.

18.4   In the consultation document *Bankruptcy: A Fresh Start*, it was reported that in the year ending 31 March 2000 it was likely that official receivers would have secured between 2,300 and 2,500 income payment orders, nearly all with the consent of the bankrupt individual. For obvious reasons, the average monthly instalment ordered to be paid is relatively small and is such that:

> 'A substantial proportion (and, in many smaller cases the whole) of what is paid may be absorbed in discharging the costs of the proceedings and of any insolvency practitioner appointed to deal with the case.'[4]

The result was that creditors often receive little benefit from income payment orders.

18.5   The EA 2002 tackles these problem by introducing the new concept of an income payment agreement (IPA) in a new s 310A of IA 1986, which provides a mechanism for reaching a binding agreement with the minimum of formality and without the cost of an application to the court. The old, familiar IPO scheme under IA 1986, s 310 is preserved and runs in tandem with the new IPA, and otherwise s 310 is slightly amended to be consistent with the more wide-ranging amendments introduced by the EA 2002.

INCOME PAYMENT ORDERS

18.6   The former 1986 regime is largely unaffected. Section 310(1) is amended and a new subs (1A) is introduced to make it plain that an IPO may only be made on the application of a trustee and has to be made before the discharge of the bankrupt.[5] Given the considerably shorter duration of bankruptcies following the Act (see Chapter 13), this creates an obvious pitfall for practitioners. In many cases, automatic discharge will be achieved within 12 months. The time for obtaining either an IPA or an IPO is therefore short. It is not a condition precedent for an application for an IPO that the trustee should have attempted to enter into an IPA, but in the usual course the court may look askance at an application for an IPO, and in particular any claim for costs included within the application, unless there has been some invitation to enter into an IPA before the application is made.

18.7   Section 310(6) is amended to provide that an IPO must specify the period during which it will have effect, that the period may end after the discharge of the bankrupt, but may not end after the end of 3 years, beginning with the date of the bankruptcy.[6] A similar period is provided for IPAs (see below). Satisfaction in full of the bankruptcy debt and costs aside, there does not appear to be any particular reason why a trustee should agree to limit an IPO to any period of less than 3 years. An amendment to the Bill was proposed in the

---

4   *Bankruptcy – A Fresh Start*, para 7.11, p 21.
5   EA 2002, s 259(1), (2) and (3).
6   Ibid, s 259(4).

House of Lords to the effect that the 3-year time-limit for IPOs should be removed, resulting in potentially longer or open-ended IPOs.[7] The Government maintained that the 3-year maximum held the correct balance between the interests of the bankrupt's creditors and the rehabilitation of the individual concerned and the amendment was rejected. In the general run of cases, there does not appear to be any reason why insolvency practitioners should take a different view. In the circumstances it seems likely that most, if not all, IPOs will be made for a period of 3 years whether the order is made soon after the commencement of the bankruptcy or shortly before discharge. In this respect, the bankrupt will feel the effects of the bankruptcy order long after his discharge, and, in fact, for a similar duration as bankruptcy orders and IPOs made under the former regime. When it comes to paying his debts it may appear to the bankrupt that nothing much has changed.

18.8   A new s 310(6A) is introduced, providing that an IPO may be varied on the application of the trustee or the bankrupt (whether before or after discharge). The court's power to vary and review an IPO had always been inferred under the former regime; this amendment makes the court's power of variation explicit.

18.9   Otherwise, s 310 remains intact and familiar.

INCOME PAYMENT AGREEMENTS

18.10   Section 260 of EA 2002 introduces a new s 310A into the IA 1986:

'**310A Income payments agreement**

(1)   In this section "income payments agreement" means a written agreement between a bankrupt and his trustee or between a bankrupt and the official receiver which provides—

    (a)   that the bankrupt is to pay to the trustee or the official receiver an amount equal to a specified part or proportion of the bankrupt's income for a specified period, or

    (b)   that a third person is to pay to the trustee or the official receiver a specified proportion of money due to the bankrupt by way of income for a specified period.

(2)   A provision of an income payments agreement of a kind specified in subsection (1)(a) or (b) may be enforced as if it were a provision of an income payments order.

(3)   While an income payments agreement is in force the Court may, on the application of the bankrupt, his trustee or the official receiver, discharge or vary an attachment of earnings order that is for the time being in force to secure payments by the bankrupt.

(4)   The following provisions of section 310 shall apply to an income payments agreement as they apply to an income payments order—

    (a)   subsection (5) (receipts to form part of an estate), and

    (b)   subsections (7) to (9) (meaning of income).

---

7   Second reading, House of Lords, 21 October 2002.

(5) An income payments agreement must specify the period during which it is to have effect; and that period—

(a) may end after the discharge of the bankrupt, but
(b) may not end after the period of three years beginning with the date on which the agreement is made.

(6) An income payments agreement may (subject to subsection 5(b)) be varied—

(a) by agreement between the parties, or
(b) by the court made on an application made by the bankrupt, the trustee, or the official receiver.

(7) The court—

(a) may not vary an income payments agreement so as to include provision of a kind which could not be included in an income payments order, and
(b) shall grant an application to vary an income payments agreement if and to the extent that the Court thinks variation necessary to avoid the effect mentioned in section 310(2).'

18.11 Where there is a valid IPA, the receipts form part of the bankrupt's estate.[8]

18.12 The new s 310A prescribes certain formalities necessary to create an IPA, but does not expressly provide a sanction if the formalities are not adhered to. The agreement is required to be 'a written agreement between a bankrupt and his trustee or between a bankrupt and the official receiver' (s 310A(1)). Plainly, a verbal agreement will not suffice under subs (1). However, the agreement is not required to be signed, nor is it required to be in a single document, and therefore it appears that an exchange of correspondence or faxes may amount to sufficient writing provided that it otherwise complies with subs (1).

18.13 Nevertheless, it may well be that rules dealing with the formation of IPAs will provide, for instance, for the provision of a draft agreement by the official receiver or the trustee, and the signature of the bankrupt and the official receiver/trustee on the draft agreement before the IPA comes into force, thereby effectively increasing the formality required to conclude an effective IPA. It is also possible that the new rules will prescribe a form for IPAs.

18.14 The written agreement must specify 'an amount equal to a specified part or proportion of the bankrupt's income for a specified period'.[9] These requirements apparently require the agreement to specify separately:

(a) a sum of money payable periodically (either weekly or monthly or otherwise usually depending upon the periods of the bankrupt's income); and
(b) the part or proportion of the bankrupt's income that the sum of money is equal to (probably best expressed as a percentage); and
(c) the period (probably best expressed with a start date and a finish date and stating the number of instalments due under the agreement).

8   IA 1986, s 310A(4)(a) referring to s 310(5).
9   Ibid, s 310A(1)(a).

18.15   It appears from s 310A(1) that it is not sufficient merely to specify (a) and (c) without (b), or (b) or (c) without (a), or any other combination of the requirements. Unless an agreement is in writing and complies with all three requirements it may not be an IPA within the meaning of s 310A, and there is a risk that it is not enforceable under the provisions of the new section (see below). One consequence of an agreement which does not satisfy the formality requirements may be that the receipts do not form part of the bankrupt's estate pursuant to s 310A(4)(a) (above).[10]

18.16   The agreement may be an agreement between the trustee and the bankrupt for a third person, typically the bankrupt's employer, 'to pay to the trustee or the official receiver a specified proportion of money due to the bankrupt by way of income for a specified period' (see subs (1)(b)). In distinction to subs (1)(a), such an agreement need not specify the sum of money required to be paid, merely:

(a)   the specified proportion of money due to the bankrupt from the third party; and

(b)   the specified period.

Again, an agreement which does not conform with these requirement is not, strictly speaking, an IPA within the meaning of s 310A with all the consequent risks (see above).[11]

18.17   It is notable that in line with the procedure relating to IPOs (see above), an IPA made in respect of a third person need not be made with the third party. As is the case with IPOs, the third party has no interest in the destination of the income or the terms of the order and the IPA may be concluded without reference to the third party.

18.18   The specified period for an IPA must not exceed 3 years from the date on which the agreement was made. The relevant period is 3 years, whether or not the period ends after the discharge of the bankrupt.[12] The period is identical to that provided for IPOs. Apart from cases where there is to be satisfaction of the bankruptcy shortfall and costs, as with IPOs there does not appear to be any particular reason for a trustee to agree to limit the duration of an IPA to less than 3 years.[13] In the circumstances, it appears likely that all IPAs (and IPOs) will be made for a straight period of 3 years, whether the order is made at the beginning of the bankruptcy, or just before discharge. In most cases the bankrupt will

---

10   Nevertheless, such an agreement might arguably be enforceable as a contract between the bankrupt and the trustee – the trustee providing consideration by forbearing to apply for an IPO. If the agreement is not an IPO what is the status of the receipt (IA 1986, ss 310A(4)(a) and 310(5) being inapplicable)?

11   Furthermore, although the agreement might arguably amount to a contract between the bankrupt and the trustee (see the note above), the third party is not party to such a contract.

12   IA 1986, s 310A(5). For agreements entered into by correspondence it may be necessary to examine the usual contractual rules of offer and acceptance in order to ascertain the precise date of the agreement.

13   Where it is the case that the bankrupt might potentially discharge the bankruptcy debts, or a significant proportion of the bankruptcy debts, through the IPA, then it may well be the case that the trustee and the bankrupt should be considering a post-bankruptcy IVA.

continue making payment under an IPA for in excess of 2 years following his discharge.

18.19   The bankrupt, the trustee or the official receiver may apply to discharge or vary an attachment of earnings order that is for the time being in force to secure payments by the bankrupt.[14]

18.20   An IPA may be varied by agreement between the parties, or upon application by the bankrupt, the trustee or the official receiver to the court.[15] As a matter of principle, the formality requirements of s 310A apply equally to variations of an existing IPA, albeit a simple exchange of correspondence should suffice (subject to anything in the rules). It is likely that the Rules will provide for the service of any application and supporting evidence any application by the bankrupt or the trustee/official receiver to the court for a variation of an IPA.

18.21   If the bankrupt's income increases, the bankrupt has a duty, at least until discharge, to disclose the increase and give notice to his trustee.[16] It is likely that, under the new regime, IPAs will continue for 3 years, often in excess of 2 years after the date of discharge of the bankrupt. After discharge, there is no duty on the bankrupt to give notice of after-acquired property or an increase in income, although the bankrupt may remain under a duty to give the trustee such information relating to his affairs as the trustee may reasonably require.[17] Well drafted IPAs should therefore contain a clause requiring the bankrupt to notify the trustee of any increases in income notwithstanding the bankrupt's discharge, thereby imposing a duty on the bankrupt to disclose an increase in income after his discharge.[18]

18.22   Consequently, a bankrupt may reasonably expect to pay the trustee or official receiver an increased sum in line with the part or proportion of the bankrupt's income specified in the agreement pursuant to s 310A(1)(a) or (b). Similarly, if the bankrupt's income decreases the trustee can reasonably expect a decrease. The IPA may not be varied so that it extends for a duration in excess of 3 years,[19] nor may the court vary an IPA to include provisions of a kind which could not be included in an IPO.[20]

18.23   The court shall grant an application to vary an IPA if and to the extent that the court thinks the variation necessary to avoid reducing the bankrupt's income (together with any payments by way of guaranteed minimum pensions or giving effect to protected rights as a member of a pension scheme) to below what appears to the court to be necessary for meeting the reasonable domestic needs of the bankrupt and his family.[21] The legislation will not hold the bankrupt to a bargain that leaves the bankrupt and his family suffering real

---

14   IA 1986, s 310A(3), mirroring s 310(3) in relation to IPOs.

15   Ibid, s 310A(6).

16   Ibid, s 333(2) and see IR 1986, r 6.200.

17   Ibid, s 333(3).

18   See Ibid, s 333(1).

19   Ibid, s 310(5)(b).

20   Ibid, s 310(7)(a).

21   Ibid, ss 310A(7)(b), 310(2), (8); and see *Re Rayatt* [1998] BPIR 495; *Kilvert v Flackett* [1998] 721; *Malcolm v Official Receiver* [1999] BPIR 97.

hardship. Obviously, good practice dictates that the trustee and the bankrupt should consider the reasonable domestic needs of the bankrupt and his family when agreeing the original terms of the IPA. A well drafted IPA may well make express reference to the sum allocated to the bankrupt and his family's reasonable domestic needs, and thereby discourage argument about the extent of the reasonable domestic needs of the bankrupt and his family at a later date, ie a well drafted IPA will be prima facie evidence of the reasonable domestic needs of a bankrupt and his family.

18.24 It is noteworthy that s 310A does not expressly provide for the IPA to be discharged by agreement or on the application of the bankrupt or anyone else. Of course, if the income ceases then a well drafted IPA should make it clear that the agreement has no effect whilst there is no income. Where income is reduced to a level where the bankrupt needs all of the income for the reasonable domestic needs of himself and his family, presumably the IPA may be effectively discharged under s 310A(6) by agreement or upon application to the court by varying the amount payable to zero or to a nominal sum, or otherwise varying the agreement so that it does not take effect unless the bankrupt's income is over a specified level. As the parties are entitled to vary an IPA by agreement, it is expected that an exchange of correspondence agreeing the variation will be sufficient (subject to anything in the rules).

18.25 'Income' for the purposes of IPAs is defined in the same manner as for IPOs by reference to s 310(7)–(9) of IA 1986.[22] The income of the bankrupt comprises every payment in the nature of income which is, from time to time, made to him or to which he, from time to time, becomes entitled, including any payment in respect of the carrying on of any business or in respect of any office or employment and (despite anything in ss 11 or 12 of the Welfare Reform and Pensions Act 1999) any payment under a pension scheme but excluding any payment by way of guaranteed minimum pension and payments giving effect to the bankrupt's protected rights as a member of a pension scheme. 'Guaranteed minimum pension' and 'protected rights' are defined in the Pension Schemes Act 1993.[23]

18.26 An IPA (whether relating to the bankrupt or a third party) may be enforced as if it were a provision of an IPO.[24] It is not necessary to apply for and obtain an IPO in order to enforce an IPA. It is worth noting that, under the former regime, the consequence of failing to adhere to an IPO would be an application, or at least the threat of an application, to postpone the bankrupt's discharge pursuant to the old s 279 of IA 1986 until all the payments due under the IPO had been made. This was a persuasive tactic. Under the new s 279 the bankrupt will be discharged within a period of 1 year, beginning with the date on which the bankruptcy commenced, unless on the application of the official receiver or the trustee the court orders that the 1-year period shall cease to run until the end of a specified period or the fulfilment of a specified condition.[25]

---

22   IA 1986, s 310A(4)(b).
23   See discussions of this definition of income in *Kilvert v Flackett* [1998] BPIR 721; *Supperstone v Lloyds Names Working Party* [1999] BPIR 832.
24   IA 1986, s 310A(2).
25   See the new IA 1986, s 279(3).

18.27   In the general run of cases the bankrupt will be discharged within 1 year, but may be subject to an IPO or an IPA for between 2–3 years after the date of discharge. If a bankrupt falls into default in respect of an IPO or IPA before discharge is obtained, the court may, in an appropriate case, postpone discharge until the fulfilment of the bankrupt's obligations under the IPO or IPA (s 279(3) as amended). However it does not appear that the court may postpone discharge by reason of a possible or probable future failure to comply with the bankrupt's obligation under an IPO or an IPA. Section 279(2) (as amended) appears to apply to past or continuing failures only.

18.28   However, after the bankrupt has obtained discharge under s 279(1) it does not appear that the court can retrospectively postpone discharge under the provisions of s 279(3). In those circumstances, short of an application for contempt of court and/or execution, the trustee may be lacking leverage after the bankrupt's discharge to ensure compliance with IPOs and IPAs. Under IR 1986, r 6.191(1), where the bankrupt fails to comply, the trustee may apply for the order to be varied so as to take effect under s 310(3)(b) as an order to the payor of the relevant income (ie an order directed to the bankrupt's employer to pay a proportion of the income directly to the trustee). It is likely that new Rules will provide a similar provision for IPAs, ie where the bankrupt is in breach of an IPA, the trustee may apply for a variation so that the payer/employer of the bankrupt pays the relevant proportion directly to the trustee. Obviously, neither IR 1986, r 6.191(1) nor any equivalent rule for IPAs will provide a solution where the bankrupt is not employed.

18.29   Presumably, rules will be made for IPAs equivalent to the existing rules under IA 1986, Chapter 16 in relation to IPOs requiring service on third parties,[26] variation of the order upon non-compliance,[27] requiring the third party to make arrangements requisite for immediate compliance,[28] allowing the third party to deduct an administrative fee,[29] requiring the third party to inform the bankrupt of the deduction of any administrative fee,[30] giving notice of any cessation of liability to the bankrupt[31] (typically cessation of employment), and a procedure for review or variation of the agreement.[32]

TRANSITIONAL PROVISIONS

18.30   The transitional provisions for IPOs existing at the date of commencement of the EA 2002 are contained in Sch 19, para 7.

18.31   Where a bankrupt is made bankrupt, but has not been discharged before the commencement of s 255 (duration of bankruptcy), he is a 'pre-

---

26   IR 1986, r 6.190.
27   Ibid, r 6.191.
28   Ibid, r 6.192(1).
29   Ibid, r 13.11.
30   Ibid, r 6.192(2).
31   Ibid, r 6.192(3).
32   Ibid, r 6.193.

commencement bankrupt'.[33] Such bankrupts are discharged under the transitional provisions upon the earlier of either:

(a) 1 year from the commencement of s 254 of the EA 2002; or
(b) the end of the former period of bankruptcy under the former provisions of IA 1986, s 279.[34]

18.32   Where an IPO is in force in respect of a pre-commencement bankrupt which does not specify a date after which it is not to have effect, the IPO will cease upon the bankrupt's discharge under the transitional provisions.[35] Therefore, the IPO ceases upon the earlier of either 1 year from the commencement of s 254 of EA 2002, or the end of the former period of bankruptcy under the former provisions of IA 1986, s 279.

18.33   Where an IPO is in force in respect of such a pre-commencement bankrupt which specifies a date after which it is not to have effect,[36] it shall remain in force until the specified date, notwithstanding the pre-commencement bankrupt's discharge under the transitional provisions, and then lapse.[37] However, the transitional provisions provide that a pre-commencement bankrupt may apply to the court to vary the IPO or to provide for the IPO to cease to have effect earlier than the date specified in the original order.[38] No doubt, applications to vary an existing IPO so that it falls into line with the new regime will be sympathetically entertained. However, it is unlikely that the general run of cases will merit any such application or variation because the maximum period of the IPO under the former regime and the new regime remains the same (ie 3 years).

DRAFTING IPAs

18.34   In due course, it is likely that a standard form agreement will evolve, or a form will be prescribed. In the meantime, it is likely that insolvency practitioners will need to draft their own IPAs, whether the IPA is concluded in correspondence, or in a more formal document.

18.35   The following checklist may be helpful:

(a)   a written agreement;
(b)   dated;
(c)   expressly stating each of the following:

   (i)   except in the case of an IPO relating to payment by a third party/employer, a sum of money and the relevant period of payment (monthly, weekly, or exceptionally singularly);

---

33   EA 2002, Sch 19, paras 1, 2.
34   EA 2002, Sch 19, para 4 (ie 3 years from the date of commencement of the bankruptcy (s 279(2)(b)), other than summary administrations (2 years) (s 279(2)(a)), or where the court intervenes in the case of a recalcitrant bankrupt (s 279(3))).
35   See IA 1986, s 310(6)(b).
36   Which will, by necessary implication, be after the discharge of the pre-commencement bankrupt. See IA 1986, s 310(6)(b).
37   EA 2002, Sch 19, para 7(2).
38   Ibid, para 7(3).

(ii) a part or portion of the bankrupt's income (in the case of an IPA relating to payment by the bankrupt personally, the part of proportion should correspond with the sum of money specified above);

(iii) the period of the IPA,[39] being not more than 3 years in any event;[40]

(d) consider specifying the method of payment and the corresponding details required by the payer (name, address of payee, bank details, etc);

(e) consider and state whether the agreement is subject to or conditional upon the discharge or variation of an existing attachment of earnings order;[41]

(f) consider the reasonable domestic needs of the bankrupt and his family and consider recording any agreed assessment of those needs in monetary terms within the agreement[42] (so as to pre-empt argument about the extent of those needs at a later date);

(g) consider how much of the bankrupt's surplus income it is wise to take under the IPA (typically, one-half to two-thirds of the surplus income is common practice in relation to IPOs, and it would appear that the same is appropriate for IPAs);

(h) consider whether one-half to two-thirds of the surplus income justified the administrative expense of collecting it (a minimum of £40 pcm was often used a rule of thumb in the case of IPOs; however, the IPA will not entail the costs of an application to court and a sum less than £40 pcm may be a viable minimum);

(i) consider the impact of the deduction of any administrative fee by a third party (which may be prescribed by the rules);

(j) the deduction of the instalments from the bankrupt's income may qualify for income tax relief – consider informing the Inland Revenue of the existence of the IPA and reserving the tax relief to the trustee under the terms of the IPA;

(k) consider whether the funds potentially available under the IPA and the relative size of the bankruptcy debts would make a post-bankruptcy IVA a more appropriate option;

(l) consider requiring the bankrupt to notify the trustee of any increase or other change in his income during the period of the IPA (whether before or after his discharge), and remind the bankrupt of the penalty for non-compliance (contempt of court – fine or prison);[43] otherwise, the bankrupt may be under no obligation to inform the trustee of an increase in income after his discharge;

(m) consider making reference to the ability of the trustee or the bankrupt to vary the IPA by agreement or by application to court;[44]

(n) execute the draft agreement in accordance with the rules;

---

39 IA 1986, s 310A(1)(a), (b).
40 Ibid, s 310A(5).
41 Ibid, s 310A(3).
42 Ibid, ss 310A(7)(b) and 310(2).
43 Ibid, s 333(1).
44 Ibid, s 310A(6).

(o)	if the agreement relates to payments by a third party, serve the IPA on the third party and otherwise comply with any rules in relation to such agreements.

Chapter 19

BANKRUPTCY RESTRICTION ORDERS/ UNDERTAKINGS

'And now for something completely different . . .'
Graham Chapman and John Cleese[1]

INTRODUCTION

19.1 One of the key themes of the EA 2002 is the encouragement of business enterprise by the removal of the stigma of failure. The consequences of the bankruptcy of the individual are the same 'whether the bankrupt was dishonest or irresponsible or whether his failure was honest and above-board'.[2] This 'one size fits all' policy is to change. Stephen Byers, the former Secretary of State for Trade and Industry, explained the approach:[3]

'For too many people the fear of failure stifles innovation and enterprise. No wonder if failure means losing everything including the family home. We need to take a fresh look at our attitude to business failure, balancing the needs of the bankrupt with the rights of the creditors.

We must come down hard on the estimated 7–12% of bankrupts who are culpable, that is those who deliberately set out to mislead and deceive. But for those who fail for reasons beyond their control and despite their best efforts to save their business we need a new attitude.'

Announcing the publication of the Department of Trade and Industry White Paper, *Productivity and Enterprise, Insolvency – A Second Chance*, his successor, Patricia Hewitt, repeated this ethos:[4]

'We must remove the stigma surrounding bankruptcy. Too many people are unwilling to set up their own business because they are worried about the consequences of failure.

We must change attitudes. Most businesses fail because of bad luck or a lack of cash. But for too long such people have been tarred with the same brush as the reckless minority whose company collapses because of fraudulent activity.'

---

1   *Monty Python's Flying Circus* (1970).
2   Department of Trade and Industry White Paper, Productivity and Enterprise, *Insolvency – A Second Chance*, July 2001, Cm 5234.
3   DTI Press Notice, 'Byers outlines details of bankruptcy study', 2 July 1999, when announcing the publication of the Insolvency Service Consultation Paper, *Bankruptcy – a Fresh Start*. This is echoed in para 741 of the Explanatory Notes.
4   DTI Press Notice, 'Radical new approach to bankruptcy law planned', 7 April 2000.

19.2   'Enterprise' is encouraged principally by shortening the standard period of discharge to only 1 year[5] and relaxing the restrictions and disqualifications placed upon bankrupts during the period of the bankruptcy.[6]

19.3   As a counter-balance, the 'rogue' bankrupts will be subjected to a regime analogous to that imposed by the Company Directors Disqualification Act 1986 (CDDA 1986).

19.4   In order to protect the public and the commercial community, the court will be able to impose a bankruptcy restriction order (BRO) on the minority of bankrupts who abuse the system, do not co-operate with the official receiver or whose conduct has been dishonest or otherwise culpable. Such orders will impose the bankruptcy restrictions upon the bankrupt for a period beyond his discharge.

19.5   At present, the only punishments available in respect of the 'rogue' bankrupts are criminal sanctions. They obviously require the criminal standard of proof – beyond reasonable doubt. These are used in about 3% of cases.[7] Therefore, at present, there are no procedures by which a bankrupt whose conduct falls short of the criminal standard may be punished. The application for a BRO will be subject to the civil standard of proof – on the balance of probabilities. With the scope to bring more cases, this will allow for the greater protection of the public and business.

19.6   Coincidentally, the regime is also similar to that which prevailed under the Bankruptcy Act 1914. Under the 1914 Act, a bankrupt had to apply for his discharge. The official receiver reported to the court as to whether the bankrupt had been guilty of any of the acts set out in the Act (the so-called 'reportable facts').[8] The court would take these into account in determining whether the bankrupt should be discharged and, if so, whether any conditions should be attached. Despite the similarity, practitioners should be exceedingly wary of citing authorities based upon a previous statutory regime.[9] It remains to be seen whether the courts will adopt a similar approach to submissions based on the analogous regime under the CDDA 1986.

19.7   Mirroring the directors' disqualification provisions, the restrictions imposed upon the bankrupt can be imposed either by a BRO or by a written undertaking (a 'bankruptcy restriction undertaking' or 'BRU'). It is anticipated that a body of law, albeit smaller, will arise in the same way as in disqualification cases.

19.8   However, it remains to be seen what impact, if any, the threat of a potential BRO might have on a trading individual. The likelihood is that those who establish themselves in business do not have failure in mind when they are

---

5   See Chapter 16.

6   See Chapter 20.

7   The White Paper, para 1.25 providing figures for the 5 years to 31 March 2001 in which there were over 100,000 bankruptcies.

8   Bankruptcy Act 1914, s 26(3).

9   *Re a Debtor (No 1 of Lancaster)* [1989] 1 WLR 271 and *Smith v Braintree District Council* [1990] 2 AC 215, where both the Court of Appeal and the House of Lords warned against the citation of pre-1986 cases in respect of bankruptcy cases under the IA 1986.

starting or running a business. Those who do think about the possibility of failure are likely to be those who have previously suffered it.

THE STATUTORY FRAMEWORK

19.9   The entirety of the new regime is brought into being by a single section. Section 246(1) of EA 2002 inserts a new s 281A into the IA 1986 and simply states:

'Schedule 4A to this Act (bankruptcy restrictions order and bankruptcy restrictions undertaking) shall have effect.'

The main body of the provisions is included within the schedules: Sch 20 for the making of the BRO or BRU, Sch 21 for their effects.

The initial stages

19.10   At the outset, the official receiver will investigate the conduct and affairs of each bankrupt, including his conduct and affairs before the making of the bankruptcy order.[10] As well as being obliged to report to the court,[11] the official receiver will also compile a report for the Bankruptcy Restrictions Order Unit at the DTI. The Unit at this stage will take over conduct of the investigation and take the necessary preliminary steps in the preparation of the application. After these issues have been dealt with, the matter will be remitted to the official receiver for the finalisation of the evidence.

19.11   It is intended that an application for a BRO will be shorter and speedier than an application for a disqualification order. Therefore, in the vast majority of cases, solicitors will not be used to assist in the preparation of the cases. In that respect, the applications will bear more relation to an application to suspend the discharge of the bankrupt than an application for a disqualification order.

The application for a BRO

19.12   The application for a BRO is made to the court.[12] The application can be made only by the Secretary of State[13] or by the official receiver acting on a direction of the Secretary of State.[14] The application cannot be made by a creditor perhaps aggrieved by the conduct of the bankrupt that the court will take into account in deciding whether to make a BRO.

19.13   The Rules will no doubt provide the details of the procedural requirements of the application. These will deal with:

---

10   See EA 2002, s 258, introducing a revised IA 1986, s 289.
11   See IA 1986, s 289(2)(b), as revised.
12   IA 1986, Sch 4A, para 1(1).
13   Ibid, para 1(2)(a).
14   Ibid, para 1(2)(b). It is anticipated that, in practice, official receivers will bring all such applications; see para 1.29 of the White Paper.

(a) the venue;
(b) the timing of the evidence of the applicant;
(c) the timing of the evidence of the bankrupt; and
(d) the manner of presentation of such evidence, whether by report or affidavit.

It is anticipated that the formalities will be similar to those for proceedings under the CDDA 1986.[15] The Rules will no doubt also set out the extent to which IR 1986, Part 7, as regards court procedure and practice generally, shall apply to such applications.

19.14   The application for a BRO must be made within 1 year of the date upon which the bankruptcy commences.[16] This is the day on which the bankruptcy order is made.[17] An application may be made out of time with the permission of the court.[18] The period shall cease to run in respect of a bankrupt during the period in which his discharge has been suspended under IA 1986, s 279(3).[19] It is anticipated that the application will be made without notice to the bankrupt.

19.15   The choice of 1 year and the automatic extension of time upon the suspension of the discharged show that this is linked to the period for the discharge of the bankruptcy. However, there is no guidance at all as to the circumstances in which the court will exercise its discretion to extend the time period for the making of the application. If the discharge has not been suspended but, by not complying with his obligations, the bankrupt has been able to conceal from the official receiver or the trustee in bankruptcy the misconduct that is likely to form the basis of the application, the court is likely to grant permission to issue the BRO application out of time.

19.16   On the other hand, it would seem unlikely that the court would be pre-disposed to grant an extension of time for the BRO application where the discharge has been granted early, within the 1 year, upon the official receiver's filing of a notice that the investigation of the conduct and affairs of the bankrupt under s 289 of IA 1986 is unnecessary or concluded.[20]

19.17   The greatest source of guidance will no doubt be provided by the line of cases under the CDDA 1986 determining the Secretary of State's application for permission to bring disqualification proceedings out of time.[21] The factors that the court considers are:[22]

(a) the length of the delay;
(b) the reason for the delay;
(c) the strength of the case; and
(d) the degree of prejudice caused to the defendant by the delay.

---

15   Insolvent Companies (Disqualification of Unfit Directors) Proceedings Rules 1987, SI 1987/2023, as amended, and the Practice Direction: Directors Disqualification Proceedings.
16   IA 1986, Sch 4A, para 3(1)(a).
17   Ibid, s 278(a).
18   Ibid, s 278(b).
19   Ibid, Sch 4A, para 3(2).
20   Ibid, s 279(2).
21   CDDA 1986, s 7(2).
22   *Re Probe Date Systems Ltd (No 3)* [1992] BCLC 405 at 416, per Scott LJ.

This is not an exhaustive list. Generally, the court will take into account all the circumstances of the case and, in particular, whether the Secretary of State has shown a good reason for an extension of time.[23]

19.18 The Act does not provide that the application for an extension of time can only be made after the expiry of the time. Thus, it is envisaged that it is possible for there to be an application for an extension of the 1-year period for issue prior to its expiry. Even though the wording is very similar, there is no practice under the directors' disqualification regime to seek an extension of time prior to the expiry of the period.[24] This may well be because 2 years is thought sufficient for the purposes of carrying out the necessary investigations and preparing the necessary evidence. The position in respect of BROs is obviously a little different. It is entirely possible that, even in the absence of any default or blameworthy conduct by the bankrupt, the official receiver might not complete the necessary investigations within the shorter 1-year period. Accordingly, there must be some question as to whether the court would be amenable to an application for an extension of time where the official receiver is able to show jusifiable reasons why the necessary investigations cannot be completed and can identify a date by which they can be completed. The official receiver either embarks on a hastily prepared application in order to issue within the 1-year period, or the proceedings are prepared appropriately and properly, but with the risk that when issued, permission to issue out of time is not granted. Whilst the court will exercise its discretion appropriately, and will always balance the merits with the prejudice, this is hardly an efficient and effective route to the commencement of proceedings to protect the interests of the public.

19.19 As will be seen below,[25] some of the facts that the court is to take into account in determining whether to grant the application for a BRO are similar to those that would found claw-back proceedings by the official receiver or trustee in bankruptcy. These are:

(a) transactions at an undervalue;
(b) preferences; and
(c) excessive pension contributions.

These are to be proved in the same way as would be required in the usual proceedings brought under the IA 1986. In those circumstances, it is difficult to see how an application can be dealt with in the short and speedy way anticipated in the White Paper. It is one thing to prove non-co-operation with the official receiver or the trustee, or a string of unpaid consumer debts that should not have been entered into. These can be shown by simple schedules. It is quite another thing to prove that a transaction amounted to a transaction at an undervalue or preference.

---

23 *Re Copecrest Ltd* [1994] 2 BCLC 284 at 287, per Hoffmann LJ.
24 This is especially the case after the introduction of Part 17.1 of the Practice Direction: Directors Disqualification Proceedings, which provides that the application for an extension of time should be sought by way of an application notice within the main disqualification proceedings.
25 See **19.27**.

19.20 The court is not apparently given a power to make a BRO after having made an order on the trustee's successful application for relief in relation to such transactions.[26] Therefore, there is a possibility that an application for a BRO might be consolidated with the claw-back proceedings, so that the cases will be heard together and the evidence in one application be treated as evidence in the other. This is a practice that has developed recently in the disqualification regime.[27] Previously, it was often the case that a liquidator would hold back on claw-back proceedings, awaiting the outcome of the disqualification proceedings to see the strength of the arguments and the performance of the director in the witness box.

19.21 It is not anticipated that the Community Legal Service will provide assistance for the funding of a defence to a BRO application. It is not clear whether this is a policy decision or, as with company director disqualification cases, it is because such applications are regarded as trade disputes. Obviously, an issue arises in relation to consumer bankrupts, who have not been engaged in a trade, or in mixed consumer/trading bankruptcies, where eligibility criteria will have to be judged separately.

19.22 Therefore, since the applications are by their very nature made against bankrupts, it is difficult to see how precisely a defence to a BRO application will be funded.

19.23 The Insolvency Service has stated that it will not be seeking costs orders against bankrupts against whom BROs are made.[28] The same will not, however, work the other way. As it is, bringing these cases in the public interest, the Insolvency Service anticipates that the applicants will face a costs order against them in the event of unsuccessful applications for BROs.

Grounds for the application

19.24 The court can only make a BRO if it thinks it appropriate having regard to the conduct of the bankrupt, whether before or after the making of the bankruptcy order.[29] It is also implicit in this that the court will have to be of the view that it is in the public interest that the bankruptcy restrictions continue notwithstanding the discharge of the bankrupt, in order to provide protection to the public and the business community.[30]

19.25 A non-exhaustive list of the matters that that court shall, in particular, take into account are set out in IA 1986, Sch 4A, para 2(2). Many of these are similar to the matters that the court is bound to take into account when

---

26 Compare the position with wrongful trading, when the court is empowered to make a disqualification order after making a declaration that a director is liable under IA 1986, s 214; see CDDA 1986, s 10.

27 See *Official Receiver v Doshi* [2001] 2 BCLC 235, where proceedings in respect of misfeasance and wrongful trading were considered with an application for a disqualification order based on the same matters.

28 Mike Chapman, of the Insolvency Practitioner Policy section of the Insolvency Service, in a presentation to the South West and Wales region of R3 on 7 October 2002.

29 IA 1986, Sch 4A, para 2(1).

30 See para 741 of the Explanatory Notes.

considering an application for a disqualification order[31] and, as stated earlier, bear some similarity with the provisions regarding the 'reportable facts' in respect of which the official receiver was obliged to report to the court on upon the bankrupt's application for a discharge under the Bankruptcy Act 1914, s 26.

19.26 It is to be emphasised that these are only matters that the court should take into account. Although the particular part of the Schedule is headed 'Grounds for making order', there is no compulsion on the court to make an order in the event that the allegations of such conduct are made out.

19.27 The matters that the court shall take into account are as follows.

'(a)   failing to keep records which account for a loss of property by the bankrupt, or by a business carried on by him, where the loss occurred in the period beginning 2 years before petition[32] and ending with the date of the application.'

(1)   This is similar to one of the historic reportable facts.[33]

(2)   The provision was formerly the subject of a criminal offence.[34] It has now been decriminalised.[35] This was for two reasons. First, the ethos of the EA 2002 is to take away the stigma of being made bankrupt, so it would be exceedingly unfair to criminalise conduct simply because a person was made bankrupt at some later stage. The second follows on from this. The effective criminalisation of conduct only in the event of a bankruptcy order being made inevitable carries with it a degree of retrospection that would be unlikely to survive a challenge under the human rights legislation.

(3)   The effectiveness of the decriminalisation and the shifting of the regime into the BRO provisions will be reviewed after the new legislation has been in operation for 3 years.[36]

(4)   The terms used are not exactly the same as those contained within the old criminal offence. Of particular note is the requirement that the records must relate to a loss suffered by the bankrupt or his business. The criminal offence was more widely drawn, referring to such records as are necessary to show and explain transactions of the financial position of the business. There is no apparent justification for the narrowing of the specified conduct, in particular when the purpose of the new provisions is to ensure that more cases can be brought.

(5)   Therefore, it will not be possible simply to base the allegation upon a failure properly to maintain the books and records in the same way that a director's disqualification application might be brought on the grounds of a

---

31   See CDDA 1986, s 9 and Sch 1.
32   IA 1986, Sch 4A, para 2(4) provides that this shall be construed in accordance with IA 1986, s 351(c).
33   Bankruptcy Act 1914, s 26(3)(b).
34   IA 1986, s 361.
35   EA 2002, s 263(a).
36   The White Paper, Annex D, Draft Regulatory Impact Assessment, para 10.1.

failure to maintain the company's books and records under the Companies Act 1985, s 221. It will be necessary to link the missing books and records to a loss of property. How exactly that is to be done when the records are not available is not obvious.

(6) The criminal offence was subject to a defence that the omission was honest and reasonable having regard to the circumstances in which he conducted his business. Whilst not expressly referred to on the face of the new sections, it remains to be seen to what extent the court will take such a defence into account in determining whether it is in the public interest to make a BRO.

'(b) failing to produce records of that kind on demand by the official receiver or the trustee'

(1) This is an obvious example of conduct to take into account, in particular as the failure to produce such relevant documents is likely to have a direct impact upon the investigations connected with the realisation of the bankrupt's estate.

(2) It is notable that this is a matter that can only arise after the bankruptcy order is made, illustrating that the purpose of these provisions is to protect the community against bankrupts whose conduct has been dishonest or culpable either before or after bankruptcy.[37]

'(c) entering into a transaction at an undervalue'[38]

Again, this is an obvious example of conduct to take into account in determining the conduct of the bankrupt. It seems here that the applicant must prove a case in the same way as would be the case in claw-back proceedings brought under IA 1986, s 339. Therefore, this would seem to exclude the possibility of the official receiver relying upon a transaction that might fall for consideration under IA 1986, s 423 (transactions defrauding creditors) because of the relevant time-limits.[39] It mirrors one of the matters that the court shall take into account in determining whether to make a disqualification order.[40]

'(d) giving a preference'[41]

(1) Again, this is an obvious example of conduct to take into account in determining the conduct of the bankrupt. It also mirrors one of the matters that the court shall take into account in determining whether to make a disqualification order.[42]

---

37 See para 741 of the Explanatory Notes.
38 IA 1986, Sch 4A, para 2(4) provides that this shall be construed in accordance with IA 1986, s 339.
39 In fact, it does not appear that such transactions would fall within any of the identified matters that the court is directed to consider.
40 See CDDA 1986, s 9 and Sch 1, Part II, paras 3 and 8(a).
41 IA 1986, Sch 4A, para 2(4) provides that this shall be construed in accordance with IA 1986, s 340.
42 See CDDA 1986, s 9 and Sch 1, Part II, paras 3 and 8(a).

(2) It seems here that the applicant must prove a case in the same way as would be the case in claw-back proceedings brought under IA 1986, s 340.

'(e)   making an excessive pension contribution'[43]

It seems here that the applicant must prove a case in the same way as would be the case in claw-back proceedings brought under IA 1986, s 342A as introduced by the Welfare Reform and Pensions Act 1999 with effect from 29 May 2000.

'(f)   a failure to supply goods or services which were wholly or partly paid for which gave rise to a claim provable in the bankruptcy'

Again, this mirrors one of the matters that the court shall take into account in determining whether to make a disqualification order.[44]

'(g)   trading at a time before commencement of the bankruptcy when the bankrupt knows himself to be unable to pay his debts'

(1) This is similar to one of the historic reportable facts.[45]

(2) Since the wholesale changes to the bankruptcy regime in 1986, this is the first introduction of the concept of an individual being criticised for a form of wrongful trading along the lines of the provisions of s 214 of IA 1986. The concept is obviously similar. Whilst a person who is trading is solvent, there are no particular qualms about how that trade is conducted, even if it is losing money. However, the moment that the business becomes insolvent, the trader is no longer trading at his own risk, but at the risk of the creditors, and therefore must be accountable for his decisions.

(3) In respect of wrongful trading, a director has a statutory defence that he took every step with a view to minimising the potential loss to the company's creditors as he ought to have taken.[46] In relation to the next ground, the slightly wider one of incurring debts, there is a defence that the bankrupt reasonably expected to be able to pay the debt.

(4) There is no such defence provided for on the face of the grounds. It remains to be seen wherever there develops a defence that, although the trader knew at the time he was unable to pay the debts, there was reasonable justification for believing that in due course, those debts would be paid. The bankrupt may refer to a reasonable business plan that established clear grounds for a decision to attempt to trade out of the difficulties, but, for some reasons, perhaps out of his control, the plan foundered. He might refer to specific professional advice that it was appropriate to continue to trade. The official receiver would no doubt have to respond with evidence

---

43   IA 1986, Sch 4A, para 2(4) provides that this shall be construed in accordance with IA 1986, s 342A.
44   See CDDA 1986, s 9 and Sch 1, Part II, para 7.
45   Bankruptcy Act 1914, s 26(3)(c).
46   See IA 1986, s 214(3).

suggesting that the expectations of such continued trade were unreasonable, or that it was not reasonable to follow the professional advice blindly without further consideration.

(5)   Although these are not expressly provided for as defences, these are matters that the court will no doubt take into account in determining whether it is in the public interest to make a BRO.

(6)   There is, however, no allied provision that grants a remedy to the official receiver or the trustee in bankruptcy to obtain an order of the court that the bankrupt make a contribution to the bankruptcy estate so as to compensate for such trading. This is no doubt because, in the absence of any substantial post-bankruptcy assets, such a remedy is likely to be worthless, the bankrupt's estate having vested in the trustee in bankruptcy. If the bankrupt has after-acquired assets, then they can be claimed by the trustee in bankruptcy.[47] If the bankrupt has a significant income, then the trustee in bankruptcy can seek an income payments order[48] or agreement.[49]

'(h)   incurring, before commencement of the bankruptcy, a debt which the bankrupt had no reasonable expectation of being able to pay'

(1)   This is similar to one of the historic reportable facts.[50] It also goes hand in hand with the previous ground, as there is strong likelihood that a business debt incurred by a trader without being able to pay it will be regarded as continuing to trade after knowledge of insolvency. However, there are some differences to note:

   (a)   the ground is not limited to traders – it will apply equally to consumers;
   (b)   the ground specifically refers to a potential defence, namely that the bankrupt had a reasonable expectation of being able to pay the debt – the precise wording of the ground suggests that the burden of proof is on the official receiver to show that the bankrupt did not have that reasonable expectation.[51]

(2)   It will always be a question of fact and degree in each case as to whether a particular transaction will be the subject of criticism. A transaction entered into on the day before a consumer unexpectedly lost his job will have to be considered differently from one that was entered into the day after the job was lost.

(3)   There are bound to be complications under this ground in respect of guarantees, in particular by company directors who are subsequently made bankrupt, commonly after the demise of the company. The court will have to have regard to the financial affairs of the company, and the likelihood

---

47   See IA 1986 s 307.
48   Ibid, s 310 as amended by EA 2002, s 259, as to which, see **18.6**.
49   Ibid, s 310A as introduced amended by EA 2002, s 260, as to which, see **18.10**.
50   Bankruptcy Act 1914, s 26(3)(d).
51   This contrasts with the position under Bankruptcy Act 1914, s 26(3)(d), which expressly provided that the onus was on the bankrupt to prove that reasonable expectation.

and extent to which the guarantee might be called upon, in considering the financial status of the director when he incurred a particular personal debt.

(4) Further complications might arise in respect of the bankrupt's dealings with debts that might otherwise have survived discharge.[52] For example, it is anticipated that the law as to student loans will be amended to provide that the obligation to repay them will survive the discharge of the bankruptcy. A cunning graduate might borrow a sum from a High Street bank, pay off the student loan with the proceeds, and then make himself bankrupt. Would such conduct fall within this ground? The bankrupt will have had no expectation of being able to repay the student loan, principally because the obligation to do so would not arise until much later in his (working) life. Is it wrong to replace such an obligation with one which might have no expectation of repaying now? And what of a bankrupt who had been facing a criminal bankruptcy order? Would he be criticised for replacing one debt that he could not immediately pay with another, in order to lessen his obligations post-discharge?

'(i)   failing to account satisfactorily to the court, the official receiver or the trustee for a loss of property or for an insufficiency of property to meet bankruptcy debts'

(1) This is similar to one of the historic reportable facts.[53]

(2) Again, this is an obvious ground of criticism, for the failure of the bankrupt properly to explain how his affairs come to be in the position that they are is bound to have an effect on the ability of the official receiver properly to realise the assets in the estate. It is also another illustration of a post-bankruptcy event that is capable of being criticised.

'(j)   carrying on any gambling, rash and hazardous speculation or unreasonable extravagance which may have materially contributed to or increased the extent of the bankruptcy or which took place between presentation of the petition and commencement of the bankruptcy'

(1) This is similar to one of the historic reportable facts.[54]

(2) This too was formerly the subject of a criminal offence.[55] It has now been decriminalised[56] for the same reasons.

(3) It will always be a question of fact and degree in each case as to whether a particular transaction was rash or hazardous in the particular circumstances of the bankrupt. It will depend upon the prevailing and likely

---

52   See **18.28**.
53   Bankruptcy Act 1914, s 26(3)(e).
54   Ibid, s 26(3)(f).
55   IA 1986, s 362.
56   EA 2002, s 263(b).

financial position of the bankrupt at the time of the transaction being entered into.

(4) The court will also have to have regard to the extent of the bankrupt's assets and debts at the time that the particular transaction was entered into. A £10,000 holiday incurred on a credit card by a consumer bankrupt with £10,000 of pressing creditors and no assets will bound to be the subject of criticism. But a similar holiday cost incurred by a consumer bankrupt with £200,000 of other assets and £250,000 of creditors, incurred at a time when there was no risk of bankruptcy might not be criticised. The debt may not have had a material effect on the extent of the bankruptcy, nor might the extravagance be regarded as unreasonable. Nonetheless, it cannot be right that a debtor can continue to live at the same standard of living despite strained financial circumstances. He must be obliged to make adjustments to the standard of living in order that creditors' claims can be met.

(5) It is notable that this covers both trading and consumer bankrupts. Therefore, applications might well be based upon rash business investments or contracts entered into by the bankrupt. Again, the exact circumstances and solvency of the business at the time of the transaction will be crucial in this determination.

'(k) neglect of business affairs of a kind which may have materially contributed to or increased the extent of the bankruptcy'

(1) This is similar to one of the historic reportable facts.[57]

(2) It is obviously only available in relation to trading bankrupts. It will cover the sort of situation where the bankrupt has, for one reason or another, failed properly to manage the business.

(3) The old allegation under the Bankruptcy Act 1914 was on the basis of 'culpable' neglect, suggesting a degree of blameworthiness. This is not reflected in the ground. This suggests that the allegation now is one of strict liability. So a trader who might have taken time off from the business to look after a sick spouse, leaving the business to the employees for a short period of time which caused or contributed to the failure of the business and the subsequent bankruptcy, may well be the subject of criticism. There does not seem to be any scope for a degree of reasonableness. That may well be a factor that the court takes into account in considering whether it is in the public interest to make a BRO.

'(l) fraud or fraudulent breach of trust'

(1) This is the same as one of the historic reportable facts.[58]

(2) It obviously carries the high standard of proof that comes with a fraud allegation. It is notable that it does not extend to simple breaches of trust – the breach must be fraudulent.

---

57 Bankruptcy Act 1914, s 26(3)(f).
58 Ibid, s 26(3)(k).

'(m)   failing to cooperate with the official receiver or the trustee.'

This mirrors one of the matters that the court shall take into account in determining whether to make a disqualification order[59] and obviously arises in relation to matters that occurred after the bankruptcy order. The bankrupt is generally obliged to assist the official receiver[60] and his trustee in bankruptcy.[61] Further, on the application of either the official receiver or the trustee in bankruptcy, the bankrupt can be ordered by the court to assist in the administration of estate in bankruptcy under IA 1986, s 363. Failure to comply with each of these is punishable as a contempt of court.

19.28   Additionally, the court is bound to consider whether the bankrupt was an undischarged bankrupt at some time during the period of 6 years ending with the date of the bankruptcy to which the application relates.[62] This was one of the previous reportable facts.[63]

19.29   The court will obviously have to take into account the circumstances in which the first bankruptcy order was made, its causes and the assets and liabilities arising in that bankruptcy. No doubt those matters will be compared with the circumstances of the later bankruptcies. This seems to suggest that the mere fact of there having been two bankruptcies within 6 years can be the subject of some criticism, which is odd. After all, the whole point of the EA 2002 is to encourage enterprise and take away the stigma of failure. It would be remarkable if two 'non-culpable' failures could, without more, result in a BRO being made against someone when the aim of the legislation is quickly to rehabilitate the honest and above-board bankrupt. Therefore, this is perhaps the best example of how the facts are taken into account depending upon the circumstances, rather than as grounds for compelling the making of a BRO.

19.30   There are undoubtedly other matters that the court will take into account, such as the relative size of the bankruptcy and the extent to which, if any, a dividend will be made available to the creditors.

Duration of the BRO

19.31   As with disqualification orders, the lower limit for the length is 2 years[64] and the upper limit is 15 years.[65] However, there is a slight difference in that the order will come into force when it is made.[66] Unless there is specific provision in the Rules, it does not appear that there will be a period of grace for the bankrupt within which he will have an opportunity to reorganise his affairs.[67] Also, the order will not specify a period of years from which it shall

---

59   See CDDA 1986, s 9 and Sch 1, Part II, para 10(g).
60   See IA 1986, s 291.
61   Ibid, s 333.
62   IA 1986, Sch 4A, para 2(3).
63   Bankruptcy Act 1914, s 26(3)(j).
64   IA 1986, Sch 4A, para 4(2)(a).
65   Ibid, para 4(2)(b).
66   Ibid, para 4(1)(a).
67   Compare the position with directors' disqualification proceedings, when the disqualification order does not take effect for 21 days; see CDDA 1986, s 1(2).

apply, but, in the way of modern drafting, will specify the date at the end of which the order shall cease to have effect.[68]

19.32   No doubt a practice will develop of brackets for the appropriate periods along the lines of those that apply in disqualification cases:[69]

(a) 2–5 years: relatively unserious cases, where the imposition of a BRO is mandatory;
(b) 5–10 years: serious cases that do not merit the top bracket;
(c) 10–15 years: particularly serious cases, including deceit and fraud and where the bankrupt has already has been the subject of a BRO in respect of an earlier bankruptcy.

INTERIM BROs

19.33   The effect of a BRO[70] is akin to an extension of the period for the automatic discharge of the bankrupt. In many cases, it is unlikely that the court will be in a position to impose a BRO within the standard 1-year period for automatic discharge.[71] It is implicitly accepted that there may be a period of time between the discharge of the bankrupt after a year (or sooner) and the full hearing of the BRO application. Therefore, the EA 2002 introduces the novel concept of an interim BRO. At any time between the institution of an application for a BRO and the determination of the application,[72] the court may make an interim BRO if it thinks that:

(a) there are prima facie grounds to suggest that an application for a BRO will be successful;[73] and
(b) it is in the public interest to make an interim order.[74]

The interim BRO will have the same effect as a BRO[75] and will come into force when it is made.[76]

19.34   Again, the application for an interim BRO can be made only by the Secretary of State[77] or by the official receiver acting on a direction of the Secretary of State.[78] This therefore excludes creditors. Rather oddly, the potential applicant for an interim BRO is not merely the applicant in the main proceedings. Theoretically, though unlikely, it is possible for the Secretary of

---

68   IA 1986, Sch 4A, para 4(1)(a). See also para 746 of the Explanatory Notes.
69   *Re Sevenoaks Stationers (Retail) Ltd* [1991] Ch 164.
70   See **19.54**.
71   See para 747 of the Explanatory Notes.
72   IA 1986, Sch 4A, para 5(1).
73   Ibid, para 5(2)(a).
74   Ibid, para 5(2)(b). Paragraph 747 of the Explanatory Notes specifically refers to the fact that the court will make such an order when it is of the view that the misconduct is so serious that that it is in the public interest to make such an order. This basis is not expressly referred to on the face of the Act.
75   Ibid, para 5(4)(a); as to which, see **19.54**.
76   Ibid, para 5(4)(b).
77   Ibid, para 1(3)(a).
78   Ibid, para 1(3)(b).

State to make an application for an interim BRO in proceedings instituted by the official receiver.

19.35 The interim BRO is not, however, available prior to the institution of the application for the BRO itself. Therefore, there is no route available to the official receiver or the Secretary of State to seek to impose the effects of a BRO prior to the issue of proceedings. It is incumbent upon the official receiver to complete the investigations in due time, in order to be able to issue the application within 1 year from the date of the bankruptcy order. If there are no grounds upon which the 1-year period for discharge will be extended, the there will have to be an application for an extension of time for the commencement of the application for the BRO.[79]

19.36 It is not simply the case that the court will make an interim BRO because there is a strong case for an order being made on the full hearing of the application. The interim BRO will be made if the court is of the view that the conduct is so serious that it is in the public interest to make such an order. However, this is not reflected in the EA 2002 itself, which refers only to the public interest. It may well be the case that post-discharge where these provisions are to be used the bankrupt is embarking on a course of conduct that would otherwise be prevented by a BRO and it is in the public interest to prevent it (eg being involved in the management of a company that is engaging in the sort of conduct which would found an application for a BRO or a disqualification order).

19.37 Ordinarily however, if the interim BRO is simply to be made on the basis that there is a very strong case, then the likelihood is that the application will be issued at the same time as the full application. After all, if the application is based on the strength of the evidence against the bankrupt, then it is unlikely that the applicant's case will get any stronger after the service of the bankrupt's evidence.

19.38 The Rules will no doubt provide the details of the procedural requirements of the application for an interim BRO. These will deal with:

(a) the venue;
(b) the timing of the evidence of the applicant;
(c) the timing of the evidence of the bankrupt;
(d) the manner of presentation of such evidence, whether by report or affidavit; and
(e) the notice that will be required to be given to the bankrupt prior to the hearing of the application.

19.39 The Rules will no doubt also set out the extent to which IR 1986, Part 7, as regards court procedure and practice generally, shall apply to such applications for an interim BRO.

19.40 There does not appear to be any scope for an interim BRU. A bankrupt may wish to defend the full BRO application but, for personal reasons, not be particularly bothered about the effect of an interim BRO pending the

---

79   IA 1986, s 278(b); see **19.14**.

hearing of the application. He may be working abroad, or taking time out from trading to look after a sick relative, but with a view to returning to trade at a later date. It may well be that, in those circumstances, it is envisaged that the bankrupt merely submits to the application for an interim BRO.

19.41   There are no provisions that set out the period for which an interim order will operate. Whilst it might be envisaged that it should operate until the trial of the full application, there is nothing that limits the court to this. It may well be that the court imposes an interim BRO for a limited period of time, with a view to encouraging the applicant to bring the application on for a speedy hearing.

19.42   If an interim order is made, then it will cease to have effect in the following circumstances:

(a)   on the determination of the full application for a BRO;[80]
(b)   on the acceptance of a BRU made by the bankrupt;[81] or
(c)   if the court discharges the interim BRO on the application of either the person who applied for it or of the bankrupt.[82]

It is easy to see why the first two should apply. Obviously, if the application for a BRO fails, then the interim order must fall away. If a BRO is made, then it will replace the interim BRO. Similarly, the BRU will replace the interim BRO.

19.43   The circumstances in which an application for a discharge might be made are more difficult to envisage. It may well be the case that, for one reason or another, the full hearing of the application for a BRO has taken so long to come to court that the applicant thinks that it is no longer in the public interest to pursue the application, particularly if the period of years that is likely to be imposed has already been exceeded since the imposition of the interim BRO.

19.44   Such a circumstance may well arise because of the provisions that apply in the event of the court making a BRO in circumstances where an interim BRO has already been made. In such a case, the date upon which the duration of the BRO begins is not the date on which it is made but is the date upon which the interim BRO was made.[83] Consequently, the time served under the duration of the interim BRO will effectively be taken into account in determining for how much longer the BRO should last.

19.45   Alternatively, it may well be that the step is included as a drafting measure, simply to enable the bankrupt to make such an application in appropriate circumstances, without any real consideration as to what those circumstances might actually be.

BANKRUPTCY RESTRICTIONS UNDERTAKING

19.46   In the same way that the Secretary of State for Trade and Industry can now accept an undertaking from a director without the formality of having to

---

80   IA 1986, Sch 4A, para 5(1).
81   Ibid, para 5(2).
82   Ibid, para 5(3).
83   Ibid, para 6(2).

issue proceedings, a similar regime will operate here. Instead of having to await the determination of the proceedings, the bankrupt may offer an undertaking to the Secretary of State.[84] In considering whether to accept the offer of an undertaking, the Secretary of State must take into account the kinds of conduct that the court would take into account in deciding whether it is appropriate to grant an application for a BRO.[85]

19.47   To all intents and purposes, the BRU takes effect as if it were a BRO.[86] It comes into force upon the date of its acceptance,[87] and lasts until the end of the date specified in the BRU.[88] The lower limit for the length is 2 years[89] and the upper limit is 15 years.[90]

19.48   The main difference is that the BRU may be brought to an end on an application by the bankrupt. He may apply for an order:

(a) annulling the BRU;[91] or
(b) providing for the BRU to come to an end on a date before that specified in the BRU.[92]

This is an odd provision. A similar provision was included in the directors' disqualification regime upon the introduction of the undertaking procedure in April 2001.[93] It may well be that it is to apply where the circumstances in which the undertaking was given have changed completely, such that it may be unfair for the BRU to continue. An example might be where an allegation has been made in the application, forming the basis upon which the undertaking is given, but it turns out that the facts and matters alleged are not accurate, either because of further evidence obtained subsequently or a misunderstanding as to the applicable law, such that an application would never have been brought.

19.49   It might be argued that such a route would be available to a discharged bankrupt who might have come into an inheritance that means that the entirety of his bankruptcy debts might be paid off. As a discharged bankrupt, an IVA would not be available to him, either on the traditional basis or under the new fast-track procedure.[94] He could only seek an annulment and there are express provisions to the effect that the annulment, brought about by and IVA or payment of the bankruptcy debts in full, shall not affect the BRU.[95] This may seem a particularly unfair basis to continue the BRU, but, since the provisions

---

84   IA 1986, Sch 4A, para 7(1).
85   Ibid, para 7(2); as to which, see **19.54**.
86   Ibid, para 8.
87   Ibid, para 9(1)(a).
88   Ibid, Sch 4A, para 9(1)(b).
89   Ibid, para 9(2)(a).
90   Ibid, para 9(2)(b).
91   bid, para 9(3)(a).
92   Ibid, para 9(3)(b).
93   See CDDA 1986, s 8A and the Practice Direction: Directors Disqualification Proceedings, paras 29–34. Due to its recent introduction, the precise scope of the provision is not entirely clear.
94   See *Wright v Official Receiver* [2001] BPIR 196.
95   See **19.52**.

make specific reference to the position, it would not seem that such would be grounds to bring the BRU to an end.

19.50   Alternatively, it may well be that the step is included as a drafting measure, copied across from the directors' disqualification procedure, simply to enable the bankrupt to make such an application in appropriate circumstances, without any real consideration as to what those circumstances might actually be.

ANNULMENT OF THE BANKRUPTCY

19.51   These complex provisions depend upon the basis upon which the bankruptcy order is annulled.

19.52   If the bankruptcy order is annulled because it ought not to have been made[96] or where a bankruptcy order has been made erroneously after a criminal bankruptcy order had been made,[97] then:

(a) any BRO, interim BRO or BRU is annulled;[98]
(b) no new BRO or interim BRO may be made in respect of the bankrupt;[99] and
(c) no new BRU by the bankrupt can be accepted.[100]

19.53   The position is different if the bankruptcy order is annulled because an individual voluntary arrangement (IVA) has been approved by the creditors[101] (either traditionally or under the new procedure)[102] or because the bankrupt has paid the bankruptcy expenses and debts in full.[103] In those circumstances:

(a) the annulment does not affect any BRO, interim BRO or BRU in respect of the bankrupt;[104]
(b) a BRO may be made by the court against the bankrupt on an application instituted before the annulment;[105] but
(c) an application for a BRO or interim BRO may not be instituted after the annulment.[106]

Again, the reasons for this are fairly obvious. A bankrupt will not be able to avoid the potential consequences of a BRO being made against him by buying off the creditors, either in full or through an IVA. Whether the general body of creditors would view this as appropriate is another matter. They may well prefer

---

96   IA 1986, s 282(1)(a).
97   Ibid, s 282(2).
98   Ibid, Sch 4A, para 10(a).
99   Ibid, para 10(b).
100 Ibid, para 10(c).
101 Ibid, s 261.
102 Ibid, s 263D(3); as to which see Chapter 21.
103 Ibid, s 282(1)(b).
104 Ibid, Sch 4A, para 11(a).
105 Ibid, para 11(b).
106 Ibid, para 11(c).

to see their debts paid, either in full or sufficiently so as to make an IVA viable, rather than see post-discharge restrictions imposed upon the bankrupt, which might inhibit the bankrupt's ability to fund an IVA.

REGISTRATION

19.54   The Secretary of State shall maintain a register of BROs, interim BROs and BRUs.[107] The Secretary of State is empowered to make rules regarding the inspection of the register.[108]

EFFECT OF BROs AND BRUs

19.55   It is only worthwhile establishing a regime of BROs and BRUs if their imposition is going to be in the public interest in protecting the public. So, what will a bankrupt be prevented from doing after the court has imposed a BRO against him?

19.56   Unfortunately, the EA 2002 does not incorporate into the IA 1986 a Schedule or section setting out the prohibited actions. Schedule 21 provides for a number of new sections to be incorporated into the IA 1986, some brand new and others in substitution of existing sections.

19.57   Essentially, the effect is to provide that particular conduct that is an offence while an undischarged bankrupt is likewise an offence if conducted by someone subject to a BRO, interim BRO or BRU. So, the bankrupt will be committing an offence if:

(a)   he acts as a receiver or manager of a company's property on behalf of a debenture-holder,[109] although he is not prevented from being a court-appointed receiver or manager;

(b)   either alone or jointly with any other person, he obtains credit above the prescribed limit[110] without disclosing that he is the subject of a BRO, interim BRO or BRU;[111]

(c)   trading in a name other than that under which he was made bankrupt without disclosing to all persons with wom he enters into any business transaction the name under which he was made bankrupt;[112]

(d)   he acts as an insolvency practitioner whilst subject to a BRO, interim BRO or BRU;[113] or

---

107 IA 1986, Sch 4A, para 12.

108 Ibid, Sch 9, para 29A.

109 Ibid, s 31(1)(b), inserted by EA 2002, Sch 21, para 1.

110 Presently £250 under IA 1986, s 360(1) and the Insolvency Proceedings (Monetary Limits) Order 1986, SI 1986/1996. It is anticipated that this level will rise to £500.

111 IA 1986, s 360(5), (6), inserted by EA 2002, Sch 21, para 3. It is not expressly stated that the bankrupt must disclose the fact that he is subject to an interim BRO or a BRU, but this must be implied from the fact that both these are to have the same effect as a BRO: see IA 1986, Sch 4A, paras 5(4) and 8, respectively.

112 IA 1986, s 360(5).

113 Ibid, s 390(5), inserted by EA 2002, Sch 21, para 4.

(e) if he acts as a director of a company or directly or indirectly takes part or is concerned in the promotion, formation or management of a company without the leave of the court whilst a BRO, interim BRO or BRU is in force against him.[114]

On conviction, he is liable to imprisonment, a fine or both.[115]

19.58   As a general rule, a bankrupt only commits offences under Part VI of IA 1986 if the acts are committed prior to discharge.[116] As the regime of BROs and BRUs is obviously intended to take effect after discharge, this is amended so as to allow prosecution for an act committed after discharge but whilst the person is subject to a BRO, interim BRO or BRU.[117]

19.59   Not surprisingly, since the ethos of the EA 2002 is to promote enterprise and allow the faster rehabilitation of bankrupts, the provisions do not go so far as to prevent the bankrupt trading completely whilst a BRO or BRU is in force. He is principally prevented from trading with the benefit of limited liability without the leave of the court, putting him on the same footing as an undischarged bankrupt.

19.60   In this respect, the new regime bears no comparison with the director's disqualification regime. If a company director is found to be unfit, the disqualification order prevents him from using the limited liability status for the benefit of continued trading. One might seriously suggest that if an individual is found to be a dishonest bankrupt, or one who abuses the system, why should he be allowed to trade at all if the public needs to be protected from him? This will be a matter that the court will no doubt take into account in so far as it faces applications for BROs against second bankrupts.[118]

19.61   The court rarely grants permission under CDDA 1986, s 11 for a bankrupt to be a director of a company. In respect of a non-culpable bankrupt, this will no longer be as much of a restriction, as the bankrupt will face his discharge in a matter of months – 12 months at the longest. It remains to be seen whether the court adopts a restrictive approach in respect of applications for permission made by those subject to a BRO.

19.62   Additionally, a person against whom a BRO is made shall be disqualified from:

(a) membership of the House of Commons;[119]
(b) sitting or voting in the House of Lords;[120] and
(c) sitting or voting in a committee of the House of Lords or a joint committee of both Houses.[121]

---

114 CDDA 1986, s 1(1)(b), substituted by EA 2002, Sch 21, para 5.
115 IA 1986, s 31(2), inserted by EA 2002, Sch 21, para 1.
116 Ibid, s 350(3).
117 Ibid, s 350(3A), inserted by EA 2002, Sch 21, para 2.
118 Ibid, Sch 4A, para 2(3).
119 Ibid, s 426A(1)(a), inserted by EA 2002, s 266.
120 Ibid, s 426A(1)(b).
121 Ibid, s 426A(1)(c).

Such disqualification means that the seat of a Member of the House of Commons shall be immediately vacated.[122] These disqualifications apply equally if the Secretary of State accepts a BRU.[123]

19.63 If the court makes a BRO or an interim BRO in respect of a Member of the House of Commons or the House of Lords, the court is required to notify the Speaker of that House.[124] Similarly, if the Secretary of State accepts a BRO in respect of a Member of the House of Commons or the House of Lords, the court is required to notify the Speaker of that House.[125]

19.64 A person who is the subject of a BRO or interim order shall be disqualified from membership of a local authority.[126] This disqualification will apply equally if the Secretary of State accepts a BRU.[127]

19.65 The Secretary of State is empowered to make regulations extending the class of offices from which a person against whom a BRO or interim BRO is made, or from whom a BRU is accepted, is disqualified.[128]

19.66 At present, most professional bodies have rules as to the impact of a bankruptcy order or a disqualification order and the requirements for such an order to be notified to the relevant body. No doubt, in due course, the professions will vary their regulations so as to provide for limitations and notification requirements in the event of a BRO being made or a BRU being offered.

POLICING

19.67 It is one thing for the court to make a BRO restricting the bankrupt. It is quite another thing to ensure that those orders are properly complied with. In the case of director disqualifications, there is little or no policing by the DTI to determine whether such orders are being complied with. The system is completely reliant upon complaints from members of the public or, quite frequently, the accident of second liquidations, when it is spotted that a director has been acting in breach of the order.

19.68 It remains to be seen whether the effect of BROs or BRUs will be effectively policed, or whether likewise the system will depend upon public reports and the accident of second bankruptcies.

HUMAN RIGHTS

19.69 The Rules may well make some provision as regards the extent to which in an application for a BRO, the applicant will be able to rely upon

---

122 IA 1986, s 426A(2).
123 Ibid, Sch 4A, para 8.
124 Ibid, s 426A(5).
125 Ibid, s 426A(6).
126 See EA 2002, s 267(1), amending the Local Government Act 1975, s 80(1)(b).
127 See IA 1986, Sch 4A, para 8.
128 See EA 2002, s 268.

information that has been given under compulsion pursuant to the bankrupt's obligations to assist the official receiver[129] and/or the trustee in bankruptcy.[130] Even if they do not, the human rights consequences of the regime and the use of the evidence had to be considered.

19.70   It has recently been held that the offence of failing to provide information so as to account for a loss of property prior to the bankruptcy[131] does not infringe the fundamental human rights of the bankrupt on the grounds that the offence breaches his rights against self-incrimination.[132] It is one thing to say that it is not unfair to require that the information be provided, but it is quite another to then use the compelled information against the bankrupt to found a case that places further restrictions upon him.

19.71   Such a complaint will not be upheld if the disqualification cases are applied by analogy. It has been held that it is unfair and in breach of Art 6 of the European Convention for the Protection of Human Rights and Fundamental Freedoms to use compelled information in criminal proceedings, on the basis that such use amounted to a breach of the director's right against self-incrimination.[133] However, the same result has not been reached when directors have complained that such compelled evidence was used against them for the purposes of disqualification applications.[134] Such proceedings were not criminal and were more of a regulatory measure. It has also been held that it is not unfair for the Secretary of State for Trade and Industry to continue to use such compelled evidence in disqualification proceedings even though a practice had been adopted not to use it in criminal proceedings.[135] Similarly, it has been held that the director disqualification regime does not infringe the director's right to a private life under Art 8 of the Convention.[136]

19.72   Therefore, it is unlikely that the court will be pre-disposed to a challenge to the new regime, whether wholly or in part, on the basis of the human rights legislation.

IMPLEMENTATION

19.73   The BRO and BRU regime will come into force when the personal insolvency provisions of the EA 2002 are introduced in April 2004. It might be assumed that a BRO or a BRU might only be sought in respect of a bankrupt whose bankruptcy order was on or after the date of the introduction of the regime. However, there is no express provision on the face of the Act that

---

129 See IA 1986, s 291.
130 Ibid, s 333.
131 Ibid, s 354(3).
132 See *R v Kearns* [2002] EWCA Crim 748, [2002] BPIR 1213.
133 See *Saunders v United Kingdom* [1997] BCC 872.
134 See *R v Secretary of State for Trade and Industry, ex p McCormick* [1998] BCC 379; *DC, HS and AD v United Kingdom (Application No 39031/97)* [2000] BCC 710 and *Re Westminster Property Management Limited, Official Receiver v Stern* [2000] 1 WLR 2230, where these human rights arguments are dealt with in detail.
135 See *R v Secretary of State for Trade and Industry, ex p McCormick* (above).
136 See *WGS and MGSL v United Kingdom (Application No 38172/97)* [2000] BCC 719.

information that has been given under compulsion pursuant to the bankrupt's obligations to assist the official receiver[137] and/or the trustee in bankruptcy.[138] Even if they do not, the human rights consequences of the regime and the use of the evidence have to be considered.

19.74 EA 2002, Sch 19 sets out the transitional provisions as regards discharge that are to apply to a pre-commencement bankrupt.[139] Commencement is defined as the date of commencement of EA 2002, s 256 (duration of bankruptcy).[140] A pre-commencement bankrupt is an individual who, immediately before commencement, has been adjudged bankrupt and not discharged.[141] Essentially, a pre-commencement bankrupt is discharged on the 1-year anniversary of commencement or the date on which he would have been discharged but for the EA 2002, whichever is the earlier.[142]

19.75 However, the terms providing for the discharge of a pre-commencement bankrupt under EA 2002, Sch 19 are specifically made subject to:

(a) any BRO or interim BRO made against the individual;[143] and
(b) any BRU entered into by that individual.[144]

This means that the automatic discharge provisions for existing bankrupts as at the date of the introduction of the personal insolvency aspects of the Act do not apply in the event of a BRO and BRU being in place. The only way that this can happen is if the new regime is applied to such an existing bankrupt.

19.76 This is an odd provision. Nowhere on the face of the Act, whether in the body or in the Schedules, is there any link between the making of a BRO or BRU and the discharge of the bankrupt. The whole point of the regime is that some (but not all) of the effects of being an undischarged bankrupt are extended beyond discharge. But, despite this, the bankrupt still gets his discharge.

19.77 This also suggests that the Act carries a degree of retrospection, the basis for which is difficult to justify. Any individual who is made bankrupt in the 12 months before commencement is at risk of a BRO application being issued without the leave of the court. He will not know at the time of the bankruptcy order whether this is the case because the precise commencement date might not be known. Further, theoretically, the BRO regime could be said to apply to an individual against whom a bankruptcy order was made prior to the Act receiving Royal Assent. The applicant would have to apply for permission to bring the application, as it would of necessity be commenced more than a year after the bankruptcy order. It may be that at this stage, the court will have an opportunity to consider the fairness of the provisions.

---

137 See IA 1986, s 291.
138 Ibid, s 333.
139 See **16.38**.
140 EA 2002, Sch 19, para 2.
141 Ibid, paras 1, 2.
142 Ibid, para 4(1). There are provisions dealing with pre-commencement bankrupts whose discharge has been suspended or who are second bankrupts; see **16.39**.
143 Ibid, para 8(a).
144 Ibid, para 8(b).

19.78   It may well be that this is an anti-avoidance measure. Without such retrospection, an individual, in the knowledge that he has committed an act that is likely to make him a target for a BRO application, might make himself bankrupt on his own petition prior to the introduction of the regime specifically provides that to be the case. In fact, by a rather complex route, it seems that the opposite is actually the case.

19.79   Alternatively, the provision may simply be a drafting error. The clause may be left over from an earlier draft when consideration was being given to the main effect of a BRO being the suspension of the bankrupt's automatic discharge.

19.80   Accordingly, every undischarged bankrupt at the date of the commencement of EA 2002, s 256 is at risk of an application for a BRO, even if the bankruptcy order was made before the draft Enterprise Bill was first presented to Parliament. There is a possibility that the official receivers may well already have started investigations with a view to issuing applications against such bankrupts immediately upon the introduction of the BRO regime.

19.81   It remains to be seen whether such retrospection will survive a challenge under the human rights legislation.

THE NEW SYSTEM IN OPERATION

19.82   The Act imposes a complex regime, albeit against the background of one with which official receivers will be readily familiar. A recurring question is the extent to which, if any, there will be additional resources available to the official receivers' offices up and down the country to take on the additional burden of this work.

19.83   The Government does not anticipate that there will be any requirement for additional resources. The new procedures will use redeployed staff, although it is not specified from where.[145] This is very difficult to understand, in particular as the White Paper predicted that the civil burden of proof will allow for a greater number of cases to be brought, up from the 3% that is currently the case to the 7–12% referred to by the then Secretary of State in 1999. That, of course, is excluding the cases that are investigated and not brought, or which are unsuccessful. Further, it is not anticipated that solicitors will have a great deal of input into the proceedings; it is likely that they will be involved in some proceedings.[146]

19.84   It is very difficult to see how the new regime can be properly and adequately administered within the existing official receivers' offices without at least some increase in staffing levels, especially if, as anticipated, there are greater numbers of bankruptcy orders.

---

145 The White Paper, Annex D, Draft Regulatory Impact Assessment, para 5.14. The finalised Regulatory Impact Assessment suggests that there will be an element of refocusing existing investigative resources, yet also acknowledges the likelihood that the number of specialist examining staff will need to be restored to 1 April 2000 levels; see **7.22**.

146 Ibid, para 5.1.

19.85 Once all these cases have been investigated and prepared by the official receivers, contested hearings will take up court time. Again, it is not in order to avoid the risk of such an application. Further, it may be the case that the imposition of the BRO regime on pre-commencement bankrupts is the price that they have to pay for the benefit of the application of the 1-year discharge provisions under the transitional provisions.

19.86 However, it has seriously to be questioned whether the new regime is worthwhile. Traders and consumers do not expect bankruptcy orders to be made against them, as human nature does not anticipate failure. Therefore, the risk of a BRO being made against him is not something that is going to be at the forefront of an individual's mind whilst conducting business or applying for another credit card. Such threats are unlikely to bring about better business practices amongst sole traders or more responsible borrowing from consumers.

19.87 Similarly, the effect of a BRO is rather toothless. Continued trading as a sole trader or in partnership is not prevented. The only trading that is prevented is that with the protection of limited liability. Accordingly, there is nothing to stop a trader simply continuing with the same conduct that justified the making of the BRO against him in the first place. Serial consumer bankrupts will be prevented only by the sophistication of the credit industry, not by the fact of a BRO against an individual. A BRO is not going to prevent fraud. With the absence of adequate policing, one has to ask the question whether a BRO will actually affect anything at all.

19.88 Also, the effect of a BRO or BRU is not to extend the bankrupt's discharge. The limitations and obligations that are imposed upon an undischarged bankrupt do not apply. Consequently, a BRO application is only likely to be defended by a person who wishes to continue to trade as a director of a company with the benefit of limited liability.

19.89 Therefore, despite the vigour with which the Government expects culpable bankrupts to be brought to account, it is tempting to conclude that the BRO regime is simply window dressing, to placate the criticism that discharge from bankruptcy in 12 months, or even sooner, is too soft on bankrupts. As a result, it is likely that the new regime will be the subject of some publicity when implemented. It is not clear whether this will be done by the instigation of a large number of cases against a wide range of bankrupts,[147] or whether there will be a smaller number of high-profile applications.

---

147 As envisaged by R3 in its written response to the White Paper.

Chapter 20

RELAXATION OF PROHIBITIONS AND OFFENCES

'Freedom's just another word for nothin' left to lose,
Nothin' ain't worth nothin', but it's free.'
Kris Kristofferson[1]

INTRODUCTION

20.1   In his illuminating work, 'Landmarks in the Reform of English Insolvency Law',[2] David Graham QC provides the historical context to (what became) the approach of the Victorians to bankruptcy as a miserable state in which punishment was the primary object. As Dickens frequently reminds us, the debtors' prison and general loss of freedom were the lot of the bankrupt. Many prohibitions and offences were spawned out of this attitude – with every walk of public life (including, for example, certain areas at Ascot Racecourse) turning its back on the ill-fated bankrupt.

20.2   In far earlier times, Mr Graham records that English society adopted what was apparently a more humanitarian approach to bankruptcy. However, on analysis, this is explicable on the basis that feudal law placed enormous weight on the vassal's duty to serve his lord. This duty was not to be interrupted at the instance of a mere unpaid creditor. Entertainingly, it is this same desire not to interrupt a debtor's ability to create wealth which informs the far-reaching new provisions concerning discharge from bankruptcy and the relaxation of prohibitions and offences. For all but the culpable, bankruptcy is to be relatively pain-free.

20.3   This approach requires a distinction to be made between culpable and non-culpable bankrupts. The EA 2002 does so by introducing BROs for the culpable, leaving it possible to relax the prohibitions and offences in respect of the rest.

Drawing the line

20.4   Traditionally, no distinction has been made between those who suffer bankruptcy through honest failure and those for whom bankruptcy results from culpable behaviour. Following on from an earlier Insolvency Service consul-

---

1   'Me and Bobby McGee' (1969).
2   (2002) 11 *International Insolvency Review* 97–119.

tation paper,[3] the Government's White Paper, 'Insolvency: A Second Chance' (July 2001), set out proposals which were to form the basis of the Enterprise Bill. As has already been discussed, the Government is keen to remove the stigma from bankruptcy; the White Paper recognised the difference between:

> 'honest failure [which] is an inevitable part of a dynamic market economy'

and reckless bankrupts in relation to whom a far more stringent regime was proposed.

20.5 The Cork Committee's Report[4] referred to the idea of distinguishing between culpable and non-culpable bankruptcy when deciding whether or not an individual should be permitted to hold some offices:

> '. . . he should, by virtue of his conduct giving rise to the bankruptcy, be disqualified from holding certain positions, particularly those of a public nature involving trust and confidence and where a record of integrity and competence is sought.'

20.6 The Government's hope is that the general liberalisation of the bankruptcy regime will actively foster economic growth. A significant proportion of the White Paper's proposals have been incorporated into the final draft of the EA 2002, including the relaxation of a number of prohibitions and offences.

PROHIBITIONS: NEW REGIME

20.7 The honest failure (including the serially improvident) will benefit in that the EA 2002 removes a number of the prohibitions which traditionally applied only to undischarged bankrupts, and applies them instead to those who are now subject to a BRO. There are literally hundreds[5] of prohibitions and restrictions which come with bankruptcy. Only a few of the more well known ones will be mentioned below.

20.8 Generally, the EA 2002 provides wide powers to the Secretary of State to review the current restrictions on bankrupts.[6]

Members of Parliament

20.9 The previous s 427 imposed a number of prohibitions upon the members of both Houses of Parliament who had been declared bankrupt. In the Commons, a member could not be elected to sit or vote in the House or on a Committee. In the Lords, a member could not sit or vote in the House or on a Committee, although all elected representatives had a 6-month period to annul the bankruptcy before being required to vacate their seat. These restrictions also applied to the devolved assemblies.

20.10 EA 2002, s 266 introduces new provisions in relation to Parliament and the devolved assemblies in relation to members who are made bankrupt or

---

3   'Bankruptcy: A Fresh Start', April 2000.
4   *Insolvency Law and Practice: Report of the Review Committee* (The Cork Report) (1982) Cmnd 8558, ch 46, 'Disabilities Attaching to Individual Insolvents', para 1839.
5   About 360 at the last count.
6   IA 1986, s 426A(3).

who are subject to a BRO.[7] It also amends IA 1986, s 427 to remove the references to England and Wales from that section, and to amend the title.

20.11 For those MPs where there is some element of culpability and in respect of whom a BRO is made, the new s 426A disqualifies them from sitting in the House of Commons for the duration of the BRO,[8] and they must vacate their seat immediately.[9] Hence, an MP who is made bankrupt is not automatically disqualified from membership, whereas one who is subject to a BRO – because of some element of culpability – is so disqualified. Those MPs subject to a BRO are not permitted the 6-month window.[10]

20.12 Section 426A also applies to members of the House of Lords. An individual in respect of whom a BRO has been made is disqualified from sitting or voting in the House of Lords,[11] or indeed sitting or voting in a committee of the House of Lords or a joint committee of both Houses,[12] for the duration of the BRO. Nor can a writ of summons be issued to a member of the House of Lords who is subject to a BRO.[13] Hence, those restrictions that previously took effect on bankruptcy are now activated by the imposition of a BRO.

20.13 If the court makes a BRO or interim order in respect of a member of either of the Houses of Parliament, the court must notify the relevant Speaker of the House.[14] Similarly, if the Secretary of State accepts a BRU from a member of either House, he must notify the Speaker of that House.[15] These provisions take effect irrespective of Parliamentary privilege.[16]

Justices of the peace

20.14 Section 265 of EA 2002 repeals s 65 of the Justices of the Peace Act 1997, so that an undischarged bankrupt will no longer be automatically disqualified from being a justice of the peace. The new provisions will mean that the position of a justice of the peace who has been adjudged bankrupt will be left to the discretion of the Lord Chancellor.[17]

Local government

20.15 Section 267 of EA 2002 amends the Local Government Act 1972[18] to the effect that where previously an individual was disqualified from holding

---

7   IA 1986, ss 426A and 426B.
8   Ibid, s 426A(1)(a).
9   Ibid, s 426A(2).
10   There will, therefore, be two regimes running concurrently, since a member who is adjudged bankrupt in Northern Ireland or sequestrated in Scotland, will automatically be disqualified, but still retain the 6-month period to have it annulled before being required to vacate his seat.
11   IA 1986, s 426A(1)(b).
12   Ibid, s 426A(1)(c).
13   Ibid, s 426A(4).
14   Ibid, s 426A(5).
15   Ibid, s 426A(6).
16   Ibid, s 426C(1).
17   Guidance Notes to the Enterprise Act 2002, para 781.
18   Local Government Act 1972, s 80(1)(b).

office in local government whilst bankrupt, or where he had made a composition or arrangement with his creditors, now he is disqualified where he is subject to a BRO or interim order against him.

Other statutory prohibitions

Prohibition on directorships

20.16   It is an offence for an individual who is an undischarged bankrupt to act as a director of, or directly or indirectly to take part in, or be concerned in the promotion, formation or management of a company, except with the leave of the court.[19] A bankrupt who is found so to have acted commits a criminal offence.[20] The EA 2002 amends the CDDA 1986 so that this restriction also applies in respect of a discharged bankrupt who is the subject of a BRO.[21]

20.17   The White Paper did not propose the removal or amendment of this prohibition on discharged bankrupts, but it did indicate that in an enterprise society:

> '... the cost of failure must not be set so high that it acts as a deterrent to economic activity'.

This is in contrast to the approach proposed by the Cork Committee, which actually recommended that the restriction on undischarged bankrupts be extended to include any other body handling funds on behalf of a large body of individuals, such as a building society, friendly society or trade union.[22]

20.18   It seems more possible that in line with the Government's stated intention to distinguish between culpable and non-culpable bankruptcies, the courts may be more ready to allow an undischarged bankrupt who is not subject to a BRO to act as a director.

Receiver or manager

20.19   Under IA 1986, s 31 (as amended by the EA 2002, Sch 21, para 1), an undischarged bankrupt remains disqualified from acting as a receiver or manager of the property of the company on behalf of debenture-holders; this has now been extended to cover a person for the duration of a BRO.[23] This prohibition does not apply to appointments made by the court.[24]

Trustees

20.20   An undischarged bankrupt is not automatically disqualified from office although, as with a number of the professional bodies (see below), the circumstances surrounding the bankruptcy may be such as to cause his removal

---

19   CDDA 1986, s 11(1). The means by which this application is made are set out in IR 1986, Chapter 20, rr 6.203–6.205.

20   Ibid, s 13.

21   CDDA 1986, s 11(1) as amended by EA 2002, Sch 21, para 5.

22   The Cork Report (1982), ch 46, 'Disabilities Attaching to Individual Insolvents', para 1847.

23   IA 1986, s 31(1)(b).

24   Ibid, s 31(3).

from office.[25] In line with the new regime, it is possible that the court will now place greater emphasis on whether the failure arose as a result of culpable or non-culpable behaviour and it is expected that the court will be less likely to remove the non-culpable bankrupt from office.

Charity trustees

20.21   An undischarged bankrupt (or an individual subject to a composition or arrangement or who has granted a trust deed to his creditors[26]) is prohibited from acting as a charity trustee or a trustee for a charity.[27] This is a mandatory provision that the EA 2002 has not amended and therefore remains unaffected by the distinctions being drawn between culpable and non-culpable bankruptcies.

20.22   Presumably, the reason for not amending this provision in line with other relaxations lies in the fact that public policy considerations require the conduct of a charity's affairs to be above criticism where possible, and it is unlikely that this restriction will be relaxed in the future.

Other restrictions

20.23   A bankrupt is still disqualified from:

(a)   being appointed as an attorney under an enduring power of attorney;[28]
(b)   election to or holding office as mayor, alderman or councillor of the City of London;[29]
(c)   membership of a local land drainage committee;[30]
(d)   appointment as a superintendent registrar or registrar of births and deaths, or registrar of marriages.[31]

Professional bodies

20.24   In addition to the statutory restrictions, a professional who is made bankrupt will also be subject to the rules of his professional body, which for the most part turn on an exercise of discretion. Generally, the approach of each professional body relates to public expectations and the requirements of each profession.

20.25   It seems likely that these bodies will relax their approaches, mirroring the general move to lessen the stigma attached to bankruptcy. As at the date of publication, some professional bodies continue to enforce mandatory expulsion following bankruptcy or entry into an IVA, although such automatic expulsion may be open to challenge under the Human Rights Act 1998.

---

25   Trustee Act 1925, s 36(1).
26   Charities Act 1993, s 72(1)(b) and (c).
27   Ibid, s 72(1)(b).
28   Enduring Powers of Attorney Act 1985, s 2(7) and (10).
29   City of London Municipal Elections Act 1849, s 8B (amended by Statute Law (Repeals) Act 1989, Sch 2).
30   Land Drainage Act 1976, s 3(9).
31   Registration of Births, Deaths and Marriages Regulations 1968, reg 5(a)(i).

Accountants

20.26   Although the bodies vary in their approach to bankruptcy and IVAs, readmission is possible in all cases.

(a) *Institute of Chartered Accountants of England and Wales* (ICA): mandatory exclusion on bankruptcy continues until at least 3 years after the date of the discharge of the bankruptcy order. It is possible that following the statutory reduction of discharge to 1 year after the date of bankruptcy, the ICA may reduce the current 3-year period. Expulsion following an IVA is discretionary.

(b) *Chartered Institute of Management Accountants*: expulsion is mandatory following either the making of a bankruptcy order or entry into an IVA.

(c) *Chartered Association of Certified Accountants and Chartered Institute of Financial Accountants*: expulsion is discretionary on either bankruptcy or an IVA and all the circumstances of the case are taken into consideration in the exercise of this discretion.

Insolvency practitioners

20.27   An insolvency practitioner is automatically disqualified from acting as such whilst bankrupt,[32] or whilst subject to a BRO.[33] In assessing whether or not an insolvency practitioner is fit and proper to act, the regulatory bodies apply similar standards as those applied by legal professional bodies to their members. The Insolvency Practitioners Association does not permit members to practise if bankrupt, but exercises its discretion in the case of an IVA.

Architects and surveyors

20.28   Expulsion for bankruptcy or entry into an IVA is discretionary and based upon the Architects Registration Board's guidelines.

Estate agents

20.29   Exclusion from the National Association of Estate Agents (NAEA) is mandatory upon either bankruptcy or an IVA. Readmission is unlikely, although membership of the NAEA is not required in order to practise as an estate agent.

Company secretary

20.30   Bankruptcy or entry into an IVA will result in automatic suspension from the Institute of Chartered Secretaries and Administrators, but may lead to expulsion in the more serious cases.

---

32   IA 1986, s 390(4).
33   Ibid, Sch 21, para 4, amending IA 1986, s 390.

Legal profession

20.31   The following rules apply in relation to the following bodies.

(a) *The Law Society*: upon bankruptcy, a solicitor's practising certificate is automatically suspended. On entry into an IVA, the solicitor must inform the Office of Supervision of Solicitors who may impose conditions upon the solicitor's practising certificate (including suspension).
(b) *The Bar Council*: A barrister must inform the Bar Council if bankruptcy proceedings are initiated against him or her and again if a bankruptcy order is made or the barrister enters into an IVA. On being informed, the Bar Council may investigate the circumstances and may impose sanctions.
(c) *The Institute of Legal Executives*: the power to expel on bankruptcy or entry into IVA is discretionary. However, members are obliged to inform the Institute should either of these events occur.
(d) *The Institute of Barristers' Clerks*: the Institute's rules do not cover bankruptcy and it does not prevent a member from practising.

Medical profession

20.32   The view taken by the medical professional bodies is that an individual's ability to practise in this field is generally not affected by personal insolvency. This applies in respect of doctors, dentists, vets and pharmacists. Exclusion is likely only where an investigation into the circumstances of the insolvency reveals some element of professional misconduct.

Armed forces and the services

20.33   The following rules apply in relation to the services:

(a) *Armed Forces*: expulsion following bankruptcy or entry into an IVA is discretionary and will depend upon all the circumstances including the officer's conduct in his financial dealings – if the officer is dismissed, readmission at a later date is very unlikely.
(b) *Metropolitan Police*: the Metropolitan Police Force will usually only expel a member where his attitude to discharging the debt is unsatisfactory; readmission is possible in theory, but unlikely.
(c) *London Fire Brigade*: providing there are no factors that could bring continued service into disrepute, such as fraud, bankruptcy and entry into an IVA do not prevent personnel remaining in employment.

Summary

20.34   The table below[34] sets out the position of various organisations in respect to the bankruptcy of their members.

---

34 Reproduced with kind permission from an article written by Lawrence Katz and Sam Tate of Holman, Fenwick & Willan, which first appeared in *Insolvency Intelligence* (Sweet & Maxwell, 2002).

Body	Expulsion on Bankruptcy	Expulsion on IVA	Criteria	Readmission
Chartered Association of Certified Accountants	Discretion	Discretion	Consideration given to all relevant circumstances. Note that there is a mandatory requirement that the bankrupt must notify the Association within 1 month of the bankruptcy. Failure to do so will result in automatic expulsion.	Possible
Institute of Chartered Accountants in England & Wales	Mandatory	Discretion	Consideration given to all relevant circumstances.	Possible
Institute of Company Accountants	Discretion	Discretion	No guidelines available.	Possible
Chartered Institute of Financial Accountants	Discretion	Discretion	Consideration given to all relevant circumstances. Personal insolvency usually leads to suspension after disciplinary hearing rather than expulsion.	Possible. Discretionary following repayment of all debts.
Chartered Institute of Management Accountants	Mandatory	Mandatory	Not applicable.	Possible
Institute of Chartered Secretaries and Administrators	Discretion	Discretion	Expulsion depends upon the recklessness of the member's behaviour. Suspension is often imposed until the bankruptcy is discharged or the IVA terminated.	Possible
Insolvency Practitioners Association	Mandatory	Discretion	Consideration will be given to all the relevant circumstances, including whether the individual made any effort to pay their debts.	Possible, but unlikely
Architects Registration Board	Discretion	Discretion	The Board will consider whether the bankrupt's conduct amounted to unacceptable professional conduct. Guidelines are available.[35]	Possible
Institute of Incorporated Engineers	Not applicable	Not applicable	Not applicable.	
National Association of Estate Agents	Mandatory	Mandatory	Not applicable.	Possible, but unlikely
General Medical Council	Discretion	Discretion	The Council will consider whether the circumstances of the bankruptcy involved medical misconduct. No guidelines.	Possible, right of appeal against dismissal
Royal College of Veterinary Surgeons	Discretion	Discretion	Members are only struck off if bankruptcy involves fraudulent acts or other misconduct.	Possible
General Dental Council	Discretion	Discretion	Members are only excluded if bankruptcy reveals other misconduct.	Possible

---

35   Architects Registration Board website: www.arb.org.uk.

Body	Expulsion on Bankruptcy	Expulsion on IVA	Criteria	Readmission
British Dental Association	Not applicable	Not applicable	Members in bankruptcy are not excluded but will be if they are excluded from practising by the GDC (see above).	Possible, following readmission to the roll of dentists
Royal Pharmaceutical Society of Great Britain	Discretion	Discretion	Personal insolvency does not affect members' registration unless misconduct involves the illegal supply of drugs, otherwise expulsion will depend on the circumstances in each case. There are no formal guidelines available.	Possible
The Law Society	Automatic suspension, expulsion discretionary	Discretion	It is possible to apply to lift the suspension.	Possible
The General Council of the Bar	Discretion	Discretion	The Council will consider whether the circumstances surrounding the bankruptcy involve professional misconduct.	Possible, although there are no guidelines specified in the Code of Conduct
Institute of Legal Executives	Discretion	Discretion	The Investigating Committee and, if necessary the Disciplinary Committee, will consider all the relevant circumstances.	Possible, although the Disciplinary Committee may suggest a minimum period in which readmission is prohibited
Institute of Barristers' Clerks	Discretion	Discretion	Breach of the Code of Conduct.	It would seem possible, although there are no guidelines specified in the Code of Conduct
Ministry of Defence	Discretion	Discretion	Attitude of individual towards discharging their debts is relevant.	Possible, but unlikely
Metropolitan Police	Discretion	Discretion	Dismissal will depend on all the circumstances of the case, including the sums involved and the effort made to repay the debts.	Possible, but unlikely
London Fire Service	Not applicable	Not applicable	Not applicable.	Not applicable

OFFENCES

Current offences

20.35   During the period of bankruptcy, the individual is bound by a number of provisions that take immediate and automatic effect and which subsist for the duration of that bankruptcy order.[36] A breach of these provisions is a criminal offence that can result in a fine, imprisonment or both.[37] The desire

---

36   The bankruptcy offences are set out in Chapter VI of IA 1986, ss 350–360.
37   IA 1986, Sch 10.

to reduce the stigma of bankruptcy in the case of 'no fault' bankruptcies is reflected in the relaxation of a number of the prohibitions and the deletion of certain offences, and this is mirrored by increased restrictions in respect of those culpable bankrupts who are subject to a BRO or BRU.

20.36　　　The current offences are:

(a)　failure to disclose property;[38]
(b)　failure to deliver up property;[39]
(c)　concealment or falsification of books and papers;[40]
(d)　giving false statements;[41]
(e)　fraudulent disposal of property;[42]
(f)　absconding;[43]
(g)　fraudulent dealing with property obtained on credit;[44]
(h)　obtaining credit and engaging in business.[45]

20.37　　　In each case of bankruptcy, the official receiver has a duty to investigate the bankrupt's conduct and affairs (including his business).[46] If, during his investigation, the official receiver identifies an actual or possible commission of a criminal offence, he must submit a report to the court. The IR 1986 impose additional duties on the official receiver to send a statement of affairs to the creditors.[47]

20.38　　　The Insolvency Service[48] has published figures showing the number of reports produced by the official receiver and the numbers of convictions obtained following the submission of these reports to the court:

Year ending[49]	*Number of reports submitted*	*Convictions obtained following official receiver reports*
1999	853	288
2000	906	273
2001	518	268

20.39　　　A detailed breakdown of bankruptcy convictions is provided below:[50]

38　IA 1986, s 353.
39　Ibid, s 354.
40　Ibid, s 355.
41　Ibid, s 356.
42　Ibid, s 357.
43　Ibid, s 358.
44　Ibid, s 359.
45　Ibid, s 360.
46　Ibid, s 289(1).
47　IR 1986, r 6.73, where the bankruptcy order is made on a creditor's petition.
48　Insolvency Service General Annual Report 2001.
49　Table compiled from figures provided in the Insolvency Service General Annual Report 2000. Figures relate to both bankruptcy and directorship offences.
50　This table is based upon the figures provided in the Insolvency Service General Annual Report (2001).

Nature of offence	Relevant section	Number of convictions obtained (2000)	Number of convictions obtained (2001)
Non-disclosure	Section 353	37	36
Concealment of property/failure to account	Section 354	53	53
Concealment of books and papers and falsification	Section 355	3	6
Material omission and false statement	Section 356	25	30
Fraudulent disposal of property	Section 357	32	23
Fraudulent dealing with property obtained on credit	Section 359	3	1
Undischarged bankrupt obtaining credit/trading under another name	Section 360	143	62
Failure to keep proper accounting records	Section 361	52	42
Gambling	Section 362	15	14

New regime

20.40   Section 263 of EA 2002 repeals the offences of failing to keep proper accounting records and gambling and speculation.[51] Although these acts will no longer be criminal offences, they will now be dealt with as part of the BRO regime and are still matters that fall to be considered in relation to the bankrupt's conduct.

20.41   Paragraph 2 of the new Sch 4A (Grounds for Making a Bankruptcy Restriction Order) expressly refers to gambling and hazardous speculation as matters to which the court will have particular regard, and failure to keep proper accounting records will no doubt still be an important consideration for the court.

Extension of offences

Concealment of property

20.42   The offence of the concealment of property[52] is extended to include any failure to account for the loss of any substantial property to the trustee.[53]

---

51   IA 1986, ss 361, 362.
52   Ibid, s 354.
53   EA 2002, Sch 23, para 12.

20.43   Under the old law, the scope of the offence of failure to account for any substantial loss of property (or give a satisfactory explanation for such losses) to the official receiver, or the court, was provided by s 354(3).[54] This offence is now extended to include failure to give such explanation to the trustee in bankruptcy as well.

Concealment and falsification of records

20.44   Section 355 is amended,[55] so that in so far as its provisions relate to a trading record, the original 12-month period is now extended to 2 years.[56] A definition of 'trading record' is also inserted.[57] The availability of adequate records is crucial to the examination of the bankrupt's estate and enquiries into his affairs.[58]

County court administration order

20.45   County court administration orders (CCAOs) are made in order to provide respite to an individual who is subject to a county court judgment and at least one other judgment, the combined total of which is less than £5,000. Under the old regime, where the debtor failed to make payment under a county court administration order, s 429 of IA 1986 permitted a court to make an order restricting the acquiring of credit and the use of a trading name for 2 years where a debtor has filed to pay under a CCAO. The power is now amended to 1 year to reflect the fact that the restrictions that follow a bankruptcy order will now only take effect for a year.[59]

Application of offences to an individual subject to a BRO

Discharge from liability

20.46   The EA 2002 inserts a new subs 350(3A) into the IA 1986 (bankruptcy offences: general: no liability of bankrupt after discharge) so that an individual will still be liable for offences committed after discharge whilst subject to a BRO.[60]

Obtaining credit

20.47   Similarly, s 360 of IA 1986 (obtaining credit and doing business) is amended so as to apply to an individual who has been discharged from bankruptcy, but is subject to a BRO.[61]

---

54   IA 1986.
55   EA 2002, Sch 23, para 13.
56   In line with the rule applicable to other basic records.
57   IA 1986, s 365(5).
58   Guidance Notes to the Enterprise Act 2002, para 786.
59   EA 2002, Sch 23, para 15.
60   Ibid, Sch 21, para 2.
61   Ibid, Sch 21, para 3.

Chapter 21

INDIVIDUAL VOLUNTARY ARRANGEMENTS

'Men keep their agreements when it is an advantage to both parties not to break them.'

Solon[1]

INTRODUCTION

21.1   The use of individual voluntary arrangements (IVAs) as an alternative to bankruptcy has been steadily increasing in recent years. The figures[2] are as follows:

Year	Bankruptcies	IVAs	Total	% IVAs
1987	6,994	404	7,398	5
1988	7,714	779	8,493	9
1989	8,138	1,224	9,362	13
1999	12,058	1,927	13,985	14
1991	22,632	3,002	25,634	12
1992	32,106	4,686	36,792	13
1993	31,016	5,679	36,695	15
1994	25,634	5,103	30,737	17
1995	21,933	4,384	26,317	17
1996	21,803	3,983	25,786	15
1997	19,892	4,211	24,103	17
1998	19,647	4,620	24,267	19
1999	21,611	7,086	28,697	25
2000	21,550	7,909	29,459	27
2001	23,477	6,286	29,775	21

Only a very small minority of the IVAs are proposed by undischarged bankrupts.[3] They are popular with debtors and creditors alike, for differing reasons. The debtor avoids bankruptcy and so is not subject to the same degree of stigma. The automatic restrictions do not apply, so that the debtor is relatively free to continue to trade – particularly important if he is a director of a

---

1   *Plutarch's Lives.*
2   Derived from the Department of Trade and Industry: *The Enterprise Bill, Insolvency Provisions – Regulatory Impact Assessment*, paras 2.2 and 3.2. See also the Department of Trade and Industry White Paper. *Productivity and Enterprise; Insolvency – A Second Chance*, July 2001, Cm 3234.
3   See para 763 of the Explanatory Notes. In 2001, there were 35.

company and wishes to avoid the automatic disqualification.[4] Like the moratoriums in company administrations, the effect of the interim order allows breathing space for the creditors to come to sensible arrangements without an unseemly scramble towards enforcement of rights. They are also popular with creditors for, as a general rule, the return to creditors is rather larger than is the case in bankruptcy.

21.2   Whilst it will usually be incumbent upon a trustee in bankruptcy at least to consider the position of the bankrupt and whether an IVA would be in the interests of the bankrupt and the creditors, the statistics show that this does not commonly happen. One reason for this is that by the time that the true position has been realised, too much of the costs that would ordinarily be saved by the IVA will have been incurred. The saving of the costs of the official receiver and the trustee in bankruptcy and the fees incurred in the bankruptcy is one of the major factors in encouraging the use of IVAs. However, if an official receiver has already been appointed, conducted some investigations, called a creditors' meeting for the appointment of an insolvency practitioner (who then incurs his own costs after his appointment), it can easily be seen that a large element of the costs of the bankruptcy will be incurred in a matter of months after the bankruptcy order. This will be at a time when, commonly, the bankrupt is not fully aware of the position and is unwilling to incur the potential cost of instructing an insolvency practitioner to assist in the preparation of a post-bankruptcy IVA.

21.3   So, in the same way that the 'one size fits all' approach to bankruptcy has been varied by the provisions of the EA 2002, the Act seeks to do likewise with IVAs. It appears that this is as a result of criticisms by creditors and debtors of the level of fees charged by insolvency practitioners, with the resultant reduction in the returns to creditors.[5] This is especially the case in 'small IVAs' where the disproportionate costs are felt most acutely.

---

4   CDDA 1986, s 11.
5   The White Paper.

21.4 Insolvency Service research[6] of 900 IVAs completed or abandoned in the period 1 August 2000–31 October 2000 shows the following breakdown of IVA receipts:

AVERAGE VALUES

Value of receipts	No of cases	Receipts	Nominee fee	Supervisor fee	Other costs*	Payments to creditors	Costs as % of receipts
Up to £15,700	202	£9,083	£1,277	£2,509	£1,189	£4,449	54.8%
£15,701–£23,800	96	£19,492	£1,431	£4,490	£1,592	£12,208	38.5%
£23,801–£33,800	64	£28,142	£1,695	£5,714	£2,538	£18,741	35.3%
£33,801–£45,380	49	£38,545	£1,798	£6,925	£3,561	£25,912	31.9%
£45,381–£58,800	37	£49,352	£1,728	£8,642	£4,797	£32,067	30.7%
£58,801–£86,800	28	£67,647	£1,673	£11,349	£4,668	£49,536	26.2%
£86,001–£112,000	21	£97,462	£1,816	£14,743	£8,923	£70,896	26.1%
£112,001–£167,000	11	£140,333	£3,143	£16,005	£21,572	£100,079	29.0%
£167,001–£350,000	9	£204,451	£2,719	£20,924	£19,687	£153,264	21.2%
Above £350,000	4	£474,342	£3,338	£17,083	£38,760	£408,818	12.5%

*other costs include VAT payments and disbursements (eg auction charges)

21.5 The EA 2002 seeks to encourage greater use of IVAs post-bankruptcy[7] by the introduction of two innovations to the current IVA regime:[8]

(1) a new fast-track scheme by which a debtor can propose to his creditors an IVA in respect of which the official receiver will act as nominee (either approved or not); and

(2) the authorisation of the official receiver to put proposals to creditors and to act as supervisor of the post-bankruptcy IVA.

Therefore, in respect of IVAs, there will be a choice between the official receiver, acting as nominee for a flat fee and as a supervisor for a percentage of the realisations, and an insolvency practitioner doing likewise, but at fees charged at market rates. The involvement of the official receiver means that the viability of an IVA can at least be considered at minimal cost shortly after the bankruptcy order is made.

21.6 The White Paper[9] specifically referred to the US experience of Chapter 13 of the US Bankruptcy Code (payment plans by debtors) as

---

6   See the Regulatory Impact Assessment, para 5.19.
7   Referred to by IR 1986, r 5.1(2) as 'Case 1'. Otherwise, it is 'Case 2'.
8   See para 765 of the Explanatory Notes.
9   Paragraph 1.44.

establishing that economies of scale had meant substantially higher returns to creditors. It is anticipated that, in each case, the official receiver would need to conduct limited research into the affairs of the debtor for the purposes of the proposal because he would already have all the details to hand. Therefore, the entry costs of the IVA, perceived hitherto as a deterrent to debtors, will be significantly reduced. The administration of the receipts and payments is likely to be undertaken centrally, thereby reducing the costs further. As a result, the Government expects that, even in smaller asset cases, the reduced fees incurred by the official receiver will lead to a greater proportionate recovery for the general body of creditors.

21.7   One of the driving forces behind these proposals is the analysis that a large number of small asset bankruptcies result specifically from the increased availability of personal credit. This has led to an increased number of consumer bankruptcies arising in cases where the bankrupt has not traded at all.[10]

Year	Total bankruptcies	Consumer bankruptcies	% Consumer
1992	32,016	12,581	39
1993	31,016	12,455	40
1994	25,634	10,520	41
1995	21,933	8,651	39
1996	21,803	9,136	42
1997	19,892	8,623	43
1998	19,647	9,227	47
1999	21,611	10,888	50
2000	21,550	11,598	53

21.8   The new scheme is advantageous to creditors, because it should secure greater returns. Whether an IVA is as attractive to the individual debtor is another matter. In view of the relaxation of the restrictions and the supposed lifting of the stigma of bankruptcy, an honest bankrupt may consider the prospect of bankruptcy and an automatic discharge after 1 year or less more attractive than a voluntary arrangement which may require his contributions beyond the 3-year period of any income payments order or agreement.

21.9   The proposals have been criticised for potentially taking away work from smaller insolvency practitioner firms. However, the likelihood is that it will have a greater impact upon cases which, currently, are dealt with completely outside the realm of insolvency practice. Debt management plans, a completely unregulated sector of the insolvency market, cater for more debtors than do IVAs. Many of the debts would be better suited to IVAs, whether pre- or post-bankruptcy.

21.10   Organisations such as Paylink and the Consumer Credit Counselling Service provide services to consumer debtors at no cost to those debtors. They are creditor-funded, in the sense that they typically levy a 15% charge on realisations as an administration fee. Basically, they arrange formal payment

---

10   See para 1.46 of the White Paper.

plans, binding on both the debtor and the creditors. About 20,000 cases per year are dealt with in this way.

21.11 On the other hand, there are professional debt managers who, at a cost to the debtor, arrange informal and non-binding arrangements. They charge an up-front fee of, typically, £450–£750 paid by the debtor, together with a percentage charge on realisations. Whilst looking like an formal IVA, there is a critical difference in that the arrangement is not contractually binding. The creditor is allowed to withdraw at any stage and instigate such enforcement action as it thinks fit. Many schemes commit the debtor to monthly payments for anything up to 10 years when, in actual fact, bankruptcy might be a better option. It is thought that another 20,000 individuals opt for this arrangement each year.

21.12 Finally, the existing county court administration regime deals with nearly 8,000 cases per year. These relate to debtors who have unsecured debts of less that £5,000, at least two debts and at least one judgment.[11] The scheme also requires that the debtor has some form of income. An amendment raising the £5,000 limit to £20,000 have yet to be brought into force,[12] presumably for fear that an extension of the regime will cause the court system to be inundated with applications by consumer debtors who can afford the court fee to apply for administration but cannot afford the fee to present their own bankruptcy petitions.[13]

21.13 Thus, there are nearly 50,000 small debt cases that are currently being dealt with beyond formal insolvency measures. It is hoped that these debtors, having been put off by the existing IVA procedures because of the cost of the up-front costs, will be attracted to bankruptcy and the small-scale fast-track IVA.

21.14 It remains to be seen whether these provisions will prove as effective in practice as they appear in theory. Official receivers will already be overburdened by having to conduct speedy investigations in order to determine whether to apply for the bankrupt's automatic discharge to be suspended[14] or for a BRO.[15] This is especially the case if, as a result of the reduction to the automatic discharge period and stigma attached to bankruptcy, the number of bankruptcies rises significantly.

21.15 Additionally, the official receiver might also be more interested in obtaining a speedy IPO or IPA rather than enter into the complication of an IVA with very similar terms. Despite the delay of 1 year in the introduction of the personal insolvency aspects of the EA 2002 to allow for the official receivers' offices to be trained and resourced, it remains to be seen whether adequate resources will be provided. The official receiver will be competing in a sophisticated marketplace with insolvency practitioners in relation to post-

---

11 See County Courts Act 1984, Part IV and County Court Rules, Order 39.
12 See Courts and Legal Services Act 1990, s 13.
13 The fee for an administration application is presently £120, whereas the fee for a debtor's own petition is £300.
14 See Chapter 16.
15 See Chapter 19.

bankruptcy IVAs. How well this operates will, no doubt, determine whether at some stage in the future the official receiver will be permitted to act as a supervisor in a Case 2 IVA (ie post-bankruptcy IVAs).

FAST-TRACK IVAS

21.16   The fast-track IVA is a new streamlined procedure to assist in the arrangement of post-bankruptcy IVAs where the debtor is an undischarged bankrupt. EA 2002, s 252 and Sch 22 insert into the IA 1986, new ss 263A–263G. These provisions apply only where:

(a)   the debtor is an undischarged bankrupt;[16]
(b)   the official receiver is specified in the proposal as the nominee in relation to the voluntary arrangement;[17] and
(c)   no interim order is applied for under IA 1986, s 253.[18]

21.17   In order to invoke the procedure, the bankrupt must submit:[19]

(a)   a document setting out the terms of the proposal for a voluntary arrangement;[20] and
(b)   a statement of his affairs containing such particulars as may be prescribed of:[21]

    (i)   creditors;
    (ii)   debts;
    (iii) other liabilities;
    (iv)   assets; and
    (v)   other information.

The bankrupt will have to pay a prescribed fee upon submitting the document.

21.18   It is unlikely that the proposal from the debtor will be delivered to the official receiver without some form of notice. After all, it is unlikely that the debtor by himself will be able to construct a persuasive proposal for consideration by the official receiver and the creditors. To the extent that the debtor will need the assistance of an insolvency practitioner to prepare the proposal, there would appear to be little or no reason why the existing (and retained) Case 1 (where the debtor is an undischarged bankrupt) procedure should not be used. If the IVA is a viable option, there can be few insolvency practitioners willing to spare the time and effort, at the cost of the bankrupt, to assist in the preparation of the proposal, yet willing to give up the opportunity to act as the nominee and supervisor.

21.19   It is therefore probable that the official receiver will provide some form of assistance to the bankrupt in the preparation of the proposal, or, at the

---

16   IA 1986, s 263A(a).
17   Ibid, s 263A(b).
18   Ibid, s 263A(c).
19   The statute actually states 'may submit' but, since the procedure cannot be invoked without these steps being taken, this is as good as 'must'.
20   IA 1986, s 263B(1)(a).
21   Ibid, s 263B(1)(b). There are no particulars provided for, so they are likely to be included in the relevant Rules. It is anticipated that they will follow IR 1986, r 5.3.

very least, advise the bankrupt to consider proposing an IVA. The likelihood is that, even at the first interview stage, the official receiver will have sufficient information to assess whether an IVA would be appropriate and may even be in a position to provide draft details. If that is the case, then the official receiver will have to be very wary of doing or saying anything that might amount to an actionable breach of duty.[22]

21.20   In particular, the official receiver will have to give some consideration as to whether the proposed IVA should be solely in relation to bankruptcy debts, or whether the bankrupt should attempt to bind in creditors with claims not provable in the bankruptcy or might otherwise survive the discharge of the bankruptcy.[23] This is important, because the next step is for the official receiver to consider whether the proposal has a reasonable prospect of being approved and implemented[24] and whether he is prepared to act as the nominee in respect of it. At this stage, the official receiver will have to consider not only the information that has been provided by the bankrupt, but also such information as may have been forthcoming from creditors in relation to the conduct and dealings of the bankrupt.

21.21   If the official receiver considers that there is a reasonable prospect of the proposal being approved, then he may make arrangements for inviting the creditors to decide whether or not to approve it.[25] For this purpose, a person is a creditor if:

(a)   he is a creditor of the debtor in respect of a bankruptcy debt;[26] and
(b)   the official receiver is aware of both his claim and his address.[27]

There would seem to be little or no point in the bankrupt submitting to the official receiver a proposal that had no chance of passing this hurdle. Therefore, a practice may develop amongst official receivers to point out the minimum requirements of such a proposal. Such guidance would have to be given at an early stage, perhaps even as early as the preliminary interview. If not, the official receiver can expect to be inundated with unacceptable proposals, followed by requests for justification as to why each proposal has not been passed by the creditors. A particularly dissatisfied bankrupt might even issue an application to the court for directions, or the reversal or modification of the official receiver's decision.[28]

21.22   There is no guidance as to any other matters that the official receiver can or might wish to take into account. No doubt they will include all the usual considerations in respect of an IVA: the level of the DTI fees, the reduction in the

---

22   As regards the potential liability in negligence, in particular negligent misstatement, and immunity from suit, see *Mond v Hyde* [1999] QB 1097.
23   For example, matrimonial debts, debts arising out of fraud or, in future, obligations under student loan agreements. See **16.29**.
24   IA 1986, s 263B(2).
25   Ibid, s 263B(2).
26   Ibid, s 263B(3)(a). 'Bankruptcy debts' are defined by IA 1986, s 382.
27   Ibid, s 263B(3)(b).
28   Either under IA 1986, s 303 or the court's jurisdiction over the official receiver as an officer of the court under s 400(3).

likely overall fees, the speedier realisation of assets and the availability of third-party funds which would not be available in bankruptcy. By the same token, there may be matters that mean a continuation of the bankruptcy might be more appropriate. There may be continuing investigations into the affairs of the bankrupt, with a view to issuing proceedings to set aside antecedent dealings as transactions at an undervalue, preferences or transactions defrauding creditors.[29] Such proceedings might already be under way. There may be onerous property that should be disclaimed.[30] Some consideration may be being given to an application for a BRO, an IPA or an IPO.

21.23   The bankrupt is likely to put forward a proposal early in the bankruptcy, at which time the official receiver will have had little or no chance to complete these considerations. If the bankruptcy order is annulled as a result of the creditors approving an IVA,[31] an application for a BRO or interim BRO may not be instituted.[32] The official receiver may want to postpone having to decide to put forward the proposal to creditors until he has completed such investigations. Consequently, there may be an unresolved conflict between the desire of the creditors to receive some money and the stated objective of the Act to punish delinquent bankrupts.[33]

21.24   The difficulty is that, in the sort of case where an IVA can be considered quite soon into the bankruptcy, where valuable assets have been identified and are speedily realisable, the likelihood is that there will have been a speedy appointment of an insolvency practitioner as trustee in bankruptcy, either by a creditors' meeting or by the official receiver off the rota. It is more likely that, in such circumstances, investigation costs will have been carried out, so that an IVA is a less attractive proposition as far as costs are concerned.

21.25   The fast-track scheme only operates with creditors with bankruptcy debts. There is no such limitation in the present scheme of Case 1 IVAs. In some cases, it may well be in the best interests of the bankrupt to propose a traditional Case 1 IVA in order to bind in post-bankruptcy creditors. This would be particularly relevant in the case of a trader who may have incurred significant further debt in relation to post-bankruptcy trading. It remains to be seen the extent to which the official receiver takes on board these points when considering the most appropriate way forward for the debtor.[34]

21.26   It is aparent that an official receiver is entitled to decline to act as nominee. After a bankrupt has filed his proposal documents with the official receiver, interim provisions apply. These state that no interim order under IA 1986, s 253 can be made until the official receiver has:

---

29   See IA 1986, ss 339, 340 and 423, respectively.

30   Ibid, s 315 and following.

31   Either by the traditional route of IA 1986, s 261 or the new fast-track procedure.

32   IA 1986, Sch 4A, para 11(c).

33   In some quarters, it is perceived that the avoidance of a BRO will be a significant inducement for the bankrupt to propose an individual voluntary arrangement; see Brougham QC and Briggs 'Current Issues In Insolvency – Bankruptcy Reform Proposals' (2002) 15 *Insolvency Intelligence* 17, referring to the response of the Insolvency Lawyers' Association to the White Paper.

34   See generally statement of Insolvency Practice 3, issued by R3.

(a) made the arrangements for inviting the creditors to decide whether or not to approve the voluntary arrangement;[35] or
(b) informed the debtor that he does not intend to make the arrangements either because:[36]

    (i) he does not think that the voluntary arrangement has a reasonable prospect of success; or
    (ii) he declines to act.

21.27 The rules are likely to stipulate a time-limit by which the official receiver must decide whether to act or not. The official receiver declines to act. The prescribed fee paid by the bankrupt will be refunded. There is no explicit provision permitting the official receiver who declines to act to recommend that the bankrupt approach an insolvency practitioner for the purposes of preparing a traditional post-bankruptcy IVA, perhaps on the basis that it takes into account post-bankruptcy creditors. This may occur informally.

21.28 The arrangements made by the official receiver for inviting creditors to approve the proposal must include the provision of:

(a) a copy of the proposal to each creditor;[37] and
(b) information to each creditor as to the criteria by reference to which the official receiver shall determine whether the creditors approve the proposal or not.[38]

29.29 Of key importance is the fact that the arrangements for consideration of the proposal must not include an opportunity for modifications to the proposed voluntary arrangement to be suggested or made.[39] Thus, it is essential for the bankrupt's proposal to be acceptable in the first place, and for the official receiver to have properly judged the likely views of the creditors. This should constitute a major cost saving, because a significant amount of the costs of preparing for the meeting of creditors arises from the to-ing and fro-ing necessary to resolve modifications suggested by creditors, in particular the Crown.

21.30 As practitioners will be aware, in March 2002, R3 issued a form of Standard Conditions for Individual Voluntary Arrangements for its members' use. They are not obligatory, and any nominee or debtor is free to use an alternative. Practitioners will also be aware of the recent practice of both the Inland Revenue and HM Customs & Excise to propose standard modifications, to stand or fall together, which, if rejected, means that their votes upon the proposal itself should be treated as rejections. The R3 Standard Conditions deal with many of these points, and it is understood that the Inland Revenue and HM Customs & Excise have already prepared draft 'standard modifications' for submission in response to the Standard Conditions.

---

35 IA 1986, s 263B(5)(a).
36 Ibid, s 263B(5)(b).
37 Ibid, s 263B(4)(a).
38 Ibid, s 263B(4)(b).
39 Ibid, s 263B(4)(c). Paragraph 767 of the Explanatory Notes describes the proposal to the creditors as being on a 'take it or leave it' basis.

21.31   Additionally, as mentioned elsewhere, the abolition of Crown preference in bankruptcies is likely to have the effect of a greater involvement of the Crown departments in voluntary arrangements. The Voluntary Arrangements Service, managed by the Inland Revenue on behalf of itself and HM Customs & Excise, has published criteria by which it will judge the proposals put to it.[40] Therefore, practitioners will have to bear these in mind to a far greater extent now that the Crown will be participating as an unsecured creditor in such voluntary arrangements. It remains to be seen whether, in practice, the Voluntary Arrangements Service will relax its criteria to any extent so as to facilitate a greater realisation for unsecured creditors in appropriate cases.

21.32   It is clear, therefore, that, where the bankrupt is putting forward a proposal to a body of creditors that includes a large element of Crown debt, these standard modifications must be borne in mind if the proposal is to stand any chance of success. As a consequence it is likely that fast-track IVAs will be used for consumer bankrupts, as opposed to trading bankrupts who may have Crown debts, especially if, as is anticipated, R3 should issue shorter and less complex standard terms for use in purely consumer-type cases.

21.33   There is no other guidance as to what steps the official receiver should take to arrange for the approval of the IVA. Although not mentioned in the EA 2002, it is anticipated that the meetings will take place entirely by correspondence.[41] Again, this is a major cost-saving measure, as the cost of the meeting significantly contributes to the size of the nominee's fee. It has already been made clear that the majorities required for approval of the IVA will remain unchanged.[42] The rules are likely to provide for:[43]

(a) time-limits for responses from the creditors;
(b) the manner in which their votes will be calculated;
(c) the extent to which the official receiver's treatment of the claims might be challenged; and
(d) how a creditor or the debtor might go about challenging that decision.

21.34   As soon as reasonably practicable after implementation of the arrangements for the approval of the IVA, the official receiver must report to the court as to whether the proposal has been approved or rejected.[44]

21.35   One approved, IA 1986, s 263D takes effect upon the official receiver reporting this outcome to the court.[45] This expressly states that the voluntary arrangement:

(a) takes effect;[46]

---

40   They are published on the Inland Revenue website at www.inlandrevenue.gov.uk/pdfs/cwl5.htm#6.
41   See para 767 of the Explanatory Notes.
42   See para 767 of the Explanatory Notes. The majorities are provided for by IA 1986, s 258 and IR 1986, r 5.18.
43   These are likely to reflect the existing position for IVAs, in so far as applicable.
44   IA 1986, s 263C.
45   Ibid, s 263D(1).
46   Ibid, s 263D(2)(a).

(b) binds the debtor;[47] and

(c) binds every person who was entitled to participate in the arrangements made by the official receiver.[48]

21.36   There then follows a hiatus of 28 days before the official receiver can apply to the court for the annulment of the bankruptcy order.[49] This is to allow a period of time for an application for an order revoking the voluntary arrangement on the ground that:

(a) it unfairly prejudices the interests of a creditor of the debtor;[50] or

(b) that a material irregularity has occurred in relation to the arrangements made by the official receiver for the arrangements for the approval of the individual voluntary arrangement.[51]

These echo the existing provisions under the IA 1986, s 262(1) upon which a challenge can be made in respect of the decision reached at the creditors' meeting.

21.37   The persons entitled to bring such revocation applications are as follows:

(a) the debtor;[52]

(b) a person who was entitled to participate in the entitled to participate in the official receiver's arrangements for the approval of the IVA;[53]

(c) the trustee of the bankrupt's estate[54]; or

(d) the official receiver.[55]

Again, these echo the existing class of persons who may make such an application, as provided for in the IA 1986, s 262(2).

21.38   The application for revocation must be made within 28 days of the official receiver's report to the court as to whether the proposal was approved or rejected.[56] This is subject to two provisos:

(a) a creditor not aware of the official receiver's arrangements for the approval of the voluntary arrangement at the time that they were made may issue an application within 28 days of becoming aware of the voluntary arrangement.[57]

(b) the court has a general discretion under IA 1986, s 376 to disregard time-limits.[58]

---

47   IA 1986, s 263D(2)(b).
48   Ibid, s 263D(2)(c). See also s 263B(2), (3).
49   Ibid, s 283D(3), (4).
50   Ibid, s 263F(1)(a).
51   Ibid, s 263F(1)(b).
52   Ibid, s 263F(2)(a).
53   Ibid, s 263F(2)(b).
54   Ibid, s 263F(2)(c).
55   Ibid, s 263F(2)(d).
56   Ibid, s 263F(3).
57   Ibid, s 263F(4).
58   *Tager v Westpac Banking Corporation* [1997] BCLC 313 and *Solomons v Williams* [2001] BPIR 1123. The court will have regard to the period of delay, the merits of the application generally, the prejudice to the parties and the reason for the delay.

Rather oddly, the statutory construction is not clear. On first reading, the extension in favour of a forgotten creditor would seem merely to be an extension of time provision. But, in so far as it refers only to 'a creditor' of the debtor, as opposed to 'a creditor of the debtor in respect of a bankruptcy debt', there is an argument for saying that the category of persons entitled to apply for a revocation is actually widened.

21.39   If a revocation application is made, then the official receiver cannot apply for the annulment of the bankruptcy order whilst the application is pending.[59] Further, the annulment application cannot be made whilst any appeal from the decision whether to revoke the IVA or not, is pending or may be brought.[60] This effectively extends the period to 14 days after the decision.[61]

21.40   Otherwise, if the 28 days pass without an application for a revocation, then the official receiver can apply for the annulment of the bankruptcy.[62]

21.41   The court is empowered to give such directions about the conduct of the bankruptcy and the administration of the bankrupt's estate as it thinks appropriate for the purposes of implementing the approved IVA.[63] There is no provision that limits the categories of person who may apply for such directions. This will include the debtor, the official receiver, the supervisor[64] and the trustee in bankruptcy. It is also possible that it might extend to a third party who has promised to put forward money or property for inclusion within the IVA.

21.42   The rules will no doubt make provision as to the manner in which either the bankrupt or the official receiver should apply for such annulment, and the information that will have to be provided.

21.43   Once implemented, to all intents and purposes, the IVA effected by this fast-track method takes effect as if it were one approved at a meeting of the creditors. Accordingly, IA 1986, s 263 (implementation and supervision of the approved voluntary arrangement) applies to it.[65] All references in the IA 1986 or any other Act to a voluntary arrangement are to be treated as including a reference to one effected by this method.[66] This therefore means that the official receiver will be in a position to present a bankruptcy petition against the debtor in the event that he has defaulted in connection with the voluntary arrange-

---

59   IA 1986, s 263D(4)(b).
60   Ibid, s 263D(4)(c).
61   As to appeals in insolvency proceedings generally, see Practice Direction Insolvency
     Proceedings 1999, para 17.
62   IA 1986, s 263D(3).
63   Ibid, s 263D(5).
64   Whether the official receiver or an insolvency practitioner.
65   IA 1986, s 263E.
66   Ibid, s 263D(7).

ment.[67] As in the case of an IVA approved in the traditional way,[68] the Deeds of Arrangement Act 1914 does not apply.[69]

21.44 In the same way that the chairman of the creditors' meeting has to provide the Secretary of State with specified information to enable the register of IVAs to be maintained,[70] the rules are likely to provide that the official receiver will have to provide the Secretary of State with the following information:

(a) the name and address of the debtor;
(b) the date on which the arrangement was approved by the creditors; and
(c) the name and address of the official receiver concerned as supervisor of the IVA.

The official receiver will also no doubt be required to notify the Secretary of State of any revocation of the IVA.

21.45 Finally, the rules are likely to provide mechanisms by which the official receiver notifies the creditors that the IVA has been completed.

OFFICIAL RECEIVER AS SUPERVISOR

21.46 The old provisions stated that in respect of an IVA, the nominee[71] and the supervisor[72] each had to be an insolvency practitioner. The official receiver was excluded from acting as a supervisor of an IVA.[73]

21.47 In relation to Case 1 IVAs, this has been changed by EA 2002, Sch 22, para 3, which inserts into the IA 1986 a new s 389B. It states simply that the official receiver is authorised to act as nominee or supervisor of an IVA provided that, at the time that the arrangement is proposed, the debtor is an undischarged bankrupt.[74] There is no amendment of the requirement to apply for an interim order in the usual way by the undischarged bankrupt, the official receiver or the trustee in bankruptcy.[75]

21.48 Further, the Secretary of State is given power to repeal the proviso regarding the debtor being an undischarged bankrupt. This can be done by statutory instrument. However, such repeal is subject to annulment by a resolution of either House of Parliament.[76]

21.49 This opens the way for the official receiver, at some stage in the future, to be a supervisor of both Case 1 and Case 2 IVAs. No doubt,

---

67 IA 2986, s 264(1)(c) and s 276. The grounds are failing to comply with the obligations
    under the IVA, providing information that was false, misleading or contained material
    omissions and failing to do things reasonably required by the supervisor in connection with
    the IVA.
68 Ibid, s 260(3).
69 Ibid, s 263D(6).
70 IR 1986, r 5.24
71 IA 1986, s 388(2)(c) and IR 1986, r 5.5(1)(e).
72 Ibid, s 255(1)(d).
73 Ibid, s 388(5).
74 Ibid, s 389B(1).
75 Ibid, s 253(3)(a).
76 Ibid, s 389B(3)(b).

consideration will be given to this proposal after analysis of how well the new provisions operate as regards Case 1 IVAs.

21.50   However, until then, the new provisions allow both debtor and creditor to choose who should administer the post-bankruptcy IVA: either the official receiver or a private sector insolvency practitioner.

21.51   One point does arise in relation to the concept of the official receiver as nominee or supervisor in whichever type of post-bankruptcy IVA is entered into. The office of nominee or supervisor has always been undertaken by an insolvency practitioner as an individual. The Act does not make clear whether the official receiver in taking on this role will do so as an individual or in the capacity of the office of official receiver. The distinction will be pertinent where an individual who vacates his engagement as official receiver is a supervisor of post-bankruptcy IVAs, for it is not clear whether this successor as official receiver will automatically assume the appointments.

ANNULMENTS

21.52   The EA 2002 amends the existing procedure for Case 1 IVAs. IA 86, s 261 (effect on undischarged bankrupt) is replaced by a completely new section (entitled 'additional effect on undischarged bankrupt'). The new provisions are set out in EA 2002, Sch 22, para 1.

21.53   The provisions apply where the creditors' meeting summoned under IA 1986, s 257 approves the proposed voluntary arrangement, whether with modifications or not,[77] and the debtor is an undischarged bankrupt.[78] Where the section applies, the court shall annul the bankruptcy order on an application made by the bankrupt[79] or, where the bankrupt has not made an application within the prescribed period, the official receiver.[80]

21.54   Such an application for an annulment cannot be made:

(a)   during the period[81] specified in IA 1986, s 262(3)(a) during which the decision of the creditors' meeting can be challenged[82] by an application for it to be revoked under IA 1986, s 262;[83]

(b)   whilst any such application is pending;[84] or

---

77   IA 1986, s 262(1)(a).
78   Ibid, s 262(1)(b).
79   Ibid, s 262(2)(a).
80   Ibid, s 262(2)(b).
81   The present period is 28 days beginning on the day on which the chairman of the creditors' meeting reported the result of the meeting to the court under IA 1986, s 259.
82   On the grounds that the approved voluntary arrangement unfairly prejudices the interests of a creditor of a debtor; or that there has been some material irregularity at or in relation to such meeting.
83   IA 1986, s 261(3)(a).
84   Ibid, s 261(3)(b).

(c) whilst any appeal from the decision whether to revoke the voluntary arrangement or not is pending or may be brought.[85] This effectively extends the period to 14 days after the decision.[86]

21.55 Where the section applies, the court is empowered to give such directions about the conduct of the bankruptcy and the administration of the bankrupt's estate as it thinks appropriate for the purposes of implementing the approved voluntary arrangement.[87] It is difficult to envisage the circumstances in which such a provision might apply, as it is unusual for the IVA and the bankruptcy to sit side by side, especially if the creditors are the same in each.[88] It is possible that there may be a particular reason to keep the bankruptcy open, such as the finalisation of some litigation. But, if that is the case, then it is unlikely to be a suitable case for an IVA in any event.

21.56 The rules will no doubt prescribe the procedure by which either the bankrupt or the official receiver should apply for such annulment, and the information that will have to be provided to the court.

21.57 This is a welcome amendment. It clears up the anomaly as to who should be making the application for an annulment of the bankruptcy in Case 1 IVAs.

21.58 In addition, the provision is mandatory. The court *shall* annul the bankruptcy order. Again, this is a welcome change for al those who like certainty. The old provisions stated that the court *may* annul the bankruptcy order.

FEES AND ACCOUNTS

21.59 As stated earlier, one of the main deterrents to the entry into a post-bankruptcy IVA is the level of the nominee's fee, which is usually difficult for a recent bankrupt to provide without third-party assistance. The official receiver, as nominee, will charge a flat rate for his time in the preparation and approval of the proposal. This will have to be paid when the bankrupt sends the proposal to the official receiver, but will be refunded in the event that the official receiver declines to act.

21.60 There was some consideration as to whether to charge a sliding-scale fee up to the maximum, depending upon the amount of work that the official receiver has done prior to any decision to reject the debtor's proposal, especially if such rejection resulted from misrepresentations or non-disclosure by the bankrupt. However, it was thought that this would be too difficult to manage and not cost-effective. It has been decided that it is easier simply to refund the full fee. In such cases, therefore, it seems that the bankrupt will be unable to argue

---

85   IA 1986, s 261(3)(c).

86   As to appeals in insolvency proceedings generally, see *Practice Direction: Insolvency Proceedings* [2000] BPIR 647, para 17.

87   IA 1986, s 263D(5).

88   There is no conceptual difficulty with an undischarged bankrupt entering into an IVA with his post-bankruptcy creditors only.

that he has suffered any loss as a result of the official receiver encouraging an IVA that turned out to be unworkable.

21.61 As supervisor, the official receiver's fees will be based upon a percentage of anticipated total receipts.

21.62 The Rules are likely to provide details of the accounts the official receiver must keep as supervisor and the circumstances in which he will have to provide details of his accounts, receipts and payments to the debtor, the creditors and the Secretary of State.

CONCLUSION

21.63 Generally, the new provisions are to be welcomed. Anything that increases the prospects of a greater recovery for the creditors is to be encouraged. The provisions allow for two types of post-bankruptcy IVAs:

(a) an old-style Case 1 IVA, in respect of which the official receiver or an insolvency practitioner acts as nominee or supervisor; and
(b) a fast-track IVA, in respect of which the official receiver will be nominee and supervisor.

21.64 The most significant development is that at a very early stage, the official receiver will be considering which route will be the most appropriate for the bankrupt. He will consider the availability of assets, in particular cash, property, income and shares, in order to determine whether an IVA, or a bankruptcy, with the prospect of an income payment order (IPO) or income payment agreement (IPA), is the more appropriate course. The Insolvency Service says that the prospect of a bankruptcy restriction order (BRO) or bankruptcy restriction undertaking (BRU) is not a matter that would arise for consideration at that stage and the possibility of such a step would not be something that would prejudice the view as to whether an IVA was an appropriate step. A cynic might suggest that one of the more significant factors in the decision as to the appropriate route would be any quarterly targets for the official receivers for the numbers of BRO applications, IPOs/IPAs and IVAs.

21.65 However, aside from such cynicism, there is a serious question to be asked as to the type of debtors who will enter into such an IVA, no matter how much they are encouraged. It is perceived that many IVAs, whether Case 1 or Case 2, relate to professionals whose regulatory bodies have specific rules as to the effect of bankruptcy on the ability to continue to practise.[89] Therefore, Case 1 IVAs are a good route out for professionals who find themselves unexpectedly bankrupt, or did not properly consider their position until after the bankruptcy order was made. But, in time, with the reduced stigma of bankruptcy, there is a strong likelihood that these professional bodies will relax their rules. Therefore, the requirement to enter into an IVA and to avoid bankruptcy will not be so pressing.

---

89 See **20.34**.

21.66   Similarly, it is difficult to see why a bankrupt would want to enter into an IVA rather than accept the consequences of the bankruptcy order. In the ordinary circumstances, under the bankruptcy provisions, he would be discharged after 1 year, with a strong chance of being discharged even earlier. He will face the prospect of a 3-year income payments order or agreement, which can be varied downwards or suspended in the event of a change of circumstances. On the other hand, if the bankrupt fails to comply with the terms of the IVA, he will be facing a bankruptcy order all over again and, as a second bankrupt, facing the prospect of a bankruptcy restrictions order being made against him. As far as a consumer bankrupt in a rented property is concerned, there will simply be no incentive to enter into a post-bankruptcy IVA. He will be better off remaining as a bankrupt.

21.67   In due course, if the professional bodies do relax the restrictions imposed as a consequence of a bankruptcy order, the majority of those who will use these provisions will be those who have a company directorship at risk from the effects of his being an undischarged bankrupt, or who wishes to avoid the consequences of a bankruptcy restrictions order being imposed for a longer period.

21.68   Finally, since one of the key themes of the EA 2002 is to ensure that non-culpable bankrupts are speedily discharged, there will be a very small class of bankrupts to whom these fast-track IVAs will be available. Post-bankruptcy IVAs, whether fast-track or traditional, are only available to undischarged bankrupts.[90] With many bankrupts to receive their discharges in as short a period as 12 weeks, it is very possible that many debtors will find themselves discharged before proper consideration has been given to an IVA, whether fast-track or traditional.

21.69   Therefore, it is possible that there will continue to be a very small market for post-bankruptcy IVAs. The extent to which they are taken up will play a significant role in the decision of the Secretary of State as to whether to exercise the power to enable official receivers to act as nominees and supervisors in all IVAs, not just post-bankruptcy ones.

21.70   It remains to be seen the extent to which the new fast-track IVAs actually bring the presently unregulated debt management plans within a formal and binding regime. A cheap IVA is bound to be a better step than an informal, non-binding and unregulated agreement.

---

90   See *Wright v Official Receiver* [2001] BPIR 196.

Part 3

OTHER REFORMS

Chapter 22

SANCTION FOR CLAW-BACK PROCEEDINGS

'When someone else was paying, generosity ceased to be a virtue and Scrooge-like parsimony ceased to be a vice'
The Honourable Mr Justice Lightman[1]

THE POSITION PRIOR TO THE EA 2002

Definitions

22.1   Two different categories of proceedings are discussed in this chapter. The first category, referred to here as 'claw-back proceedings', includes the following:

(a)   as regards corporate insolvency, proceedings pursuant to ss 213 (fraudulent trading), 214 (wrongful trading), 238 (transactions at an undervalue), 239 (preferences) and 423 (transactions defrauding creditors) of IA 1986, which are brought in the name of the liquidator;
(b)   as regards personal insolvency, proceedings brought by the trustee in bankruptcy under ss 339 (transactions at an undervalue), 340 (preferences) and 423 (transactions defrauding creditors) of IA 1986.

22.2   The second category, referred to here as 'civil recovery proceedings', includes the following:

(a)   as regards corporate insolvency, proceedings brought, or defended, in the company's name and on the company's behalf;
(b)   as regards personal insolvency, proceedings relating to the property comprised in the bankrupt's estate.

22.3   In some circumstances, an office-holder is required to obtain sanction in order to bring civil recovery proceedings and/or claw-back proceedings which will be dealt with below. Sanction may be obtained from different persons dependent upon the insolvency procedure. As regards corporate insolvency, sanction may be obtained from:

(a)   in the case of a creditors' voluntary winding-up, the court, or liquidation committee or if there is no such committee, a meeting of the company's creditors;[2]

---

1   *Insolvency Intelligence* 1998 (Vol 1).
2   IA 1986, s 165(2).

(b) in the case of a compulsory winding-up, the court or liquidation committee.[3] Where there is no liquidation committee sanction may be obtained
from the Secretary of State.[4]

22.4   As regards personal insolvency, sanction may be obtained from the
court or creditors committee. Where there is no creditors committee, sanction
may be obtained from the Secretary of State.[5]

22.5   For the rest of this chapter, a reference to the need to obtain sanction
should be read accordingly.

Corporate

22.6   Prior to the commencement of the EA 2002, where a liquidator has
been appointed in a voluntary liquidation no sanction is required to bring any
proceedings.[6]

22.7   The position has been different in compulsory liquidations. Sanction
has not been required to bring claw-back proceedings,[7] but has been required to
bring or defend civil recovery proceedings.[8]

22.8   Prior to the changes to the IR 1986 described below, if an office-holder
in a corporate insolvency has commenced claw-back proceedings and has been
unsuccessful he has been liable to pay the costs of the successful party but he was
not entitled to an indemnity from the estate.[9]

Personal

22.9   In bankruptcy a trustee has required sanction in order to bring civil
recovery proceedings.[10] There has been no express provision dealing with
whether or not sanction is required in respect of claw-back proceedings. It has
therefore been presumed that a trustee in bankruptcy does not require sanction
to commence claw-back proceedings.

THE REASONS FOR CHANGE

The anomalies

22.10   There is no obvious reason why sanction has been required to bring
civil recovery proceedings if a company is wound-up by the court, yet no
sanction is required in the case of a company in voluntary liquidation. Further,

---

3   IA 1986, s 167(1)(a).
4   Ibid, s 141(5) and IR 1986, r 4.172.
5   Ibid, s 302(2) and IR 1986, r 6.166.
6   Ibid, Sch 4, Part II, para 4.
7   See *Dear IP* Chap 7(4); www.insolvency.gov.uk.
8   IA 1986, ss 165, 67 and Sch 4, Part II, para 4.
9   *Lewis v Commissioners of the Inland Revenue* [1999] 2 BCLC 666 – the risk of being
     personally liable for the costs of an action without an indemnity from the estate has been
     too great for some insolvency practitioners and potentially good claims have been thwarted
     as a result.
10   IA 1986, Sch 5, Part I.

there is no apparent justification as to why no sanction has been required to commence claw-back proceedings yet sanction has been required in respect of civil recovery proceedings in compulsory liquidations. The EA 2002 now brings a consistency of approach. There is no longer a distinction drawn between claw-back and civil recovery proceedings or between compulsory and voluntary liquidations.

The creation of a top-slice for unsecured creditors initiates change

22.11 The EA 2002 seeks to improve the position of unsecured creditors by abolishing Crown preferences and by introducing 'top-slicing'.[11] The prescribed part of the net property ('the top-slice'), which is to be distributed to the unsecured creditors, is likely to be at risk (or may be reduced) if claw-back proceedings are unsuccessful.[12] In addition, unsecured creditors may decide that they would prefer the certainty of a small amount of money immediately rather than opt for the chance of greater recoveries at a more distant point in time. It was therefore proposed that unsecured creditors should have a say in the decision of whether or not claw-back proceedings would be commenced. This was succinctly explained by Lord McIntosh (the Minister for the Government in the House of Lords) during the third reading in the House of Lords:[13]

> 'Consideration of that matter [the anomaly between compulsory and voluntary liquidations] led us to look at the impact of the removal of the Crown's preference, whose abolition is aimed at generating funds for unsecured creditors. We would not want any such sums to be used by the liquidator in pursuing legal action unless the creditors approve. After all it is a commercial decision for the creditor to choose between, say, a five pence in the pound dividend payable now, or whether to allow the liquidator to pursue a claim which may result in a 50 pence in the pound dividend at a later stage.'

Personal insolvency

22.12 Whilst top-slicing does not apply to personal insolvency, it is thought that the principles of consistency of approach and accountability are equally important in this context.

CHANGES MADE BY THE EA 2002

Corporate

22.13 Section 253 of EA 2002 inserts a new para 3A into Part I of Sch 4 to IA 1986 (powers exercisable only with sanction). This change means that the liquidator can only exercise the power to bring claw-back proceedings with

---

11 See Chapters 3 and 5 respectively.
12 Assuming that the expenses of the office-holder (including costs of proceedings) would be payable out of the net property; see the discussion in Chapter 5 on Top-Slicing.
13 21 October 2002, col 1123.

sanction. This is the case whether the company is wound-up by the court or wound-up voluntarily. Thus, the unwarranted distinction between claw-back proceedings and civil recovery proceedings in compulsory liquidations is removed. The EA 2002 has not sought to alter the power of a liquidator of a company in voluntary liquidation to bring civil recovery proceedings without sanction.

Personal

22.14   Consistent with the change in the rules regarding corporate insolvency, EA 2002, s 262 inserts a new para 2A into Part I of Sch 5 to IA 1986 (powers of a trustee in bankruptcy exercisable with sanction). This change will mean that a trustee in bankruptcy will only be able to exercise the power to bring claw-back proceedings with prior sanction.

THE RULE CHANGES

Corporate

22.15   From 1 January 2003, r 23 of the Insolvency (Amendment) (No 2) Rules 2002, SI 2002/2712, amends r 4.218 of IR 1986. The amended r 4.218 provides that costs properly chargeable in relation to any legal proceedings which the official receiver or liquidator has power to bring, whether in his own name or that of the company, are payable as a first priority out of the assets.[14] This is intended to 'ameliorate the difficulties caused by the Court of Appeal decision in *Lewis v Commissioners of Inland Revenue*'.[15] The amended rule provides:

> '(1) The expenses of the liquidation are payable out of the assets in the following order of priority—
>
> (a)   expenses or costs which—
>
> (i)   are properly chargeable or incurred by the official receiver or the liquidator in preserving, realising or getting in any of the assets of the company *or otherwise relating to the conduct of any legal proceedings which he has power to bring or defend whether in his own name or the name of the company*'. (emphasis added)

Personal

22.16   A similar amendment is made to r 6.224 of IR 1986 concerning bankruptcy proceedings, which amended rule provides:

> '(1) The expenses of the bankruptcy are payable out of the estate in the following order of priority—
>
> (a)   expenses or costs which—

---

14   R3 *Technical Bulletin* (Institute of Business Recovery Professionals) No 54, December 2002.
15   Ibid.

(i) are properly chargeable or incurred by the official receiver or the trustee in preserving, realising or getting in any of the assets of the bankrupt *or otherwise relating to the conduct of any legal proceedings which he has power to bring (whether the claim on which the proceedings are based forms part of the estate or otherwise) or defend*' (emphasis supplied).

SUMMARY

Corporate

22.17   In all cases of corporate insolvency, the office-holder will now have to seek, and obtain, sanction before bringing claw-back proceedings. This removes the anomaly between claw-back proceedings and civil recovery proceedings in compulsory liquidations. The change can be seen as part of a wider move by the Government to give creditors, and in particular unsecured creditors, a greater say in the decision as to whether or not proceedings should be issued.

22.18   Nevertheless, the new provisions introduce a fresh anomaly in voluntary liquidations in that sanction is required in claw-back proceedings but not in civil recovery proceedings. The grounds for maintaining this distinction are no longer obvious.

Personal

22.19   In personal insolvency, a trustee in bankruptcy will also have to seek sanction in order to bring claw-back proceedings.

Costs of claw-back proceedings

22.20   The change of the rules effected on the 1 January 2003 enables liquidators and trustees in bankruptcy to recoup expenses of claw-back litigation out of the assets of the estate where proceedings have been properly brought.

Conclusion

22.21   As regards corporate insolvency, the rationale behind the changes is that liquidators cannot assume that funds made available to the unsecured creditors by reason of the abolition of Crown preferences and creation of the top-slice, may be used as a fighting fund to pursue errant former directors. Equally, however, the changes suggest that the Government is not intending to prevent the top-slice from being used as a fighting fund, if the same is agreed by the creditors. This is good news for practitioners.

22.22   Generally, the changes ought to be welcomed in that they increase consultation with creditors in the decision-making process and make compulsory that which was good practice prior to the introduction of the EA 2002.

Chapter 23

MONEY AND FEES

'Put not your trust in money, but put your money in trust'
OW Holmes[1]

INTRODUCTION

23.1   The Insolvency Service is to become more of a business. To use a phrase borrowed from the world of property developers, it will soon be able to 'wash its own face'. Implementation of the sea-change introduced by the EA 2002 described in this book must be funded. Whether it is the introduction of BROs, post-bankruptcy IVAs or the new emphasis on front-loading costs in bankruptcies, the new statutory scheme will be more costly.

23.2   In the Insolvency Service's Strategic Plan for 2002–2005,[2] it is recognised that at a high level the principal risks for the Service during that period include inadequate resources/funding. The same plan discloses that the Service has been allocated an additional £10 million over 2 years to fund its plans.

23.3   There are also provisions of the EA 2002 which create new income for the Service from the insolvency profession and rewrite the statutory scheme for managing funds derived from insolvent estates. These last-mentioned reforms have been a long time coming.

THE NEED FOR REFORM

23.4   The way in which the Insolvency Service holds funds and is funded is neither apparent nor easy to understand. There has been pressure to reform the Insolvency Service's financial regime to bring increased transparency and simplicity and to ensure that the maximum possible investment return goes to insolvent estates.

23.5   In 1982, the Cork Committee[3] deplored the fact that the State (through the Consolidated Fund) was receiving the benefit of surplus sums held in the Insolvency Services Account (ISA) into which liquidators and trustees in

---

1   *The Autocrat of the Breakfast-Table* II.
2   Signed off by the Chief Executive, Desmond Flynn, in March 2002 and appearing on the web in October 2002 at: http://www.insolvency.gov.uk/pdfs/strategicplan2002final.pdf.
3   *Report of the Review Committee on Insolvency Law and Practice* Cmnd 8558 (1982), para 857.

bankruptcy were obliged to pay realisations. Nothing was done about it. Years later, the annual State windfall had become large. For example, in the financial year 2000/01, the excess income (ie from the investment of creditors' moneys) paid from the ISA into the Consolidated Fund for the benefit of the State amounted to £43 million. By then, it was recognised that this benefit at the expense of unsecured creditors was not justifiable.[4]

23.6   In para 1.51 of the White Paper,[5] the Government expressed the desire to reform the financial regime which governs insolvency:

> 'The financial regime under which the Insolvency Service operates was established in the 19th Century. Whilst it produces large revenues for the government (and, indeed, surpluses in recent years) it does not enable income generated by dealing with cases to be used to provide resources to enable such cases to be properly dealt with. The requirement that funds from voluntary liquidations be placed in the Insolvency Services Account does not recognise the regulatory regime that has existed since 1986 and the payment of the bulk of the interest generated on insolvency funds to the Consolidated Fund can no longer be justified. The Enterprise Bill will contain proposals for substantial reforms in this area.'

THE NEW PROVISIONS OF THE EA 2002[6]

23.7   In broad terms, the Government has set the scene for introducing the promised reforms by ss 270 ('Fees'), 271 ('Insolvency Services Account') and 272 ('Insolvency Services Account') of EA 2002. These provisions pave the way for secondary legislation to be introduced. Since the secondary legislation is yet to appear, this book can only deal briefly with 'the headlines'. First, it is necessary to mention how the ISA operates.

The ISA

23.8   Regulation 5(1) (winding-up by the court) and reg 20 (bankruptcy) of the Insolvency Regulations 1994, SI 1994/2507 require that, subject to the exception for local bank accounts, a liquidator or trustee in bankruptcy is required, at specified times, to pay all moneys received by him in the course of carrying out his functions as such into the ISA. In the case of a voluntary winding-up, reg 5(2) requires the liquidator, at specified times, to pay into the ISA the balance of funds in his hands or under his control relating to the company.

ISA: Transparency

23.9   The current financial regime comprises numerous fees charged by the Insolvency Service covering a spectrum of services ranging from case administration to a Secretary of State fee. They are set out in the Insolvency Fees Order 1986, SI 1986/2030. None of the fees operates in such a way as to achieve full cost recovery of the activity in question undertaken by the Insolvency Service. This may be contrasted with the more commercial approach of the private sector.

---

4   IA 2000 provided for payment of interest into bankruptcy estates.
5   *Insolvency – A Second Chance* (Cmnd 5234).
6   Explanatory Notes, paras 788–797.

23.10 EA 2002, s 270 introduces a new s 415A into the IA 1986. Section 415A(3) provides for payment of fees that relate to the operation of the ISA by the Insolvency Service and money paid into and out of the ISA. The idea is that the Insolvency Service will separate out the costs that relate to the operation of the ISA so that these costs are met by the insolvent estates. The effects of the proposals are summarised in para 793 of the Explanatory Notes as follows:

> 'This will allow for clear identification of those banking services that are carried out in respect of all cases, and that will be charged through an annual service fee, and those that relate to specific estates and transactions such as investment requests by IPs or the volume of payments out of the account through cheques or bank transfers. These changes will also enable the ending of the current arrangements whereby a number of different fees are used to meet these costs and to cross-subsidise other functions.'

23.11 Thus, it is envisaged that the pooling of funds in the ISA and their application for disparate and unrelated purposes will come to an end. The re-allocation of costs and fees and the avoidance of 'cross-subsidy' are designed to benefit creditors and are expected to do so. That said, it is not possible to calculate a direct comparison between current and the proposed new regimes. This is because the current system of fees is so complicated and unrelated to costs. It is sufficient to say that it is intended that the new administration fees will reflect the actual cost of an official receiver's administration, and will be charged on a full cost-recovery basis.

23.12 The level of specific fees has not been determined as yet, but each will reflect the full cost of the services covered.

ISA: Surplus income

23.13 IA 1986, s 405(1) has been revoked by EA 2002, s 272(1) with the effect that there is no longer a requirement to pay excess income in the ISA into the Consolidated Fund. As already mentioned, this will be of immediate benefit to creditors – approximately £40–50 million per annum. As a reform, this is consistent with the policy which drove the abolition of Crown preference and is likely to have more immediate effect in that the Crown preference moneys will not flow to the unsecured creditors for some time.

ISA: Insufficient funds

23.14 EA 2002, s 272(2) revokes IA 1986, s 408 and introduces a new s 408 entitled 'Adjustment of Balances' which provides wider powers to make adjustments to be made between the ISA and the Insolvency Services Investment Account and the Consolidated Fund. Due to fluctuations in interest rates and other variables, it has become necessary to create a 'buffer' to deal with such fluctuations and to cater for occasions when adjustments need to be made between the accounts.

ISA: Interest

23.15 Since 24 October 1994, company balances in excess of £2 held in the ISA have automatically attracted interest at the rate of 3.5% per annum in accordance with reg 9(6) of the Insolvency Regulations 1994. The interest is applied in April and October each year. Any surplus income has been transferred to the Consolidated Fund.

23.16   Under the regime introduced by EA 2002, s 271, the rate of interest will be set by notice, and will be able to be adjusted more often. Additionally, the provision requiring liquidators to deposit funds in the ISA in voluntary liquidations is to be revoked. The new rates will be set as competitively as possible in line with the returns on the Insolvency Service Investment Account.

Additional fees/charges levied on the licensing bodies

23.17   As already mentioned, EA 2002, s 270 introduces a new s 415A into the IA 1986. Section 415A(1) enables the Secretary of State to charge a fee to bodies recognised under IA 1986, s 391 as a professional body for the purposes of licensing IPs. The idea is that the fees to be prescribed will cover both the cost of recognition and also the cost of monitoring the bodies' activities.[7] The fee will also cover the cost of general regulatory functions carried out by the Insolvency Service.[8]

23.18   The costs of these functions is currently met by the DTI but the new policy is that they are to fall to the profession. The fee, which will be set out in secondary legislation, will be charged to each body based on the number of IPs licensed by them.

Additional fees/charges levied on insolvency practitioners

23.19   New s 415A(2) provides for a fee to be charged to those insolvency practitioners licensed by the Secretary of State under IA 1986, s 392 and will be based on the costs of granting and maintaining authorisation.

The wider picture

23.20   There is a sense that these reforms are but one small step in the overall restructure of the Insolvency Service. There is a tension between fulfilling the role imposed upon the Insolvency Service by the insolvency legislation and keeping within budgetary limitations. Thankfully, issues such as cross-financing and principles of cost-recovery are beyond this book. Nevertheless, it is worth signing off from this text on a positive note. The UK public benefits from an effective and just insolvency system that can be trusted. Whilst it is sensible to maximise the income generated by carrying out its statutory function, it is equally logical that the taxpayer should absorb some of the costs – especially in the area of compliance. As the Insolvency Service achieves greater transparency and becomes more accountable for its results, so it should become easier to rationalise and justify a greater level of funding.

---

7   Ie overseeing their procedures and ensuring that licensing is carried out properly.
8   Ie representation on the Joint Insolvency Council and keeping IPs informed of legislative and other developments through the issuing of newsletters and guidance such as the (much-used) 'Dear IP' service.

Appendix

ENTERPRISE ACT 2002

PART 10

INSOLVENCY

Companies etc

248 Replacement of Part II of Insolvency Act 1986

(1) The following shall be substituted for Part II of the Insolvency Act 1986 (administration orders) –

'PART II

ADMINISTRATION

8 Administration

Schedule B1 to this Act (which makes provision about the administration of companies) shall have effect.'

(2) The Schedule B1 set out in Schedule 16 to this Act shall be inserted after Schedule A1 to the Insolvency Act 1986.

(3) Schedule 17 (minor and consequential amendments relating to administration) shall have effect.

(4) The Secretary of State may by order amend an enactment in consequence of this section.

(5) An order under subsection (4) –

  (a) must be made by statutory instrument, and
  (b) shall be subject to annulment in pursuance of a resolution of either House of Parliament.

249 Special administration regimes

(1) Section 248 shall have no effect in relation to –

  (a) a company holding an appointment under Chapter I of Part II of the Water Industry Act 1991 (water and sewerage undertakers),
  (b) a protected railway company within the meaning of section 59 of the Railways Act 1993 (railway administration order) (including that section as it has effect by virtue of section 19 of the Channel Tunnel Rail Link Act 1996 (administration)),
  (c) a licence company within the meaning of section 26 of the Transport Act 2000 (air traffic services),
  (d) a public–private partnership company within the meaning of section 210 of the Greater London Authority Act 1999 (public–private partnership agreement), or

(e) a building society within the meaning of section 119 of the Building Societies Act 1986 (interpretation).

(2) A reference in an Act listed in subsection (1) to a provision of Part II of the Insolvency Act 1986 (or to a provision which has effect in relation to a provision of that Part of that Act) shall, in so far as it relates to a company or society listed in subsection (1), continue to have effect as if it referred to Part II as it had effect immediately before the coming into force of section 248.

(3) But the effect of subsection (2) in respect of a particular class of company or society may be modified by order of –

(a) the Treasury, in the case of building societies, or
(b) the Secretary of State, in any other case.

(4) An order under subsection (3) may make consequential amendment of an enactment.

(5) An order under subsection (3) –

(a) must be made by statutory instrument, and
(b) may not be made unless a draft has been laid before and approved by resolution of each House of Parliament.

(6) An amendment of the Insolvency Act 1986 made by this Act is without prejudice to any power conferred by Part VII of the Companies Act 1989 (financial markets) to modify the law of insolvency.

250 Prohibition of appointment of administrative receiver

(1) The following shall be inserted after Chapter III of Part III of the Insolvency Act 1986 (receivership: receivers' powers) –

'CHAPTER IV

PROHIBITION OF APPOINTMENT OF ADMINISTRATIVE RECEIVER

72A Floating charge holder not to appoint administrative receiver

(1) The holder of a qualifying floating charge in respect of a company's property may not appoint an administrative receiver of the company.

(2) In Scotland, the holder of a qualifying floating charge in respect of a company's property may not appoint or apply to the court for the appointment of a receiver who on appointment would be an administrative receiver of property of the company.(3) In subsections (1) and (2) –

'holder of a qualifying floating charge in respect of a company's property' has the same meaning as in paragraph 14 of Schedule B1 to this Act, and
'administrative receiver' has the meaning given by section 251.

(4) This section applies –

(a) to a floating charge created on or after a date appointed by the Secretary of State by order made by statutory instrument, and
(b) in spite of any provision of an agreement or instrument which purports to empower a person to appoint an administrative receiver (by whatever name).

(5) An order under subsection (4)(a) may –

(a) make provision which applies generally or only for a specified purpose;

(b) make different provision for different purposes;
(c) make transitional provision.

(6) This section is subject to the exceptions specified in sections 72B to 72G.

72B First exception: capital market

(1) Section 72A does not prevent the appointment of an administrative receiver in pursuance of an agreement which is or forms part of a capital market arrangement if –

(a) a party incurs or, when the agreement was entered into was expected to incur, a debt of at least £50 million under the arrangement, and

(b) the arrangement involves the issue of a capital market investment.

(2) In subsection (1) –

'capital market arrangement' means an arrangement of a kind described in paragraph 1 of Schedule 2A, and
'capital market investment' means an investment of a kind described in paragraph 2 or 3 of that Schedule.

72C Second exception: public–private partnership

(1) Section 72A does not prevent the appointment of an administrative receiver of a project company of a project which –

(a) is a public-private partnership project, and
(b) includes step-in rights.

(2) In this section 'public-private partnership project' means a project –

(a) the resources for which are provided partly by one or more public bodies and partly by one or more private persons, or
(b) which is designed wholly or mainly for the purpose of assisting a public body to discharge a function.

(3) In this section –

'step-in rights' has the meaning given by paragraph 6 of Schedule 2A, and
'project company' has the meaning given by paragraph 7 of that Schedule.

72D Third exception: utilities

(1) Section 72A does not prevent the appointment of an administrative receiver of a project company of a project which –

(a) is a utility project, and
(b) includes step-in rights.

(2) In this section –

(a) 'utility project' means a project designed wholly or mainly for the purpose of a regulated business,
(b) 'regulated business' means a business of a kind listed in paragraph 10 of Schedule 2A,

(c) 'step-in rights' has the meaning given by paragraph 6 of that Schedule, and
(d) 'project company' has the meaning given by paragraph 7 of that Schedule.

72E Fourth exception: project finance

(1) Section 72A does not prevent the appointment of an administrative receiver of a project company of a project which –

(a) is a financed project, and
(b) includes step-in rights.

(2) In this section –

(a) a project is 'financed' if under an agreement relating to the project a project company incurs, or when the agreement is entered into is expected to incur, a debt of at least £50 million for the purposes of carrying out the project,
(b) 'project company' has the meaning given by paragraph 7 of Schedule 2A, and
(c) 'step-in rights' has the meaning given by paragraph 6 of that Schedule.

72F Fifth exception: financial market

Section 72A does not prevent the appointment of an administrative receiver of a company by virtue of –

(a) a market charge within the meaning of section 173 of the Companies Act 1989 ,
(b) a system-charge within the meaning of the Financial Markets and Insolvency Regulations 1996,
(c) a collateral security charge within the meaning of the Financial Markets and Insolvency (Settlement Finality) Regulations 1999.

72G Sixth exception: registered social landlord

Section 72A does not prevent the appointment of an administrative receiver of a company which is registered as a social landlord under Part I of the Housing Act 1996 or under Part 3 of the Housing (Scotland) Act 2001.

72H Sections 72A to 72G: supplementary

(1) Schedule 2A (which supplements sections 72B to 72G) shall have effect.

(2) The Secretary of State may by order –

(a) insert into this Act provision creating an additional exception to section 72A(1) or (2);
(b) provide for a provision of this Act which creates an exception to section 72A(1) or (2) to cease to have effect;
(c) amend section 72A in consequence of provision made under paragraph (a) or (b);
(d) amend any of sections 72B to 72G;
(e) amend Schedule 2A.

(3) An order under subsection (2) must be made by statutory instrument.

(4) An order under subsection (2) may make –

(a) provision which applies generally or only for a specified purpose;
(b) different provision for different purposes;

(c) consequential or supplementary provision;

(d) transitional provision.

(5) An order under subsection (2) –

(a) in the case of an order under subsection (2)(e), shall be subject to annulment in pursuance of a resolution of either House of Parliament,

(b) in the case of an order under subsection (2)(d) varying the sum specified in section 72B(1)(a) or 72E(2)(a) (whether or not the order also makes consequential or transitional provision), shall be subject to annulment in pursuance of a resolution of either House of Parliament, and

(c) in the case of any other order under subsection (2)(a) to (d), may not be made unless a draft has been laid before and approved by resolution of each House of Parliament.'

(2) The Schedule 2A set out in Schedule 18 to this Act shall be inserted after Schedule 2 to the Insolvency Act 1986.

251 Abolition of Crown preference

(1) The following paragraphs of Schedule 6 to the Insolvency Act 1986 (categories of preferential debts) shall cease to have effect –

(a) paragraphs 1 and 2 (debts due to Inland Revenue),

(b) paragraphs 3 to 5C (debts due to Customs and Excise), and

(c) paragraphs 6 and 7 (social security contributions).

(2) The following paragraphs of Schedule 3 to the Bankruptcy (Scotland) Act 1985 (list of preferred debts) shall cease to have effect –

(a) paragraph 1 (debts due to Inland Revenue),

(b) paragraph 2 (debts due to Customs and Excise), and

(c) paragraph 3 (social security contributions).

(3) In section 386 of the Insolvency Act 1986 (categories of preferential debts) for the parenthetical words after 'Schedule 6 to this Act' there shall be substituted '(contributions to occupational pension schemes; remuneration, &c. of employees; levies on coal and steel production)'.

252 Unsecured creditors

The following shall be inserted after section 176 of the Insolvency Act 1986 (winding up: preferential debt) –

'Property subject to floating charge

176A Share of assets for unsecured creditors

(1) This section applies where a floating charge relates to property of a company –

(a) which has gone into liquidation,

(b) which is in administration,

(c) of which there is a provisional liquidator, or

(d) of which there is a receiver.

(2) The liquidator, administrator or receiver –

(a) shall make a prescribed part of the company's net property available for the satisfaction of unsecured debts, and

(b) shall not distribute that part to the proprietor of a floating charge except in so far as it exceeds the amount required for the satisfaction of unsecured debts.

(3) Subsection (2) shall not apply to a company if –

(a) the company's net property is less than the prescribed minimum, and
(b) the liquidator, administrator or receiver thinks that the cost of making a distribution to unsecured creditors would be disproportionate to the benefits.

(4) Subsection (2) shall also not apply to a company if or in so far as it is disapplied by –

(a) a voluntary arrangement in respect of the company, or
(b) a compromise or arrangement agreed under section 425 of the Companies Act (compromise with creditors and members).

(5) Subsection (2) shall also not apply to a company if –

(a) the liquidator, administrator or receiver applies to the court for an order under this subsection on the ground that the cost of making a distribution to unsecured creditors would be disproportionate to the benefits, and
(b) the court orders that subsection (2) shall not apply.

(6) In subsections (2) and (3) a company's net property is the amount of its property which would, but for this section, be available for satisfaction of claims of holders of debentures secured by, or holders of, any floating charge created by the company.

(7) An order under subsection (2) prescribing part of a company's net property may, in particular, provide for its calculation –

(a) as a percentage of the company's net property, or
(b) as an aggregate of different percentages of different parts of the company's net property.

(8) An order under this section –

(a) must be made by statutory instrument, and
(b) shall be subject to annulment pursuant to a resolution of either House of Parliament.

(9) In this section –

'floating charge' means a charge which is a floating charge on its creation and which is created after the first order under subsection (2)(a) comes into force, and 'prescribed' means prescribed by order by the Secretary of State.

(10) An order under this section may include transitional or incidental provision.'

253 Liquidator's powers

The following shall be inserted in Part I of Schedule 4 to the Insolvency Act 1986 (liquidator's powers in winding up: powers exercisable only with sanction) after paragraph 3 –

'3A

Power to bring legal proceedings under section 213, 214, 238, 239, 242, 243 or 423.'

254 Application of insolvency law to foreign company

(1) The Secretary of State may by order provide for a provision of the Insolvency Act 1986 to apply (with or without modification) in relation to a company incorporated outside Great Britain.

(2) An order under this section –

(a) may make provision generally or for a specified purpose only,
(b) may make different provision for different purposes, and
(c) may make transitional, consequential or incidental provision.

(3) An order under this section –

(a) must be made by statutory instrument, and
(b) shall be subject to annulment in pursuance of a resolution of either House of Parliament.

255 Application of law about company arrangement or administration to non-company

(1) The Treasury may with the concurrence of the Secretary of State by order provide for a company arrangement or administration provision to apply (with or without modification) in relation to –

(a) a society registered under the Industrial and Provident Societies Act 1965 ,
(b) a society registered under section 7(1)(b), (c), (d), (e) or (f) of the Friendly Societies Act 1974 ,
(c) a friendly society within the meaning of the Friendly Societies Act 1992 , or
(d) an unregistered friendly society.

(2) In subsection (1) 'company arrangement or administration provision' means –

(a) a provision of Part I of the Insolvency Act 1986 (company voluntary arrangements),
(b) a provision of Part II of that Act (administration), and
(c) section 425 of the Companies Act 1985 (compromise or arrangement with creditors).

(3) An order under this section may not provide for a company arrangement or administration provision to apply in relation to a society which is registered as a social landlord under Part I of the Housing Act 1996 or under Part 3 of the Housing (Scotland) Act 2001.

(4) An order under this section –

(a) may make provision generally or for a specified purpose only,
(b) may make different provision for different purposes, and
(c) may make transitional, consequential or incidental provision.

(5) Provision by virtue of subsection (4)(c) may, in particular –

(a) apply an enactment (with or without modification);
(b) amend an enactment.

(6) An order under this section –

(a) must be made by statutory instrument, and
(b) shall be subject to annulment in pursuance of a resolution of either House of Parliament.

Individuals

256 Duration of bankruptcy

(1) The following shall be substituted for section 279 of the Insolvency Act 1986 (duration of bankruptcy) –

'279 Duration

(1) A bankrupt is discharged from bankruptcy at the end of the period of one year beginning with the date on which the bankruptcy commences.

(2) If before the end of that period the official receiver files with the court a notice stating that investigation of the conduct and affairs of the bankrupt under section 289 is unnecessary or concluded, the bankrupt is discharged when the notice is filed.

(3) On the application of the official receiver or the trustee of a bankrupt's estate, the court may order that the period specified in subsection (1) shall cease to run until –

   (a) the end of a specified period, or
   (b) the fulfilment of a specified condition.

(4) The court may make an order under subsection (3) only if satisfied that the bankrupt has failed or is failing to comply with an obligation under this Part.

(5) In subsection (3)(b) 'condition' includes a condition requiring that the court be satisfied of something.

(6) In the case of an individual who is adjudged bankrupt on a petition under section 264(1)(d) –

   (a) subsections (1) to (5) shall not apply, and
   (b) the bankrupt is discharged from bankruptcy by an order of the court under section 280.

(7) This section is without prejudice to any power of the court to annul a bankruptcy order.'

(2) Schedule 19 (which makes transitional provision in relation to this section) –

  (a) shall have effect, and
  (b) is without prejudice to the generality of section 276.

257 Post-discharge restrictions

(1) The following shall be inserted after section 281 of the Insolvency Act 1986 (bankruptcy: effect of discharge) –

'281A Post-discharge restrictions

Schedule 4A to this Act (bankruptcy restrictions order and bankruptcy restrictions undertaking) shall have effect.'

(2) The Schedule 4A set out in Schedule 20 to this Act shall be inserted after Schedule 4 to the Insolvency Act 1986.

(3) The amendments set out in Schedule 21 (which specify the effect of a bankruptcy restrictions order or undertaking) shall have effect.

258 Investigation by official receiver

The following shall be substituted for section 289 of the Insolvency Act 1986 (official receiver's duty to investigate) –

'289 Investigatory duties of official receiver

(1) The official receiver shall –

(a) investigate the conduct and affairs of each bankrupt (including his conduct and affairs before the making of the bankruptcy order), and
(b) make such report (if any) to the court as the official receiver thinks fit.

(2) Subsection (1) shall not apply to a case in which the official receiver thinks an investigation under that subsection unnecessary.

(3) Where a bankrupt makes an application for discharge under section 280 –

(a) the official receiver shall make a report to the court about such matters as may be prescribed, and
(b) the court shall consider the report before determining the application.

(4) A report by the official receiver under this section shall in any proceedings be prima facie evidence of the facts stated in it.'

259 Income payments order

(1) Section 310 of the Insolvency Act 1986 (income payments order) shall be amended as follows.

(2) In subsection (1) omit ', on the application of the trustee,'.

(3) After subsection (1) insert –

'(1A) An income payments order may be made only on an application instituted –

(a) by the trustee, and
(b) before the discharge of the bankrupt.'

(4) For subsection (6) substitute –

'(6) An income payments order must specify the period during which it is to have effect; and that period –

(a) may end after the discharge of the bankrupt, but
(b) may not end after the period of three years beginning with the date on which the order is made.

(6A) An income payments order may (subject to subsection (6)(b)) be varied on the application of the trustee or the bankrupt (whether before or after discharge).'

260 Income payments agreement

The following shall be inserted after section 310 of the Insolvency Act 1986 (income payments order) –

'310A Income payments agreement

(1) In this section 'income payments agreement' means a written agreement between a bankrupt and his trustee or between a bankrupt and the official receiver which provides –

(a) that the bankrupt is to pay to the trustee or the official receiver an amount equal to a specified part or proportion of the bankrupt's income for a specified period, or

(b) that a third person is to pay to the trustee or the official receiver a specified proportion of money due to the bankrupt by way of income for a specified period.

(2) A provision of an income payments agreement of a kind specified in subsection (1)(a) or (b) may be enforced as if it were a provision of an income payments order.

(3) While an income payments agreement is in force the court may, on the application of the bankrupt, his trustee or the official receiver, discharge or vary an attachment of earnings order that is for the time being in force to secure payments by the bankrupt.

(4) The following provisions of section 310 shall apply to an income payments agreement as they apply to an income payments order –

(a) subsection (5) (receipts to form part of estate), and
(b) subsections (7) to (9) (meaning of income).

(5) An income payments agreement must specify the period during which it is to have effect; and that period –

(a) may end after the discharge of the bankrupt, but
(b) may not end after the period of three years beginning with the date on which the agreement is made.

(6) An income payments agreement may (subject to subsection (5)(b)) be varied –

(a) by written agreement between the parties, or
(b) by the court on an application made by the bankrupt, the trustee or the official receiver.

(7) The court –

(a) may not vary an income payments agreement so as to include provision of a kind which could not be included in an income payments order, and
(b) shall grant an application to vary an income payments agreement if and to the extent that the court thinks variation necessary to avoid the effect mentioned in section 310(2).'

261 Bankrupt's home

(1) The following shall be inserted after section 283 of the Insolvency Act 1986 (definition of bankrupt's estate) –

'283A Bankrupt's home ceasing to form part of estate

(1) This section applies where property comprised in the bankrupt's estate consists of an interest in a dwelling-house which at the date of the bankruptcy was the sole or principal residence of –

(a) the bankrupt,
(b) the bankrupt's spouse, or
(c) a former spouse of the bankrupt.

(2) At the end of the period of three years beginning with the date of the bankruptcy the interest mentioned in subsection (1) shall –

(a) cease to be comprised in the bankrupt's estate, and

(b) vest in the bankrupt (without conveyance, assignment or transfer).

(3) Subsection (2) shall not apply if during the period mentioned in that subsection –

(a) the trustee realises the interest mentioned in subsection (1),

(b) the trustee applies for an order for sale in respect of the dwelling-house,

(c) the trustee applies for an order for possession of the dwelling-house,

(d) the trustee applies for an order under section 313 in Chapter IV in respect of that interest, or

(e) the trustee and the bankrupt agree that the bankrupt shall incur a specified liability to his estate (with or without the addition of interest from the date of the agreement) in consideration of which the interest mentioned in subsection (1) shall cease to form part of the estate.

(4) Where an application of a kind described in subsection (3)(b) to (d) is made during the period mentioned in subsection (2) and is dismissed, unless the court orders otherwise the interest to which the application relates shall on the dismissal of the application –

(a) cease to be comprised in the bankrupt's estate, and

(b) vest in the bankrupt (without conveyance, assignment or transfer).

(5) If the bankrupt does not inform the trustee or the official receiver of his interest in a property before the end of the period of three months beginning with the date of the bankruptcy, the period of three years mentioned in subsection (2) –

(a) shall not begin with the date of the bankruptcy, but

(b) shall begin with the date on which the trustee or official receiver becomes aware of the bankrupt's interest.

(6) The court may substitute for the period of three years mentioned in subsection (2) a longer period –

(a) in prescribed circumstances, and

(b) in such other circumstances as the court thinks appropriate.

(7) The rules may make provision for this section to have effect with the substitution of a shorter period for the period of three years mentioned in subsection (2) in specified circumstances (which may be described by reference to action to be taken by a trustee in bankruptcy).

(8) The rules may also, in particular, make provision –

(a) requiring or enabling the trustee of a bankrupt's estate to give notice that this section applies or does not apply;

(b) about the effect of a notice under paragraph (a);

(c) requiring the trustee of a bankrupt's estate to make an application to the Chief Land Registrar.

(9) Rules under subsection (8)(b) may, in particular –

(a) disapply this section;

(b) enable a court to disapply this section;

(c) make provision in consequence of a disapplication of this section;

(d) enable a court to make provision in consequence of a disapplication of this section;

(e) make provision (which may include provision conferring jurisdiction on a court or tribunal) about compensation.'

(2) Section 313 of the Insolvency Act 1986 (charge on bankrupt's home) shall be amended as follows –

    (a) in subsection (2) for ', up to the value from time to time of the property secured,' substitute ', up to the charged value from time to time,',

    (b) after subsection (2) insert –

'(2A) In subsection (2) the charged value means –

      (a) the amount specified in the charging order as the value of the bankrupt's interest in the property at the date of the order, plus

      (b) interest on that amount from the date of the charging order at the prescribed rate.

(2B) In determining the value of an interest for the purposes of this section the court shall disregard any matter which it is required to disregard by the rules.', and

      (c) at the end insert –

'(5) But an order under section 3(5) of that Act may not vary a charged value.'

(3) The following shall be inserted after section 313 of that Act –

'313A Low value home: application for sale, possession or charge

    (1) This section applies where –

      (a) property comprised in the bankrupt's estate consists of an interest in a dwelling-house which at the date of the bankruptcy was the sole or principal residence of –
        (i) the bankrupt,
        (ii) the bankrupt's spouse, or
        (iii) a former spouse of the bankrupt, and

      (b) the trustee applies for an order for the sale of the property, for an order for possession of the property or for an order under section 313 in respect of the property.

(2) The court shall dismiss the application if the value of the interest is below the amount prescribed for the purposes of this subsection.

(3) In determining the value of an interest for the purposes of this section the court shall disregard any matter which it is required to disregard by the order which prescribes the amount for the purposes of subsection (2).'

(4) The following shall be inserted after section 307(2)(a) of the Insolvency Act 1986 (after-acquired property: exclusions) –

'(aa)any property vesting in the bankrupt by virtue of section 283A in Chapter II,'.

(5) In section 384(2) of that Act (prescribed amounts) after 'section 273;' insert –

'section 313A;'.

(6) In section 418(1) of that Act (monetary limits in bankruptcy) after the entry for section 273 insert –

'section 313A (value of property below which application for sale, possession or charge to be dismissed);'.

(7) In subsection (8) –

    (a) 'pre-commencement bankrupt' means an individual who is adjudged bankrupt on a petition presented before subsection (1) above comes into force, and

(b) 'the transitional period' is the period of three years beginning with the date on which subsection (1) above comes into force.

(8) If a pre-commencement bankrupt's estate includes an interest in a dwelling-house which at the date of the bankruptcy was the sole or principal residence of him, his spouse or a former spouse of his, at the end of the transitional period that interest shall –

(a) cease to be comprised in the estate, and
(b) vest in the bankrupt (without conveyance, assignment or transfer).

(9) But subsection (8) shall not apply if before or during the transitional period –

(a) any of the events mentioned in section 283A(3) of the Insolvency Act 1986 (inserted by subsection (1) above) occurs in relation to the interest or the dwelling-house, or
(b) the trustee obtains any order of a court, or makes any agreement with the bankrupt, in respect of the interest or the dwelling-house.

(10) Subsections 283A(4) to (9) of that Act shall have effect, with any necessary modifications, in relation to the provision made by subsections (7) to (9) above; in particular –

(a) a reference to the period mentioned in section 283A(2) shall be construed as a reference to the transitional period,
(b) in the application of section 283A(5) a reference to the date of the bankruptcy shall be construed as a reference to the date on which subsection (1) above comes into force, and
(c) a reference to the rules is a reference to rules made under section 412 of the Insolvency Act 1986 (for which purpose this section shall be treated as forming part of Parts VIII to XI of that Act).

262 Powers of trustee in bankruptcy

The following shall be inserted in Part I of Schedule 5 to the Insolvency Act 1986 (powers of trustee in bankruptcy: powers exercisable only with sanction) after paragraph 2 –

'2A

Power to bring legal proceedings under section 339, 340 or 423.'

263 Repeal of certain bankruptcy offences

The following sections of the Insolvency Act 1986 shall cease to have effect –

(a) section 361 (offence of failure to keep proper accounting records), and
(b) section 362 (offence of gambling and speculation).

264 Individual voluntary arrangement

(1) Schedule 22 (which makes provision about individual voluntary arrangements) shall have effect.

(2) The Secretary of State may by order amend the Insolvency Act 1986 so as to extend the provisions of sections 263B to 263G (which are inserted by Schedule 22 and provide a fast-track procedure for making an individual voluntary arrangement) to some or all cases other than those specified in section 263A as inserted by Schedule 22.

(3) An order under subsection (2) –

(a) must be made by statutory instrument, and

(b) may not be made unless a draft has been laid before and approved by each House of Parliament.

(4) An order under subsection (2) may make –

(a) consequential provision (which may include provision amending the Insolvency Act 1986 or another enactment);

(b) transitional provision.

265 Disqualification from office: justice of the peace

Section 65 of the Justices of the Peace Act 1997 (disqualification of bankrupt from appointment as justice of the peace) shall cease to have effect.

266 Disqualification from office: Parliament

(1) The following shall be inserted before section 427 of the Insolvency Act 1986 (the title to which becomes 'Disqualification from Parliament (Scotland and Northern Ireland)') –

'426A Disqualification from Parliament (England and Wales)

(1) A person in respect of whom a bankruptcy restrictions order has effect shall be disqualified –

(a) from membership of the House of Commons,

(b) from sitting or voting in the House of Lords, and

(c) from sitting or voting in a committee of the House of Lords or a joint committee of both Houses.

(2) If a member of the House of Commons becomes disqualified under this section, his seat shall be vacated.

(3) If a person who is disqualified under this section is returned as a member of the House of Commons, his return shall be void.

(4) No writ of summons shall be issued to a member of the House of Lords who is disqualified under this section.

(5) If a court makes a bankruptcy restrictions order or interim order in respect of a member of the House of Commons or the House of Lords the court shall notify the Speaker of that House.

(6) If the Secretary of State accepts a bankruptcy restrictions undertaking made by a member of the House of Commons or the House of Lords, the Secretary of State shall notify the Speaker of that House.

426B Devolution

(1) If a court makes a bankruptcy restrictions order or interim order in respect of a member of the Scottish Parliament, the Northern Ireland Assembly or the National Assembly for Wales, the court shall notify the presiding officer of that body.

(2) If the Secretary of State accepts a bankruptcy restrictions undertaking made by a member of the Scottish Parliament, the Northern Ireland Assembly or the National Assembly for Wales, the Secretary of State shall notify the presiding officer of that body.

426C Irrelevance of privilege

(1) An enactment about insolvency applies in relation to a member of the House of Commons or the House of Lords irrespective of any Parliamentary privilege.

(2) In this section 'enactment' includes a provision made by or under –

    (a) an Act of the Scottish Parliament, or
    (b) Northern Ireland legislation.'

(2) In section 427 of the Insolvency Act 1986 the following shall cease to have effect –

    (a) in subsection (1), the words 'England and Wales or', and
    (b) subsection (7).

(3) The Secretary of State may by order –

    (a) provide for section 426A or 426B of that Act (as inserted by subsection (1) above) to have effect in relation to orders made or undertakings accepted in Scotland or Northern Ireland under a system which appears to the Secretary of State to be equivalent to the system operating under Schedule 4A to that Act (as inserted by section 257 of this Act);
    (b) make consequential amendment of section 426A or 426B of that Act (as inserted by subsection (1) above);
    (c) make other consequential amendment of an enactment.

(4) An order under this section may make transitional, consequential or incidental provision.

(5) An order under this section –

    (a) must be made by statutory instrument, and
    (b) may not be made unless a draft has been laid before and approved by resolution of each House of Parliament.

267 Disqualification from office: local government

(1) The following shall be substituted for section 80(1)(b) of the Local Government Act 1972 (disqualification for membership of local authority: bankrupt) –

    '(b) is the subject of a bankruptcy restrictions order or interim order;'.

(2) Section 81(1) and (2) of that Act (which amplify the provision substituted by subsection (1) above) shall cease to have effect.

268 Disqualification from office: general

(1) The Secretary of State may make an order under this section in relation to a disqualification provision.

(2) A 'disqualification provision' is a provision which disqualifies (whether permanently or temporarily and whether absolutely or conditionally) a bankrupt or a class of bankrupts from –

    (a) being elected or appointed to an office or position,
    (b) holding an office or position, or
    (c) becoming or remaining a member of a body or group.

(3) In subsection (2) the reference to a provision which disqualifies a person conditionally includes a reference to a provision which enables him to be dismissed.

(4) An order under subsection (1) may repeal or revoke the disqualification provision.

(5) An order under subsection (1) may amend, or modify the effect of, the disqualification provision –

  (a) so as to reduce the class of bankrupts to whom the disqualification provision applies;
  (b) so as to extend the disqualification provision to some or all individuals who are subject to a bankruptcy restrictions regime;
  (c) so that the disqualification provision applies only to some or all individuals who are subject to a bankruptcy restrictions regime;
  (d) so as to make the application of the disqualification provision wholly or partly subject to the discretion of a specified person, body or group.

(6) An order by virtue of subsection (5)(d) may provide for a discretion to be subject to –

  (a) the approval of a specified person or body;
  (b) appeal to a specified person or body.

(7) An order by virtue of subsection (5)(d) made with the concurrence of the Lord Chancellor may provide for a discretion to be subject to appeal to a specified court or tribunal.

(8) The Secretary of State may specify himself for the purposes of subsection (5)(d) or (6)(a) or (b).

(9) In this section 'bankrupt' means an individual –

  (a) who has been adjudged bankrupt by a court in England and Wales or in Northern Ireland,
  (b) whose estate has been sequestrated by a court in Scotland, or
  (c) who has made an agreement with creditors of his for a composition of debts, for a scheme of arrangement of affairs, for the grant of a trust deed or for some other kind of settlement or arrangement.

(10) In this section 'bankruptcy restrictions regime' means an order or undertaking –

  (a) under Schedule 4A to the Insolvency Act 1986 (bankruptcy restrictions orders), or
  (b) under any system operating in Scotland or Northern Ireland which appears to the Secretary of State to be equivalent to the system operating under that Schedule.

(11) In this section –

'body' includes Parliament and any other legislative body, and
'provision' means –

  (a) a provision made by an Act of Parliament passed before or in the same Session as this Act, and
  (b) a provision made, before or in the same Session as this Act, under an Act of Parliament.

(12) An order under this section –

  (a) may make provision generally or for a specified purpose only,
  (b) may make different provision for different purposes, and
  (c) may make transitional, consequential or incidental provision.

(13) An order under this section –

  (a) must be made by statutory instrument, and
  (b) may not be made unless a draft has been laid before and approved by resolution of each House of Parliament.

(14) A reference in this section to the Secretary of State shall be treated as a reference to the National Assembly for Wales in so far as it relates to a disqualification provision which –

    (a) is made by the National Assembly for Wales, or
    (b) relates to a function of the National Assembly.

(15) Provision made by virtue of subsection (7) is subject to any order of the Lord Chancellor under section 56(1) of the Access to Justice Act 1999 (appeals: jurisdiction).

269 Minor and consequential amendments

Schedule 23 (minor and consequential amendments relating to individual insolvency) shall have effect.
Money

270 Fees

(1) The following shall be inserted after section 415 of the Insolvency Act 1986 (fees orders: individual insolvency) –

'415A Fees orders (general)

(1) The Secretary of State –

    (a) may by order require a body to pay a fee in connection with the grant or maintenance of recognition of the body under section 391, and
    (b) may refuse recognition, or revoke an order of recognition under section 391(1) by a further order, where a fee is not paid.

(2) The Secretary of State –

    (a) may by order require a person to pay a fee in connection with the grant or maintenance of authorisation of the person under section 393, and
    (b) may disregard an application or withdraw an authorisation where a fee is not paid.

(3) The Secretary of State may by order require the payment of fees in respect of –

    (a) the operation of the Insolvency Services Account;
    (b) payments into and out of that Account.

(4) The following provisions of section 414 apply to fees under this section as they apply to fees under that section –

    (a) subsection (3) (manner of payment),
    (b) subsection (5) (additional provision),
    (c) subsection (6) (statutory instrument),
    (d) subsection (7) (payment into Consolidated Fund), and
    (e) subsection (9) (saving for rules of court).'

(2) An order made by virtue of subsection (1) may relate to the maintenance of recognition or authorisation granted before this section comes into force.

(3) At the end of section 392 of the Insolvency Act 1986 (authorisation of insolvency practitioner) there shall be added –

'(9) Subsection (3)(c) shall not have effect in respect of an application made to the Secretary of State (but this subsection is without prejudice to section 415A).'

(4) In section 440(2)(c) of that Act (provisions not extending to Scotland) after '415,' there shall be inserted '415A(3),'.

271 Insolvency Services Account: interest

(1) The following shall be inserted after paragraph 16 of Schedule 8 to the Insolvency Act 1986 (company insolvency rules: money) –

'16A

Provision enabling the Secretary of State to set the rate of interest paid on sums which have been paid into the Insolvency Services Account.'

(2) The following shall be inserted after paragraph 21 of Schedule 9 to the Insolvency Act 1986 (individual insolvency rules: money) –

'21A

Provision enabling the Secretary of State to set the rate of interest paid on sums which have been paid into the Insolvency Services Account.'

272 Insolvency Services Accounts

(1) Section 405 of the Insolvency Act 1986 (operation of Investment Account) shall cease to have effect.

(2) The following shall be substituted for section 408 of that Act (recourse to Consolidated Fund) –

'**408 Adjustment of balances**

(1) The Treasury may direct the payment out of the Consolidated Fund of sums into –

   (a) the Insolvency Services Account;
   (b) the Investment Account.

(2) The Treasury shall certify to the House of Commons the reason for any payment under subsection (1).

(3) The Secretary of State may pay sums out of the Insolvency Services Account into the Consolidated Fund.

(4) The National Debt Commissioners may pay sums out of the Investment Account into the Consolidated Fund.'

...

SCHEDULE 16

Section 248

SCHEDULE B1 TO INSOLVENCY ACT 1986

'SCHEDULE B1
ADMINISTRATION

Arrangement of Schedule

Nature of Administration

Administration

1 (1) For the purposes of this Act 'administrator' of a company means a person appointed under this Schedule to manage the company's affairs, business and property.

(2) For the purposes of this Act –

- (a) a company is 'in administration' while the appointment of an administrator of the company has effect,
- (b) a company 'enters administration' when the appointment of an administrator takes effect,
- (c) a company ceases to be in administration when the appointment of an administrator of the company ceases to have effect in accordance with this Schedule, and
- (d) a company does not cease to be in administration merely because an administrator vacates office (by reason of resignation, death or otherwise) or is removed from office.

2 A person may be appointed as administrator of a company –

- (a) by administration order of the court under paragraph 10,
- (b) by the holder of a floating charge under paragraph 14, or
- (c) by the company or its directors under paragraph 22.

Purpose of administration

3 (1) The administrator of a company must perform his functions with the objective of –

- (a) rescuing the company as a going concern, or
- (b) achieving a better result for the company's creditors as a whole than would be likely if the company were wound up (without first being in administration), or

(c) realising property in order to make a distribution to one or more secured or preferential creditors.

(2) Subject to sub-paragraph (4), the administrator of a company must perform his functions in the interests of the company's creditors as a whole.

(3) The administrator must perform his functions with the objective specified in sub-paragraph (1)(a) unless he thinks either –

(a) that it is not reasonably practicable to achieve that objective, or
(b) that the objective specified in sub-paragraph (1)(b) would achieve a better result for the company's creditors as a whole.

(4) The administrator may perform his functions with the objective specified in sub-paragraph (1)(c) only if –

(a) he thinks that it is not reasonably practicable to achieve either of the objectives specified in sub-paragraph (1)(a) and (b), and
(b) he does not unnecessarily harm the interests of the creditors of the company as a whole.

4 The administrator of a company must perform his functions as quickly and efficiently as is reasonably practicable.

Status of administrator

5 An administrator is an officer of the court (whether or not he is appointed by the court).

General restrictions

6 A person may be appointed as administrator of a company only if he is qualified to act as an insolvency practitioner in relation to the company.

7 A person may not be appointed as administrator of a company which is in administration (subject to the provisions of paragraphs 90 to 97 and 100 to 103 about replacement and additional administrators).

8 (1) A person may not be appointed as administrator of a company which is in liquidation by virtue of –

(a) a resolution for voluntary winding up, or
(b) a winding-up order.

(2) Sub-paragraph (1)(a) is subject to paragraph 38.

(3) Sub-paragraph (1)(b) is subject to paragraphs 37 and 38.

9 (1) A person may not be appointed as administrator of a company which –

(a) has a liability in respect of a deposit which it accepted in accordance with the Banking Act 1979 or 1987, but
(b) is not an authorised deposit taker.

(2) A person may not be appointed as administrator of a company which effects or carries out contracts of insurance.

(3) But sub-paragraph (2) does not apply to a company which –

(a) is exempt from the general prohibition in relation to effecting or carrying out contracts of insurance, or

(b) is an authorised deposit taker effecting or carrying out contracts of insurance in the course of a banking business.

(4) In this paragraph –

'authorised deposit taker' means a person with permission under Part IV of the Financial Services and Markets Act 2000 to accept deposits, and
'the general prohibition' has the meaning given by section 19 of that Act.

(5) This paragraph shall be construed in accordance with –

(a) section 22 of the Financial Services and Markets Act 2000 (classes of regulated activity and categories of investment),
(b) any relevant order under that section, and
(c) Schedule 2 to that Act (regulated activities).

Appointment Of Administrator By Court

Administration order

10 An administration order is an order appointing a person as the administrator of a company.

Conditions for making order

11 The court may make an administration order in relation to a company only if satisfied –

(a) that the company is or is likely to become unable to pay its debts, and
(b) that the administration order is reasonably likely to achieve the purpose of administration.

Administration application

12 (1) An application to the court for an administration order in respect of a company (an 'administration application') may be made only by –

(a) the company,
(b) the directors of the company,
(c) one or more creditors of the company,
(d) the justices' chief executive for a magistrates' court in the exercise of the power conferred by section 87A of the Magistrates' Courts Act 1980 (fine imposed on company), or
(e) a combination of persons listed in paragraphs (a) to (d).

(2) As soon as is reasonably practicable after the making of an administration application the applicant shall notify –

(a) any person who has appointed an administrative receiver of the company,
(b) any person who is or may be entitled to appoint an administrative receiver of the company,
(c) any person who is or may be entitled to appoint an administrator of the company under paragraph 14, and
(d) such other persons as may be prescribed.

(3) An administration application may not be withdrawn without the permission of the court.

(4) In sub-paragraph (1) 'creditor' includes a contingent creditor and a prospective creditor.

Powers of court

13 (1) On hearing an administration application the court may –

   (a) make the administration order sought;
   (b) dismiss the application;
   (c) adjourn the hearing conditionally or unconditionally;
   (d) make an interim order;
   (e) treat the application as a winding-up petition and make any order which the court could make under section 125;
   (f) make any other order which the court thinks appropriate.

(2) An appointment of an administrator by administration order takes effect –

   (a) at a time appointed by the order, or
   (b) where no time is appointed by the order, when the order is made.

(3) An interim order under sub-paragraph (1)(d) may, in particular –

   (a) restrict the exercise of a power of the directors or the company;
   (b) make provision conferring a discretion on the court or on a person qualified to act as an insolvency practitioner in relation to the company.

(4) This paragraph is subject to paragraph 39.

Appointment of Administrator by Holder of Floating Charge

Power to appoint

14 (1) The holder of a qualifying floating charge in respect of a company's property may appoint an administrator of the company.

(2) For the purposes of sub-paragraph (1) a floating charge qualifies if created by an instrument which –

   (a) states that this paragraph applies to the floating charge,
   (b) purports to empower the holder of the floating charge to appoint an administrator of the company,
   (c) purports to empower the holder of the floating charge to make an appointment which would be the appointment of an administrative receiver within the meaning given by section 29(2), or
   (d) purports to empower the holder of a floating charge in Scotland to appoint a receiver who on appointment would be an administrative receiver.

(3) For the purposes of sub-paragraph (1) a person is the holder of a qualifying floating charge in respect of a company's property if he holds one or more debentures of the company secured –

   (a) by a qualifying floating charge which relates to the whole or substantially the whole of the company's property,
   (b) by a number of qualifying floating charges which together relate to the whole or substantially the whole of the company's property, or
   (c) by charges and other forms of security which together relate to the whole or substantially the whole of the company's property and at least one of which is a qualifying floating charge.

Restrictions on power to appoint

15 (1) A person may not appoint an administrator under paragraph 14 unless –

(a) he has given at least two business days' written notice to the holder of any prior floating charge which satisfies paragraph 14(2), or

(b) the holder of any prior floating charge which satisfies paragraph 14(2) has consented in writing to the making of the appointment.

(2) One floating charge is prior to another for the purposes of this paragraph if –

(a) it was created first, or

(b) it is to be treated as having priority in accordance with an agreement to which the holder of each floating charge was party.

(3) Sub-paragraph (2) shall have effect in relation to Scotland as if the following were substituted for paragraph (a) –

'(a) it has priority of ranking in accordance with section 464(4)(b) of the Companies Act 1985,'.

16 An administrator may not be appointed under paragraph 14 while a floating charge on which the appointment relies is not enforceable.

17 An administrator of a company may not be appointed under paragraph 14 if –

(a) a provisional liquidator of the company has been appointed under section 135, or

(b) an administrative receiver of the company is in office.

Notice of appointment

18 (1) A person who appoints an administrator of a company under paragraph 14 shall file with the court –

(a) a notice of appointment, and

(b) such other documents as may be prescribed.

(2) The notice of appointment must include a statutory declaration by or on behalf of the person who makes the appointment –

(a) that the person is the holder of a qualifying floating charge in respect of the company's property,

(b) that each floating charge relied on in making the appointment is (or was) enforceable on the date of the appointment, and

(c) that the appointment is in accordance with this Schedule.

(3) The notice of appointment must identify the administrator and must be accompanied by a statement by the administrator –

(a) that he consents to the appointment,

(b) that in his opinion the purpose of administration is reasonably likely to be achieved, and

(c) giving such other information and opinions as may be prescribed.

(4) For the purpose of a statement under sub-paragraph (3) an administrator may rely on information supplied by directors of the company (unless he has reason to doubt its accuracy).

(5) The notice of appointment and any document accompanying it must be in the prescribed form.

(6) A statutory declaration under sub-paragraph (2) must be made during the prescribed period.

(7) A person commits an offence if in a statutory declaration under sub-paragraph (2) he makes a statement –

  (a) which is false, and
  (b) which he does not reasonably believe to be true.

Commencement of appointment

19 The appointment of an administrator under paragraph 14 takes effect when the requirements of paragraph 18 are satisfied.

20 A person who appoints an administrator under paragraph 14 –

  (a) shall notify the administrator and such other persons as may be prescribed as soon as is reasonably practicable after the requirements of paragraph 18 are satisfied, and
  (b) commits an offence if he fails without reasonable excuse to comply with paragraph (a).

Invalid appointment: indemnity

21 (1) This paragraph applies where –

  (a) a person purports to appoint an administrator under paragraph 14, and
  (b) the appointment is discovered to be invalid.

(2) The court may order the person who purported to make the appointment to indemnify the person appointed against liability which arises solely by reason of the appointment's invalidity.

Appointment of Administrator by Company or Directors

Power to appoint

22 (1) A company may appoint an administrator.

(2) The directors of a company may appoint an administrator.

Restrictions on power to appoint

23 (1) This paragraph applies where an administrator of a company is appointed –

  (a) under paragraph 22, or
  (b) on an administration application made by the company or its directors.

(2) An administrator of the company may not be appointed under paragraph 22 during the period of 12 months beginning with the date on which the appointment referred to in sub-paragraph (1) ceases to have effect.

24 (1) If a moratorium for a company under Schedule A1 ends on a date when no voluntary arrangement is in force in respect of the company, this paragraph applies for the period of 12 months beginning with that date.

(2) This paragraph also applies for the period of 12 months beginning with the date on which a voluntary arrangement in respect of a company ends if –

  (a) the arrangement was made during a moratorium for the company under Schedule A1, and

(b) the arrangement ends prematurely (within the meaning of section 7B).

(3) While this paragraph applies, an administrator of the company may not be appointed under paragraph 22.

25 An administrator of a company may not be appointed under paragraph 22 if –

(a) a petition for the winding up of the company has been presented and is not yet disposed of,
(b) an administration application has been made and is not yet disposed of, or
(c) an administrative receiver of the company is in office.

Notice of intention to appoint

26 (1) A person who proposes to make an appointment under paragraph 22 shall give at least five business days' written notice to –

(a) any person who is or may be entitled to appoint an administrative receiver of the company, and
(b) any person who is or may be entitled to appoint an administrator of the company under paragraph 14.

(2) A person who proposes to make an appointment under paragraph 22 shall also give such notice as may be prescribed to such other persons as may be prescribed.

(3) A notice under this paragraph must –

(a) identify the proposed administrator, and
(b) be in the prescribed form.

27 (1) A person who gives notice of intention to appoint under paragraph 26 shall file with the court as soon as is reasonably practicable a copy of –

(a) the notice, and
(b) any document accompanying it.

(2) The copy filed under sub-paragraph (1) must be accompanied by a statutory declaration made by or on behalf of the person who proposes to make the appointment –

(a) that the company is or is likely to become unable to pay its debts,
(b) that the company is not in liquidation, and
(c) that, so far as the person making the statement is able to ascertain, the appointment is not prevented by paragraphs 23 to 25, and
(d) to such additional effect, and giving such information, as may be prescribed.

(3) A statutory declaration under sub-paragraph (2) must –

(a) be in the prescribed form, and
(b) be made during the prescribed period.

(4) A person commits an offence if in a statutory declaration under sub-paragraph (2) he makes a statement –

(a) which is false, and
(b) which he does not reasonably believe to be true.

28 (1) An appointment may not be made under paragraph 22 unless the person who makes the appointment has complied with any requirement of paragraphs 26 and 27 and –

(a) the period of notice specified in paragraph 26(1) has expired, or

(b) each person to whom notice has been given under paragraph 26(1) has consented in writing to the making of the appointment.

(2) An appointment may not be made under paragraph 22 after the period of ten business days beginning with the date on which the notice of intention to appoint is filed under paragraph 27(1).

Notice of appointment

29 (1) A person who appoints an administrator of a company under paragraph 22 shall file with the court –

(a) a notice of appointment, and
(b) such other documents as may be prescribed.

(2) The notice of appointment must include a statutory declaration by or on behalf of the person who makes the appointment –

(a) that the person is entitled to make an appointment under paragraph 22,
(b) that the appointment is in accordance with this Schedule, and
(c) that, so far as the person making the statement is able to ascertain, the statements made and information given in the statutory declaration filed with the notice of intention to appoint remain accurate.

(3) The notice of appointment must identify the administrator and must be accompanied by a statement by the administrator –

(a) that he consents to the appointment,
(b) that in his opinion the purpose of administration is reasonably likely to be achieved, and
(c) giving such other information and opinions as may be prescribed.

(4) For the purpose of a statement under sub-paragraph (3) an administrator may rely on information supplied by directors of the company (unless he has reason to doubt its accuracy).

(5) The notice of appointment and any document accompanying it must be in the prescribed form.

(6) A statutory declaration under sub-paragraph (2) must be made during the prescribed period.

(7) A person commits an offence if in a statutory declaration under sub-paragraph (2) he makes a statement –

(a) which is false, and
(b) which he does not reasonably believe to be true.

30 In a case in which no person is entitled to notice of intention to appoint under paragraph 26(1) (and paragraph 28 therefore does not apply) –

(a) the statutory declaration accompanying the notice of appointment must include the statements and information required under paragraph 27(2), and
(b) paragraph 29(2)(c) shall not apply.

Commencement of appointment

31 The appointment of an administrator under paragraph 22 takes effect when the requirements of paragraph 29 are satisfied.

32 A person who appoints an administrator under paragraph 22 –

(a) shall notify the administrator and such other persons as may be prescribed as soon as is reasonably practicable after the requirements of paragraph 29 are satisfied, and

(b) commits an offence if he fails without reasonable excuse to comply with paragraph (a).

33 If before the requirements of paragraph 29 are satisfied the company enters administration by virtue of an administration order or an appointment under paragraph 14 –

(a) the appointment under paragraph 22 shall not take effect, and

(b) paragraph 32 shall not apply.

Invalid appointment: indemnity

34 (1) This paragraph applies where –

(a) a person purports to appoint an administrator under paragraph 22, and

(b) the appointment is discovered to be invalid.

(2) The court may order the person who purported to make the appointment to indemnify the person appointed against liability which arises solely by reason of the appointment's invalidity.

Administration Application – Special Cases

Application by holder of floating charge

35 (1) This paragraph applies where an administration application in respect of a company –

(a) is made by the holder of a qualifying floating charge in respect of the company's property, and

(b) includes a statement that the application is made in reliance on this paragraph.

(2) The court may make an administration order –

(a) whether or not satisfied that the company is or is likely to become unable to pay its debts, but

(b) only if satisfied that the applicant could appoint an administrator under paragraph 14.

Intervention by holder of floating charge

36 (1) This paragraph applies where –

(a) an administration application in respect of a company is made by a person who is not the holder of a qualifying floating charge in respect of the company's property, and

(b) the holder of a qualifying floating charge in respect of the company's property applies to the court to have a specified person appointed as administrator (and not the person specified by the administration applicant).

(2) The court shall grant an application under sub-paragraph (1)(b) unless the court thinks it right to refuse the application because of the particular circumstances of the case.

Application where company in liquidation

37 (1) This paragraph applies where the holder of a qualifying floating charge in respect of a company's property could appoint an administrator under paragraph 14 but for paragraph 8(1)(b).

(2) The holder of the qualifying floating charge may make an administration application.

(3) If the court makes an administration order on hearing an application made by virtue of sub-paragraph (2) –

   (a) the court shall discharge the winding-up order,
   (b) the court shall make provision for such matters as may be prescribed,
   (c) the court may make other consequential provision,
   (d) the court shall specify which of the powers under this Schedule are to be exercisable by the administrator, and
   (e) this Schedule shall have effect with such modifications as the court may specify.

38 (1) The liquidator of a company may make an administration application.

(2) If the court makes an administration order on hearing an application made by virtue of sub-paragraph (1) –

   (a) the court shall discharge any winding-up order in respect of the company,
   (b) the court shall make provision for such matters as may be prescribed,
   (c) the court may make other consequential provision,
   (d) the court shall specify which of the powers under this Schedule are to be exercisable by the administrator, and
   (e) this Schedule shall have effect with such modifications as the court may specify.

Effect of administrative receivership

39 (1) Where there is an administrative receiver of a company the court must dismiss an administration application in respect of the company unless –

   (a) the person by or on behalf of whom the receiver was appointed consents to the making of the administration order,
   (b) the court thinks that the security by virtue of which the receiver was appointed would be liable to be released or discharged under sections 238 to 240 (transaction at undervalue and preference) if an administration order were made,
   (c) the court thinks that the security by virtue of which the receiver was appointed would be avoided under section 245 (avoidance of floating charge) if an administration order were made, or
   (d) the court thinks that the security by virtue of which the receiver was appointed would be challengeable under section 242 (gratuitous alienations) or 243 (unfair preferences) or under any rule of law in Scotland.

(2) Sub-paragraph (1) applies whether the administrative receiver is appointed before or after the making of the administration application.

Effect of Administration

Dismissal of pending winding-up petition

40 (1) A petition for the winding up of a company –

   (a) shall be dismissed on the making of an administration order in respect of the company, and

(b) shall be suspended while the company is in administration following an appointment under paragraph 14.

(2) Sub-paragraph (1)(b) does not apply to a petition presented under –

(a) section 124A (public interest), or
(b) section 367 of the Financial Services and Markets Act 2000 (petition by Financial Services Authority).

(3) Where an administrator becomes aware that a petition was presented under a provision referred to in sub-paragraph (2) before his appointment, he shall apply to the court for directions under paragraph 63.

Dismissal of administrative or other receiver

41 (1) When an administration order takes effect in respect of a company any administrative receiver of the company shall vacate office.

(2) Where a company is in administration, any receiver of part of the company's property shall vacate office if the administrator requires him to.

(3) Where an administrative receiver or receiver vacates office under sub-paragraph (1) or (2) –

(a) his remuneration shall be charged on and paid out of any property of the company which was in his custody or under his control immediately before he vacated office, and
(b) he need not take any further steps under section 40 or 59.

(4) In the application of sub-paragraph (3)(a) –

(a) 'remuneration' includes expenses properly incurred and any indemnity to which the administrative receiver or receiver is entitled out of the assets of the company,
(b) the charge imposed takes priority over security held by the person by whom or on whose behalf the administrative receiver or receiver was appointed, and
(c) the provision for payment is subject to paragraph 43.

Moratorium on insolvency proceedings

42 (1) This paragraph applies to a company in administration.

(2) No resolution may be passed for the winding up of the company.

(3) No order may be made for the winding up of the company.

(4) Sub-paragraph (3) does not apply to an order made on a petition presented under –

(a) section 124A (public interest), or
(b) section 367 of the Financial Services and Markets Act 2000 (petition by Financial Services Authority).

(5) If a petition presented under a provision referred to in sub-paragraph (4) comes to the attention of the administrator, he shall apply to the court for directions under paragraph 63.

Moratorium on other legal process

43 (1) This paragraph applies to a company in administration.

(2) No step may be taken to enforce security over the company's property except –

(a) with the consent of the administrator, or

(b) with the permission of the court.

(3) No step may be taken to repossess goods in the company's possession under a hire-purchase agreement except –

(a) with the consent of the administrator, or

(b) with the permission of the court.

(4) A landlord may not exercise a right of forfeiture by peaceable re-entry in relation to premises let to the company except –

(a) with the consent of the administrator, or

(b) with the permission of the court.

(5) In Scotland, a landlord may not exercise a right of irritancy in relation to premises let to the company except –

(a) with the consent of the administrator, or

(b) with the permission of the court.

(6) No legal process (including legal proceedings, execution, distress and diligence) may be instituted or continued against the company or property of the company except –

(a) with the consent of the administrator, or

(b) with the permission of the court.

(7) Where the court gives permission for a transaction under this paragraph it may impose a condition on or a requirement in connection with the transaction.

(8) In this paragraph 'landlord' includes a person to whom rent is payable.

Interim moratorium

44 (1) This paragraph applies where an administration application in respect of a company has been made and –

(a) the application has not yet been granted or dismissed, or

(b) the application has been granted but the administration order has not yet taken effect.

(2) This paragraph also applies from the time when a copy of notice of intention to appoint an administrator under paragraph 14 is filed with the court until –

(a) the appointment of the administrator takes effect, or

(b) the period of five business days beginning with the date of filing expires without an administrator having been appointed.

(3) Sub-paragraph (2) has effect in relation to a notice of intention to appoint only if it is in the prescribed form.

(4) This paragraph also applies from the time when a copy of notice of intention to appoint an administrator is filed with the court under paragraph 27(1) until –

(a) the appointment of the administrator takes effect, or

(b) the period specified in paragraph 28(2) expires without an administrator having been appointed.

(5) The provisions of paragraphs 42 and 43 shall apply (ignoring any reference to the consent of the administrator).

(6) If there is an administrative receiver of the company when the administration application is made, the provisions of paragraphs 42 and 43 shall not begin to apply by

virtue of this paragraph until the person by or on behalf of whom the receiver was appointed consents to the making of the administration order.

(7) This paragraph does not prevent or require the permission of the court for –

  (a) the presentation of a petition for the winding up of the company under a provision mentioned in paragraph 42(4),
  (b) the appointment of an administrator under paragraph 14,
  (c) the appointment of an administrative receiver of the company, or
  (d) the carrying out by an administrative receiver (whenever appointed) of his functions.

Publicity

45 (1) While a company is in administration every business document issued by or on behalf of the company or the administrator must state –

  (a) the name of the administrator, and
  (b) that the affairs, business and property of the company are being managed by him.

(2) Any of the following commits an offence if without reasonable excuse he authorises or permits a contravention of sub-paragraph (1) –

  (a) the administrator,
  (b) an officer of the company, and
  (c) the company.

(3) In sub-paragraph (1) 'business document' means –

  (a) an invoice,
  (b) an order for goods or services, and
  (c) a business letter.

Process of Administration

Announcement of administrator's appointment

46 (1) This paragraph applies where a person becomes the administrator of a company.

(2) As soon as is reasonably practicable the administrator shall –

  (a) send a notice of his appointment to the company, and
  (b) publish a notice of his appointment in the prescribed manner.

(3) As soon as is reasonably practicable the administrator shall –

  (a) obtain a list of the company's creditors, and
  (b) send a notice of his appointment to each creditor of whose claim and address he is aware.

(4) The administrator shall send a notice of his appointment to the registrar of companies before the end of the period of 7 days beginning with the date specified in sub-paragraph (6).

(5) The administrator shall send a notice of his appointment to such persons as may be prescribed before the end of the prescribed period beginning with the date specified in sub-paragraph (6).

(6) The date for the purpose of sub-paragraphs (4) and (5) is –

  (a) in the case of an administrator appointed by administration order, the date of the order,

(b) in the case of an administrator appointed under paragraph 14, the date on which he receives notice under paragraph 20, and

(c) in the case of an administrator appointed under paragraph 22, the date on which he receives notice under paragraph 32.

(7) The court may direct that sub-paragraph (3)(b) or (5) –

(a) shall not apply, or

(b) shall apply with the substitution of a different period.

(8) A notice under this paragraph must –

(a) contain the prescribed information, and

(b) be in the prescribed form.

(9) An administrator commits an offence if he fails without reasonable excuse to comply with a requirement of this paragraph.

Statement of company's affairs

47 (1) As soon as is reasonably practicable after appointment the administrator of a company shall by notice in the prescribed form require one or more relevant persons to provide the administrator with a statement of the affairs of the company.

(2) The statement must –

(a) be verified by a statement of truth in accordance with Civil Procedure Rules,

(b) be in the prescribed form,

(c) give particulars of the company's property, debts and liabilities,

(d) give the names and addresses of the company's creditors,

(e) specify the security held by each creditor,

(f) give the date on which each security was granted, and

(g) contain such other information as may be prescribed.

(3) In sub-paragraph (1) 'relevant person' means –

(a) a person who is or has been an officer of the company,

(b) a person who took part in the formation of the company during the period of one year ending with the date on which the company enters administration,

(c) a person employed by the company during that period, and

(d) a person who is or has been during that period an officer or employee of a company which is or has been during that year an officer of the company.

(4) For the purpose of sub-paragraph (3) a reference to employment is a reference to employment through a contract of employment or a contract for services.

(5) In Scotland, a statement of affairs under sub-paragraph (1) must be a statutory declaration made in accordance with the Statutory Declarations Act 1835 (and sub-paragraph (2)(a) shall not apply).

48 (1) A person required to submit a statement of affairs must do so before the end of the period of 11 days beginning with the day on which he receives notice of the requirement.

(2) The administrator may –

(a) revoke a requirement under paragraph 47(1), or

(b) extend the period specified in sub-paragraph (1) (whether before or after expiry).

(3) If the administrator refuses a request to act under sub-paragraph (2) –

(a) the person whose request is refused may apply to the court, and

(b) the court may take action of a kind specified in sub-paragraph (2).

(4) A person commits an offence if he fails without reasonable excuse to comply with a requirement under paragraph 47(1).

Administrator's proposals

49 (1) The administrator of a company shall make a statement setting out proposals for achieving the purpose of administration.

(2) A statement under sub-paragraph (1) must, in particular –

(a) deal with such matters as may be prescribed, and
(b) where applicable, explain why the administrator thinks that the objective mentioned in paragraph 3(1)(a) or (b) cannot be achieved.

(3) Proposals under this paragraph may include –

(a) a proposal for a voluntary arrangement under Part I of this Act (although this paragraph is without prejudice to section 4(3));
(b) a proposal for a compromise or arrangement to be sanctioned under section 425 of the Companies Act (compromise with creditors or members).

(4) The administrator shall send a copy of the statement of his proposals –

(a) to the registrar of companies,
(b) to every creditor of the company of whose claim and address he is aware, and
(c) to every member of the company of whose address he is aware.

(5) The administrator shall comply with sub-paragraph (4) –

(a) as soon as is reasonably practicable after the company enters administration, and
(b) in any event, before the end of the period of eight weeks beginning with the day on which the company enters administration.

(6) The administrator shall be taken to comply with sub-paragraph (4)(c) if he publishes in the prescribed manner a notice undertaking to provide a copy of the statement of proposals free of charge to any member of the company who applies in writing to a specified address.

(7) An administrator commits an offence if he fails without reasonable excuse to comply with sub-paragraph (5).

(8) A period specified in this paragraph may be varied in accordance with paragraph 107.

Creditors' meeting

50 (1) In this Schedule 'creditors' meeting' means a meeting of creditors of a company summoned by the administrator –

(a) in the prescribed manner, and
(b) giving the prescribed period of notice to every creditor of the company of whose claim and address he is aware.

(2) A period prescribed under sub-paragraph (1)(b) may be varied in accordance with paragraph 107.

(3) A creditors' meeting shall be conducted in accordance with the rules.

Requirement for initial creditors' meeting

51 (1) Each copy of an administrator's statement of proposals sent to a creditor under paragraph 49(4)(b) must be accompanied by an invitation to a creditors' meeting (an 'initial creditors' meeting').

(2) The date set for an initial creditors' meeting must be –

(a) as soon as is reasonably practicable after the company enters administration, and
(b) in any event, within the period of ten weeks beginning with the date on which the company enters administration.

(3) An administrator shall present a copy of his statement of proposals to an initial creditors' meeting.

(4) A period specified in this paragraph may be varied in accordance with paragraph 107.

(5) An administrator commits an offence if he fails without reasonable excuse to comply with a requirement of this paragraph.

52 (1) Paragraph 51(1) shall not apply where the statement of proposals states that the administrator thinks –

(a) that the company has sufficient property to enable each creditor of the company to be paid in full,
(b) that the company has insufficient property to enable a distribution to be made to unsecured creditors other than by virtue of section 176A(2)(a), or
(c) that neither of the objectives specified in paragraph 3(1)(a) and (b) can be achieved.

(2) But the administrator shall summon an initial creditors' meeting if it is requested –

(a) by creditors of the company whose debts amount to at least 10% of the total debts of the company,
(b) in the prescribed manner, and
(c) in the prescribed period.

(3) A meeting requested under sub-paragraph (2) must be summoned for a date in the prescribed period.

(4) The period prescribed under sub-paragraph (3) may be varied in accordance with paragraph 107.

Business and result of initial creditors' meeting

53 (1) An initial creditors' meeting to which an administrator's proposals are presented shall consider them and may –

(a) approve them without modification, or
(b) approve them with modification to which the administrator consents.

(2) After the conclusion of an initial creditors' meeting the administrator shall as soon as is reasonably practicable report any decision taken to –

(a) the court,
(b) the registrar of companies, and
(c) such other persons as may be prescribed.

(3) An administrator commits an offence if he fails without reasonable excuse to comply with sub-paragraph (2).

Revision of administrator's proposals

54 (1) This paragraph applies where –

(a) an administrator's proposals have been approved (with or without modification) at an initial creditors' meeting,

(b) the administrator proposes a revision to the proposals, and

(c) the administrator thinks that the proposed revision is substantial.

(2) The administrator shall –

(a) summon a creditors' meeting,

(b) send a statement in the prescribed form of the proposed revision with the notice of the meeting sent to each creditor,

(c) send a copy of the statement, within the prescribed period, to each member of the company of whose address he is aware, and

(d) present a copy of the statement to the meeting.

(3) The administrator shall be taken to have complied with sub-paragraph (2)(c) if he publishes a notice undertaking to provide a copy of the statement free of charge to any member of the company who applies in writing to a specified address.

(4) A notice under sub-paragraph (3) must be published –

(a) in the prescribed manner, and

(b) within the prescribed period.

(5) A creditors' meeting to which a proposed revision is presented shall consider it and may –

(a) approve it without modification, or

(b) approve it with modification to which the administrator consents.

(6) After the conclusion of a creditors' meeting the administrator shall as soon as is reasonably practicable report any decision taken to –

(a) the court,

(b) the registrar of companies, and

(c) such other persons as may be prescribed.

(7) An administrator commits an offence if he fails without reasonable excuse to comply with sub-paragraph (6).

Failure to obtain approval of administrator's proposals

55 (1) This paragraph applies where an administrator reports to the court that –

(a) an initial creditors' meeting has failed to approve the administrator's proposals presented to it, or

(b) a creditors' meeting has failed to approve a revision of the administrator's proposals presented to it.

(2) The court may –

(a) provide that the appointment of an administrator shall cease to have effect from a specified time;

(b) adjourn the hearing conditionally or unconditionally;

(c) make an interim order;

(d) make an order on a petition for winding up suspended by virtue of paragraph 40(1)(b);

(e) make any other order (including an order making consequential provision) that the court thinks appropriate.

Further creditors' meetings

56 (1) The administrator of a company shall summon a creditors' meeting if –

(a) it is requested in the prescribed manner by creditors of the company whose debts amount to at least 10% of the total debts of the company, or
(b) he is directed by the court to summon a creditors' meeting.

(2) An administrator commits an offence if he fails without reasonable excuse to summon a creditors' meeting as required by this paragraph.

Creditors' committee

57 (1) A creditors' meeting may establish a creditors' committee.

(2) A creditors' committee shall carry out functions conferred on it by or under this Act.

(3) A creditors' committee may require the administrator –

(a) to attend on the committee at any reasonable time of which he is given at least seven days' notice, and
(b) to provide the committee with information about the exercise of his functions.

Correspondence instead of creditors' meeting

58 (1) Anything which is required or permitted by or under this Schedule to be done at a creditors' meeting may be done by correspondence between the administrator and creditors –

(a) in accordance with the rules, and
(b) subject to any prescribed condition.

(2) A reference in this Schedule to anything done at a creditors' meeting includes a reference to anything done in the course of correspondence in reliance on sub-paragraph (1).

(3) A requirement to hold a creditors' meeting is satisfied by conducting correspondence in accordance with this paragraph.

Functions of Administrator

General powers

59 (1) The administrator of a company may do anything necessary or expedient for the management of the affairs, business and property of the company.

(2) A provision of this Schedule which expressly permits the administrator to do a specified thing is without prejudice to the generality of sub-paragraph (1).

(3) A person who deals with the administrator of a company in good faith and for value need not inquire whether the administrator is acting within his powers.

60 The administrator of a company has the powers specified in Schedule 1 to this Act.

61 The administrator of a company –

(a) may remove a director of the company, and
(b) may appoint a director of the company (whether or not to fill a vacancy).

62 The administrator of a company may call a meeting of members or creditors of the company.

63 The administrator of a company may apply to the court for directions in connection with his functions.

64 (1) A company in administration or an officer of a company in administration may not exercise a management power without the consent of the administrator.

(2) For the purpose of sub-paragraph (1) –

(a) 'management power' means a power which could be exercised so as to interfere with the exercise of the administrator's powers,
(b) it is immaterial whether the power is conferred by an enactment or an instrument, and
(c) consent may be general or specific.

Distribution

65 (1) The administrator of a company may make a distribution to a creditor of the company.

(2) Section 175 shall apply in relation to a distribution under this paragraph as it applies in relation to a winding up.

(3) A payment may not be made by way of distribution under this paragraph to a creditor of the company who is neither secured nor preferential unless the court gives permission.

66 The administrator of a company may make a payment otherwise than in accordance with paragraph 65 or paragraph 13 of Schedule 1 if he thinks it likely to assist achievement of the purpose of administration.

General duties

67 The administrator of a company shall on his appointment take custody or control of all the property to which he thinks the company is entitled.

68 (1) Subject to sub-paragraph (2), the administrator of a company shall manage its affairs, business and property in accordance with –

(a) any proposals approved under paragraph 53,
(b) any revision of those proposals which is made by him and which he does not consider substantial, and
(c) any revision of those proposals approved under paragraph 54.

(2) If the court gives directions to the administrator of a company in connection with any aspect of his management of the company's affairs, business or property, the administrator shall comply with the directions.

(3) The court may give directions under sub-paragraph (2) only if –

(a) no proposals have been approved under paragraph 53,
(b) the directions are consistent with any proposals or revision approved under paragraph 53 or 54,
(c) the court thinks the directions are required in order to reflect a change in circumstances since the approval of proposals or a revision under paragraph 53 or 54, or
(d) the court thinks the directions are desirable because of a misunderstanding about proposals or a revision approved under paragraph 53 or 54.

Administrator as agent of company

69　In exercising his functions under this Schedule the administrator of a company acts as its agent.

Charged property: floating charge

70　(1) The administrator of a company may dispose of or take action relating to property which is subject to a floating charge as if it were not subject to the charge.

(2) Where property is disposed of in reliance on sub-paragraph (1) the holder of the floating charge shall have the same priority in respect of acquired property as he had in respect of the property disposed of.

(3) In sub-paragraph (2) 'acquired property' means property of the company which directly or indirectly represents the property disposed of.

Charged property: non-floating charge

71　(1) The court may by order enable the administrator of a company to dispose of property which is subject to a security (other than a floating charge) as if it were not subject to the security.

(2) An order under sub-paragraph (1) may be made only –

    (a)　on the application of the administrator, and
    (b)　where the court thinks that disposal of the property would be likely to promote the purpose of administration in respect of the company.

(3) An order under this paragraph is subject to the condition that there be applied towards discharging the sums secured by the security –

    (a)　the net proceeds of disposal of the property, and
    (b)　any additional money required to be added to the net proceeds so as to produce the amount determined by the court as the net amount which would be realised on a sale of the property at market value.

(4) If an order under this paragraph relates to more than one security, application of money under sub-paragraph (3) shall be in the order of the priorities of the securities.

(5) An administrator who makes a successful application for an order under this paragraph shall send a copy of the order to the registrar of companies before the end of the period of 14 days starting with the date of the order.

(6) An administrator commits an offence if he fails to comply with sub-paragraph (5) without reasonable excuse.

Hire-purchase property

72　(1) The court may by order enable the administrator of a company to dispose of goods which are in the possession of the company under a hire-purchase agreement as if all the rights of the owner under the agreement were vested in the company.

(2) An order under sub-paragraph (1) may be made only –

    (a)　on the application of the administrator, and
    (b)　where the court thinks that disposal of the goods would be likely to promote the purpose of administration in respect of the company.

(3) An order under this paragraph is subject to the condition that there be applied towards discharging the sums payable under the hire-purchase agreement –

(a) the net proceeds of disposal of the goods, and

(b) any additional money required to be added to the net proceeds so as to produce the amount determined by the court as the net amount which would be realised on a sale of the goods at market value.

(4) An administrator who makes a successful application for an order under this paragraph shall send a copy of the order to the registrar of companies before the end of the period of 14 days starting with the date of the order.

(5) An administrator commits an offence if he fails without reasonable excuse to comply with sub-paragraph (4).

Protection for secured or preferential creditor

73 (1) An administrator's statement of proposals under paragraph 49 may not include any action which –

(a) affects the right of a secured creditor of the company to enforce his security,

(b) would result in a preferential debt of the company being paid otherwise than in priority to its non-preferential debts, or

(c) would result in one preferential creditor of the company being paid a smaller proportion of his debt than another.

(2) Sub-paragraph (1) does not apply to –

(a) action to which the relevant creditor consents,

(b) a proposal for a voluntary arrangement under Part I of this Act (although this sub-paragraph is without prejudice to section 4(3)), or

(c) a proposal for a compromise or arrangement to be sanctioned under section 425 of the Companies Act (compromise with creditors or members).

(3) The reference to a statement of proposals in sub-paragraph (1) includes a reference to a statement as revised or modified.

Challenge to administrator's conduct of company

74 (1) A creditor or member of a company in administration may apply to the court claiming that –

(a) the administrator is acting or has acted so as unfairly to harm the interests of the applicant (whether alone or in common with some or all other members or creditors), or

(b) the administrator proposes to act in a way which would unfairly harm the interests of the applicant (whether alone or in common with some or all other members or creditors).

(2) A creditor or member of a company in administration may apply to the court claiming that the administrator is not performing his functions as quickly or as efficiently as is reasonably practicable.

(3) The court may –

(a) grant relief;

(b) dismiss the application;

(c) adjourn the hearing conditionally or unconditionally;

(d) make an interim order;

(e) make any other order it thinks appropriate.

(4) In particular, an order under this paragraph may –

(a) regulate the administrator's exercise of his functions;
(b) require the administrator to do or not do a specified thing;
(c) require a creditors' meeting to be held for a specified purpose;
(d) provide for the appointment of an administrator to cease to have effect;
(e) make consequential provision.

(5) An order may be made on a claim under sub-paragraph (1) whether or not the action complained of –

(a) is within the administrator's powers under this Schedule;
(b) was taken in reliance on an order under paragraph 71 or 72.

(6) An order may not be made under this paragraph if it would impede or prevent the implementation of –

(a) a voluntary arrangement approved under Part I,
(b) a compromise or arrangement sanctioned under section 425 of the Companies Act (compromise with creditors and members), or
(c) proposals or a revision approved under paragraph 53 or 54 more than 28 days before the day on which the application for the order under this paragraph is made.

Misfeasance

75 (1) The court may examine the conduct of a person who –

(a) is or purports to be the administrator of a company, or
(b) has been or has purported to be the administrator of a company.

(2) An examination under this paragraph may be held only on the application of –

(a) the official receiver,
(b) the administrator of the company,
(c) the liquidator of the company,
(d) a creditor of the company, or
(e) a contributory of the company.

(3) An application under sub-paragraph (2) must allege that the administrator –

(a) has misapplied or retained money or other property of the company,
(b) has become accountable for money or other property of the company,
(c) has breached a fiduciary or other duty in relation to the company, or
(d) has been guilty of misfeasance.

(4) On an examination under this paragraph into a person's conduct the court may order him –

(a) to repay, restore or account for money or property;
(b) to pay interest;
(c) to contribute a sum to the company's property by way of compensation for breach of duty or misfeasance.

(5) In sub-paragraph (3) 'administrator' includes a person who purports or has purported to be a company's administrator.

(6) An application under sub-paragraph (2) may be made in respect of an administrator who has been discharged under paragraph 98 only with the permission of the court.

Ending Administration

Automatic end of administration

76 (1) The appointment of an administrator shall cease to have effect at the end of the period of one year beginning with the date on which it takes effect.

(2) But –

(a) on the application of an administrator the court may by order extend his term of office for a specified period, and
(b) an administrator's term of office may be extended for a specified period not exceeding six months by consent.

77 (1) An order of the court under paragraph 76 –

(a) may be made in respect of an administrator whose term of office has already been extended by order or by consent, but
(b) may not be made after the expiry of the administrator's term of office.

(2) Where an order is made under paragraph 76 the administrator shall as soon as is reasonably practicable notify the registrar of companies.

(3) An administrator who fails without reasonable excuse to comply with sub-paragraph (2) commits an offence.

78 (1) In paragraph 76(2)(b) 'consent' means consent of –

(a) each secured creditor of the company, and
(b) if the company has unsecured debts, creditors whose debts amount to more than 50% of the company's unsecured debts, disregarding debts of any creditor who does not respond to an invitation to give or withhold consent.

(2) But where the administrator has made a statement under paragraph 52(1)(b) 'consent' means –

(a) consent of each secured creditor of the company, or
(b) if the administrator thinks that a distribution may be made to preferential creditors, consent of –
  (i) each secured creditor of the company, and
  (ii) preferential creditors whose debts amount to more than 50% of the preferential debts of the company, disregarding debts of any creditor who does not respond to an invitation to give or withhold consent.

(3) Consent for the purposes of paragraph 76(2)(b) may be –

(a) written, or
(b) signified at a creditors' meeting.

(4) An administrator's term of office –

(a) may be extended by consent only once,
(b) may not be extended by consent after extension by order of the court, and
(c) may not be extended by consent after expiry.

(5) Where an administrator's term of office is extended by consent he shall as soon as is reasonably practicable –

(a) file notice of the extension with the court, and
(b) notify the registrar of companies.

(6) An administrator who fails without reasonable excuse to comply with sub-paragraph (5) commits an offence.

Court ending administration on application of administrator

79 (1) On the application of the administrator of a company the court may provide for the appointment of an administrator of the company to cease to have effect from a specified time.

(2) The administrator of a company shall make an application under this paragraph if –

  (a) he thinks the purpose of administration cannot be achieved in relation to the company,
  (b) he thinks the company should not have entered administration, or
  (c) a creditors' meeting requires him to make an application under this paragraph.

(3) The administrator of a company shall make an application under this paragraph if –

  (a) the administration is pursuant to an administration order, and
  (b) the administrator thinks that the purpose of administration has been sufficiently achieved in relation to the company.

(4) On an application under this paragraph the court may –

  (a) adjourn the hearing conditionally or unconditionally;
  (b) dismiss the application;
  (c) make an interim order;
  (d) make any order it thinks appropriate (whether in addition to, in consequence of or instead of the order applied for).

Termination of administration where objective achieved

80 (1) This paragraph applies where an administrator of a company is appointed under paragraph 14 or 22.

(2) If the administrator thinks that the purpose of administration has been sufficiently achieved in relation to the company he may file a notice in the prescribed form –

  (a) with the court, and
  (b) with the registrar of companies.

(3) The administrator's appointment shall cease to have effect when the requirements of sub-paragraph (2) are satisfied.

(4) Where the administrator files a notice he shall within the prescribed period send a copy to every creditor of the company of whose claim and address he is aware.

(5) The rules may provide that the administrator is taken to have complied with sub-paragraph (4) if before the end of the prescribed period he publishes in the prescribed manner a notice undertaking to provide a copy of the notice under sub-paragraph (2) to any creditor of the company who applies in writing to a specified address.

(6) An administrator who fails without reasonable excuse to comply with sub-paragraph (4) commits an offence.

Court ending administration on application of creditor

81 (1) On the application of a creditor of a company the court may provide for the appointment of an administrator of the company to cease to have effect at a specified time.

(2) An application under this paragraph must allege an improper motive –

  (a) in the case of an administrator appointed by administration order, on the part of the applicant for the order, or

(b) in any other case, on the part of the person who appointed the administrator.

(3) On an application under this paragraph the court may –

(a) adjourn the hearing conditionally or unconditionally;
(b) dismiss the application;
(c) make an interim order;
(d) make any order it thinks appropriate (whether in addition to, in consequence of or instead of the order applied for).

Public interest winding-up

82 (1) This paragraph applies where a winding-up order is made for the winding up of a company in administration on a petition presented under –

(a) section 124A (public interest), or
(b) section 367 of the Financial Services and Markets Act 2000 (petition by Financial Services Authority).

(2) This paragraph also applies where a provisional liquidator of a company in administration is appointed following the presentation of a petition under any of the provisions listed in sub-paragraph (1).

(3) The court shall order –

(a) that the appointment of the administrator shall cease to have effect, or
(b) that the appointment of the administrator shall continue to have effect.

(4) If the court makes an order under sub-paragraph (3)(b) it may also –

(a) specify which of the powers under this Schedule are to be exercisable by the administrator, and
(b) order that this Schedule shall have effect in relation to the administrator with specified modifications.

Moving from administration to creditors' voluntary liquidation

83 (1) This paragraph applies in England and Wales where the administrator of a company thinks –

(a) that the total amount which each secured creditor of the company is likely to receive has been paid to him or set aside for him, and
(b) that a distribution will be made to unsecured creditors of the company (if there are any).

(2) This paragraph applies in Scotland where the administrator of a company thinks –

(a) that each secured creditor of the company will receive payment in respect of his debt, and
(b) that a distribution will be made to unsecured creditors (if there are any).

(3) The administrator may send to the registrar of companies a notice that this paragraph applies.

(4) On receipt of a notice under sub-paragraph (3) the registrar shall register it.

(5) If an administrator sends a notice under sub-paragraph (3) he shall as soon as is reasonably practicable –

(a) file a copy of the notice with the court, and

(b) send a copy of the notice to each creditor of whose claim and address he is aware.

(6) On the registration of a notice under sub-paragraph (3) –

    (a) the appointment of an administrator in respect of the company shall cease to have effect, and

    (b) the company shall be wound up as if a resolution for voluntary winding up under section 84 were passed on the day on which the notice is registered.

(7) The liquidator for the purposes of the winding up shall be –

    (a) a person nominated by the creditors of the company in the prescribed manner and within the prescribed period, or

    (b) if no person is nominated under paragraph (a), the administrator.

(8) In the application of Part IV to a winding up by virtue of this paragraph –

    (a) section 85 shall not apply,

    (b) section 86 shall apply as if the reference to the time of the passing of the resolution for voluntary winding up were a reference to the beginning of the date of registration of the notice under sub-paragraph (3),

    (c) section 89 does not apply,

    (d) sections 98, 99 and 100 shall not apply,

    (e) section 129 shall apply as if the reference to the time of the passing of the resolution for voluntary winding up were a reference to the beginning of the date of registration of the notice under sub-paragraph (3), and

    (f) any creditors' committee which is in existence immediately before the company ceases to be in administration shall continue in existence after that time as if appointed as a liquidation committee under section 101.

Moving from administration to dissolution

84 (1) If the administrator of a company thinks that the company has no property which might permit a distribution to its creditors, he shall send a notice to that effect to the registrar of companies.

(2) The court may on the application of the administrator of a company disapply sub-paragraph (1) in respect of the company.

(3) On receipt of a notice under sub-paragraph (1) the registrar shall register it.

(4) On the registration of a notice in respect of a company under sub-paragraph (1) the appointment of an administrator of the company shall cease to have effect.

(5) If an administrator sends a notice under sub-paragraph (1) he shall as soon as is reasonably practicable –

    (a) file a copy of the notice with the court, and

    (b) send a copy of the notice to each creditor of whose claim and address he is aware.

(6) At the end of the period of three months beginning with the date of registration of a notice in respect of a company under sub-paragraph (1) the company is deemed to be dissolved.

(7) On an application in respect of a company by the administrator or another interested person the court may –

    (a) extend the period specified in sub-paragraph (6),

    (b) suspend that period, or

    (c) disapply sub-paragraph (6).

(8) Where an order is made under sub-paragraph (7) in respect of a company the administrator shall as soon as is reasonably practicable notify the registrar of companies.

(9) An administrator commits an offence if he fails without reasonable excuse to comply with sub-paragraph (5).

Discharge of administration order where administration ends

85 (1) This paragraph applies where –

- (a) the court makes an order under this Schedule providing for the appointment of an administrator of a company to cease to have effect, and
- (b) the administrator was appointed by administration order.

(2) The court shall discharge the administration order.

Notice to Companies Registrar where administration ends

86 (1) This paragraph applies where the court makes an order under this Schedule providing for the appointment of an administrator to cease to have effect.

(2) The administrator shall send a copy of the order to the registrar of companies within the period of 14 days beginning with the date of the order.

(3) An administrator who fails without reasonable excuse to comply with sub-paragraph (2) commits an offence.

Replacing Administrator

Resignation of administrator

87 (1) An administrator may resign only in prescribed circumstances.

(2) Where an administrator may resign he may do so only –

- (a) in the case of an administrator appointed by administration order, by notice in writing to the court,
- (b) in the case of an administrator appointed under paragraph 14, by notice in writing to the person who appointed him,
- (c) in the case of an administrator appointed under paragraph 22(1), by notice in writing to the company, or
- (d) in the case of an administrator appointed under paragraph 22(2), by notice in writing to the directors of the company.

Removal of administrator from office

88 The court may by order remove an administrator from office.

Administrator ceasing to be qualified

89 (1) The administrator of a company shall vacate office if he ceases to be qualified to act as an insolvency practitioner in relation to the company.

(2) Where an administrator vacates office by virtue of sub-paragraph (1) he shall give notice in writing –

- (a) in the case of an administrator appointed by administration order, to the court,
- (b) in the case of an administrator appointed under paragraph 14, to the person who appointed him,

(c) in the case of an administrator appointed under paragraph 22(1), to the company, or

(d) in the case of an administrator appointed under paragraph 22(2), to the directors of the company.

(3) An administrator who fails without reasonable excuse to comply with sub-paragraph (2) commits an offence.

Supplying vacancy in office of administrator

90 Paragraphs 91 to 95 apply where an administrator –

(a) dies,
(b) resigns,
(c) is removed from office under paragraph 88, or
(d) vacates office under paragraph 89.

91 (1) Where the administrator was appointed by administration order, the court may replace the administrator on an application under this sub-paragraph made by –

(a) a creditors' committee of the company,
(b) the company,
(c) the directors of the company,
(d) one or more creditors of the company, or
(e) where more than one person was appointed to act jointly or concurrently as the administrator, any of those persons who remains in office.

(2) But an application may be made in reliance on sub-paragraph (1)(b) to (d) only where –

(a) there is no creditors' committee of the company,
(b) the court is satisfied that the creditors' committee or a remaining administrator is not taking reasonable steps to make a replacement, or
(c) the court is satisfied that for another reason it is right for the application to be made.

92 Where the administrator was appointed under paragraph 14 the holder of the floating charge by virtue of which the appointment was made may replace the administrator.

93 (1) Where the administrator was appointed under paragraph 22(1) by the company it may replace the administrator.

(2) A replacement under this paragraph may be made only –

(a) with the consent of each person who is the holder of a qualifying floating charge in respect of the company's property, or
(b) where consent is withheld, with the permission of the court.

94 (1) Where the administrator was appointed under paragraph 22(2) the directors of the company may replace the administrator.

(2) A replacement under this paragraph may be made only –

(a) with the consent of each person who is the holder of a qualifying floating charge in respect of the company's property, or
(b) where consent is withheld, with the permission of the court.

95 The court may replace an administrator on the application of a person listed in paragraph 91(1) if the court –

(a) is satisfied that a person who is entitled to replace the administrator under any of paragraphs 92 to 94 is not taking reasonable steps to make a replacement, or

(b) that for another reason it is right for the court to make the replacement.

Substitution of administrator: competing floating charge-holder

96 (1) This paragraph applies where an administrator of a company is appointed under paragraph 14 by the holder of a qualifying floating charge in respect of the company's property.

(2) The holder of a prior qualifying floating charge in respect of the company's property may apply to the court for the administrator to be replaced by an administrator nominated by the holder of the prior floating charge.

(3) One floating charge is prior to another for the purposes of this paragraph if –

(a) it was created first, or

(b) it is to be treated as having priority in accordance with an agreement to which the holder of each floating charge was party.

(4) Sub-paragraph (3) shall have effect in relation to Scotland as if the following were substituted for paragraph (a) –

'(a) it has priority of ranking in accordance with section 464(4)(b) of the Companies Act 1985,'.

Substitution of administrator appointed by company or directors: creditors' meeting

97 (1) This paragraph applies where –

(a) an administrator of a company is appointed by a company or directors under paragraph 22, and

(b) there is no holder of a qualifying floating charge in respect of the company's property.

(2) A creditors' meeting may replace the administrator.

(3) A creditors' meeting may act under sub-paragraph (2) only if the new administrator's written consent to act is presented to the meeting before the replacement is made.

Vacation of office: discharge from liability

98 (1) Where a person ceases to be the administrator of a company (whether because he vacates office by reason of resignation, death or otherwise, because he is removed from office or because his appointment ceases to have effect) he is discharged from liability in respect of any action of his as administrator.

(2) The discharge provided by sub-paragraph (1) takes effect –

(a) in the case of an administrator who dies, on the filing with the court of notice of his death,

(b) in the case of an administrator appointed under paragraph 14 or 22, at a time appointed by resolution of the creditors' committee or, if there is no committee, by resolution of the creditors, or

(c) in any case, at a time specified by the court.

(3) For the purpose of the application of sub-paragraph (2)(b) in a case where the administrator has made a statement under paragraph 52(1)(b), a resolution shall be taken as passed if (and only if) passed with the approval of –

(a) each secured creditor of the company, or
(b) if the administrator has made a distribution to preferential creditors or thinks that a distribution may be made to preferential creditors –
  (i) each secured creditor of the company, and
  (ii) preferential creditors whose debts amount to more than 50% of the preferential debts of the company, disregarding debts of any creditor who does not respond to an invitation to give or withhold approval.

(4) Discharge –

(a) applies to liability accrued before the discharge takes effect, and
(b) does not prevent the exercise of the court's powers under paragraph 75.

Vacation of office: charges and liabilities

99 (1) This paragraph applies where a person ceases to be the administrator of a company (whether because he vacates office by reason of resignation, death or otherwise, because he is removed from office or because his appointment ceases to have effect).

(2) In this paragraph –

'the former administrator' means the person referred to in sub-paragraph (1), and 'cessation' means the time when he ceases to be the company's administrator.

(3) The former administrator's remuneration and expenses shall be –

(a) charged on and payable out of property of which he had custody or control immediately before cessation, and
(b) payable in priority to any security to which paragraph 70 applies.

(4) A sum payable in respect of a debt or liability arising out of a contract entered into by the former administrator or a predecessor before cessation shall be –

(a) charged on and payable out of property of which the former administrator had custody or control immediately before cessation, and
(b) payable in priority to any charge arising under sub-paragraph (3).

(5) Sub-paragraph (4) shall apply to a liability arising under a contract of employment which was adopted by the former administrator or a predecessor before cessation; and for that purpose –

(a) action taken within the period of 14 days after an administrator's appointment shall not be taken to amount or contribute to the adoption of a contract,
(b) no account shall be taken of a liability which arises, or in so far as it arises, by reference to anything which is done or which occurs before the adoption of the contract of employment, and
(c) no account shall be taken of a liability to make a payment other than wages or salary.

(6) In sub-paragraph (5)(c) 'wages or salary' includes –

(a) a sum payable in respect of a period of holiday (for which purpose the sum shall be treated as relating to the period by reference to which the entitlement to holiday accrued),
(b) a sum payable in respect of a period of absence through illness or other good cause,
(c) a sum payable in lieu of holiday,
(d) in respect of a period, a sum which would be treated as earnings for that period for the purposes of an enactment about social security, and
(e) a contribution to an occupational pension scheme.

General

Joint and concurrent administrators

100 (1) In this Schedule –

(a) a reference to the appointment of an administrator of a company includes a reference to the appointment of a number of persons to act jointly or concurrently as the administrator of a company, and

(b) a reference to the appointment of a person as administrator of a company includes a reference to the appointment of a person as one of a number of persons to act jointly or concurrently as the administrator of a company.

(2) The appointment of a number of persons to act as administrator of a company must specify –

(a) which functions (if any) are to be exercised by the persons appointed acting jointly, and

(b) which functions (if any) are to be exercised by any or all of the persons appointed.

101 (1) This paragraph applies where two or more persons are appointed to act jointly as the administrator of a company.

(2) A reference to the administrator of the company is a reference to those persons acting jointly.

(3) But a reference to the administrator of a company in paragraphs 87 to 99 of this Schedule is a reference to any or all of the persons appointed to act jointly.

(4) Where an offence of omission is committed by the administrator, each of the persons appointed to act jointly –

(a) commits the offence, and

(b) may be proceeded against and punished individually.

(5) The reference in paragraph 45(1)(a) to the name of the administrator is a reference to the name of each of the persons appointed to act jointly.

(6) Where persons are appointed to act jointly in respect of only some of the functions of the administrator of a company, this paragraph applies only in relation to those functions.

102 (1) This paragraph applies where two or more persons are appointed to act concurrently as the administrator of a company.

(2) A reference to the administrator of a company in this Schedule is a reference to any of the persons appointed (or any combination of them).

103 (1) Where a company is in administration, a person may be appointed to act as administrator jointly or concurrently with the person or persons acting as the administrator of the company.

(2) Where a company entered administration by administration order, an appointment under sub-paragraph (1) must be made by the court on the application of –

(a) a person or group listed in paragraph 12(1)(a) to (e), or

(b) the person or persons acting as the administrator of the company.

(3) Where a company entered administration by virtue of an appointment under paragraph 14, an appointment under sub-paragraph (1) must be made by –

(a) the holder of the floating charge by virtue of which the appointment was made, or

(b) the court on the application of the person or persons acting as the administrator of the company.

(4) Where a company entered administration by virtue of an appointment under paragraph 22(1), an appointment under sub-paragraph (1) above must be made either by the court on the application of the person or persons acting as the administrator of the company or –

(a) by the company, and
(b) with the consent of each person who is the holder of a qualifying floating charge in respect of the company's property or, where consent is withheld, with the permission of the court.

(5) Where a company entered administration by virtue of an appointment under paragraph 22(2), an appointment under sub-paragraph (1) must be made either by the court on the application of the person or persons acting as the administrator of the company or –

(a) by the directors of the company, and
(b) with the consent of each person who is the holder of a qualifying floating charge in respect of the company's property or, where consent is withheld, with the permission of the court.

(6) An appointment under sub-paragraph (1) may be made only with the consent of the person or persons acting as the administrator of the company.

Presumption of validity

104 An act of the administrator of a company is valid in spite of a defect in his appointment or qualification.

Majority decision of directors

105 A reference in this Schedule to something done by the directors of a company includes a reference to the same thing done by a majority of the directors of a company.

Penalties

106 (1) A person who is guilty of an offence under this Schedule is liable to a fine (in accordance with section 430 and Schedule 10).

(2) A person who is guilty of an offence under any of the following paragraphs of this Schedule is liable to a daily default fine (in accordance with section 430 and Schedule 10) –

(a) paragraph 20,
(b) paragraph 32,
(c) paragraph 46,
(d) paragraph 48,
(e) paragraph 49,
(f) paragraph 51,
(g) paragraph 53,
(h) paragraph 54,
(i) paragraph 56,
(j) paragraph 71,
(k) paragraph 72,
(l) paragraph 77,

(m) paragraph 78,
(n) paragraph 80,
(o) paragraph 84,
(p) paragraph 86, and
(q) paragraph 89.

Extension of time limit

107 (1) Where a provision of this Schedule provides that a period may be varied in accordance with this paragraph, the period may be varied in respect of a company –

(a) by the court, and
(b) on the application of the administrator.

(2) A time period may be extended in respect of a company under this paragraph –

(a) more than once, and
(b) after expiry.

108 (1) A period specified in paragraph 49(5), 50(1)(b) or 51(2) may be varied in respect of a company by the administrator with consent.

(2) In sub-paragraph (1) 'consent' means consent of –

(a) each secured creditor of the company, and
(b) if the company has unsecured debts, creditors whose debts amount to more than 50% of the company's unsecured debts, disregarding debts of any creditor who does not respond to an invitation to give or withhold consent.

(3) But where the administrator has made a statement under paragraph 52(1)(b) 'consent' means –

(a) consent of each secured creditor of the company, or
(b) if the administrator thinks that a distribution may be made to preferential creditors, consent of –
  (i) each secured creditor of the company, and
  (ii) preferential creditors whose debts amount to more than 50% of the total preferential debts of the company, disregarding debts of any creditor who does not respond to an invitation to give or withhold consent.

(4) Consent for the purposes of sub-paragraph (1) may be –

(a) written, or
(b) signified at a creditors' meeting.

(5) The power to extend under sub-paragraph (1) –

(a) may be exercised in respect of a period only once,
(b) may not be used to extend a period by more than 28 days,
(c) may not be used to extend a period which has been extended by the court, and
(d) may not be used to extend a period after expiry.

109 Where a period is extended under paragraph 107 or 108, a reference to the period shall be taken as a reference to the period as extended.

Amendment of provision about time

110 (1) The Secretary of State may by order amend a provision of this Schedule which –

(a) requires anything to be done within a specified period of time,

(b) prevents anything from being done after a specified time, or

(c) requires a specified minimum period of notice to be given.

(2) An order under this paragraph –

(a) must be made by statutory instrument, and

(b) shall be subject to annulment in pursuance of a resolution of either House of Parliament.

Interpretation

111 (1) In this Schedule –

'administrative receiver' has the meaning given by section 251,

'administrator' has the meaning given by paragraph 1 and, where the context requires, includes a reference to a former administrator,

'company' includes a company which may enter administration by virtue of Article 3 of the EC Regulation,

'correspondence' includes correspondence by telephonic or other electronic means,

'creditors' meeting' has the meaning given by paragraph 50,

'enters administration' has the meaning given by paragraph 1,

'floating charge' means a charge which is a floating charge on its creation,

'in administration' has the meaning given by paragraph 1,

'hire-purchase agreement' includes a conditional sale agreement, a chattel leasing agreement and a retention of title agreement,

'holder of a qualifying floating charge' in respect of a company's property has the meaning given by paragraph 14,

'market value' means the amount which would be realised on a sale of property in the open market by a willing vendor,

'the purpose of administration' means an objective specified in paragraph 3, and

'unable to pay its debts' has the meaning given by section 123.

(2) A reference in this Schedule to a thing in writing includes a reference to a thing in electronic form.

(3) In this Schedule a reference to action includes a reference to inaction.

Scotland

112–116 (*Apply to Scotland only*).

SCHEDULE 17
ADMINISTRATION: MINOR AND CONSEQUENTIAL AMENDMENTS

Section 248

General

1 In any instrument made before section 248(1) to (3) of this Act comes into force –

(a) a reference to the making of an administration order shall be treated as including a reference to the appointment of an administrator under paragraph 14 or 22 of Schedule B1 to the Insolvency Act 1986 (inserted by section 248(2) of this Act), and

(b) a reference to making an application for an administration order by petition shall be treated as including a reference to making an administration application under that Schedule, appointing an administrator under paragraph 14 or 22 of that Schedule or giving notice under paragraph 15 or 26 of that Schedule.

Magistrates' Courts Act 1980

2 In section 87A(1) of the Magistrates' Court Act 1980 (fine imposed on company) for 'section 9 or 124 of the Insolvency Act 1986' substitute 'section 124 of, or paragraph 12 of Schedule B1 to, the Insolvency Act 1986'.

Companies Act 1985

3 The Companies Act 1985 shall be amended as follows.

4 In section 225 (alteration of accounting reference date) –

(a) in subsection (4) for 'an administration order is in force' substitute 'the company is in administration', and

(b) in subsection (6) for 'An accounting reference period may not in any case, unless an administration order is in force' substitute 'A company's accounting reference period may not in any case, unless the company is in administration'.

5 In section 425(1) (power of company to compromise) for 'an administration order being in force in relation to a company' substitute 'in administration'.

6 In section 427A(3) (mergers and divisions of public companies) for 'an administration order being in force in relation to the company' substitute 'where the company is in administration'.

7 In section 652B(3) (duty when applying to strike off defunct company) for paragraph (c) substitute –

'(c) the company is in administration under Part II of that Act;

(ca) an application to the court for an administration order in respect of the company has been made and not finally dealt with or withdrawn;

(cb) a copy of notice of intention to appoint an administrator of the company under paragraph 14 of Schedule B1 to that Act has been filed with the court and neither of the events mentioned in paragraph 44(2)(a) and (b) of that Schedule has occurred;

(cc) a copy of notice of intention to appoint an administrator of the company under paragraph 22 of that Schedule has been filed with the court and neither of the events mentioned in paragraph 44(4)(a) and (b) of that Schedule has occurred;'.

8 In section 652C(4) (director's duty following application to strike off defunct company) for paragraph (d) substitute –

'(d) an application to the court for an administration order in respect of the company is made under paragraph 12 of Schedule B1 to that Act;

(da) an administrator is appointed in respect of the company under paragraph 14 or 22 of that Schedule;

(db) a copy of notice of intention to appoint an administrator of the company under paragraph 14 or 22 of that Schedule is filed with the court;'.

Insolvency Act 1986

9 The Insolvency Act 1986 shall be amended as follows.

10 In section 1 (proposal for company voluntary arrangement) –

(a) in subsection (1) for '(other than one for which an administration order is in force, or which is being wound up)' substitute '(other than one which is in administration or being wound up)', and

(b) in subsection (3) for paragraph (a) substitute –

'(a) where the company is in administration, by the administrator,'.

11 In section 5(3) (approval of company voluntary arrangement) –

(a) for 'an administration order is in force' substitute 'is in administration', and
(b) for 'discharge the administration order' substitute 'provide for the appointment of the administrator to cease to have effect'.

12 In section 6(2)(c) (challenge of decision in relation to company voluntary arrangement) for 'an administration order is in force' substitute 'is in administration'.

13 In section 51 (power to appoint receiver: Scotland) after subsection (2) insert –

'(2A) Subsections (1) and (2) are subject to section 72A.'

14 At the end of section 100 (creditors' voluntary winding up of company: appointment of liquidator) add –

'(4) The court shall grant an application under subsection (3) made by the holder of a qualifying floating charge in respect of the company's property (within the meaning of paragraph 14 of Schedule B1) unless the court thinks it right to refuse the application because of the particular circumstances of the case.'

15 At the end of section 127 (winding-up: avoidance of property disposition) (which becomes subsection (1)) add –

'(2) This section has no effect in respect of anything done by an administrator of a company while a winding-up petition is suspended under paragraph 40 of Schedule B1.'

16 After section 129(1) (commencement of winding up) insert –

'(1A) Where the court makes a winding-up order by virtue of paragraph 13(1)(e) of Schedule B1, the winding up is deemed to commence on the making of the order.'

17 In section 140 (appointment by court of liquidator following administration or voluntary arrangement) for subsection (1) substitute –

'(1) Where a winding-up order is made immediately upon the appointment of an administrator ceasing to have effect, the court may appoint as liquidator of the company the person whose appointment as administrator has ceased to have effect.'

18 In section 212 (misfeasance of officers) –

(a) in subsection (1)(b) omit ', administrator',
(b) in subsection (2) omit (in each place) 'or administrator', and
(c) in subsection (4) –
   (i)   omit 'or administrator', and
   (ii) for 'that person' substitute 'he'.

19 Section 230(1) (administrator to be qualified insolvency practitioner) shall cease to have effect.

20 In section 231(1) and (2) (appointment to office of two or more persons) omit the word 'administrator,'.

21 In section 232 (validity of office-holder's act) omit the word 'administrator,'.

22 In section 233 (utility supplies) –

(a) for subsection (1)(a) substitute –

'(a) the company enters administration,', and

(b) for subsection (4)(a) substitute –

'(a) the date on which the company entered administration'.

23 For section 234(1)(a) (getting in the company's property) substitute –

'(a) the company enters administration,'.

24 For section 235(4)(a) (co-operation with office-holder) substitute –

'(a) the date on which the company entered administration,'.

25 For section 238(1)(a) (transactions at an undervalue: England and Wales) substitute –

'(a) the company enters administration,'.

26 (1) Section 240 (relevant time for sections 238 and 239) shall be amended as follows.

(2) For subsection (1)(c) substitute –

'(c) in either case, at a time between the making of an administration application in respect of the company and the making of an administration order on that application, and
(d) in either case, at a time between the filing with the court of a copy of notice of intention to appoint an administrator under paragraph 14 or 22 of Schedule B1 and the making of an appointment under that paragraph.'

(3) The word 'and' after subsection (1)(b) shall cease to have effect.

(4) For subsection (3)(a), (aa) and (b) substitute –

'(a) in a case where section 238 or 239 applies by reason of an administrator of a company being appointed by administration order, the date on which the administration application is made,
(b) in a case where section 238 or 239 applies by reason of an administrator of a company being appointed under paragraph 14 or 22 of Schedule B1 following filing with the court of a copy of a notice of intention to appoint under that paragraph, the date on which the copy of the notice is filed,
(c) in a case where section 238 or 239 applies by reason of an administrator of a company being appointed otherwise than as mentioned in paragraph (a) or (b), the date on which the appointment takes effect,
(d) in a case where section 238 or 239 applies by reason of a company going into liquidation either following conversion of administration into winding up by virtue of Article 37 of the EC Regulation or at the time when the appointment of an administrator ceases to have effect, the date on which the company entered administration (or, if relevant, the date on which the application for the administration order was made or a copy of the notice of intention to appoint was filed), and
(e) in a case where section 238 or 239 applies by reason of a company going into liquidation at any other time, the date of the commencement of the winding up.'

27 (1) Section 241 (order under section 238 or 239) shall be amended as follows.

(2) For subsection (3A) substitute –

'(3A) Where section 238 or 239 applies by reason of a company's entering administration, a person has notice of the relevant proceedings if he has notice that –

(a) an administration application has been made,

  (b) an administration order has been made,
  (c) a copy of a notice of intention to appoint an administrator under paragraph
       14 or 22 of Schedule B1 has been filed, or
  (d) notice of the appointment of an administrator has been filed under paragraph
       18 or 29 of that Schedule.'

(3) For subsection (3B) substitute –

'(3B) Where section 238 or 239 applies by reason of a company's going into
liquidation at the time when the appointment of an administrator of the company
ceases to have effect, a person has notice of the relevant proceedings if he has notice
that –

  (a) an administration application has been made,
  (b) an administration order has been made,
  (c) a copy of a notice of intention to appoint an administrator under paragraph
       14 or 22 of Schedule B1 has been filed,
  (d) notice of the appointment of an administrator has been filed under paragraph
       18 or 29 of that Schedule, or
  (e) the company has gone into liquidation.'

28 (1) Section 242 (gratuitous alienations: Scotland) shall be amended as follows.

(2) In subsection (1)(b) for 'an administration order is in force in relation to a company'
substitute 'a company enters administration'.

(3) In subsection (3)(a)(ii) for 'the administration order is made' substitute 'the company
enters administration'.

29 (1) Section 243 (unfair preferences: Scotland) shall be amended as follows.

(2) In subsection (1) for 'the making of an administration order in relation to the
company' substitute 'the company enters administration'.

(3) In subsection (4)(b) for 'in the case of an administration order' substitute 'where the
company has entered administration'.

30 In section 244(2) (extortionate credit transaction) for 'the day on which the
administration order was made or (as the case may be) the company went into
liquidation' substitute 'the day on which the company entered administration or went
into liquidation'.

31 (1) Section 245 (avoidance of floating charge) shall be amended as follows.

(2) The word 'or' after subsection (3)(b) shall cease to have effect.

(3) For subsection (3)(c) substitute –

  '(c) in either case, at a time between the making of an administration application
        in respect of the company and the making of an administration order on that
        application, or
   (d) in either case, at a time between the filing with the court of a copy of notice of
        intention to appoint an administrator under paragraph 14 or 22 of Schedule
        B1 and the making of an appointment under that paragraph.'

(4) For subsection (5)(a) and (b) substitute –

  '(a) in a case where this section applies by reason of an administrator of a
        company being appointed by administration order, the date on which the
        administration application is made,

(b) in a case where this section applies by reason of an administrator of a company being appointed under paragraph 14 or 22 of Schedule B1 following filing with the court of a copy of notice of intention to appoint under that paragraph, the date on which the copy of the notice is filed,

(c) in a case where this section applies by reason of an administrator of a company being appointed otherwise than as mentioned in paragraph (a) or (b), the date on which the appointment takes effect, and

(d) in a case where this section applies by reason of a company going into liquidation, the date of the commencement of the winding up.'

32 For section 246(1)(a) (unenforceability of lien on records) substitute –

'(a) the company enters administration,'.

33 (1) Section 247 (meaning of 'insolvency' and 'go into liquidation') shall be amended as follows.

(2) In subsection (1) for 'the making of an administration order or the appointment of an administrative receiver' substitute 'or the appointment of an administrator or administrative receiver'.

(3) For subsection (3) substitute –

'(3) The reference to a resolution for voluntary winding up in subsection (2) includes a reference to a resolution which is deemed to occur by virtue of –

(a) paragraph 83(6)(b) of Schedule B1, or

(b) an order made following conversion of administration or a voluntary arrangement into winding up by virtue of Article 37 of the EC Regulation.'

34 (1) Section 387 (preferential debts: 'the relevant date') shall be amended as follows.

(2) In subsection (2) for paragraphs (a) and (b) substitute –

'(a) if the company is in administration, the date on which it entered administration, and

(b) if the company is not in administration, the date on which the voluntary arrangement takes effect.'

(3) In subsection (3) –

(a) in paragraphs (a), (aa) and (ab) for 'the date of the making of the administration order' substitute 'the date on which the company entered administration',

(b) after paragraph (b) insert –

'(ba) if the case does not fall within paragraph (a), (aa), (ab) or (b) and the company is being wound up following administration pursuant to paragraph 83 of Schedule B1, the relevant date is the date on which the company entered administration;', and

(c) in paragraph (c) for 'paragraph (a), (aa), (ab) or (b)' substitute 'paragraph (a), (aa), (ab), (b) or (ba)'.

(4) After subsection (3) insert –

'(3A) In relation to a company which is in administration (and to which no other provision of this section applies) the relevant date is the date on which the company enters administration.'

35 In section 422 (power to apply first Group of Parts to banks, etc) for subsection (1) substitute –

'(1) The Secretary of State may by order made with the concurrence of the Treasury and after consultation with the Financial Services Authority provide that specified provisions in the first Group of Parts shall apply with specified modifications in relation to any person who –

    (a) has a liability in respect of a deposit which he accepted in accordance with the Banking Act 1979 or 1987, but

    (b) does not have permission under Part IV of the Financial Services and Markets Act 2000 (regulated activities) to accept deposits.

(1A) Subsection (1)(b) shall be construed in accordance with –

    (a) section 22 of the Financial Services and Markets Act 2000 (classes of regulated activity and categories of investment),

    (b) any relevant order under that section, and

    (c) Schedule 2 to that Act (regulated activities).'

36 In section 424(1)(a) (application for order in relation to transaction defrauding creditor) for 'in relation to which an administration order is in force' substitute 'is in administration'.

37 (1) Schedule A1 (moratorium where directors propose voluntary arrangement) shall be amended as follows.

(2) In paragraph 4(1) (exclusion from eligibility for moratorium) –

    (a) for paragraph (a) substitute –

    '(a) the company is in administration,', and

    (b) after paragraph (f) (and before the word 'or') insert –

    '(fa) an administrator appointed under paragraph 22 of Schedule B1 has held office in the period of 12 months ending with the date of filing,'.

(3) In paragraph 12(1) (effect of moratorium on creditor) for paragraph (d) substitute –

    '(d)   no administration application may be made in respect of the company,

    (da) no administrator of the company may be appointed under paragraph 14 or 22 of Schedule B1,'.

(4) In paragraph 40 (challenge of directors' actions during moratorium) for sub-paragraph (7) substitute –

    '(7) Sub-paragraph (8) applies where –

    (a) the appointment of an administrator has effect in relation to the company and the appointment took effect before the moratorium came into force, or

    (b) the company is being wound up in pursuance of a petition presented before the moratorium came into force.

(8) No application for an order under this paragraph may be made by a creditor or member of the company; but such an application may be made instead by the administrator or (as the case may be) the liquidator.'

38 (1) Schedule 8 (scope of insolvency rules) shall be amended as follows.

(2) At the end of paragraph 2 (which becomes sub-paragraph (1)) add –

    '(2) Rules made by virtue of this paragraph about the consequence of failure to comply with practice or procedure may, in particular, include provision about the termination of administration.'

(3) In paragraph 10 (provision as to committees) for 'section 26, 49, 68, 101, 141 or 142 of this Act' substitute 'section 49, 68, 101, 141 or 142 of, or paragraph 57 of Schedule B1 to, this Act'.

(4) After paragraph 14 insert –

'**14A** Provision about the application of section 176A of this Act which may include, in particular –

(a) provision enabling a receiver to institute winding up proceedings;
(b) provision requiring a receiver to institute winding up proceedings.'

(5) After paragraph 14A (inserted by sub-paragraph (4) above) insert –

'**Administration**

14B Provision which –

(a) applies in relation to administration, with or without modifications, a provision of Parts IV to VII of this Act, or
(b) serves a purpose in relation to administration similar to a purpose that may be served by the rules in relation to winding up by virtue of a provision of this Schedule.'

(6) In paragraph 29 (general provision) for 'section 22, 47, 66, 131, 143(2) or 235 of this Act' substitute 'section 47, 66, 131, 143(2) or 235 of, or paragraph 47 of Schedule B1 to, this Act'.

39 (1) Schedule 10 (punishment of offences) shall be amended as follows.

(2) After the entries for Schedule A1 insert –

'Sch. B1, para. 18(7).	Making false statement in statutory declaration where administrator appointed by holder of floating charge.	1. On indictment. 2. Summary.	2 years, or a fine or both. 6 months, or the statutory maximum or both.	
Sch. B1, para. 20.	Holder of floating charge failing to notify administrator or others of commencement of appointment.	1. On indictment. 2. Summary.	2 years, or a fine or both. 6 months, or the statutory maximum or both.	One-tenth of the statutory maximum.
Sch. B1, para. 27(4).	Making false statement in statutory declaration where appointment of administrator proposed by company or directors.	1. On indictment. 2. Summary.	2 years, or a fine or both. 6 months, or the statutory maximum or both.	
Sch. B1, para. 29(7).	Making false statement in statutory declaration where administrator appointed by company or directors.	1. On indictment. 2. Summary.	2 years, or a fine or both. 6 months, or the statutory maximum or both.	

Sch. B1, para. 32.	Company or directors failing to notify administrator or others of commencement of appointment.	1. On indictment. 2. Summary.	2 years, or a fine or both. 6 months, or the statutory maximum or both.	One-tenth of the statutory maximum.
Sch. B1, para. 45(2).	Administrator, company or officer failing to state in business document that administrator appointed.	Summary.	One-fifth of the statutory maximum.	
Sch. B1, para. 46(9).	Administrator failing to give notice of his appointment.	Summary.	One-fifth of the statutory maximum.	One-fiftieth of the statutory maximum.
Sch. B1, para. 48(4).	Failing to comply with provisions about statement of affairs where administrator appointed.	1. On indictment. 2. Summary.	A fine. The statutory maximum.	One-tenth of the statutory maximum.
Sch. B1, para. 49(7).	Administrator failing to send out statement of his proposals.	Summary.	One-fifth of the statutory maximum.	One-fiftieth of the statutory maximum.
Sch. B1, para. 51(5).	Administrator failing to arrange initial creditors' meeting.	Summary.	One-fifth of the statutory maximum.	One-fiftieth of the statutory maximum.
Sch. B1, para. 53(3).	Administrator failing to report decision taken at initial creditors' meeting.	Summary.	One-fifth of the statutory maximum.	One-fiftieth of the statutory maximum.
Sch. B1, para. 54(7).	Administrator failing to report decision taken at creditors' meeting summoned to consider revised proposal.	Summary.	One-fifth of the statutory maximum.	One-fiftieth of the statutory maximum.
Sch. B1, para. 56(2).	Administrator failing to summon creditors' meeting.	Summary.	One-fifth of the statutory maximum.	One-fiftieth of the statutory maximum.
Sch. B1, para. 71(6).	Administrator failing to file court order enabling disposal of charged property.	Summary.	One-fifth of the statutory maximum.	One-fiftieth of the statutory maximum.
Sch. B1, para. 72(5).	Administrator failing to file court order enabling disposal of hire-purchase property.	Summary.	One-fifth of the statutory maximum.	One-fiftieth of the statutory maximum.
Sch. B1, para. 77(3).	Administrator failing to notify Registrar of Companies of automatic end of administration.	Summary.	One-fifth of the statutory maximum.	One-fiftieth of the statutory maximum.

Sch. B1, para. 78(6).	Administrator failing to give notice of extension by consent of term of office.	Summary.	One-fifth of the statutory maximum.	One-fiftieth of the statutory maximum.
Sch. B1, para. 80(6).	Administrator failing to give notice of termination of administration where objective achieved.	Summary.	One-fifth of the statutory maximum.	One-fiftieth of the statutory maximum.
Sch. B1, para. 84(9).	Administrator failing to comply with provisions where company moves to dissolution.	Summary.	One-fifth of the statutory maximum.	One-fiftieth of the statutory maximum.
Sch. B1, para. 86(3).	Administrator failing to notify Registrar of Companies where court terminates administration.	Summary.	One-fifth of the statutory maximum.	One-fiftieth of the statutory maximum.
Sch. B1, para. 89(3).	Administrator failing to give notice on ceasing to be qualified.	Summary.	One-fifth of the statutory maximum.	One-fiftieth of the statutory maximum.'

(3) Omit the entries for the following provisions –

(a) section 12(2),
(b) section 15(8),
(c) section 18(5),
(d) section 21(3),
(e) section 22(6),
(f) section 23(3),
(g) section 24(7), and
(h) section 27(6).

Company Directors Disqualification Act 1986

40 The Company Directors Disqualification Act 1986 shall be amended as follows.

41 In section 6 (duty of court to disqualify unfit director of insolvent company) –

(a) for subsection (2)(b) substitute –

'(b) the company enters administration,',

(b) for subsection (3)(c) substitute –

'(c) where neither paragraph (a) nor (b) applies but an administrator or administrative receiver has at any time been appointed in respect of the company in question, any court which has jurisdiction to wind it up.', and

(c) for subsection (3A)(b) substitute –

'(b) in a case within paragraph (c) of that subsection, to the appointment of the administrator or (as the case may be) administrative receiver.'

42 In section 7(3) (duty of office-holder to report to Secretary of State) for paragraph (c) substitute –

'(c) in the case of a company which is in administration, the administrator,'.

Companies Act 1989

43 The Companies Act 1989 shall be amended as follows.

44 In section 158 (modification of insolvency law) –

(a) in subsection (3) for paragraph (b) substitute –

'(b) the application for an administration order or the presentation of a winding-up petition or the passing of a resolution for voluntary winding up,', and

(b) after subsection (3) insert –

'(3A) In subsection (3)(b) the reference to an application for an administration order shall be taken to include a reference to –

(a) in a case where an administrator is appointed under paragraph 14 or 22 of Schedule B1 to the Insolvency Act 1986 (appointment by floating charge holder, company or directors) following filing with the court of a copy of a notice of intention to appoint under that paragraph, the filing of the copy of the notice, and

(b) in a case where an administrator is appointed under either of those paragraphs without a copy of a notice of intention to appoint having been filed with the court, the appointment of the administrator.'

45 In section 161(4) (disapplication of enactments to default proceedings) for 'sections 10(1)(c), 11(3), 126, 128, 130, 185 or 285 of the Insolvency Act 1986' substitute 'section 126, 128, 130, 185 or 285 of, or paragraph 42 or 43 (including paragraph 43(6) as applied by paragraph 44) of Schedule B1 to, the Insolvency Act 1986'.

46 After section 167(1) (application by exchange or clearing house about taking default proceedings) insert –

'(1A) In subsection (1) a reference to an administration order shall be taken to include a reference to the appointment of an administrator under –

(a) paragraph 14 of Schedule B1 to the Insolvency Act 1986 (c.45) (appointment by holder of qualifying floating charge), or

(b) paragraph 22 of that Schedule (appointment by company or directors).'

47 (1) Section 175 (financial markets: administration) shall be amended as follows.

(2) For subsection (1) substitute –

'(1) The following provisions of Schedule B1 to the Insolvency Act 1986 (administration) do not apply in relation to a market charge –

(a) paragraph 43(2) and (3) (restriction on enforcement of security or repossession of goods) (including that provision as applied by paragraph 44 (interim moratorium)), and

(b) paragraphs 70, 71 and 72 (power of administrator to deal with charged or hire-purchase property).

(1A) Paragraph 41(2) of that Schedule (receiver to vacate office at request of administrator) does not apply to a receiver appointed under a market charge.'

(3) In subsection (2) for 'an administration order has been made or a petition for an administration order has been presented' substitute 'the occurrence of an event to which subsection (2A) applies'.

(4) After subsection (2) insert –

'(2A) This subsection applies to –

    (a) making an administration application under paragraph 12 of Schedule B1 to the Insolvency Act 1986,

    (b) appointing an administrator under paragraph 14 or 22 of that Schedule (appointment by floating charge holder, company or directors),

    (c) filing with the court a copy of notice of intention to appoint an administrator under either of those paragraphs.'

Coal Industry Act 1994

48 (1) Section 36 of the Coal Industry Act 1994 (insolvency of licensed operator) shall be amended as follows.

(2) After subsection (2) insert –

'(2A) Where the administrator of a company which is or has been a licensed operator files a notice with the registrar of companies under paragraph 84(1) of Schedule B1 to the Insolvency Act 1986 (administration: moving to dissolution), he shall at the same time send a copy to the Authority.'

(3) In subsection (3) –

    (a) after 'liquidator' insert 'or administrator', and

    (b) after 'subsection (2)' insert 'or (2A)'.

Employment Rights Act 1996

49 (1) The Employment Rights Act 1996 shall be amended as follows.

(2) In section 166(7) (application by employee for payment by Secretary of State) –

    (a) in paragraph (a) omit 'or an administration order', and

    (b) after paragraph (a) insert –

'(aa) if the company is in administration for the purposes of the Insolvency Act 1986,'.

(3) In section 183(3)(a) (insolvency of employer) –

    (a) in paragraph (a) omit 'or an administration order', and

    (b) after paragraph (a) insert –

'(aa) if the company is in administration for the purposes of the Insolvency Act 1986,'.

(4) Omit section 189(4) (transfer to Secretary of State of rights and remedies: priority of preferential debts).

Housing Act 1996

50 The Housing Act 1996 shall be amended as follows.

51 At the end of section 40 (initial notice to be given to Housing Corporation or Housing for Wales) add –

'(7) Subsections (8) and (9) apply in relation to the reference in subsection (3) to applying for an administration order.

(8) In a case where an administrator is appointed under paragraph 14 or 22 of Schedule B1 to the Insolvency Act 1986 (appointment by floating charge holder, company or directors) –

(a) the reference includes a reference to appointing an administrator under that paragraph, and

(b) in respect of an appointment under either of those paragraphs the reference to the applicant shall be taken as a reference to the person making the appointment.

(9) In a case where a copy of a notice of intention to appoint an administrator under either of those paragraphs is filed with the court –

(a) the reference shall be taken to include a reference to the filing of the copy of the notice, and

(b) in respect of the filing of a copy of a notice of intention to appoint under either of those paragraphs the reference to the applicant shall be taken as a reference to the person giving the notice.'

52 At the end of section 41 (further notice to be given to Housing Corporation or Housing for Wales) add –

'(6) In subsection (3) –

(a) the reference to the making of an administration order includes a reference to appointing an administrator under paragraph 14 or 22 of Schedule B1 to the Insolvency Act 1986 (administration), and

(b) in respect of an appointment under either of those paragraphs the reference to the applicant shall be taken as a reference to the person making the appointment.'

Financial Services and Markets Act 2000

53 The Financial Services and Markets Act 2000 shall be amended as follows.

54 (1) Section 215 (provision of Financial Services Compensation Scheme in relation to insolvency) shall be amended as follows.

(2) In subsection (3) for 'presents a petition under section 9 of the 1986 Act or Article 22 of the 1989 Order' substitute 'makes an administration application under Schedule B1 to the 1986 Act or presents a petition under Article 22 of the 1989 Order'.

(3) After subsection (3) insert –

'(3A) In subsection (3) the reference to making an administration application includes a reference to –

(a) appointing an administrator under paragraph 14 or 22 of Schedule B1 to the 1986 Act, or

(b) filing with the court a copy of notice of intention to appoint an administrator under either of those paragraphs.'

55 For section 359 (administration order) substitute –

'359 Administration order

(1) The Authority may make an administration application under Schedule B1 to the 1986 Act (or present a petition under Article 22 of the 1989 Order) in relation to a company or insolvent partnership which –

(a) is or has been an authorised person,

(b) is or has been an appointed representative, or

(c) is carrying on or has carried on a regulated activity in contravention of the general prohibition.

(2) Subsection (3) applies in relation to an administration application made (or a petition presented) by the Authority by virtue of this section.

(3) Any of the following shall be treated for the purpose of paragraph 11(a) of Schedule B1 to the 1986 Act (or Article 21(1)(a) of the 1989 Order) as unable to pay its debts –

(a) a company or partnership in default on an obligation to pay a sum due and payable under an agreement, and

(b) an authorised deposit taker in default on an obligation to pay a sum due and payable in respect of a relevant deposit.

(4) In this section –

'agreement' means an agreement the making or performance of which constitutes or is part of a regulated activity carried on by the company or partnership,

'authorised deposit taker' means a person with a Part IV permission to accept deposits (but not a person who has a Part IV permission to accept deposits only for the purpose of carrying on another regulated activity in accordance with that permission),

'company' means a company –

(a) in respect of which an administrator may be appointed under Schedule B1 to the 1986 Act, or

(b) to which Article 21 of the 1989 Order applies, and

'relevant deposit' shall, ignoring any restriction on the meaning of deposit arising from the identity of the person making the deposit, be construed in accordance with –

(a) section 22,

(b) any relevant order under that section, and

(c) Schedule 2.

(5) The definition of 'authorised deposit taker' in subsection (4) shall be construed in accordance with –

(a) section 22,

(b) any relevant order under that section, and

(c) Schedule 2.'

56 For section 361 (administrator to report to Authority) substitute –

'361 Administrator's duty to report to Authority

(1) This section applies where a company or partnership is –

(a) in administration within the meaning of Schedule B1 to the 1986 Act, or

(b) the subject of an administration order under Part III of the 1989 Order.

(2) If the administrator thinks that the company or partnership is carrying on or has carried on a regulated activity in contravention of the general prohibition, he must report to the Authority without delay.

(3) Subsection (2) does not apply where the administration arises out of an administration order made on an application made or petition presented by the Authority.'

57 In section 362 (Financial Services Authority's right to participate in proceedings) –

- (a) in subsection (1) for 'presents a petition to the court under section 9 of the 1986 Act (or Article 22 of the 1989 Order)' substitute 'makes an administration application under Schedule B1 to the 1986 Act (or presents a petition under Article 22 of the 1989 Order)',
- (b) after subsection (1) insert –

'(1A) This section also applies in relation to –

- (a) the appointment under paragraph 14 or 22 of Schedule B1 to the 1986 Act of an administrator of a company of a kind described in subsection (1)(a) to (c), or
- (b) the filing with the court of a copy of notice of intention to appoint an administrator under either of those paragraphs.',
- (c) in subsection (2)(a) for 'petition' substitute 'administration application or the petition',

(d) for subsection (4) substitute –

'(4) The Authority may apply to the court under paragraph 74 of Schedule B1 to the 1986 Act (or Article 39 of the 1989 Order).

(4A) In respect of an application under subsection (4) –

- (a) paragraph 74(1)(a) and (b) shall have effect as if for the words 'harm the interests of the applicant (whether alone or in common with some or all other members or creditors)' there were substituted the words 'harm the interests of some or all members or creditors', and
- (b) Article 39 of the 1989 Order shall have effect with the omission of the words '(including at least himself)'.',

and

- (e) in subsection (5)(b) for 'section 26 of the 1986 Act' substitute 'paragraph 57 of Schedule B1 to the 1986 Act'.

58 After section 362 insert –

'362A Administrator appointed by company or directors

(1) This section applies in relation to a company of a kind described in section 362(1)(a) to (c).

(2) An administrator of the company may not be appointed under paragraph 22 of Schedule B1 to the 1986 Act without the consent of the Authority.

(3) Consent under subsection (2) –

- (a) must be in writing, and
- (b) must be filed with the court along with the notice of intention to appoint under paragraph 27 of that Schedule.

(4) In a case where no notice of intention to appoint is required –

- (a) subsection (3)(b) shall not apply, but

(b) consent under subsection (2) must accompany the notice of appointment filed under paragraph 29 of that Schedule.'

59 In section 427A(3) (mergers and divisions of public companies) for 'an administration order being in force in relation to the company' substitute 'where the company is in administration'.

SCHEDULE 18

SCHEDULE 2A TO INSOLVENCY ACT 1986

Section 250

'SCHEDULE 2A

EXCEPTIONS TO PROHIBITION ON APPOINTMENT OF ADMINISTRATIVE RECEIVER: SUPPLEMENTARY PROVISIONS

Capital market arrangement

1 (1) For the purposes of section 72B an arrangement is a capital market arrangement if –

(a) it involves a grant of security to a person holding it as trustee for a person who holds a capital market investment issued by a party to the arrangement, or

(b) at least one party guarantees the performance of obligations of another party, or

(c) at least one party provides security in respect of the performance of obligations of another party, or

(d) the arrangement involves an investment of a kind described in articles 83 to 85 of the Financial Services and Markets Act 2000 (Regulated Activities) Order 2001 (SI 2001/544) (options, futures and contracts for differences).

(2) For the purposes of sub-paragraph (1) –

(a) a reference to holding as trustee includes a reference to holding as nominee or agent,

(b) a reference to holding for a person who holds a capital market investment includes a reference to holding for a number of persons at least one of whom holds a capital market investment, and

(c) a person holds a capital market investment if he has a legal or beneficial interest in it.

(3) In section 72B(1) and this paragraph 'party' to an arrangement includes a party to an agreement which –

(a) forms part of the arrangement,

(b) provides for the raising of finance as part of the arrangement, or

(c) is necessary for the purposes of implementing the arrangement.

Capital market investment

2 (1) For the purposes of section 72B an investment is a capital market investment if it –

(a) is within article 77 of the Financial Services and Markets Act 2000 (Regulated Activities) Order 2001 (SI 2001/544) (debt instruments), and

(b) is rated, listed or traded or designed to be rated, listed or traded.

(2) In sub-paragraph (1) –

'rated' means rated for the purposes of investment by an internationally recognised rating agency,

'listed' means admitted to the official list within the meaning given by section 103(1) of the Financial Services and Markets Act 2000 (interpretation), and
'traded' means admitted to trading on a market established under the rules of a recognised investment exchange or on a foreign market.

(3) In sub-paragraph (2) –

'recognised investment exchange' has the meaning given by section 285 of the Financial Services and Markets Act 2000 (recognised investment exchange), and
'foreign market' has the same meaning as 'relevant market' in article 67(2) of the Financial Services and Markets Act 2000 (Financial Promotion) Order 2001 (SI 2001/1335) (foreign markets).

3 (1) An investment is also a capital market investment for the purposes of section 72B if it consists of a bond or commercial paper issued to one or more of the following –

(a) an investment professional within the meaning of article 19(5) of the Financial Services and Markets Act 2000 (Financial Promotion) Order 2001,
(b) a person who is, when the agreement mentioned in section 72B(1) is entered into, a certified high net worth individual in relation to a communication within the meaning of article 48(2) of that order,
(c) a person to whom article 49(2) of that order applies (high net worth company, etc),
(d) a person who is, when the agreement mentioned in section 72B(1) is entered into, a certified sophisticated investor in relation to a communication within the meaning of article 50(1) of that order, and
(e) a person in a State other than the United Kingdom who under the law of that State is not prohibited from investing in bonds or commercial paper.

(2) In sub-paragraph (1) –

'bond' shall be construed in accordance with article 77 of the Financial Services and Markets Act 2000 (Regulated Activities) Order 2001 (SI 2001/544), and
'commercial paper' has the meaning given by article 9(3) of that order.

(3) For the purposes of sub-paragraph (1) –

(a) in applying article 19(5) of the Financial Promotion Order for the purposes of sub-paragraph (1)(a) –
　(i) in article 19(5)(b), ignore the words after 'exempt person',
　(ii) in article 19(5)(c)(i), for the words from 'the controlled activity' to the end substitute 'a controlled activity', and
　(iii) in article 19(5)(e) ignore the words from 'where the communication' to the end, and
(b) in applying article 49(2) of that order for the purposes of sub-paragraph (1)(c), ignore article 49(2)(e).

'Agreement'

4 For the purposes of sections 72B and 72E and this Schedule 'agreement' includes an agreement or undertaking effected by –

(a) contract,
(b) deed, or
(c) any other instrument intended to have effect in accordance with the law of England and Wales, Scotland or another jurisdiction.

Debt

5 The debt of at least £50 million referred to in section 72B(1)(a) or 72E(2)(a) –

(a) may be incurred at any time during the life of the capital market arrangement or financed project, and
(b) may be expressed wholly or partly in foreign currency (in which case the sterling equivalent shall be calculated as at the time when the arrangement is entered into or the project begins).

Step-in rights

6 (1) For the purposes of sections 72C to 72E a project has 'step-in rights' if a person who provides finance in connection with the project has a conditional entitlement under an agreement to –

(a) assume sole or principal responsibility under an agreement for carrying out all or part of the project, or
(b) make arrangements for carrying out all or part of the project.

(2) In sub-paragraph (1) a reference to the provision of finance includes a reference to the provision of an indemnity.

Project company

7 (1) For the purposes of sections 72C to 72E a company is a 'project company' of a project if –

(a) it holds property for the purpose of the project,
(b) it has sole or principal responsibility under an agreement for carrying out all or part of the project,
(c) it is one of a number of companies which together carry out the project,
(d) it has the purpose of supplying finance to enable the project to be carried out, or
(e) it is the holding company of a company within any of paragraphs (a) to (d).

(2) But a company is not a 'project company' of a project if –

(a) it performs a function within sub-paragraph (1)(a) to (d) or is within sub-paragraph (1)(e), but
(b) it also performs a function which is not –
    (i)   within sub-paragraph (1)(a) to (d),
    (ii) related to a function within sub-paragraph (1)(a) to (d), or
    (iii) related to the project.

(3) For the purposes of this paragraph a company carries out all or part of a project whether or not it acts wholly or partly through agents.

'Resources'

8 In section 72C 'resources' includes –

(a) funds (including payment for the provision of services or facilities),
(b) assets,
(c) professional skill,
(d) the grant of a concession or franchise, and

(e) any other commercial resource.

'Public body'

9 (1) In section 72C 'public body' means –

(a) a body which exercises public functions,
(b) a body specified for the purposes of this paragraph by the Secretary of State, and
(c) a body within a class specified for the purposes of this paragraph by the Secretary of State.

(2) A specification under sub-paragraph (1) may be –

(a) general, or
(b) for the purpose of the application of section 72C to a specified case.

Regulated business

10 (1) For the purposes of section 72D a business is regulated if it is carried on –

(a) in reliance on a licence granted to a person under section 7 of the Telecommunications Act 1984 (telecommunications service),
(b) in reliance on a licence under section 7 or 7A of the Gas Act 1986 (transport and supply of gas),
(c) in reliance on a licence granted by virtue of section 41C of that Act (power to prescribe additional licensable activity),
(d) in reliance on a licence under section 6 of the Electricity Act 1989 (supply of electricity),
(e) by a water undertaker,
(f) by a sewerage undertaker,
(g) by a universal service provider within the meaning given by section 4(3) and (4) of the Postal Services Act 2000,
(h) by the Post Office company within the meaning given by section 62 of that Act (transfer of property),
(i) by a relevant subsidiary of the Post Office Company within the meaning given by section 63 of that Act (government holding),
(j) in reliance on a licence under section 8 of the Railways Act 1993 (railway services),
(k) in reliance on a licence exemption under section 7 of that Act (subject to sub-paragraph (2) below),
(l) by the operator of a system of transport which is deemed to be a railway for a purpose of Part I of that Act by virtue of section 81(2) of that Act (tramways, etc), or
(m) by the operator of a vehicle carried on flanged wheels along a system within paragraph (l).

(2) Sub-paragraph (1)(k) does not apply to the operator of a railway asset on a railway unless on some part of the railway there is a permitted line speed exceeding 40 kilometres per hour.

'Person'

11 A reference to a person in this Schedule includes a reference to a partnership or another unincorporated group of persons.'

SCHEDULE 19

DURATION OF BANKRUPTCY: TRANSITIONAL PROVISIONS

Section 256

Introduction

1 This Schedule applies to an individual who immediately before commencement –

(a) has been adjudged bankrupt, and
(b) has not been discharged from the bankruptcy.

2 In this Schedule –

'commencement' means the date appointed under section 279 for the commencement of section 256, and
'pre-commencement bankrupt' means an individual to whom this Schedule applies.

Neither old law nor new law to apply

3 Section 279 of the Insolvency Act 1986 (bankruptcy: discharge) shall not apply to a pre-commencement bankrupt (whether in its pre-commencement or its post-commencement form).

General rule for discharge from pre-commencement bankruptcy

4 (1) A pre-commencement bankrupt is discharged from bankruptcy at whichever is the earlier of –

(a) the end of the period of one year beginning with commencement, and
(b) the end of the relevant period applicable to the bankrupt under section 279(1)(b) of the Insolvency Act 1986 (duration of bankruptcy) as it had effect immediately before commencement.

(2) An order made under section 279(3) of that Act before commencement –

(a) shall continue to have effect in respect of the pre-commencement bankrupt after commencement, and
(b) may be varied or revoked after commencement by an order under section 279(3) as substituted by section 256 of this Act.

(3) Section 279(3) to (5) of that Act as substituted by section 256 of this Act shall have effect after commencement in relation to the period mentioned in sub-paragraph (1)(a) or (b) above.

Second-time bankruptcy

5 (1) This paragraph applies to a pre-commencement bankrupt who was an undischarged bankrupt at some time during the period of 15 years ending with the day before the date on which the pre-commencement bankruptcy commenced.

(2) The pre-commencement bankrupt shall not be discharged from bankruptcy in accordance with paragraph 4 above.

(3) An order made before commencement under section 280(2)(b) or (c) of the Insolvency Act 1986 (discharge by order of the court) shall continue to have effect after commencement (including any provision made by the court by virtue of section 280(3)).

(4) A pre-commencement bankrupt to whom this paragraph applies (and in respect of whom no order is in force under section 280(2)(b) or (c) on commencement) is discharged –

(a) at the end of the period of five years beginning with commencement, or

(b) at such earlier time as the court may order on an application under section 280 of the Insolvency Act 1986 (discharge by order) heard after commencement.

(5) Section 279(3) to (5) of the Insolvency Act 1986 as substituted by section 256 of this Act shall have effect after commencement in relation to the period mentioned in sub-paragraph (4)(a) above.

(6) A bankruptcy annulled under section 282 shall be ignored for the purpose of sub-paragraph (1).

Criminal bankruptcy

6 A pre-commencement bankrupt who was adjudged bankrupt on a petition under section 264(1)(d) of the Insolvency Act 1986 (criminal bankruptcy) –

(a) shall not be discharged from bankruptcy in accordance with paragraph 4 above, but

(b) may be discharged from bankruptcy by an order of the court under section 280 of that Act.

Income payments order

7 (1) This paragraph applies where –

(a) a pre-commencement bankrupt is discharged by virtue of paragraph 4(1)(a), and

(b) an income payments order is in force in respect of him immediately before his discharge.

(2) If the income payments order specifies a date after which it is not to have effect, it shall continue in force until that date (and then lapse).

(3) But the court may on the application of the pre-commencement bankrupt –

(a) vary the income payments order;

(b) provide for the income payments order to cease to have effect before the date referred to in sub-paragraph (2).

Bankruptcy restrictions order or undertaking

8 A provision of this Schedule which provides for an individual to be discharged from bankruptcy is subject to –

(a) any bankruptcy restrictions order (or interim order) which may be made in relation to that individual, and

(b) any bankruptcy restrictions undertaking entered into by that individual.

SCHEDULE 20

SCHEDULE 4A TO INSOLVENCY ACT 1986

Section 257

'SCHEDULE 4A

BANKRUPTCY RESTRICTIONS ORDER AND UNDERTAKING

Bankruptcy restrictions order

1 (1) A bankruptcy restrictions order may be made by the court.

(2) An order may be made only on the application of –

(a) the Secretary of State, or
(b) the official receiver acting on a direction of the Secretary of State.

Grounds for making order

2 (1) The court shall grant an application for a bankruptcy restrictions order if it thinks it appropriate having regard to the conduct of the bankrupt (whether before or after the making of the bankruptcy order).

(2) The court shall, in particular, take into account any of the following kinds of behaviour on the part of the bankrupt –

(a) failing to keep records which account for a loss of property by the bankrupt, or by a business carried on by him, where the loss occurred in the period beginning 2 years before petition and ending with the date of the application;
(b) failing to produce records of that kind on demand by the official receiver or the trustee;
(c) entering into a transaction at an undervalue;
(d) giving a preference;
(e) making an excessive pension contribution;
(f) a failure to supply goods or services which were wholly or partly paid for which gave rise to a claim provable in the bankruptcy;
(g) trading at a time before commencement of the bankruptcy when the bankrupt knew or ought to have known that he was himself to be unable to pay his debts;
(h) incurring, before commencement of the bankruptcy, a debt which the bankrupt had no reasonable expectation of being able to pay;
(i) failing to account satisfactorily to the court, the official receiver or the trustee for a loss of property or for an insufficiency of property to meet bankruptcy debts;
(j) carrying on any gambling, rash and hazardous speculation or unreasonable extravagance which may have materially contributed to or increased the extent of the bankruptcy or which took place between presentation of the petition and commencement of the bankruptcy;
(k) neglect of business affairs of a kind which may have materially contributed to or increased the extent of the bankruptcy;
(l) fraud or fraudulent breach of trust;
(m) failing to cooperate with the official receiver or the trustee.

(3) The court shall also, in particular, consider whether the bankrupt was an undischarged bankrupt at some time during the period of six years ending with the date of the bankruptcy to which the application relates.

(4) For the purpose of sub-paragraph (2) –

'before petition' shall be construed in accordance with section 351(c),
'excessive pension contribution' shall be construed in accordance with section 342A,
'preference' shall be construed in accordance with section 340, and
'undervalue' shall be construed in accordance with section 339.

Timing of application for order

3 (1) An application for a bankruptcy restrictions order in respect of a bankrupt must be made –

(a) before the end of the period of one year beginning with the date on which the bankruptcy commences, or
(b) with the permission of the court.

(2) The period specified in sub-paragraph (1)(a) shall cease to run in respect of a bankrupt while the period set for his discharge is suspended under section 279(3).

Duration of order

4 (1) A bankruptcy restrictions order –

- (a) shall come into force when it is made, and
- (b) shall cease to have effect at the end of a date specified in the order.

(2) The date specified in a bankruptcy restrictions order under sub-paragraph (1)(b) must not be –

- (a) before the end of the period of two years beginning with the date on which the order is made, or
- (b) after the end of the period of 15 years beginning with that date.

Interim bankruptcy restrictions order

5 (1) This paragraph applies at any time between –

- (a) the institution of an application for a bankruptcy restrictions order, and
- (b) the determination of the application.

(2) The court may make an interim bankruptcy restrictions order if the court thinks that –

- (a) there are prima facie grounds to suggest that the application for the bankruptcy restrictions order will be successful, and
- (b) it is in the public interest to make an interim order.

(3) An interim order may be made only on the application of –

- (a) the Secretary of State, or
- (b) the official receiver acting on a direction of the Secretary of State.

(4) An interim order –

- (a) shall have the same effect as a bankruptcy restrictions order, and
- (b) shall come into force when it is made.

(5) An interim order shall cease to have effect –

- (a) on the determination of the application for the bankruptcy restrictions order,
- (b) on the acceptance of a bankruptcy restrictions undertaking made by the bankrupt, or
- (c) if the court discharges the interim order on the application of the person who applied for it or of the bankrupt.

6 (1) This paragraph applies to a case in which both an interim bankruptcy restrictions order and a bankruptcy restrictions order are made.

(2) Paragraph 4(2) shall have effect in relation to the bankruptcy restrictions order as if a reference to the date of that order were a reference to the date of the interim order.

Bankruptcy restrictions undertaking

7 (1) A bankrupt may offer a bankruptcy restrictions undertaking to the Secretary of State.

(2) In determining whether to accept a bankruptcy restrictions undertaking the Secretary of State shall have regard to the matters specified in paragraph 2(2) and (3).

8 A reference in an enactment to a person in respect of whom a bankruptcy restrictions order has effect (or who is 'the subject of' a bankruptcy restrictions order) includes a reference to a person in respect of whom a bankruptcy restrictions undertaking has effect.

9 (1) A bankruptcy restrictions undertaking –

(a) shall come into force on being accepted by the Secretary of State, and
(b) shall cease to have effect at the end of a date specified in the undertaking.

(2) The date specified under sub-paragraph (1)(b) must not be –

(a) before the end of the period of two years beginning with the date on which the undertaking is accepted, or
(b) after the end of the period of 15 years beginning with that date.

(3) On an application by the bankrupt the court may –

(a) annul a bankruptcy restrictions undertaking;
(b) provide for a bankruptcy restrictions undertaking to cease to have effect before the date specified under sub-paragraph (1)(b).

Effect of annulment of bankruptcy order

10 Where a bankruptcy order is annulled under section 282(1)(a) or (2) –

(a) any bankruptcy restrictions order, interim order or undertaking which is in force in respect of the bankrupt shall be annulled,
(b) no new bankruptcy restrictions order or interim order may be made in respect of the bankrupt, and
(c) no new bankruptcy restrictions undertaking by the bankrupt may be accepted.

11 Where a bankruptcy order is annulled under section 261, 263D or 282(1)(b) –

(a) the annulment shall not affect any bankruptcy restrictions order, interim order or undertaking in respect of the bankrupt,
(b) the court may make a bankruptcy restrictions order in relation to the bankrupt on an application instituted before the annulment,
(c) the Secretary of State may accept a bankruptcy restrictions undertaking offered before the annulment, and
(d) an application for a bankruptcy restrictions order or interim order in respect of the bankrupt may not be instituted after the annulment.

Registration

12 The Secretary of State shall maintain a register of –

(a) bankruptcy restrictions orders,
(b) interim bankruptcy restrictions orders, and
(c) bankruptcy restrictions undertakings.'

SCHEDULE 21

EFFECT OF BANKRUPTCY RESTRICTIONS ORDER AND UNDERTAKING

Section 257

Disqualification for acting as receiver or manager

1 The following shall be substituted for section 31 of the Insolvency Act 1986 (receiver and manager: disqualification) –

'31 Disqualification of bankrupt

(1) A person commits an offence if he acts as receiver or manager of the property of a company on behalf of debenture holders while –

(a) he is an undischarged bankrupt, or
(b) a bankruptcy restrictions order is in force in respect of him.

(2) A person guilty of an offence under subsection (1) shall be liable to imprisonment, a fine or both.

(3) This section does not apply to a receiver or manager acting under an appointment made by the court.'

Bankruptcy offences after discharge

2 After section 350(3) of the Insolvency Act 1986 (bankruptcy offences: general: no liability after discharge) there shall be inserted –

'(3A) Subsection (3) is without prejudice to any provision of this Chapter which applies to a person in respect of whom a bankruptcy restrictions order is in force.'

3 At the end of section 360 of that Act (obtaining credit and doing business) there shall be inserted –

'(5) This section applies to the bankrupt after discharge while a bankruptcy restrictions order is in force in respect of him.

(6) For the purposes of subsection (1)(a) as it applies by virtue of subsection (5), the relevant information about the status of the person in question is the information that a bankruptcy restrictions order is in force in respect of him.'

Disqualification for acting as insolvency practitioner

4 At the end of section 390 of that Act (disqualification for insolvency practitioner) there shall be added –

'(5) A person is not qualified to act as an insolvency practitioner while a bankruptcy restrictions order is in force in respect of him.'

Prohibition against involvement in company

5 The following shall be substituted for section 11(1) of the Company Directors Disqualification Act 1986 (bankrupt) –

'(1) It is an offence for a person to act as director of a company or directly or indirectly to take part in or be concerned in the promotion, formation or management of a company, without the leave of the court, at a time when –

(a) he is an undischarged bankrupt, or
(b) a bankruptcy restrictions order is in force in respect of him.'

SCHEDULE 22

INDIVIDUAL VOLUNTARY ARRANGEMENT

Section 264

Annulment of bankruptcy on making of voluntary arrangement

1 The following shall be substituted for section 261 of the Insolvency Act 1986 (effect of voluntary arrangement: undischarged bankrupt) –

'261 Additional effect on undischarged bankrupt

(1) This section applies where –

- (a) the creditors' meeting summoned under section 257 approves the proposed voluntary arrangement (with or without modifications), and
- (b) the debtor is an undischarged bankrupt.

(2) Where this section applies the court shall annul the bankruptcy order on an application made –

- (a) by the bankrupt, or
- (b) where the bankrupt has not made an application within the prescribed period, by the official receiver.

(3) An application under subsection (2) may not be made –

- (a) during the period specified in section 262(3)(a) during which the decision of the creditors' meeting can be challenged by application under section 262,
- (b) while an application under that section is pending, or
- (c) while an appeal in respect of an application under that section is pending or may be brought.

(4) Where this section applies the court may give such directions about the conduct of the bankruptcy and the administration of the bankrupt's estate as it thinks appropriate for facilitating the implementation of the approved voluntary arrangement.'

Fast-track for making voluntary arrangement

2 The following shall be inserted after section 263 of that Act (implementation of voluntary arrangement) –

'Fast-track voluntary arrangement

263A Availability

Section 263B applies where an individual debtor intends to make a proposal to his creditors for a voluntary arrangement and –

- (a) the debtor is an undischarged bankrupt,
- (b) the official receiver is specified in the proposal as the nominee in relation to the voluntary arrangement, and
- (c) no interim order is applied for under section 253.

263B Decision

(1) The debtor may submit to the official receiver –

- (a) a document setting out the terms of the voluntary arrangement which the debtor is proposing, and
- (b) a statement of his affairs containing such particulars as may be prescribed of his creditors, debts, other liabilities and assets and such other information as may be prescribed.

(2) If the official receiver thinks that the voluntary arrangement proposed has a reasonable prospect of being approved and implemented, he may make arrangements for inviting creditors to decide whether to approve it.

(3) For the purposes of subsection (2) a person is a 'creditor' only if –

(a) he is a creditor of the debtor in respect of a bankruptcy debt, and

(b) the official receiver is aware of his claim and his address.

(4) Arrangements made under subsection (2) –

(a) must include the provision to each creditor of a copy of the proposed voluntary arrangement,

(b) must include the provision to each creditor of information about the criteria by reference to which the official receiver will determine whether the creditors approve or reject the proposed voluntary arrangement, and

(c) may not include an opportunity for modifications to the proposed voluntary arrangement to be suggested or made.

(5) Where a debtor submits documents to the official receiver under subsection (1) no application under section 253 for an interim order may be made in respect of the debtor until the official receiver has –

(a) made arrangements as described in subsection (2), or

(b) informed the debtor that he does not intend to make arrangements (whether because he does not think the voluntary arrangement has a reasonable prospect of being approved and implemented or because he declines to act).

263C Result

As soon as is reasonably practicable after the implementation of arrangements under section 263B(2) the official receiver shall report to the court whether the proposed voluntary arrangement has been approved or rejected.

263D Approval of voluntary arrangement

(1) This section applies where the official receiver reports to the court under section 263C that a proposed voluntary arrangement has been approved.

(2) The voluntary arrangement –

(a) takes effect,

(b) binds the debtor, and

(c) binds every person who was entitled to participate in the arrangements made under section 263B(2).

(3) The court shall annul the bankruptcy order in respect of the debtor on an application made by the official receiver.

(4) An application under subsection (3) may not be made –

(a) during the period specified in section 263F(3) during which the voluntary arrangement can be challenged by application under section 263F(2),

(b) while an application under that section is pending, or

(c) while an appeal in respect of an application under that section is pending or may be brought.

(5) The court may give such directions about the conduct of the bankruptcy and the administration of the bankrupt's estate as it thinks appropriate for facilitating the implementation of the approved voluntary arrangement.

(6) The Deeds of Arrangement Act 1914 does not apply to the voluntary arrangement.

(7) A reference in this Act or another enactment to a voluntary arrangement approved under this Part includes a reference to a voluntary arrangement which has effect by virtue of this section.

263E Implementation

Section 263 shall apply to a voluntary arrangement which has effect by virtue of section 263D(2) as it applies to a voluntary arrangement approved by a creditors' meeting.

263F Revocation

(1) The court may make an order revoking a voluntary arrangement which has effect by virtue of section 263D(2) on the ground –

(a) that it unfairly prejudices the interests of a creditor of the debtor, or
(b) that a material irregularity occurred in relation to the arrangements made under section 263B(2).

(2) An order under subsection (1) may be made only on the application of –

(a) the debtor,
(b) a person who was entitled to participate in the arrangements made under section 263B(2),
(c) the trustee of the bankrupt's estate, or
(d) the official receiver.

(3) An application under subsection (2) may not be made after the end of the period of 28 days beginning with the date on which the official receiver makes his report to the court under section 263C.

(4) But a creditor who was not made aware of the arrangements under section 263B(2) at the time when they were made may make an application under subsection (2) during the period of 28 days beginning with the date on which he becomes aware of the voluntary arrangement.

263G Offences

(1) Section 262A shall have effect in relation to obtaining approval to a proposal for a voluntary arrangement under section 263D.

(2) Section 262B shall have effect in relation to a voluntary arrangement which has effect by virtue of section 263D(2) (for which purposes the words 'by a creditors' meeting summoned under section 257' shall be disregarded).'

Role of official receiver

3 The following shall be inserted after section 389A of that Act (authorisation of nominees and supervisors) –

'389B Official receiver as nominee or supervisor

(1) The official receiver is authorised to act as nominee or supervisor in relation to a voluntary arrangement approved under Part VIII provided that the debtor is an undischarged bankrupt when the arrangement is proposed.

(2) The Secretary of State may by order repeal the proviso in subsection (1).

(3) An order under subsection (2) –

(a) must be made by statutory instrument, and
(b) shall be subject to annulment in pursuance of a resolution of either House of Parliament.'

SCHEDULE 23

INDIVIDUAL INSOLVENCY: MINOR AND CONSEQUENTIAL AMENDMENTS

Section 269

1 The Insolvency Act 1986 shall be amended as follows.

2 Section 275 (bankruptcy: summary administration) shall cease to have effect.

3 In section 280(1) (bankruptcy: discharge by order of court) –

(a) for 'section 279(1)(a)' substitute 'section 279(6)', and
(b) for 'commencement of the bankruptcy' substitute 'date on which the bankruptcy commences'.

4 In section 282 (annulment of bankruptcy) –

(a) in subsection (4) (effect of annulment) after 'section 261' insert 'or 263D', and
(b) omit subsection (5) (previous bankruptcy: disregard of annulled bankruptcy).

5 For section 291(4) (co-operation with official receiver) substitute –

'(4) The bankrupt shall give the official receiver such inventory of his estate and such other information, and shall attend on the official receiver at such times, as the official receiver may reasonably require –

(a) for a purpose of this Chapter, or
(b) in connection with the making of a bankruptcy restrictions order.'

6 In section 292(1)(a) (trustee in bankruptcy: power to appoint) omit the words 'except at a time when a certificate for the summary administration of the bankrupt's estate is in force,'.

7 In section 293(1) (trustee in bankruptcy: meeting to appoint) omit the words 'and no certificate for the summary administration of the bankrupt's estate has been issued,'.

8 In section 294(1) (power of creditors to requisition meeting) omit the words – 'and
(b) a certificate for the summary administration of the estate is not for the time being in force,'.

9 In section 297 (trustee: special cases) –

(a) omit subsections (2) and (3), and
(b) in subsection (4) omit the words 'but no certificate for the summary administration of the estate is issued'.

10 Omit section 298(3) (removal of trustee: summary administration).

11 In section 300 (trustee: vacancy) –

(a) omit subsection (5), and
(b) in subsections (6) and (7) omit the words 'or (5)'.

12 In section 354(3) (concealment of property) after 'the official receiver' insert ', the trustee'.

13 At the end of section 355 (concealment and falsification of records) add –

'(4) In their application to a trading record subsections (2)(d) and (3)(b) shall have effect as if the reference to 12 months were a reference to two years.

(5) In subsection (4) 'trading record' means a book, document or record which shows or explains the transactions or financial position of a person's business, including –

(a) a periodic record of cash paid and received,
(b) a statement of periodic stock-taking, and
(c) except in the case of goods sold by way of retail trade, a record of goods sold and purchased which identifies the buyer and seller or enables them to be identified.'

14 In the following provisions of section 399 (appointment of official receiver) for 'or winding up' substitute ', winding up or individual voluntary arrangement' –

(a) subsection (1) (twice), and
(b) subsection (4).

15 In section 429(2)(b) (disability imposed on revoking administration order under County Courts Act 1984) for 'not exceeding 2 years' there shall be substituted 'not exceeding one year'.

16 (1) Schedule 9 (scope of insolvency rules) shall be amended as follows.

(2) After paragraph 8 (registration of voluntary arrangements) insert –

'Official receiver acting on voluntary arrangement

8A Provision about the official receiver acting as nominee or supervisor in relation to a voluntary arrangement under Part VIII of this Act, including –

(a) provision requiring the official receiver to act in specified circumstances;
(b) provision about remuneration;
(c) provision prescribing terms or conditions to be treated as forming part of a voluntary arrangement in relation to which the official receiver acts as nominee or supervisor;
(d) provision enabling those terms or conditions to be varied or excluded, in specified circumstances or subject to specified conditions, by express provision in an arrangement.'

(3) After paragraph 29 (records) insert –

'Bankruptcy restrictions orders and undertakings

29A Provision about bankruptcy restrictions orders, interim orders and undertakings, including –

(a) provision about evidence;
(b) provision enabling the amalgamation of the register mentioned in paragraph 12 of Schedule 4A with another register;
(c) provision enabling inspection of that register by the public.'

17 In Schedule 10 (punishment of offences) –

(a) in the entry for section 31 omit 'Undischarged', and
(b) omit the entries for sections 361 and 362.

INDEX

References are to paragraph numbers